Theme Lotus

1956 – 1986

From Chapman to Ducarouge

DOUG NYE

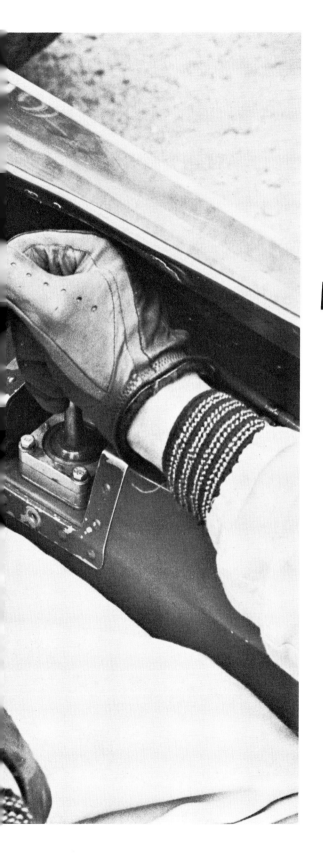

Theme Lotus

1956-1986

From Chapman to Ducarouge

MOTOR RACING PUBLICATIONS LTD
Unit 6, The Pilton Estate, 46 Pitlake, Croydon CRO 3RY, England

ISBN 0 947981 09 8
First published 1978
Second Edition 1986

Photosetting by Tek-Art Ltd, West Wickham, Kent
Printed in Great Britain by Netherwood, Dalton & Co. Ltd,
Bradley Mills, Huddersfield, West Yorkshire

Contents

Foreword to original edition

Doug Nye tells me that it was his publisher, John Blunsden, who proposed that the milestone of 21 years of Lotus involvement in Grand Prix racing should be marked by a book featuring every Formula One Lotus, as well as the various Tasman derivatives and the cars we built for our years at Indianapolis.

The result is THEME LOTUS, a book for which the author has worked very hard to achieve both accuracy and detail, but which I venture to suggest has been published somewhat prematurely. I have always held the view that our first true Formula One car was the Lotus 18, which made its debut in the 1960 Argentine Grand Prix. Both the Lotus 12 and the Lotus 16 — our first single-seater designs — were really Formula Two cars, which subsequently we adapted for Formula One racing. They led us, almost by accident, into the exacting world of Grand Prix racing, and they taught us a great deal. We have been learning ever since!

If there is a theme running through the design of the cars featured in this book it is that each of them has been conceived after a long and careful study of the current state of the art. I like to think that we have never been over-concerned by the design solutions of other teams or by what has become accepted as standard practice, other than perhaps using these as starting points from which performance improvements can be made.

Our years of involvement in top-level motor racing have, I believe, coincided with the most technically interesting and demanding in the history of the sport. Technological progress has enabled us to achieve levels of performance which seemed far beyond reach only a few years earlier, yet every advance invariably brings with it new problems demanding new solutions. This, of course, is as it should be, for Grand Prix racing in general and winning in particular is all about pushing forward the boundaries of knowledge.

Although this is essentially a book about cars, it is people who have made them work, and I am ever mindful of the contribution which so many of them have made to the Lotus success story. I have been fortunate over the years in securing the services of some of the greatest drivers the sport has ever known, who have been able to extract from our cars their ultimate potential. Equally, I have been well served by highly talented and dedicated teams of engineers, designers, researchers and mechanics who, whether working at the trackside or back at base, have striven so hard to attain the levels of accomplishment which, these days more than ever before, success in Grand Prix racing demands.

The problems of today — and their solution — tend to be so time-consuming that there seems to be far too little time to look back. Yet to do so can often be a rewarding experience. In researching THEME LOTUS Doug Nye recalled for me so much which had been lost to memory but which now seems as though it happened only yesterday. In motor racing 21 years pass all too quickly, and it is only right that they should be recorded before memory fails completely. I hope readers of this book will enjoy looking back over the most interesting period of racing car design the sport has ever experienced, and through reading it will gain a better understanding of how much effort goes into creating a race-winner.

A.C.B. Chapman

On top of the World! Jim Clark gives his friend and entrant Colin Chapman and his teammate Mike Spence a ride on the back of his Lotus-Climax type 25 after his victory in the 1963 Italian Grand Prix at Monza — a success which clinched for Clark his first World Championship and for Lotus their first Constructors' title.

Introduction

Lotus cars began racing in Formula 1 eight World Championship seasons after the fabled Italian Ferrari team, and yet they beat them to a half-century of title-qualifying Grand Prix victories. This is a chronicle of Lotus design and achievement from 1956 to 1986 and as such it does not so much end as merely provide what I hope is a remarkably comprehensive 30-year beginning.

The Lotus story is indeed quite remarkable, and in these pages I offer a history of their premier-league racing cars — Formula 1, Indianapolis and Tasman — these three types of racing being so closely interlinked as to be virtually inseparable if I am to produce a 'proper job'. Appendices list every significant race in which Lotus have competed. Although this is essentially a nuts-and-bolts story, none of it would have happened without the extraordinary personality and genius of the late Colin Chapman, and in this new and greatly expanded edition we have included extra chapters on 'The Guv', on the various design engineers who worked under him, and on Peter Warr and Gerard Ducarouge, who revived Team Lotus fortunes so ably after Colin's death.

So what follows is a history of Lotus achievement, and of the quite remarkably dynamic talents and inspiration of the company's founder. It would not have been possible to provide as full a picture without Colin Chapman's help, and my prime acknowledgement must be to him for finding so much time to talk about yesterday when he was really only interested in the future.

Special thanks, also, must go to Peter Warr, Gerard Ducarouge, Tony Rudd and Martin Ogilvie, and to Dick Scammell, David Lazenby, Bob Dance, Bobby Clarke, Ted Woodley, Arthur Birchall, Dale Porteus, Jim Endruweit, Roy Badcock, Peter Brand, Steve Sanville, John Lambert, Maurice Phillippe, Ralph Bellamy, Brian Spooner, Andrew Ferguson, Peter Warr and Nigel Bennett for talking of their current or past Team Lotus involvement. Similarly to Mike Costin, former Lotus technical director and today the 'Cos' of Cosworth, to Frank Coltman, formerly of Progress Chassis, and to Len Terry, former Lotus chief designer, for spending so much time helping me unravel this particular story's technical aspects. Thanks also to drivers Innes Ireland, Cliff Allison, Trevor Taylor, Bruce Halford (lately the proud owner of two Type 16s), David Piper, Tony Marsh, Mario Andretti and Ronnie Peterson for current and previous assistance; to former Lotus owners Rob Walker, John Fisher, Bill Wilks, Mike Taylor, David Boorer, Keith Finney and John Roberts; to current owners Bruce Halford (again), the Hon. John Dawson-Damer, Nigel Woollett, Brian Eckersley and Tom Wheatcroft; and to outside team mechanics John Chisman (of Walker Racing), Wally Varley (of John Fisher's team) and Brit Pearce (of Innes Ireland Ltd).

Geoff Goddard made the solution of the Lotus 16 mystery possible by printing literally hundreds of race photographs from his huge collection knowing that very few of them could possibly be published, and access to his enormous library was invaluable when I couldn't find references in my own. Denis Jenkinson of *Motor Sport* was extremely helpful in allowing me to study his original notebooks where 12s and 16s were concerned, and for help with information and photographs I must also thank Maurice Rowe and *Motor* magazine for providing so much research material, plus Nigel Snowdon, Euan Sarginson, Nigel Roebuck of *Autosport* magazine, Eoin Young, John Dunbar, David Phipps, David Hodges, Cyril Posthumus, Ford Photographic, London Art Tech and last, but most definitely not least, Al Bloemker and Ron McQueeney of the Indianapolis Motor Speedway. I hope I have been able to squeeze Team Lotus' 29 Formula 1 seasons of brimfull working days (and at times nights!) between the covers of this book – all the achievements are their's, the omissions and errors are mine.

DOUG NYE

Lower Bourne
Farnham
Surrey
June 1986

LOTUS 12

The first step (1957)

**'That first little Formula 2 car got everybody excited, but what sank
it was the dreaded five-speed Lotus queerbox . . .'**

Mike Costin

Saturday, July 14, 1956 was dull and overcast but dry as a huge crowd jammed into Silverstone circuit for the British Grand Prix. Juan Fangio was to win for Ferrari after the British BRMs of Mike Hawthorn and Tony Brooks had caused sensation by leading early on, only to retire, Brooks' in a fiery roll-over crash. But for the cause of British motor racing the major supporting event to the GP was of more significance. A new 1½-litre unsupercharged Formula 2 class was to take effect in the coming year, and at Silverstone the organizing British Racing Drivers' Club had decided to run a 25-lap 'Formula 2' dress-rehearsal race as a foretaste.

To some small extent they were disappointed. Only one prototype F2 car appeared amongst a field of 1,500cc sports-racers stripped of lights, dynamo and battery. Roy Salvadori's works mid-engined Cooper was the lone newcomer, powered by a single-ohc 1,460cc Coventry Climax FWB 4-cylinder engine. It offered around 100bhp at 6,000rpm, and the bottle-green car was neat and pert, if not exactly pretty.

Salvadori made a slow start as Colin Chapman, the 28-year-old creator of Team Lotus and the Lotus sports-racing cars, led the first nine laps in his stripped type 11 roadster. As *Motor Sport* observed, '...the Cooper was obviously very fast...up from fourth place on the first lap to second place on the ninth, to take the lead on lap ten. It then drew well away to win comfortably its first race — but as Chapman was driving virtually a sports car...the F2 Lotus should be formidable!'.

Chapman was a stress-master of outstanding perception. His expertise in the design of multi-tubular spaceframe chassis and advanced suspension systems had been vividly demonstrated by Lotus' immense sports-racing success. Mr G.A. Vandervell had hired his services as consultant to redesign the Vanwall GP car for 1956. Chapman had drawn a lightweight chassis-frame and supple suspension system, and had introduced Frank Costin (an aerodynamicist responsible for the Lotus bodies whose brother, Mike, was Colin's development engineer) who devised the definitive Vanwall teardrop body-shape. These cars were soon to win GP races and, in 1958, the World Manufacturers' Championship. Peter Berthon of BRM also hired Chapman to tame his P25 design, and Colin succeeded where such industry establishment 'heavies' as Alec Issigonis and Alex Moulton had failed...

Early in October, 1956 Chapman invited the press to a modest function at the Lotus works. Here, tucked into outbuildings behind his father's Railway Hotel, in Tottenham Lane, Hornsey, North London, Colin unveiled his prototype single-seat Lotus type 12.

It was slim, neat and sparkling — glisteningly prepared for the London Motor Show at Earls Court. It was incomplete, its engine merely a mock-up of the new 1,475cc twin-cam Climax FPF, and its all-new Lotus transaxle just a wooden maquette. But as a front-engined racing car it looked sensational — as by then was expected from Lotus.

Its spaceframe chassis was typical of Lotus lightweight practice, but it included some new features. The bottom chassis longerons, for example, were to be in aircraft-spec Reynolds 531 tube, nominally 1-inch square 20-gauge, but with ⅜-inch-radius corners in section to give an almost round-tube appearance. This was very strong for its weight, but was also expensive and in short supply. Lotus normally specified ERW tube, rolled and seamed from flat sheet — and cheap. This was a new departure, and chassis-builder Frank Coltman didn't particularly like it, for joints were tricky to form.

Frank managed the Progress Chassis Company, founded by John Teychenne ('Taychnee') and housed behind his home in a side turning opposite Stan Chapman's 'pub'. The prototype 12 frame was made there, then assembled into the Show car by

The first serious tests of a Lotus single-seater took place at Silverstone in March, 1957 — and Geoff Goddard was there. Ron Flockhart is seen here swinging '351' out on to the circuit. This was a De Dion-axled car, with BMC gearbox in unit with the engine. The tail cone itself was tested experimentally as a fuel tank, sealed off above the suspension compartment by an internal diaphragm and lined with 'slushing compound' — it was unsuccessful, and separate tail and scuttle tanks were used instead.

Colin Chapman testing his second prototype De Dion-axled Lotus 12 — the first Lotus single-seater to run — at Silverstone in March, 1957.

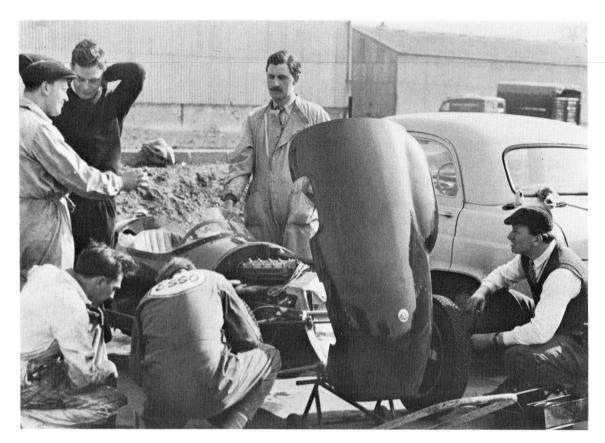

Team Lotus conference during the Silverstone tests, with chief mechanic Willie Griffiths kneeling (left), Colin Chapman making a point to Ron Flockhart, Graham Hill and (right) a sceptical Mike Costin. Note the inclined engine mounting which dropped the propeller-shaft low beneath the driver's seat.

Box of tricks — the dreaded Lotus 'queerbox' shown in its original form as fitted in the Formula 2 and Formula 1 type 12s with its inboard disc brakes and their forward calipers. The actual gearbox is that tiny section beneath the domed housing — the rest is final-drive.

The first Formula 1 entry — Graham Hill handling the prototype 1,960cc Lotus 12 in the BRDC International Trophy race at Silverstone in May 1958. This car was probably '353'. Strut rear suspension is used, with the forward radius-rod pick-up bolt supported at its outboard end by an additional steady-bar (this was standard on strut-type 12s). Scuttle tanks have now been fitted.

Colin Chapman, Mike Costin and John Lambert, working against the clock. Lotus Engineering knew no other way!

Curved inch-square cross-members linked the main longerons, while the upper rails were of inch-round 20-gauge linked by similar-size verticals to the lower members. All triangulation was in ¾-inch tube, and those curved bottom cross-members persuaded Progress to build this and subsequent 12 chassis upside-down, on the perfectly straight toprail run. In those days practicality was the watchword — the Lotus 6 production chassis had been 'jigged' on a double-bed frame.

Torsional rigidity was a problem in such a narrow frame as the 12's so Colin attached the undertray rigidly to its bottom bay and spooned it slightly for extra stiffness. He also mounted the engine rigidly by using a rear engine plate of 10-gauge alloy fitted as a bulkhead at four points, while the front engine bearers bolted direct to the frame with 5/16-inch high-tensile bolts.

Front suspension was something new for Lotus — in effect a double-wishbone system. The lower member was very wide-based, while the upper wishbone consisted of a tubular transverse link located by a forward-mounted anti-roll bar. A combined coil-spring/damper unit, cut and shut from proprietary parts, inclined from an outboard mount on the bottom wishbone to a bracket on the top chassis rail. This system's non-parallel geometry retained the characteristics of a 40-inch effective-length swing-axle (the layout used on preceding Lotus sports cars)

but Chapman and Mike Costin suspected that the higher speed potential of the 'F2' would exceed gyroscopic loading limits of a true swing-axle.

At the rear they used a similar De Dion arrangement to the sports-racer's, but with single radius rods providing fore-and-aft location on either side and with the right-side rod forming part of an A-bracket, the other element of which angled beneath the seat to pick-up on the left side of the chassis — inboard on the radius-rod mount. This located the De Dion tube transversely, while a single central link pivoted the tube around a pick-up on a frame diagonal just above the new transmission.

Half-shafts passed through the ends of the De Dion tube rather than the more normal system of the tube merely uniting separate hub carriers. This typical Chapman refinement of an accepted system allowed the outer half-shaft UJ to be part of the short hub-shaft. Apart from weight-saving this provided longer effective half-shaft lengths and so minimized angularity changes in its twin UJs. Coil/damper units were mounted between the outboard ends of the De Dion tube and pick-ups high on the chassis.

Girling disc brakes were used, outboard front and inboard rear, with calipers mounted high on the disc leading edge instead of on the trailing edge as normal. Reason had always dictated the latter mounting, for the retarding force at the disc edge then imparted a downward wheel reaction against its spindle — opposite to normal wheel loading. This relieved the bearings under braking rather than risk overloading them.

13

Early failings with the strut suspension centred upon the seamed-tube half-shafts. This Innes Ireland photograph shows the result of an early test at Goodwood when Innes — having his first Lotus single-seater outing — had one shaft knot itself. An identical failure put Cliff Allison out of the type 12's debut race. When Bill Wilks raced his 16 in VSCC events in the 1960s he soon found that his tubular half-shafts were developing a spiral seam!

In earlier cars Lotus had found that consistent heavy braking induced front-wheel chatter, traced to play in the front-wheel bearings. As the calipers moved forward, without going right to the front of the disc, they induced unidirectional bearing loadings, which eliminated much of that chatter. The calipers cooled better, too.

The wheels were another Lotus first, as the 12 introduced the famous 'wobbly-webs'. These were cast magnesium-alloy discs, chosen by Chapman for their light weight and strength since minimum unsprung weight would be vital on such a feathery vehicle. The wheel casting had to be of minimum thickness consistent with strength and ease of manufacture since the foundry preferred uniform thickness. To meet this requirement while achieving the necessary variation in bending strength throughout the wheel, Lotus opted for the wobbly-web, in which peripheral distance at varying radii from the hub was kept approximately constant, producing deep folds near the hub where most strength was required and merging into a near uniform plane at the rim. There were no perforations, thereby minimizing stress-raisers and improving fatigue life. A six-bolt fixing was used, the front wheels incorporating integral hubs and their wheel-bolts doubling to locate the brake discs. Colin believed that with a dry weight of 620lb the 12 was unlikely to wear out tyres even in a 300-mile GP, and that was far beyond his ambitions at that time. He was only interested in F2, and in those sprint-type events a wheel-change would

blow one's chances in any case. So bolt-fixing had replaced the heavyweight tradition of the knock-off hub.

Power in the shape of the Coventry Climax FPF came from the drawing boards and brains of Walter Hassan and Harry Mundy. It had been developed virtually as one half of the still-born FPE 'Godiva' 2½-litre V8 which they had laid out in 1952-53 for Formula 1. It used the V8's cylinder-head, and similar rods and pistons, but had an all-new crankcase and block. Once in production it was guaranteed to produce 141bhp at 7,300rpm on F2 regulation 100-octane pump petrol. It scaled just 280lb, while the 12 spaceframe itself accounted for only 47lb, complete with all brackets.

Harry Mundy had left Coventry Climax in 1955 to become the most significant British motoring journalist. He was appointed Technical Editor of *The Autocar* and always remained the practical and experienced engineer. Chapman consulted him regularly, and from their discussions emerged the controversial five-speed Lotus transmission — remembered by Mike Costin as 'the five-speed Lotus queerbox'.

Colin had had enough of struggling with proprietary production transmissions and attempting to make them live in racing. To progress, Lotus needed a pure-bred racing gearbox of their own. The problem with front-engined single-seaters, however, was that the driver sat on the centre-line — pushed up into the air by the propeller-shaft beneath him. If one wanted to minimize such a car's frontal area and size, then the prop-shaft had to be dropped as low as possible or offset to one side. In the 12 Colin opted for the first expedient. He had toyed with an American Halibrand final-drive, which had drop-gears to step-down the transmission line from a forward engine and which also offered speedy ratio changes; he realised that what he required in effect was five pairs of drop-gears. Selection could be simplified by moving the bottom of the two shafts required through the stack of gears, carrying one set of dogs which would engage successively with each gear. He schemed a transmission using a Volvo ring-gear-and-pinion, made by ENV with pronounced hypoid form.

He discussed this project in depth with Mundy, who introduced a gifted detail engineer he had known since his days on the V16 BRM design staff. This was an expatriate Austrian named Richard Ansdale. He was briefed to produce a gearbox of minimum size and weight, and their now tripartite discussions reasoned that since most racing gear-changes were sequential (*ie*, drivers tended not to miss out gears but to change up 1-2-3-4-5 and back down again through all five) then a motorcycle-style progressive change would suffice.

The gearing was to be all-indirect, with the drive entering the 'box on one shaft and leaving it on the other. Five gear-sets were fitted, each simple spur gear being thin like a timing gear and interchange-

Team Lotus' first Grand Prix entries were made at Monaco on May 18, 1958. Here Cliff Allison — probably in his regular '357) — shoots the chicane while Graham Hill — probably in '353' — locks over for the Tabac. Both used 1,960cc Coventry Climax FPF power.

Cliff Allison settled well into Formula 1 and found the very high-speed curves at Spa-Francorchamps no great problem during the 1958 Belgian GP. He was fourth at the finish, behind three cars which could not have completed another lap. The fragile little 12, incredibly, was still very healthy. This car, '357', used a 2.2-litre Climax engine in this event, while Hill's sister machine ran a 1.9-litre.

Team's first British GP yielded little of note apart from Cliff Allison's quite remarkable fifth-fastest time in practice on the Silverstone circuit of 1m 40.4s, which equalled Mike Hawthorn's best in his Ferrari Dino 246. Note the difference in size between the 12 and the Maserati.

able with those on the other shaft, thus allowing maximum intermediate ratio choice from a minimum number of spares. Those on the output shaft were splined to it, while those on the input shaft were free to rotate around what was in effect a long hollow sleeve housing a set of dogs which would engage the centre of the desired gear by sliding the dogs to and fro. To produce a neutral position between each gear — and to prevent selection of two at once — the dogs were half gear-wheel thickness.

To lower the input and provide as low a prop-shaft as possible beneath the driver, Ansdale separated the shaft-centres as widely as possible, and achieved a total driveline offset (drop) of 5 inches. In the 12 the FPF engine was raked downwards towards the clutch end, with the prop-shaft passing through a centre steady-bearing to the new transaxle. The Chapman-Mundy-Ansdale gearbox was tiny and light — scaling only 49lb in original form — it had lugs to carry the inboard rear brakes on either side, acting on the half-shafts, and it was to enjoy a long if controversial career.

Its creators liked the idea of a positive-stop change, in which the gear-change lever would be moved in one direction for up-changes and in the other for down-changes, but would always return to a central position after each selection. However, they were frightened of its complication and they settled for a migratory change in the original 12 with simple left-hand lever mounted in a straight quadrant with a gate arranged in a series of 'Z's. There was a gear to be engaged in the bottom right corner of each 'Z'. The driver therefore notched the lever forwards to change-up, and back to change-down. The story was that reverse was selected by a separate lever when the main shift was in neutral...

Frank Costin's body design for the 12 aimed at untroubled airflow, minimal frontal area and adequate cooling. Unlike his teardrop Vanwall styling he cowled the 12 as closely as possible and the radiator was laid back to reduce bonnet height and to place the mass of its coolant — it had an integral header tank — over the front axle.

The overall effect was startling for that era. With a weight of around 700lb ready to run and 141bhp to push it along, its power/weight ratio looked like 451bhp/ton. Harry Mundy had a small vested interest but with good reason he wrote, '...based on these figures the latest Lotus will be able to challenge the Formula 1 cars, and has the promise of becoming one of the most remarkable racing cars ever produced...'. Uncharacteristically, he was being over-optimistic.

During 1957 Team Lotus ran a restricted F2 programme, continued racing their sports cars, sold some 12s and made relatively little impression in a formula dominated by the mid-engined Coopers — which could themselves be put in their place in Europe when Porsche or Ferrari ran cars.

The original Motor Show prototype was never man enough to be raced, John Lambert recalling how its joint welds had been ground away and the whole frame beautifully stove-enamelled for display. 'There wasn't enough weld left to hold it all together...' The car went to the Montagu Motor Museum at Beaulieu for several years, was finally returned to Lotus and is retained today by Colin Chapman.

A second De Dion car was completed for development testing at Silverstone in March, 1957, and subsequently raced by Herbert Mackay-Fraser at the Whitsun Brands Hatch and Crystal Palace meetings, where it picked up a third place. Meanwhile, the type's debut had come at Goodwood, on Easter Monday, when Cliff Allison drove a third car — the first to employ 'Chapman strut' rear suspension.

It had become very evident that reacting engine and gearbox torques at opposite ends of a very lightweight spaceframe gave it a hard time, and concentrated suspension loads were a straw which could break the chassis' back. Colin pencilled his stunningly simple strut system to distribute loads more widely through the frame and so minimize their destructive effect. Each hub now had three locating members — a tall coil/damper strut rigidly aligned with a beefy hub-casting to control vertical motion, a fabricated forward radius arm to transmit driving force to the frame and locate the hub fore-and-aft, and a fixed-length half-shaft to provide lateral location.

After studying the horrendous effects of sticking sliding splines on rear suspensions like the BRM, and distrusting the cost of ball-spline shafts, Colin had a horror of such devices. With the strut system many expected the half-shaft UJs to become overloaded, but Lotus reasoned that at rest the car's weight placed the shafts under tension, which the joints could easily accommodate, and when cornering the loaded outside wheel would tend to compress its half-shaft, whereupon the two loads (vehicle weight and cornering force) effectively cancelled out in view of the spring pillar angle. Equally, the inside wheel was very lightly loaded by both vehicle weight and cornering force in this condition, so once again the UJs could handle the situation. So it proved, although early on — as in Allison's debut with the 12 — the seamed-tube half-shafts proved too fragile for the FPF's power. Accelerating out of the Goodwood chicane in pursuit of two Coopers Cliff suddenly became aware that the left rear wheel had come closer to his elbow! Looking round he saw that the half-shaft had knotted itself and had pulled the wheel inboard. His 'drive' had failed.

The new gearbox also proved unreliable. Ring-gear-and-pinion failures were traced to inefficient lubrication as oil was held in suspension by the gear train at high rpm and effectively ceased to flow. Pressure-pump delivery was accelerated once this was discovered and deflectors were fitted to throw oil direct on to the ring-gear teeth.

During 1957 a London University graduate named

17

Stripped-out — one of Team's two 12s in the garage at Reims, in 1958, showing the inclined engine mounting, water radiator header tank above the front-axle line, propeller-shaft passing through the under-seat chassis cross-member (beneath a bolted-on channel section) and generally light and simple space-frame. The 'square-section' bottom rails are actually round-edge Reynolds aviation tube.

Unusual Lotus 12 — Dennis Taylor's was the first single-seat Lotus to race internationally in private hands. It was maintained for the Eltham off-licence proprietor by Mike Costin and Keith Duckworth, who added the high tail with Frank Coltman's assistance at Progress Chassis. The F2 1,500cc car was numbered '355', having started life as 'F2/6' and is seen here with its popular gentle giant of a driver trying hard at Crystal Palace. Taylor was killed in an FJ Lola during Monaco practice in 1962.

Tony Marsh hill-climbing his ex-Michael Christie single-cam Climax Lotus 12 '358' as the 'Motus' in 1959. It was fitted with a very lightweight sprint body and had the engine moved back in the frame. After crashing heavily in a Welsh hill-climb the car was re-chassised, then sold to Hector Graham in Ireland. Marsh hated the Lotus gearbox and during 1960 he bought an 18 kit and went well at Zeltweg first time out until the transmission jammed in fifth. Thereafter he modified the 18 to use a Cooper-Knight five-speed gearbox, added top links to the rear suspension to relieve the half-shafts of lateral-location loads (before Lotus did so on their type 21) and adopted positive Ackermann steering in place of the Chapman anti-Ackermann. As the 'Marsh Special' this unusual type 18 was quite successful, Marsh driving it very well.

Keith Duckworth joined Lotus, working at first under Graham Hill, who was in charge of gearbox preparation. After an initial period of vacation work with the company Duckworth returned as a gearbox development engineer, and he devised the positive-stop gear-change mechanism which superseded the original prototype quadrant change. After the 1957 season a spiral-bevel final-drive was adopted without the offset of the hypoid original. A ZF limited-slip differential was fitted and the 'boxes were manu-factured for Lotus by 'Zahn Fabrik Friedrichshafen', in Germany, once the idea had been 'production-ized'. Type 12s fitted with the positive-stop change appeared at Goodwood, 1958 (Allison's car only), while at Monaco (as F1 entries) both works 12s had the new gear-change, and the transmission was becoming reliable.

There were also chassis failures. The drivers -- Allison, Keith Hall (after Mac Fraser was killed in an F2 Lotus 11 at Reims), Dennis Taylor in the first customer car and Graham Hill — weren't terribly fond of sitting astride a thin propeller-shaft, and Cliff recalls the gearbox breaking free on one occasion and bashing against his seat in an attempt to throw him overboard. Another time Coltman was smuggled into the Goodwood paddock with his welding bottles to fix

cracked frames, and was given strict orders not to weld if anybody was looking!

Cracks were easy to spot. Progress frames were brush-painted by a character named Irving Danvers, who lived next door to Teychenne and painted Mark 6 chassis in the evenings for 7s 6d (37½p) a time. Later, he 'put the squeeze on and the price went up to a Pound'. Single-seaters were special, and there was a further surcharge. The paint used was Valspar light battleship grey which starred if the metal beneath should twist or crack.

I must mention the delightful fantasy of Christmas Day, 1957, when a certain racing car constructor might have taken a Formula 2 car on a trailer to the Phoenix at Hartley Wintney, where a certain bearded journalist might have attached trade plates registered '007 MH' and might have set off on a 100-mile-plus loop around the silent and deserted Hampshire countryside, reasoning that 'the law' would be otherwise engaged that day. After 17 miles or so, when howling up Kempshott Hill near Basing-stoke at near 90mph, a rear-end output-shaft snapped. Rather than abandon the single-seater on the open road for a passing patrol car to spot, the driver coasted into a driveway to interrupt a family Christmas lunch and asked if he might use their

'Ivor the Driver' — Ivor Bueb's curiously-bodied 12 was number '359' and is seen here at Crystal Palace, where it always went well. Bueb campaigned the car widely in Europe and won the Finnish Elaintarhanajo-Djurgaardsloppet with it in Helsinki. He entered as 'Ecurie Demi-Litre', revealing his 500cc F3 background. For 1959 '359' was sold to an American syndicate which included Steve Wilder.

telephone. Suddenly there was a squeal from the dining room. 'Look, daddy, there's a racing car outside!' The story goes that the broken shaft and the trade-plate authorization still survive today and that the car's chassis number was listed as 'F2/2'. But surely this was pure fantasy...a racing car on the road is just too ridiculous...

The full racing record and subsequent histories of the Lotus 12s, as for the later models, will be found in the appendices, but come 1958 and Lotus were into Formula 1. Today Chapman maintains that he didn't want to do it. 'I was only interested in Formula 2 and sports cars, and the Elite. I didn't want to get involved in Formula 1, we weren't ready for it, but the drivers were all fired up and Climax were doing bigger engines, so away we went.'

Coventry Climax had stretched an FPF to 1,960cc for Cooper to run Jack Brabham in the 1957 Monaco GP, and he had held third place. Later events that

season proved that over-sized F2 cars were a workable proposition in GP racing. For 1958 Rob Walker commissioned an intermediate 2,015cc variant of the FPF, and supposedly in deference to his drivers' ambitions Colin joined John Cooper in ordering a pair of 2,207cc units each to put their F2 cars into Formula 1 with a better chance. More 1.96-litre units were available as a second-string, and in the BRDC International Trophy race at Silverstone, on May 3, Graham Hill drove a Team Lotus 12 with the 1,960cc engine installed to give them their Formula 1 debut. Two weeks later he and Cliff drove a pair of 2-litre 12s in the Monaco GP, while the team's first 2.2 was held back as a spare, earmarked for Allison's car in the Dutch GP at Zandvoort. The 1,960cc engines offered only 176bhp at 6,500rpm, and the 2,207s 194bhp at 6,250. It was a modest start, but it was the start of something big.

Before the triumphs, however, there were to be more trials and tribulations...

LOTUS 16

The 'Mini-Vanwall' (1958-59)

'When the brakes weren't failing the chassis was breaking, and
when the chassis wasn't breaking then wheels were falling off — no
wonder Graham got peed-off with it . . .'

Innes Ireland

A works drawing survives today, drafted by Ian D. Jones, dated 28/1/58 and entitled 'Lotus F1 and F2'. It depicts a tubular single-seat space-frame as shallow as the type 12's, but broader. Effectively it marks the birth of the Lotus 16. Embodying remarkable sophistication, this was perhaps the most advanced front-engined 2½-litre GP car to be raced, but the 'Vanwall' Lotus was to become one of the last of the front-engined Dinosaurs — though by any standards it was a small, svelte and extremely lightweight little saurian.

It made the simple type 12 look crude as a test-bed for ideas now crystallized by Chapman as chassis designer and Frank Costin as aerodynamicist. Their work was carefully integrated to match a frame similar in general principles but wider and stiffer than the type 12's to an elliptical bodyshell presenting the Costin-Vanwall theme in more compact form.

Again the chassis used Reynolds round-edge tube bottom longerons, and side bays formed into simple trusses with square uprights up front to ease suspension mounting and similar-section curved beams beneath the gearbox at the rear. A sling arrangement supported the weight of fuel and oil tanks in the tail, located by simple rubber 'bungees' in the lightest manner possible. Later, detachable frame tubes were to feature as tank and gearbox supports, and once the vexed problem of engine mounting became settled another detachable tube was to form a diagonal in the engine bay. But this was to come later, after one of the most hectic and confused development programmes ever applied to a Grand Prix car — which in the light of later Lotuses says a lot.

Colin specified a frame formed mainly from 20-gauge tube with some 18-gauge members in high-stress areas, while the Costin bodyshell was formed by Williams & Pritchard from the lightest 22-gauge aluminium sheet. It was easily damaged and distorted, vibration caused cracks and splits which had to be welded-up, but Colin insisted. 'Use thick 24-

gauge' he would say — light weight was all-important and the 'seven' type 16s built by Lotus through 1958-59 split bodies and chassis alike with virtual abandon.

Costin's Lotus shells had included ducted radiator systems since the days of the Mark 8 sports-racer. This feature allowed a matrix of minimum size to reject the maximum degree of heat to air with minimum drag. A tiny nose aperture admitted air to the 16's duct, where it passed through the radiator to exit beneath the car. To minimize drag two side-ducts were formed in the bodyshell — the righthand enclosing the exhaust pipe until it discharged ahead of the right-rear wheel, and the left-hand housing two long alloy oil-pipes which formed the main cooler. This duct drew air from a high-pressure area outside the skin at its *rear* end and discharged into the cockpit low-pressure area. The right-side duct was intended to draw hot air away from both engine bay and cockpit, but this was to prove a faint hope, much to the drivers' discomfort. There was also a front-mounted oil cooler supplementing the pipe-run system, in which oil passed through an element immersed in the engine coolant.

Front suspension was a standard Lotus wishbone system with the single link/anti-roll bar arrangement at the top, while the rear strut layout was modified with longer radius-rods, which were oval-section at the chassis end, tapered and welded into 1½-inch 10-gauge round tube and picking-up on the bottom chassis rails beneath the car's belly. Girling disc brakes, of 9-inches diameter, were mounted outboard at the front and inboard at the rear, and retained the forward caliper mounting of the type 12.

It had been Colin's declared intention to minimize overall height and present a clean body profile in his 1958 sports and single-seater cars by using 'lay-down' engine mountings, with the Climax FPF in its several forms canted at some 62 degrees to the right. With an offset of 5½ degrees from the chassis

The prototype Formula 1 Lotus 16 '363' on the starting grid at Reims before the French GP. Steve Sanville, Lotus' transmission development engineer, has his hand on the rear tyre, while Allison's type 12 '357' is in the background. Note the anti-roll bar-cum-top link front-suspension location, forward-mounted brake calipers and smooth bonnet top with only a small blister to clear the 60-degree 'lay-down' engine's cambox.

Cliff Allison's F2 prototype 16 '362' in the Reims paddock with Hill's F2 type 12 and the famous Team Lotus open transporter '903 PMT' behind. This F2 16 had its engine inclined at only 17-degrees to the left, necessitating the large near-central 'power bulge' seen here. The exhaust ran in a right-side body duct, exiting just above the radius-rod pick-up, as visible here.

*Graham Hill unamused after squashing the nose of Allison's F1 '362' in German GP practice at the Nurburgring in 1958. After repairs Cliff ran fourth in the race until the damaged radiator burst. Graham drove '363', with 17-degree F2 engine, in the 1,500cc class at this event. He spun in practice when something locked-up. 'Jenks' and Cyril Posthumus saw the incident, and Cyril recalls the silence after the Lotus' engine stalled being broken by an exasperated Graham: 'Wot the bloody 'ell's happened **now?**'. It really was one problem after another . . .*

The apparent end of the first '362' — Cliff Allison lost control of the car during practice for the 1958 Portuguese GP at Oporto, when he ran on to loose asphalt plucked from the tramlines it had been intended to fill. The frame was probably rebuilt and sold to Anthony Brooke.

centreline the prop-shaft ran back from the clutch to the driver's left, alongside his seat, and into the latest variation of the 'queerbox'. This installation demanded a lateral offset between the gearbox input and output shafts as compared to the vertical offset in the type 12. Internals similar to the original box were housed in a new elektron casting, which effectively laid Ansdale's original system on its side. Steve Sanville was now responsible for gearbox developments, and the new transmission retained the pinion mounting to the left of the ring-gear, which was itself spaced away from the diff as far to the left as possible within the final-drive case to offer a little extra offset. Some fudgery thus succeeded in adding 3 inches to the original offset, making 8-inches side-step in all. Inserted between this assembly and the prop-shaft coupling was a large box housing the latest positive-stop mechanism, a box of tricks which dwarfed the gearbox proper. An attempt was made to use the first gear-train as an oil pump, but this was to prove unsatisfactory, and two later systems were to use an external pump, and then to rely on simple splash from the crownwheel and wet sump. An external gearbox oil cooler was fitted. Whereas the hypoid final-drive in the original gearbox demanded special oil, the later spiral-bevel type was to use the same oil as the engine.

Two prototype 16s were produced and entered for the French GP meeting at Reims, in early July. One was to accompany Team Lotus' 12 in the Grand Prix itself, powered by a 1.96-litre FPF, while the other would run in the Formula 2 *Coupe de Vitesse* race with a 1,500cc unit.

However, early-season experience of the 'lay-down' engines in sports chassis showed up lubrication problems and power loss. Climax frowned

23

Nuts and bolts of the 1958 Lotus 16s. The sideways variation of the queerbox, with the positive-stop selector box actually claiming more space than the gearbox itself, which is merely the part with 'LOTUS' lettering. At the rear the Chapman strut suspension used the large-diameter half-shafts as lateral location; note the struts and inboard disc brakes with trailing calipers.

The Reims prototype cars used the 17-degree F2 engine seen above in '362' with SU carburettors, and the 60-degree (other way) F1 engine seen below with Weber carburettors in '363'. The bent induction tracts robbed too much power. The Reynolds-tube bottom chassis rail is clearly visible in '363'. Note the Lotus 7 suspension top links.

upon the mounting, while Colin claimed they had approved it, and anyway if Offenhauser's 'big four' worked so well in that position at Indianapolis and Mercedes had dominated racing with it, why shouldn't the FPF work as well lying on its side in the Lotus? For Le Mans the team opted for safety and their 15s were reworked to mount their engines at a more modest cant of 17 degrees to the left. This allowed straight induction pipes between carburettors and inlet ports and the results were startlingly good.

In a typical Lotus panic one of the prototype 16s —

the original '362' — was hacked about and its 1,500cc F2 engine was remounted at 17-degrees cant to the left, angled across the frame's centreline at 6½ degrees (from right-front to left-rear) and its prop-shaft was aligned to pass beneath the driver's left leg into a gearbox at 4 degrees to the transverse. This created some awkward transmission angles, fostered extra power loss and tucked the hot gearbox against the driver's left hip — and he was hot enough already.

Reims, in the Champagne country, is noted for its blistering summer heat and the tightly-fared type

'363' in private hands, being raced at Goodwood on Easter Monday in 1959 by David Piper. Colours were 'sage-green-and-white', though David insists today they were actually blue-and-white. Later in the season the car reappeared painted BP green overall.

Debut of the 1959 prototype 16 with assymmetric chassis, steering ahead of the front axle and anti-roll bar and brake calipers behind, and lower rear wishbones relieving the half-shafts of location duties, driven by Hill at the 1959 Easter Goodwood meeting. The new 2.5-litre F1 Climax engine demanded a larger radiator, the lower corners of which protruded from the Williams & Pritchard body-panelling; fairings were quickly added. This is the car which carried the serial 'F1/X', later '368' and which the author refers to as simply '16/1'.

16s, with their tiny cockpit openings and inboard exhaust and oil-cooler piping, almost stifled their drivers. Allison handled his 2.2-litre type 12 in the Grand Prix while Graham Hill drove the 2-litre 16 with lay-down engine, and in the *Coupe de Vitesse* Cliff took the 1.5 type 16 and Graham his trusty type 12, and was the only classified finisher from Team's four starts, in 13th place. The F2 16 was shunted mildly at the start of its race, closing up the air intake and holing its oil tank. Steve Sanville hared around the paddock looking for something to stop the leak, and the only thing he could find was a Champagne cork! Then the scrutineers objected....

For the British GP the F1 type 16 from Reims, '363', was handed to Alan Stacey, while Graham drove the F2 car re-engined with a 2-litre FPF mounted 'upright' and Cliff retained his 'Old Faithful' type 12 '357'. The team were in agony, for the 16s cooked again, the 12 lost its oil pressure and all three retired.

In Germany Cliff took over the original F2 car, Graham crashed it mildly in practice, then settled into the Reims 'lay-down' car '363' which had now been hacked to accommodate a 1,500cc F2-engine canted 17 degrees to the left, with a 10½-degree rake across the car's centreline and a kinked propeller shaft with central UJ allowing the gearbox to move back into alignment with the half-shafts. Graham's race in the F2 class ended when an oil pipe broke, but Allison ran very well in fourth place only for his car's radiator — damaged in Hill's practice incident — to split and lose its coolant.

Worse followed in practice for the Portuguese GP where Cliff spun on asphalt filler plucked out of tramlines where they crossed the Oporto street circuit, and crashed heavily. The 16 — the Reims F2 car — was written-off by Lotus and for the remainder of the year Cliff drove his old type 12 while Graham soldiered on with the surviving type 16 and ended up with sixth place in the Italian GP.*

The 16's racing up to this point had been purely experimental. Colin had abandoned the 61/62-degrees 'lay-down' engine mounting, and with the 17-degrees cant/10½-degrees offset engine mount more or less standardized for 1959 the first customer car was finally completed in time for the 1958 London Motor Show, where it shared its stand with the prototype Lotus Elite which had consumed so much of Colin's time.

John Fisher, the Portsmouth motor trader, bought the car for Bruce Halford to drive in Formula 2 events in the new year, while Lotus were to use it in the meantime until their own 1959 cars became available. The Fisher car's frame (originally '364' but renumbered '362' after the Portuguese write-off) was similar in essentials to those of the Reims prototypes, but it featured the detachable tail and engine-bay members and had its sheet firewall-bulkhead angled across the frame in order to match the engine's rear mounts and to improve stiffness. After the Motor Show this car was taken to Brands Hatch for testing by prospective team drivers and customers. Down from Scotland came a youthful sports car pilot named Jim Clark, whose backers were considering Formula 2. It was his first drive in a Lotus, his first in a single-seater car and his first time at Brands, but although he found the 16's cockpit very confined he was quick and neat. Count Stephen Ouvaroff, all 6ft 6in of him, tried next and brought the car in with its brake discs glowing cherry red, his

* See Appendix

The Fisher car — Bruce Halford leading the 1959 British Empire Trophy F2 race at Oulton Park in the second '362' which actually started life serialled '364' and appeared on the 1958 London Motor Show stand. It was purely a 1,500cc F2 car, its colours being Lotus 'customer green' (a very dark shade) with chrome-yellow nose flash.

Pete Lovely apparently enjoying his one-off Team Lotus race in '16/1' at the Silverstone International Trophy. Since Goodwood the car has been painted, and fairings added over the radiator corners. The tall 2.5-litre engine demanded a small bonnet-top blister. The pure F2 cars driven by Ireland and Stacey during 1959 did not require that feature with their shorter 1.5-litre power units.

large feet having flattened the throttle and brake pedals together. Then Hill took out the car to show them all how it should be done, promptly threw a wheel at Paddock Hill Bend and capsized against the safety bank! The Scots were unimpressed and Fisher was to remain Lotus' only new type 16 customer.

John Lambert and Peter Warr (then of Lotus Components and later Team Lotus manager) recall that Brands crash. The errant wheel soared into the woods and it took a two-day search to find it. During Bruce Halford's luckless 1959 season with the Fisher car he crashed heavily at Clermont-Ferrand after a puncture. In practice he had lost a rear wheel, complete with strut, which bounded over the bank and down into one of the deep Auvergne valleys. There was no time to look for it then and it may still be there in the undergrowth today. In fact the Fisher car had a hard life, for it was involved in the famous collision at Monaco that year which eliminated all three F2 entries and its front-end was well and truly collapsed. Progress cut the damaged frame in half and built on a new front.

Len Terry had joined Lotus as designer-draughts-man by this time, and one of his drawings dated 29/9/58 is one of the first to show the angled firewall and kinked top-left chassis rail of what became known as the 'assymmetric' type 16 chassis. The rail mod had been made to '363' to clear the carburettors when the engine was swung upright. Still this layout — as seen in Fisher's '362' — was not the definitive 1959 type 16 frame, for these were stiffened amidships by a fabricated perforated-sheet hoop which formed an elliptical peripheral bulkhead around the dash-panel area. This bay could not be stiffened by a diagonal as the driver's legs passed through there,

and he already had enough to contend with from the propeller-shaft and steering column! Terry had used a similar sheet hoop in his Terrier sports-car design, and it was to become something of a Lotus feature.

Progress made the chassis, fusion-welded like all Lotus spaceframes up to the Formula Junior type 20 of 1961. This method melted both the parent steel and a steel filler rod into a common pool at 1,495 degrees C. It was replaced by bronze-welding, a low-temperature (690 degrees C) method in which Progress used 9 per cent nickel-bronze filler to unite the mating steel surfaces. Therefore, genuine early Lotus frames and parts may be identified by their fusion welds, bearing in mind later bronzed repairs...

At that time Colin had an expression that anything made for Team Lotus must not be merely 'near enough', it must be absolutely 'spot-bollock'. To keep their time-sheets, the Progress lads responded by applying 'SB' numbers to Lotus frames, so the 1959 type 16 chassis had small tags on the forward face of their stress panels, numbered 'SB 16/1', 'SB 16/2' and so on.

When the 16s finally became sought-after for historic racing in Britain in the mid-'sixties, their works careers became much-discussed. Records were apparently non-existent, and owners' enthusiasm in some cases fudged the issue. Seven type 16 chassis numbers were noted at Cheshunt in the early-'sixties when John Thompson of the Formula 1 Register did some research. They showed '363' and '364' as the Reims 1958 prototypes, '362' as Fisher's and '365-368' as the works' 1959 machines. Late in April 1978 the original Lotus specification cards came to light for '362-364', showing that the Reims cars were the earlier numbers, and that Fisher's car

— laid down as '364' — was renumbered '362' only after the original bearer of that number had been written-off. Not that numbers mean much, for those actually appearing on the cars during 1959 included such non-committal serials as 'F1/X' and '59/X'! Anthony Brooke was to build-up a special 16 around a 1958-style frame, and this was probably Allison's Oporto wreckage straightened-out. The surviving 1958 works 16 went to David Piper for 1959, and at the end of that season four Team cars and Fisher's private F2 model were sold, leaving one 16 which lived on the mezzanine floor at Cheshunt until as late as 1964, when it was acquired for £500 by Bob King amongst a batch of other bits. Whereas it has generally been considered that four 1959 cars were built (excluding Fisher's) there were actually five...

In 1958 Coventry Climax had won two GPs using under-sized engines in Cooper cars and with relatively little effort, so Leonard Lee, the Climax chief, authorized development of a full 2.5-litre FPF for 1959 '...to give Cooper and Lotus a proper chance'... It used a new block and revised twin-cam head and displaced 2,495cc. Output was around 220-230bhp, but with development it reached nearer 240bhp at 6,750rpm. This was a great leap forward, and one which proved the essentially 20-gauge Lotus 16 chassis to be marginal in the extreme.

The 1959 specification cars (excluding Fisher's, of course) featured a three-element lower rear wishbone in place of the original fixed-length half-shaft and radius-rod arrangement, which had been insufficiently rigid to prevent toe-steer variations. Len Terry, at least, also considered that lateral forces on the strut rear suspension caused binding within the strut itself. The effect was then as bad as that of sticking splines in a half-shaft, for the car would roll, its suspension would lock-up and it would remain 'rolled' until the load came off — as in a gear-change.

Front suspension was reversed, with the anti-roll bar going behind the Lotus 7 top link, which was itself soon replaced by a tubular link with threaded ends to adjust camber. The steering went ahead of the axle and brake calipers were placed behind to clasp the trailing edges of the discs. More voluptuous bodyshells appeared, less elliptical in section than the 1958 versions and housing enlarged radiators, the lower corners of which demanded blister fairings beneath the nose. Outside exhausts were standard and the drivers still needed universally-jointed legs as the driveline passed under their left shin. They sat in moulded glass-fibre seats with legs spread to the clutch pedal on the left of the bellhousing and to brake and throttle pedals to the right.

Cliff Allison moved to Ferrari, leaving Graham Hill as team leader. The American Lotus driver Pete Lovely began the season as Graham's number two, but his car was not available until the International Trophy race at Silverstone, then at Monaco it arrived too late for him to qualify. He went home — for ten years — and was later to reappear in F1 with a Lotus 49. Innes Ireland took his place, making his F1 debut at Zandvoort in 1959 after driving his new private F2 16 at Silverstone. This car was assembled by Innes' mechanic Britt Pearce (formerly with the Hawthorn family) and was supplied in bits on the basis that Innes Ireland Ltd were to prepare the car in their premises at Golden Acres, Elstead, Surrey, while Team provided parts at cost and took something like

50 per cent of its earnings. Alan Stacey had another F2 car on a similar deal, his being prepared in Essex by Bill Basson, who had cared for all his cars. While Stacey had an artificial leg, Basson had no left hand, yet both were extremely effective as driver and engineer and were immensely popular.

Innes's F2 season was punctuated at Rouen as he lost his 16's brakes into the left-handed *Virage Sanson,* and hit the outside bank at around 100mph. That launched car and driver through the tree tops to

Innes Ireland making his GP debut in Team's '16/2' at Zandvoort where after a hard drive he finished a worthy fourth. This car has small radiator bulges and a very characteristic pinch mark amidships on the waistline. It was also notorious for having its bonnet blow half-open during races, without breaking the retainers.

Len Terry's perforated 'stress panel' bulkhead, which appeared in 1959 16s to stiffen the chassis' cockpit area. Note that these cars carried front brake calipers behind the axle as the steering had been moved ahead.

plunge 60 feet or so into the notorious Rouen ravine. Innes scrambled down a tree surprisingly little hurt, and found the car on its nose, ticking over nicely! Stacey's car was little raced as he concentrated on sports events, and is the one which was later lodged at Cheshunt.

In Formula 1 the season's highlights were Ireland's fourth place at Zandvoort on his debut and sixth at Sebring, where Stacey drove the second car as Hill was moving (in disgust) to BRM. In Formula 2 Graham notched a good second place at Brands Hatch while Innes had been fourth on his type 16 debut in the F2 class at Silverstone.

At other times chassis cracked, gearboxes failed and at Reims in a new car Ireland had a front wheel fold down on to the roadway at full-chat towards the pits! Mike Costin was the ace chassis inspector, who never wasted time looking at areas which would never break. He knew where the frame was vulnerable, and every time he looked it was cracked! In

Understeer was a feature of all 16s until they began using oversize rims and tyres in historic-car racing. Here at Reims Ireland's own F2 16 leads a Cooper; the comparison in size is interesting. This car has 'pyramid' radiator fairings and a cranked waistline; Innes took it down Rouen's ravine the following weekend. It went to the USA in 1961.

Costin tail of '16/5' at Aintree prior to the 1959 British GP. The bottom wishbone members are visible here, relieving the half-shafts of lateral location, and also removing some side-load from the Chapman struts. The unusual-pattern tyres are wet-weather Dunlops.

31

New car for the new boy. For the 1959 French GP Ireland was put into this brand-new '16/5' which was a 'small radiator bulge' car with cranked waistline (plunging downwards from the bonnet/scuttle joint). During the race a front wheel folded down. . . . Watching thoughtfully here at Reims is Cliff Allison, then with Ferrari.

practice at AVUS for the German GP Innes' car dropped its engine down on to the roadway. On the grid in Lisbon he noticed its front wheels were at odd angles; sure enough a main tube had cracked. Stan Elsworth, who had taken over from Willie Griffiths as chief mechanic early that year, smiled his toothy smile. 'Don't worry, Innes, we'll weld that for you' — and they did, on the pit apron, moments before the start. At Monza, on raceday eve, Mike Costin found over 14 cracks where the spaceframes had been pounded by the speedbowl bankings. They were welded-up. After another brake failure in the race Innes felt 'the handling go, well, funny...'. At the pits his crew found the chassis-frame breaking completely in two.

Graham fared no better. His car caught fire at Monaco, and at Aintree he took over the new one which Ireland had driven at Reims. His early-season F1 car was then demoted to F2 trim. More recent owners of Lotus 16s talk much of the 'F2' and 'F1' variants, and differences in frame-tube gauge. In fact the only essential difference is between the 1958-frame cars and the 1959 'assymmetrics'. In any case the 2½ and 1½-litre engines were interchanged

quite often, so every car could race in F1 or F2 at will. Ireland and Stacey had the only two pure F2 cars and these did have slightly reduced diameter top chassis rails, but of the same-gauge tube.

In Graham's case his new F1 car survived Aintree and AVUS, but at Lisbon's Monsanto Park he spun when his fuel tank split and dumped its load over the car's rear tyres. Phil Hill was next along in his Ferrari and he torpedoed the Lotus, striking one rear wheel and burying it within the frame. For Monza Graham fell back on his early-season car and it was this machine which David Piper subsequently bought for 1960. At Monza a transmission quill-shaft had failed and put Graham out and at Snetterton he was challenging Ron Flockhart's BRM hard for the Silver City Trophy when the same shaft failed again. For Graham Hill — without a single 1959 World Championship point — that was the last straw; he had done better in the Lotus 12...

For Sebring, in December, and the first United States GP, Graham's Portugal wreck was rebuilt with double-wishbone front suspension and a remote, low-mounted anti-roll bar as drawn for the new type 18. Ireland drove, nursed the car home

32

A Graham Hill expression in the cockpit of '16/5' at Aintree. Visible here are the high header tank and right-hand cambox of the 2.5 engine (which demanded a bonnet blister for clearance), the kinked top chassis rail for carburettor clearance, the combination water-and-oil radiator and left-side oil-cooler rails. Top front suspension links with camber adjustment later replaced the Lotus forgings used here.

Just before the accident at Lisbon, Graham's '16/5' leads Shelby and Salvadori in their Aston Martins and Flockhart's BRM. He was soon to spin and be torpedoed by Phil Hill's Ferrari.

sixth and was subsequently elevated to fifth as the Von Trips Ferrari's last lap was disallowed. Stacey drove the ex-Ireland F1 car similarly modified. The old link-cum-rollbar system (now reversed) had flexed as the car's Standard-Triumph uprights tried to twist forward under braking, and the stiffer top wishbones controlled this effect. Piper modified his new car in this way, welding-in a new top cross-beam to brace the rear wishbone pick-up. It didn't look pretty, as the beam had to be kinked like a dog's hind leg to avoid the engine water pump.

Early in 1960 the Sebring cars were taken to Argentina, then Stacey handled the ex-Ireland 1959-season car in F2 at Syracuse, and used his own at Oulton Park — then the 16s joined their sisters in private hands. By this time few potential customers would even look at a front-engined racing car, and the main reason was Colin Chapman's Lotus 18...

'16/5' revived with double-front-wishbone suspension and low anti-roll bar for Ireland to nurse into sixth place at Sebring in the first US GP of modern times. Phil Hill goes howling by in his Ferrari, blissfully unaware that this was the car he had demolished in Portugal four months earlier.

Changing times — British GP 1960 with David Piper's '16/1' (converted to double-wishbone front suspension with low anti-roll bar) understeering and about to be lapped by Ireland's works mid-engined Lotus 18. The letter-box cockpit cooler on David's car had been a special 1959 tweak for Graham Hill and was copied on the Team 16s which went to Argentina early in 1960.

LOTUS 18

The good times begin (1960)

'With the 16 we were in such desperate trouble we didn't know
where we were. I'd keep rushing home and drawing something, and
they'd build it, and I'd rush home again and in the end I threw it all
up in the air and we built the 18 and started properly . . .'
Colin Chapman

Failure concentrates the mind, and towards the close of 1959 the front-engined cars' failures were all too apparent. But after two years' struggle the Elite was in production, in October the new Lotus factory had opened in Delamare Road, Cheshunt, to the north of London, and Colin had the time to think seriously of Formula 1.

Jack Brabham's works Coopers had just stormed away with the World Championship. They had inherited their mid-engined layout from the chain-drive F3 Coopers of the late-'forties and early-'fifties, and were using identical power units to Lotus.

With this example before him, Colin Chapman thought with typical clarity, and the mid-engined Lotus 18 was the result. Twenty years later he was adamant: 'In 1958-59 we were playing around with Formula 1. The front-engined cars were Formula 2 designs and nothing more. As far as I'm concerned the first Formula 1 car I ever designed and built was the type 18...'

The fine theories embodied in the Lotus 16 had never shone in practice. It was small, light and held the road well, though prone to understeer, and Cooper had proved that the Climax engine gave adequate power. But the 16s' drunken drive-line was inefficient. It had been impossible to obtain suitable constant-velocity joints to improve matters, and then there was the over-light chassis. Even when Progress had secretly built 18-gauge tubes into frames where 20-gauge was specified the breakages had continued — and doubtless a few had been caused. Reacting 2½-litre engine torques at one end of an ultra-light spaceframe and transmission loads at the other had proved unworkable.

For 1960 Colin produced a scheme (at home in his usual style), and set his team to work upon its detailing and production. He aimed to minimize power losses, to reduce frontal area to its workable minimum and to maintain the lowest possible centre of gravity. The answer, essentially, was to follow Cooper's lead, to react transmission loads direct against the engine, to seat the driver in front of both and to make his seated form the target for frontal area. The car was to be a 'Cooper', but built with Lotus expertise. One major structural lesson was apparent. This time there was to be no 'thick 22-gauge' tubing. Instead, the frame was mainly robust 18-gauge with some 16-gauge mild-steel round tube, mainly in straight 1-inch and ¾-inch diameter sections. Terry-style perforated stress-panel diaphragms appeared around the scuttle, where the perforations doubled as instrument mounts, and in the car's tail.

The chassis' front suspension bay was fully triangulated to form an integral structure, carrying a lighter forward subframe to support a very large tripartite radiator, oil tank and body mounts. Brake and clutch master-cylinders were attached here, while the rear members of this bay carried rear pick-ups for the front suspension and also the pedal mounts.

A cross-braced chassis bay united this front frame and the scuttle· panel, while the necessarily open cockpit area drew its strength from the bays on either side. The engine bulkhead was braced, while below the engine itself two straight tubes converged to meet the rear suspension pick-ups near the rear diaphragm. A detachable Y-frame, combined with the diaphragm's top beam, could be unbolted for engine and gearbox removal.

The frame was virtually square in section, moving far from the sensuous ellipse of the type 16, and the body panels — which were to be formed in glass-fibre by Williams & Pritchard from aluminium prototype shells — were designed to clothe the frame as tightly as possible, like a box. To house over 30 gallons of fuel within this confined envelope Colin located an enormous 22-gallon aluminium tank above the driver's legs (they wouldn't stand for that today) with a further 9½-gallon tank wrapped behind and to

A Lotus leads a World Championship-qualifying Grand Prix for the first time: Buenos Aires, February 7, 1960 — Innes Ireland in the Lotus 18 F1 prototype '369'. This car had an aluminium body and was subsequently sold to Mike Taylor in England. It was destroyed in his Belgian GP practice crash caused by a steering column weld failure. Bonnier, Graham Hill, Phil Hill, Trips, Brabham and Menditeguy give chase.

the right of the seat. This concentrated the fuel-load well within the wheelbase to minimize handling changes from full to empty. The large forward oil tank, water-cum-oil cooler and forward-extending top fuel tank contributed to the remarkable weight distribution of 44/56% front to rear — remarkable because the front-engined (but rear-tanked) 16s turned the scales at 40/60% and 'rear-engined' cars were meant to be tail-heavy...

The Lotus 18's suspension was a new departure. Colin opted for unequal-length double wishbones at the front, as seen in the late-'59 experiment on the 16s, and with geometry placing the instantaneous roll-centre close to road-level. A total rethink of rear-suspension philosophy dropped the roll-centre there to a similar level. In a partial reversion to 1957-58 practice, lateral location was provided by fixed-length half-shafts, but this time they formed merely the upper member of a double-link system. New cast light-alloy hub carriers extended to within an inch or two of the roadway to pick-up long tubular wishbones pivoted well underneath the gearbox, almost on the car's centre-line. This system ensured that pronounced negative camber would be adopted on bump — as at the front — so maintaining the outer tyres' contact area on the road surface even under conditions of extreme roll. Twin parallel

radius-rods on either side located the rear wheels longitudinally.

In practice much of the suspension was similar to that used previously. The machined steel front hubs, Triumph proprietary uprights and bolt-on wheels were all type 16-style, though the bottom knuckle utilized a nylon bush bearing instead of the screwed steel-type used previously. Armstrong adjustable dampers were as before and steering was similar (though a straight steering column to the 14-inch leather-trimmed wheel could now be used since there was no front engine to circumvent). Once again the rear suspension fed little tensile or compressive load through the drive-shaft, so it was not over-worked even though it was a structural suspension member. The lateral links were threaded at their inner end for alteration of camber angle, and at the outer end for toe-in, while the tubular top front wishbones had a threaded ball-joint outer end to provide camber adjustment there. Anti-roll bars were fitted at both ends to trim the car and to provide the merest degree of inherent oversteer, which would give this essentially 'neutral' device the driver-feel necessary if it was to be taken to its true limits of cornering power.

Colin explained that he had adopted the new rear-suspension layout, '...because there is insufficient height at the rear for a strut', while the cast

Innes' great day — Easter Monday Goodwood, 1960 — when his F1 and F2 18s twice beat the great Stirling Moss' Coopers. This was Lotus' first-ever Formula 1 victory, and it followed rapidly on Innes' first F2 win for them in the Oulton Park Spring meeting with the 'Buenos Aires' 18. This car at Goodwood is '371', brand-new and with moulded glass-fibre bodywork. One gets an impression of Chapman anti-Ackermann steering here with the outside front wheel turning more sharply into the corner relative to the nearside, generating greater slip-angles and generating more 'bite'. The system held good in racing car design well into the 1970s, when modern tyres began to demand true parallel steering, or even conventional positive Ackermann, with the outside wheel describing a wider arc than the inside. In 1978 Colin admitted freely, 'we're not really sure about steering any more — we've got to learn again . . .'.

Jimmy Clark's first World Championship points came from this, his second GP drive, at Spa in 1960. Here his 18 — '373' — hurtles through one of the circuit's super-fast curves. Note the absence of any roll-over protection. Accidents at this meeting killed teammate Alan Stacey and Chris Bristow, and injured Moss and Mike Taylor. Clark feared and hated Spa — but he was to return and conquer.

37

Ron Flockhart handled the brand-new Team 18 '374' in the 1960 French GP at Reims. Here the car is seen with its tapered 'fast-circuit' nose section and enclosed carburettors, achieved by canting the engine to its right. This pulled the bellmouths out of turbulent air ahead of the rear wheel and was hoped to improve carburation. The streamlined nose was tried after Ireland found he was losing as much as 800rpm on the straights at Spa when he moved out of a slipstream to run alone. The 18s were slow in a straight line.

wobbly-web rear wheels had been modified in rim-section, '...to complement the overall suspension design'. They were to carry 6.50-15 Dunlop tyres as compared to 5.00-15s on the front.

Braking was through outboard front/inboard rear discs, with provision for outboard rears if they became overheated in the standard position. Calipers were by Girling, clasping 10½-inch front and 9½-inch rear discs, and were mounted ahead of the axle, in a reversion to 1958 practice. Provision was made to carry outboard rear brakes on the new hub-carriers with calipers either ahead of the axle or behind it.

The latest gearbox was based on the 'gears-behind-the-axle' type which ran at Le Mans in 1959 on the Hill/Jolly type 15 sports car. This reverted to the 'vertical offset' of the type 12 transmission, with the gear cluster behind the ring-gear chamber and a front casting redesigned to incorporate the clutch bellhousing, throw-out mechanism and starter mount and housing. When bolted-up to the engine-clutch assembly, the drive entered this third-generation gearbox beneath the diff unit, where the positive-stop mechanism was located, then into the input shaft at the bottom of the gearbox, and through to the output-cum-pinion shaft at the top, driving forwards to the final-drive, which once more was of the hypoid-bevel type. This reversion dictated the use of the gearbox's own lubrication oil once again, whereas the 1959 transmissions, with their spiral-bevel final-drives, had used engine oil. The great advantage of the third-generation 'queerbox' was speedy ratio-changing, for the rear cover could be removed and the gears slid-out rearwards. On the 12s, the propeller-shaft had to be disconnected first, and it was a fiddly job working upside-down inside the cockpit. The 16s were tricky, too.

The Lotus 18 was to be an all-purpose racing car, the version described doubling as a Formula 1 and 2 car with 2½-litre or 1½-litre FPFs installed, while a simplified variant carried an 1,100cc engine for Formula Junior. This model was the first to appear, at the Boxing Day Brands Hatch meeting in 1959, with Alan Stacey driving. Soon after this the proto-type F1 car was crated in component form and sent to Buenos Aires for the Argentine GP, where Innes Ireland led sensationally before all manner of problems beset the hastily-assembled car; finally he nursed it home, sixth, with a shattered brake disc and only one front wheel steering properly.

It was to be Innes' year for Lotus as the 18 made its

John Surtees, still motorcycle racing at the time, made a remarkable motor racing debut in 1960. After driving Tyrrell's FJ Cooper at Easter he became Team's number-three, was second in the British GP ahead of troubled Ireland, and then started on pole here in Portugal and set fastest race lap in '373' before retirement. Clark crashed '374' in practice at Oporto and Team used all their welding rod repairing it, finally having to use fence wire as filler! Jimmy was told to take it easy in the race, yet he finished third.

mark, first in Formula 2 and then in Formula 1. At Syracuse, to open the European season, Innes brought the aluminium-bodied Argentine 18 home fourth, while Alan Stacey retired his works 16 from its last serious motor race.

Then, at Oulton Park in early-March, Innes scored Team's maiden F2 victory, the first for a Lotus single-seater, and amputated 5.2 seconds from the lap record! This made everyone sit-up and take notice, and 16 days later Innes had his triumphant day at the Easter Goodwood meeting as he drove 18s to win both F2 *and* F1 races, beating Moss' Cooper both times to give Team Lotus their first GP-class victory. Moss had been impressed with the 18's performance in Buenos Aires, Syracuse and Oulton Park, and having now witnessed that unusual open-ended tail-cowl at close-quarters at Goodwood, he wanted a Lotus, and Rob Walker ordered him one. It was completed after a hasty build the week before the Monaco GP, and with the Lotus 'queerbox' installed it carried Moss to victory at Monte Carlo to give the marque their first *Grande Epreuve* success.

Later, Walker fitted their cars with a Colotti transmission, which demanded a modified rear diaphragm and outboard rear brakes, but Team remained undecided on rear-brake mounting. Essentially, their queerbox-transmitted cars carried inboard rear brakes, but as the season progressed problems of gearbox-transmitted heat and oil leaks made outboard brakes look more attractive. In practice for the Portuguese GP Innes' 18 appeared with both inboard and outboard brakes mounted at its rear, and they were piped-up to choice.

But tragedy intruded on this 1960 season at the Belgian GP, where a hub failure sent the Walker car to oblivion in practice (seriously injuring Moss) and subsequent inspection showed that cracks were forming on the works-car hubs, which were replaced by new components flown out that evening. Mike Taylor crashed his newly-acquired ex-Argentine prototype 18 virtually simultaneously with Moss, but on a distant part of the circuit. In his case a faulty steering column weld had failed. He was also severely injured, and subsequently he received damages in settlement from Lotus. Worse followed in the race, as popular Alan Stacey was apparently struck by a bird. Stunned, he lost control of his works 18 and crashed fatally. A shocked Jimmy Clark finished fifth in this his second GP for the team, while Innes felt he had the measure of the leaders early on, only to lose time,

Team's Formula 1 18s stripped out in the paddock showing their leading-edge front brake calipers, square-section chassis form and huge scuttle fuel tanks. '374' is in the rear with its canted engine and inboard carburettor bellmouths. The cut-out tail of the engine cover was designed to draw in cool air over the gearbox and inboard brakes, not to let hot air out.

Jim Endruweit, Team's ace gearbox fitter, and from 1960 their chief mechanic, changing ratios in an 18's 'queerbox'. Note the inboard disc brakes.

Stirling Moss won at Monaco in 1960 with this brand-new Rob Walker 18 '376' (above); it was this car which lost a wheel and crashed to injure Moss in practice at Spa. Its replacement was running in the Portuguese GP (below) which Moss led. This car has a white screen surround, and when both Walker 18s appeared at Riverside in 1960 they were known to their mechanics as 'black' and 'white' from these surrounds.

At Oulton Park, for the September 1960 Gold Cup race, Moss won in 'black' (see previous page) while in 1961 he won again at Monaco in 'white', which has gone into history as '912'. The 1960 Monaco victory was Lotus' first World Championship success, though Team's cars failed and Ireland pushed his round most of one lap. The Gold Cup race which Moss won was perhaps one of Ireland's greatest races, for he led before flying up an escape road, rejoined and caught Moss and Brabham once more, only for mechanical failure to put him out.

first with a slipping clutch and then with an horrendous high-speed spin while trying to make up time.

The Moss car was replaced by one assembled at Cheshunt by the Walker crew, and Stirling was racing again at the Portuguese GP. He won the US GP to end the season at Riverside, California, where Walker Racing appeared with a spare 18 to match their second car. Thus Stirling Moss gave Lotus their first two Grand Prix victories that season, while Innes Ireland's extrovert driving (which was actually more heady than he has subsequently been given credit for) gave the works team three non-championship F1 victories, and Moss added the Oulton Park Gold Cup and Watkins Glen Libre race in Walker's car, and Team Lotus Formula Junior men Trevor Taylor and Jim Clark achieved F2 victories at Crystal Palace and Brands Hatch to add to Ireland's early-season successes.

So the Lotus 18 made its name, presenting Cooper practicality in the form of advanced Chapman theory, but unfortunately adding fuel to the controversy of Lotus building too light, and then beefing-up what broke after it had broken. Still, the 18 was supremely successful both as a works and a customer car, and many ran on through 1961-62, including the Walker cars. Politics intruded here as Moss was contracted to run on BP fuel and oil, whereas Esso backed Lotus. When Moss scored his Lotus successes in 1960 Esso were not amused, and in 1961 he was not to be allowed the latest Lotus equipment until the F1 season was over. Yet Moss' skills were to reign supreme, and as Team Lotus introduced their type 21 many 18s were updated with 21-style ideas, and Colin Chapman's marque made further impact in World Championship motor racing.

Clark's first Formula 1 victory came at Pau, in 1961, when his Team 18 '371' made an early appearance in 1.5-litre form — with a makeshift roll-over bar 'protecting' his head. The very low outboard mount for the 18's bottom rear wishbone is very evident in this shot.

Sheer genius — Moss in the rebodied, modified-rear-suspension, Colotti-gearbox Walker 18/21, supposedly '912', at Nurburgring in 1961, when he won the German GP.

43

The bodywork used on the Walker 18/21 mirrored that developed by UDT-Laystall's chief mechanic Tony Robinson for his 18s. Frank Coltman, at Progress Chassis, modified the frames and dash-panels to match the new profile. Above, in the Lombank Trophy at Snetterton in April 1962, Masten Gregory broadsides '917' ahead of his new teammate Innes Ireland in '916'. Driving such a car was a great leap backwards for Ireland, having lost his works seat at the close of the previous season. Below, the ultimate '18' — Stirling Moss heading for catastrophe at Goodwood on Easter Monday, 1962, in the Rob Walker-owned, UDT-entered '906' with Climax V8 power.

LOTUS 21

Best of the Climax 'fours' (1961)

'The thing which struck me, in those early days with Lotus, was the doggedness of the mechanics. They would work on through thick and thin where any normal human being would give up and say "To hell with it, you're not getting a car for this race!" . . .'

Jim Clark

In 1961 slippery bodies were 'back in' with Lotus. This was apparent as early as the Racing Car Show held in London, in January, at which the new Formula Junior type 20 was released to replace the immensely-successful 18. The biscuit-box bodywork had been replaced by a slim and graceful glass-fibre shell of elliptical section. The high-slung scuttle tank of the F1 type-18s was replaced by an aluminium pannier slung in the chassis side bay to lower the fuel-load C of G. Suspension was similar in principle to that of the 18, with the twin-link rear-end using the half-shafts as a lateral locating member, but further Formula 1 development was afoot...

It was positively helped, though delayed, by the type 20 development programme. Colin's design team discovered how steep a 'lay-down' driving position was acceptable, for example, and also tested the practicality of using chassis tubes to double as oil and water pipes. The Junior programme over-ran by two months, so pushing back the new F1 car, and there were other problems, too.

The old 2½-litre formula had died at the close of 1960 as the governing CSI decreed a 1½-litre Formula 1 to take effect from 1961-65. British constructors in general howled at the decision, and attempted to maintain a 2½-litre class in an Intercontinental Formula to which a handful of races were to be organized during the new season. This effectively provided a stamping ground for obsolete machinery, but Colin considered, ...'Formula 1 was going to be 1.5-litres, and there wasn't much we could do about it'. Coventry Climax and BRM had both started work — late — on V8 engines for the new Formula, but for this season Ferrari were to dominate with their powerful V6s, while the British teams struggled with what relatively feeble 1.5-litre 'fours' Climax could offer.

The original concept for the Lotus 21 had included Climax's new V8 engine, which was scheduled for May 1961. However, it rapidly became apparent that

the engine would not be available, and Lotus were forced to redesign the car for the 4-cylinder FPF, using the ZF gearbox intended for the V8. The new transmission had an increased centre-line offset when compared with the Lotus gearbox it replaced. This necessitated a suspension redesign, which Colin schemed around 6.50-section tyres. Then Dunlop ceased development of this tyre, and a further redesign was necessary to accommodate 6.00s. Meanwhile, FJ testing convinced Colin that outboard brakes were better than inboards, since they cooled so effectively, and another rear-end rejig took place to move the brake mountings outboard.

It was clear that the car would be down on power compared with Ferrari, so one aim was to present as clean a section as possible to the airstream. Pannier fuel tanks, like the FJ design but larger, dropped one mass within the car. The rear-suspension redesign to accommodate 6.00-section tyres dictated the fitting of a top link to produce the required roll-centre height. This relieved the half-shaft of lateral wheel-location duties, but provision was now required for changing the shaft length as the wheel rose and fell. Colin had always had a horror of sliding splines, and newly-developed Metalastik rubber couplings seemed ideal. They were lighter than conventional UJs, they overcame the problem of splines sticking, they acted as a drive-train cushion which would protect the gearbox from shock loads and they also reduced the abrupt alteration of traction between tyre and road during a gear-change.

Lotus' familiar and troublesome old 'queerbox' was dropped. Using one tiny set of dogs to pick-up every gear was too much, for as they wilted under the strain selection became hit-and-miss. As the gearbox wore, so shafts would float gears in and out of mesh, while rough roads caused the internal gearbox bulk-head to flex and so vary the final-drive mesh. In the Tasman races at the beginning of the year mechanic Dick Scammell found himself changing ring-gears

Jimmy Clark at Monaco, in 1961, in his brand-new type 21. Note the remarkably clean shape, fabricated top rocker-arms actuating inboard coil/dampers, top-link rear suspension relieving the half-shaft of lateral location duty, and air intakes cowled by the engine cover on either side. Ireland wrote-off his brand-new sister car here during practice after becoming confused by its unfamiliar gear-change pattern.

and pinions between race heats! Colin toyed with going to a system of ball-selection for the new year, but meanwhile a visit to ZF had attracted him to the idea of using a transmission which they could supply in its entirety. Ball-selection and continued development of the Lotus gearbox was to be set aside for a small matter of 15 years...

At Friedrichshafen, Colin spotted a transaxle casing lying in ZF's experimental shop, intended for something like the Haflinger light truck. He decided it would prove ideal for F1 use, and it was to transmit Lotus power for several years to come.

It had been hoped to put the new type 21s on the grid for the Aintree 200. This was not quite possible, but still the prototype was built from scratch in six weeks and was on test at Silverstone two days after the Aintree race. Trevor Taylor, new FJ ace Peter Arundell, Mike Costin and Chapman himself drove the car, and at Snetterton, on International Trophy race day, Colin test-drove it by himself. New Mark II Climax engines, using the more beefy 2.5 bottom-end, were to be used, but they did not arrive until two days before departure for Monte Carlo. Team eventually set off with two complete new 21s and a third in component form.

Essentially, the 21 was a stronger 20 FJ rather than a sleeker type 18. It was heavier, to match the new F1 minimum weight limit of 450Kg (990lb compared with the 18's *circa* 940lb), but its space-frame construction followed 18 principles, complete with the perforated stress-panel diaphragms at dash-board and rear-end. Once again a Y-frame bolted across the top of the engine bay, but the FPF engine was installed with an 18-degrees cant to the right to provide a lower 'bonnet' line. The last Team Lotus 18, number 374, had a similar installation and had become Jim Clark's regular 1960 car. The cant served to pull the carburettor bell-mouths inboard, out of the turbulent airstream, on the 18, while the exhaust system moved inboard low down on the right side, and required an assymmetric cut-out in the rear diaphragm to accommodate it. The installation was similar on the 21, although its shapely engine cover cowled into dual air intakes beside the driver's shoulders, and the carburettor trumpets were exposed within a bulged cowl cut-out.

In section, the 21 was more voluptuous than the 20 FJ to accommodate 30-gallons fuel tankage in shaped aluminium cells 'bungeed' on to the frame. Steering and brake systems were similar to those of the 18, although the rear brakes were placed outboard as standard and calipers now clasped the trailing edges of the discs.

Once again Colin proved himself the trend-setting suspension designer of the time. To clean-up airflow around the car's small-section front-end he tucked the coil-spring/damper units inboard, mounting them vertically within the chassis and actuating them by fabricated cantilever arms pivoting on the top chassis rail. They had adjustable ball-joints at their outboard ends to locate the top of the Triumph Herald uprights, which Lotus still used. The rocker-arm was streamlined in section to create minimum turbulence, while a more conventional wide-based bottom wishbone was formed from round-section tubing. This wishbone located the foot of the Triumph upright in a spherical bearing, and in prototype form its chassis pick-ups were inclined down towards the nose and up towards the driver to produce a degree of 'anti-dive' in the suspension geometry. Under braking, as the wheels 'pulled back', they would tend to droop on their suspension, forcing the car's front-end to maintain something like its normal ride-height and fight the tendency to dive. This controlled pitch within the car as the driver danced from brake to accelerator, and theoretically it improved its general handling. But Ireland didn't like the sensation of anti-dive at all, for without the car's nose dipping under braking it felt like the brake failures to which he had become accustomed in the bad old days of the type 16! A short

anti-roll bar linked the inboard ends of the top rocker-arms, tucking another suspension component neatly away out of the breeze.

At the rear, new hub-carriers rose above axle-height to meet upper lateral links which raked steeply down to low chassis pick-ups, thereby maintaining negative-camber geometry similar to that at the front. Twin radius-rods provided longitudinal location, with a reversed bottom wishbone fitted down below.

In the cockpit the driver leaned back steeply, lowering his head 2 inches or so to cut frontal area by 'a quarter of a square-foot'. Cockpit space was limited, dictating the use of frame tubes to carry oil and water, while a final change from the FJ design was the use of 15-inch instead of 13-inch 'wobbly-web' wheels.

The type 21's Monaco debut was fraught. Jimmy Clark was a sensation in early practice as he was the only man to lap below 1 minute 40 seconds, but trying to improve his time he crashed heavily at Ste Devote and his car had to be repaired for the race using parts from 'number three' and labour flown out specially from Cheshunt. Then Ireland crashed in the tunnel, writing-off his brand-new car after losing his way through the new ZF change and selecting second instead of fourth under full power. Innes was badly hurt, and cursed the confusion of sampling both four- and five- speed gearboxes in one practice.

Clark was to race his cobbled-up Monaco car for much of the season as a new car completed for him in

Typical Lotus spaceframe — the 21. The assymmetrical rear diaphragm bulkhead has a right-side cutout for the exhaust system which drew inboard as the engine canted to the right.

Type 21 unveiled, showing the front end of one of the 1961 Monaco cars, with its large elliptical radiator, proprietary Standard-Triumph uprights, cantilever top arm actuating inboard coil/damper units and aluminium fuel tanks strapped into place by rubber bungees. Burn marks on the front chassis cross-member show where an additional diagonal has been welded-in after initial testing revealed flexion.

Innes Ireland won the non-championship Solitude and Zeltweg GPs in Team's 21s during the 1961 season. Here at Solitude he hares for the finish line having overtaken Bonnier's works Porsche, right behind him, on the grass verge into the last major corner! When he had disappeared from his pit-crew's sight into that last lap, driving furiously behind the Porsches of Bonnier and Gurney, Chapman turned and said to his men: 'Either old Innes is going to win this race, or that's the last we'll ever see of him . . .'. It was a drive which had 'motor racing' written all over it — no holds barred.

Ireland could use his head as well when necessary. After a practice crash at Watkins Glen his 21 would not fuel to capacity before the 1961 US GP, yet he won, going as slowly as he dared, to give Team Lotus their maiden Championship-race success. Here, he is joined by Colin and mechanic Ted Woodley. Ted remembers Innes: '. . . slipped me 25-quid for winning . . .'

time for the German GP was promptly written-off in practice when a Thompson joint failed in the steering. Innes had his car catch fire during that race, and had to watch while it apparently burned-out completely, leaving the engine and gearbox melted with harder camshafts, gears, rods and crank protruding from the mess. Incredibly, the chassis frame was salvaged, it proved remarkably true in the jig and was reassembled into a replacement car. It was a case of, 'don't tell the drivers', and mechanics Dave Lazenby, Dick Scammell and Ted Woodley recall that the frame did not appear to be embrittled, just '.. beautifully annealed'. Team had a second new 21 in time for the Modena GP, where Innes tried it in practice, then Clark raced it in the Italian GP and was involved in the tragic Von Trips collision, which left the new car mangled and in Italian police custody. After his 'old nail' had dropped pieces at Oulton Park Jim refused to drive it again, but did so in the USA, where Innes scored Team's first Grand Prix victory!

Earlier in the year Ireland had won the non-championship Solitude and Austrian GPs (the former in an incredible win-or-bust battle against two works Porsches). Stirling Moss, meanwhile, had been forced to rely upon the updated but still obsolete Walker 18s (one of which carried a new Climax V8 late in the year) and his incredible virtuoso season included victories in the Monaco and German GPs

and in two minor F1 races for Rob Walker, while in UDT-Laystall's 18/21 he won three more. In addition, Jimmy Clark won the Pau GP in a Team Lotus 18. At Monza, Moss' machinery was tired, and Ireland offered him his works 21 with Chapman's approval. Innes had grown in racing as a Lotus man and the marque's success was genuinely important to him. If Moss could beat the Ferraris at Monza the Manufacturers' Championship could be Lotus'. As it was, both Moss and Ireland had their exchanged cars fail beneath them, and Ferrari were beyond reach as the circus journeyed to Watkins Glen without the Italian team. Innes' victory there, however, confirmed Lotus as runners-up in the Championship, yet within days the extrovert Scot found himself dismissed from Team Lotus in a manner which effectively wrecked his racing career and left him deeply resentful. Quite simply his unruly life-style and less-than-single-minded dedication made the burgeoning skills of Jim Clark a better bet for Chapman. The UDT team was to continue through 1962 using Lotus customer F1 machinery and Ireland was to join them; it was a cold decision, hard on Innes, but probably right in retrospect. Trevor Taylor became Jimmy's teammate for a late-season South African tour with the 21s, in which they raided the results, the Scot winning three and Taylor stealing the fourth. The last 4-cylinder Formula 1 Lotus was a fine little car...

LOTUS 24

The spaceframe '25' (1962)

**'I quite liked the old 24; I had some moments with it but it gave me
my best race I suppose — second place in the Dutch GP. People
seemed to think that was quite good really . . .'**

Trevor Taylor

Colin Chapman and his design team had something
up their sleeve for 1962, but it was not apparant
early in the season. Coventry Climax were in small-
quantity production of their FWMV V8 dohc
engine, and Lotus built on their type 21 experience
to produce their customer F1 car for the new V8-
powered season. The customers did not realise
immediately that Team were to be racing something
rather different, which would not be offered for sale...

The Lotus 24 spaceframe was the first to be
produced in quantity for Lotus by Arch Motors, who
had successfully underbid the traditional supplier,
Progress Chassis, for the 23 sports-racing frame.
Progress made one 24, but the rest were Arch-
produced for sale while Team made their own. The

prototype made its racing debut in April, at Heysel
for the Brussels GP, where Team Lotus gained their
first experience of the new Climax V8 under race
conditions.

The 24 was hailed as the sleekest and lightest
Lotus yet produced, which claims should be considered in relation to the minimum weight limit then
in force. Externally the car was similar to the late
type 21, although no components were interchange-
able. Brand-new cast front uprights replaced the
faithful Triumph components employed for so long,
and they mated with new high-mounted rack-and-
pinion steering gear, which lifted the track-rod on to
a level with the top rocker-arm, cleaning-up airflow
through the front suspension area where the mid-

*Trevor Taylor's best Grand Prix: Zandvoort 1962, where he brought his Team 24 '948' home in second place. The suspension is
absolutely type 25, attached to a spaceframe chassis with detachable glass-fibre bodywork. Note the new cast front uprights,
replacing the Triumph type used for so long and steering arms level with the top rockers.*

mounted steering gear of the 21 had intruded. Rear-suspension geometry was similar to that of the 21 and rubber-doughnut couplings reappeared on the inboard end of the half-shafts, where they had been replaced by conventional sliding-splines — with which Colin never felt at ease — during the 21's season. The V8 was more thirsty than the FPF of yore, and increased fuel tankage was accommodated by a return to scuttle tanks mounted above the driver's legs in addition to tanks shaped around and bungeed to the frame tubes on either side.

Team's prototype 24-V8 started Heat One of the Brussels GP from pole position with Clark driving, but valve-gear failure retired it on the opening lap. Two weeks later Jimmy won in the car at Snetterton, where Taylor gave Team's second 24 its debut with a 4-cylinder FPF installed. Easter weekend saw Moss' tragic acident in the Walker-owned, UDT-entered 18/21 V8 'special' at Goodwood, while at Pau Jimmy started from pole and led until the 24's gearshift broke adrift. Everything held together for him to win the Aintree '200' from pole after shattering the lap record, and then at Silverstone, for the International Trophy, the first customer 24s appeared for UDT-Laystall and Jack Brabham. Clark was beaten by a nose by Graham Hill's BRM, and that was the start of a season-long battle between these two for the world title. Next race was the Dutch GP, opening the Championship at Zandvoort, and there the '1963' Lotus appeared, which made some of Chapman's customers — notably UDT-Laystall — rather angry...

Still, Ireland won the Crystal Palace F1 race and Masten Gregory the Karlskoga Kanonloppet in UDT's BRM V8-engine 24s, while Jack Brabham's 24-Climax won at Roskilde, in Denmark, and Trevor Taylor gave the type its best GP result with second place to Graham Hill in the opening event at Zandvoort. At least 15 type 24s were produced by Lotus, and by the Parnell team, who confected several F1 Lotus 'entities' from the parts tray, and they continued their non-championship F1 successes in 1963 when Ireland won the Glover Trophy at Goodwood, and immense satisfaction was derived in beating Team's entries with his obsolete car at Aintree, where Innes was second to Hill's BRM. He started from pole in the Silverstone International Trophy and set a new lap record after a lurid high-speed spin out of Woodcote Corner! He led much of the Austrian non-championship race at Zeltweg in a titanic battle with Brabham's new Brabham-Climax, only to suffer a BRM engine failure. Swiss privateer Jo Siffert won at Syracuse in his Ecurie Filipinetti 24-BRM to complete the type's success story. Meanwhile, however, the Lotus 25 had proved itself to be in a class of its own...

The 24 leads a Grand Prix — at Spa, Belgium, in 1962, with Trevor Taylor driving like fury ahead of the Belgian Ferrari driver Willy Mairesse. This remarkable dice ended in a lurid accident when the cars touched, the Ferrari rolled and burned and Taylor's 24 hit a telegraph pole. Neither driver was badly hurt but Trevor's '948' was scrap.

The BRP Lotus 24-BRMs of Innes Ireland and Jim Hall line-up on the Zeltweg airfield grid for the 1963 non-championship Austrian GP. Innes' car is '944', Hall's '945', and the ex-Lotus number-one dominated a great battle with Jack Brabham only to lose his engine with six laps to go. He was awarded a 'bad luck' trophy by the Austrian organizers. Note the BRM V8's low exhaust system.

What Chapman described as 'quite the cleanest and nicest-looking car we'd ever made . . .' — the prototype Lotus 25 monocoque in the garage at Zandvoort prior to the Dutch GP of 1962, which saw its racing debut. Compare the suspension arrangement with that of the Taylor Lotus 24 pictured on page 50.

LOTUS 25

Monocoques and World Championships (1962-65)

'Despite people telling me ever since that there were monocoque racing cars in 1911 or whenever, the 25 was the first as far as I was concerned — I had never seen one before, and we didn't know if it would work . . .'

Colin Chapman

The early months of 1962 had seen mechanics Dick Scammell and Ted Woodley working closely with Mike Costin, Colin Chapman and the Cheshunt panelbeaters in a corner of the Team Lotus workshop. They were putting together the prototype Lotus 25, which was to revolutionize Grand Prix car design by replacing what had become the traditional multi-tubular spaceframe chassis by an aviation-style stressed-skin fuselage.

For 50 years this so-called 'monocoque' construction had been the most significant structural element of aviation engineering. Credit for the first aeronautical application of such principles may go to Frederick Handley Page for his aircraft shown at Olympia in 1911, or to Ruchonnet, in France, but it was another French engineer — Louis Bechereau — who produced the first streamlined fuselage employing a load-bearing skin in his Deperdussin racer of 1912. Bechereau employed a skin of three 1.5mm laminations of tulip-wood veneer glued together around a mould. When cured the resultant structure offered inherent rigidity without resort to internal framing, rather like an eggshell. This similarity coined the nickname *monocoque*, a bastard term mongrelized from the Greek *monos* and the Latin *coccum* — or single-shell.

In 1915 a futuristic light car had run at Indianapolis. This Cornelian employed a monocoque body-chassis unit and just for good measure it also had all-independent suspension! In 1923 the aviating motor manufacturer Gabriel Voisin produced a monocoque GP car at Tours for the French Grand Prix, and in Britain, around the time of the Second World War, Alec Issigonis and Laurie Bond both built monocoque hill-climb cars. Unitary construction rapidly replaced separate chassis frames in the production motor industry postwar, Jaguar's famous D-Types used a monocoque centre-section, and in 1962 Colin Chapman reintroduced the theme to Grand Prix racing without realising that others had unsuccess-fully trod this path before.

Tests with the prototype backbone chassis for the road-going Elan had shown this type of structure to be immensely rigid for its weight. This set Colin thinking, and in planning lunches at a local restaurant he literally sketched on a table napkin his original scheme to apply a backbone chassis to a single-seater. 'I thought, "Why not space the sides of the backbone far enough apart for a driver to sit between them?". At the same time we'd had years of trouble with wrapping aluminium fuel tanks around tubular spaceframes and trying to stop them chafing through. So if we made the sides of the backbone as box-sections we could carry fuel inside them in rubber bags...it was the first monocoque racing car so far as I was concerned. I'd never seen one before, and we didn't know if it would work. So then we drew the 24 spaceframe car to pick-up the 25 suspension. The spaceframe was a known quantity and so we sold it to our customers. We couldn't be expected to sell them a revolutionary car which might not work at all, and might need a long and expensive development programme. At that time the monocoque — if that's what you want to call it — was really an unknown animal...'.

The Lotus 25 'bath-tub' chassis structure was effectively two monocoque booms linked by an undertray, a bulkhead between cockpit and engine bay, a dash-panel frame and a forward bulkhead which provided front suspension mounts and included a hefty cross-beam to tie the bottom wishbone mounts across the car.

Since the advent of independent-suspension systems the torsional rigidity of a chassis frame had become vitally important to handling qualities. With beam-axles the beam governed the angular relationship of one wheel to the other. Without the beam the car's own chassis provided the link, and if wheel angles and suspension geometries were to be governed accurately then that chassis' stiffness

When Zandvoort still had woodland — the 1962 Dutch GP with Clark's brand-new Lotus 25 introducing a new dimension to Grand Prix car design before being delayed to finish ninth. Jimmy drove peakless quite often early in his career, tinted goggles aiding him here against a low late-afternoon sun.

With its glass-fibre nosecone-cum-cockpit surround and engine cowl removed the 25 shows off its twin-boom monocoque construction, inboard damper-cooling ducts on either side of the radiator core, lagged water return pipe along the left-side pontoon top and fuel-filler neck piped to both pontoons ahead of the dash panel. This shot actually shows 'R3' at Indianapolis late in 1962, fresh from winning the US GP in Clark's hands at Watkins Glen.

became the ultimate arbiter of cornering power.

Tests showed the type 21 chassis-frame to have a torsional stiffness of only 700lb ft/degree, for a bare weight of 82lb, which rose to 130lb complete with brackets and the separate aluminium fuel tanks. The type 24 frame was to scale 72lb for barely improved rigidity, but the Lotus monocoque finally scaled a mere 65lb bare, yet offered 1,000lb ft/degree stiffness, rising to 2,400lb ft/degree when the Climax V8 engine was installed in its rear bay. Such outstanding improvement was not to show in practice against the half-as-stiff spaceframe Brabhams and Ferraris on faster corners, but it allowed Lotus to adopt more supple suspension systems matching their monocoque's stiffness, which paid off in slower, tighter turns.

In detail the type 25 monocoque was based upon two D-section side pontoons, each about 12 inches

The first Grand Epreuve victory — Jimmy Clark storms 'R1' over the top of Eau Rouge hill at Spa during the 1962 Belgian GP, when he overcame his personal dislike of the circuit and misgivings about racing there to win and set fastest lap at 133.9mph. He was also to win the next three Belgian GPs — often with luck squarely on his side. Below: the unusual sight of Clark, as a mature driver, having to run 'ten-tenths' in a Grand Prix — Nurburgring, 1962, after inadvertently flicking-off his fuel-pump switches at the start. He tore back through the field from last place to finish fourth, but his lapse was to cost him the World Championship that year. The car is 'R2'.

Drama in the non-championship 1963 Aintree '200', as Clark's ailing 25 'R5' is called-in for Jimmy to take over Trevor Taylor's healthy sister car, 'R3'. Ted Woodley and Colin Chapman (in his famous 'used-car dealers' coat) wave Clark to a halt to await Taylor's arrival; Trev is heaving himself out almost before his car has stopped, while Ted has Clark's seat ready; the drivers change over; Jimmy has the clutch home and 'R3's rear wheels are spinning before Woodley is clear, yet he actually got away without hitting him! 'R3' streaked home third at record pace while Taylor brought 'R5' into seventh place. Team also changed drivers like this at Aintree in 1960, in the 1962 Mexican GP, when Clark won in Taylor's car, and in the 1964 US GP, when Clark retired Spence's car but was classified seventh.

deep and 6 inches wide, rivetted-up from 16-gauge L72 Alclad aluminium-alloy sheet and united by a curved undertray panel. Rubberized FPT fuel bags were inserted within these pontoons, while a third filled a wedge-shaped cavity formed by the engine bulkhead, the pontoon inner sides and the driver's backrest panel, which was inclined at some 35 degrees to the horizontal. The fuel bags were inserted through openings in the pontoons, secured by press-stud fasteners and filled through a common neck and vent on a cross-pipe ahead of the dash panel. Two Bendix electric pumps on the cockpit floor supplied the V8 engine's quadruple Weber carburettors. Tank capacity was 26 gallons, and a light-alloy 5½-gallon tank was made-up to fit over the driver's legs for longer, more thirsty events like the Belgian GP, though it proved unnecessary.

The rear horns of the pontoons provided mounts to which the V8 engine was rigidly bolted to contribute to chassis stiffness; this would not have been possible with the 4-cylinder FPF unit owing to its vibration and relatively weaker crankcase design. The inner faces of the pontoon horns were in steel sheet to accept suspension loads and resist engine heat.

Welded-steel fabrications formed cross-members to brace the frame at front and rear and by the dash panel, while the box-section front member incorporated front-suspension pick-ups and steering gear *a la* 24. Lightweight outriggers supported the combined water-and-oil radiator. Shallow triangular channels were formed in the frame's underside to accommodate oil, water and hydraulic and electric circuits. The gearchange linkage tunnelled through the right-hand pontoon to emerge through the fabricated rear frame. Suspension was as for the 24, although the rear coil/damper units were mounted ahead of the half-shafts instead of behind them, allowing the frame length to be reduced. The drive passed through a twin-plate Borg & Beck diaphragm clutch to a ZF 5DS10 five-speed transaxle, as before with synchromesh on all forward ratios except first and with a spiral-bevel final-drive. Metalastik bonded-rubber bungee couplings reappeared to avoid using sliding-spline half-shafts. Space in the cockpit, visible once the moulded glass-fibre nose cone-cum-windscreen surround had been removed, was so limited that drivers of larger than Jim Clark/ Trevor Taylor stature could barely be accommodated. A 12-inch diameter steering wheel helped to provide more space and pendant pedals were essential to provide sufficient leverage within the confined and shallow forward section.

This remarkable device was constructed in an air of muted excitement at Cheshunt. Ted Woodley recalled Colin seating himself in the mock-up and complaining, '...this cockpit's too wide, take an inch-and-a-half out of it!', so they sliced the undertray and had another go. Dick Scammell recalled, 'None of us really knew quite what we were doing, but it all took shape very nicely and it certainly

So far as photographers were concerned, Jim Clark had a lot to answer for since his lightning starts ruined so many good pictures. Here at Reims in 1963 'R4' hung fire with spinning wheels as Dan Gurney's Brabham (far side) led away and Graham Hill's new monocoque BRM P61 also spun its wheels. At the end of lap one, however, Clark had scratched like mad to give himself a huge and growing lead back towards the pits — so great that he wondered just where the rest had got to. This third shot of 'R4' clearly shows its needle-like Reims nose, with small air-intake, and the damper-cooling ducts on either side of it. Jimmy won this French GP and set the fastest lap at 131.1mph during the third of his record seven World Championship-round victories that season.

looked right. Mike Costin was in there wielding a rivetter because he had experience in the aircraft industry, so we all thought he must know what he was doing...it was that kind of project!'

The result Colin described as, '...quite the cleanest and nicest-looking car we'd ever made. There were no holes in the bodywork, the engine and gearbox were beautifully cowled-in and it all worked very well...'. At Zandvoort, the UDT-Laystall team — who were to operate 1962 cars — were cock-a-hoop when they saw the latest Lotus emerge from its transporter. 'This is beautiful, Colin' enthused Innes Ireland, still simmering from his dismissal six months before, '...when do we get our's? The

Trevor Taylor's 25 'R2' at Reims in 1963, showing off its classical lines, the comprehensive engine cowling, mesh injection-trumpet cover, 15-inch wobbly-web wheels and hub-height top radius-rod — all typical of early-series Lotus 25s. Trevor wore a yellow helmet, matching the car's yellow wheels, and often yellow overalls too. He was unlucky to write-off three 25s through little fault of his own, and when he finally left Team for BRP it was an entirely amicable arrangement as Colin suggested that his battered driver should take a few months' rest from Formula 1, but the Yorkshireman wanted to stay in it. Today, Trevor looks back affectionately on his years with Team, and still uses Jimmy Clark ('that fine man') as his standard to judge character. Below, a world-beating combination. The working relationship between Jimmy Clark and Colin Chapman was remarkably close during their great years in the mid-'sixties, driver and driving-engineer complementing one another perfectly.

Follow-my-leader through Monza's Curva Parabolica during the 1963 Italian GP, which assured Clark and Lotus of their first World Championship titles. Here Jimmy leads teammate Mike Spence, their cars respectively being 'R4' and 'R3'. Spence was driving in place of Taylor, injured when he wrote-off 'R2' at Enna in his third unlucky Lotus 25-destroying accident. Below, the 1964 Monaco GP, with Clark's 25B 'R6' leading the field into the Tabac on the first lap. The modified 25 has 13-inch wheels to carry Dunlop's new-generation 'doughnut' wide-tread tyres, plus the latest type 33 suspension and steering.

Up from the Juniors. Peter Arundell made a remarkable start to his first Formula 1 season in 1964 as Clark's new teammate, taking third place at Monaco and Zandvoort and then fourth in the French GP at Rouen. Soon afterwards he suffered vicious injuries in a Formula 2 accident at Reims and was not to return to racing until 1966, sadly as a shadow of his former self. Here at Spa in 1964 the red-helmeted driver is in 'R4', back on 15-inch wheels and narrow Dunlops for this ultra-high-speed circuit.

answer was that they wouldn't, because this was the experimental 1963 car. Relations did not improve...

From its debut race at Zandvoort, which Clark led, the Lotus 25 established itself as the car to beat. Repeatedly it led all opposition, and when it survived to the finish it won. The story was to be repeated — in spades — in 1963 when Jimmy at last brought the World Championship titles to Lotus, having finished narrowly second to Graham Hill and BRM in that 1962 season after losing the race lead and with it their title hopes in the South African GP which ended the season, after a Climax V8 bolt in the distributor housing had unwound and let the oil out.

In essence the 25s took their 1963 World Championship changed only in detail from their developed 1962 form, plus the use of Climax's now fuel-injected V8s in place of the original carburettor units. Early alarm had been caused by Leonard Lee, Chairman and Managing Director of Coventry Climax Engines Ltd, announcing the cessation of F1 engine production for economic reasons, but two months later this decision was rescinded, which allowed the British battalions to heave hearty sighs of relief and prepare for the 1963 season.

Later Lotus 25 tubs were formed in lighter-gauge sheet than the prototype. Thickness was not constant throughout, but basically a reduction of 2swg was made all round, which saved considerable weight. Whereas the 1962 cars had channelled the air from the nose intake through the radiator matrix and also round the coil/damper units, it was found that this had impaired cooling. For 1963, side ducts appeared on the nose cones, providing individual feeds to the coil/dampers while complete enclosure of the radiator ensured that it received the full benefit of the nose intake. This increased efficiency so much that smaller radiators were adopted with six tube rows instead of ten, saving some 15lb of weight. This study of internal aerodynamics also pin-pointed the round-front forward oil tank as impeding radiator airflow, so a smaller vee-front tank was adopted, saving another 12-15lb and bringing the car closer to the 450Kg (992.25lb) minimum-weight limit.

When R6 emerged for the Austrian F1 race, in September 1963, it carried the latest flat-crank Climax V8 engine with low-level exhaust system mated to a VW-derived Hewland five-speed gearbox. The front wishbone inboard pivots worked in solid eyes instead of rubber bushes, and Uniball joints replaced rubber bushes in the radius-rods. While older monocoques carried outgoing and return pipes in the vee recess beneath the car, lubrication problems had forced the use of larger pipes up to 1⅛-inch diameter which crammed the vee and protruded untidily beneath the hull. Colin's answer, typically, was to use ⅞-inch and 1¾-inch diameter aluminium oil pipes, one running within the other.

Since bag tanks were not baffled at the time, the use of fuel-injection brought problems as fuel surged when the level dropped low; as the uptakes were uncovered the fuel pump gulped air, and air is anathema to a PI system. The initial answer was to

'Mike the Bike', sixth at Monaco in 1964 in Parnell's BRM V8-engined Lotus 25 'R7'. This team eventually ran three 25s and built themselves a quasi-33 for drivers like Hailwood — who helped financially — Chris Amon, Dick Attwood, Innes Ireland and, in 1966, Mike Spence. Colours as here were dark blue with a maroon noseband.

Simple but effective — the Lotus air-deflector windscreen gave the driver clear vision over the perspex while producing a curtain of air pressure strong enough to deflect most bugs and rain-drops.

Tails of old Lotuses. Above, Mercedes-derived sliding-spline half-shafts and ZF 5DS10 five-speed transaxle on a late 25/33 with 90-degree crank fuel-injected Climax V8 and the later abbreviated engine cover. Below, a rare Colotti transaxle with Metalastik inboard joints on the half-shafts to accommodate plunge, outboard Hooke joints and the early-series hub-height top-radius-rod rear suspension.

Above, a very early experiment with the transmission which was to rule in Formula 1, the early Hewland five-speed on one of Team's 1963 25s. Below, the Parnell way — BRM V8 power, Hewland gearbox and Metalastik joints (outboard this time) on one of the Tim Parnell 25s raced during 1964-65. These cars, 'R3' and 'R7', were later modified with type 33 rear suspension in line with 'R4', which Tim originally acquired from Team Lotus for the 1964 Austrian GP.

All mod cons — Lotus works drivers were wedged firmly into their 'monocoquepits' early on by taped rolls of foam rubber, and later they occasionally had the luxury of full upholstery, as here. Once Colin had decreed that everything should sparkle, it did! The cockpit metalwork was mid-grey, with red upholstery and leather steering wheel rim contrasting with the bodywork's sparkling green-and-yellow paintwork.

load an extra 5 gallons of fuel, but the extra 35lb weight was anathema to the Chapman system. So a fuel de-aerator was devised in the form of a tall, thin rectangular tank fitted in the cockpit as a pad for the driver's knee. Improved Dunlop R6 tyres this season gave a jolt to lap times, and Jimmy's matured driving artistry made the most of Team Lotus' now outstanding machinery.

Len Terry was back with the Cheshunt team after a spell producing the Gilby cars for Syd Greene, and it had been partly his responsibility to build reliability into the 25s for 1963. Then, into 1964, work began on the updated type 33, built around new 13-inch wheels carrying the first 'doughnut' Dunlop tyres, and the Team 25s were progressively updated using type 33 features.

The first of these so-called 25Bs appeared at Snetterton in March 1964 with new rear uprights, smaller brake discs buried within the 13-inch cast-magnesium spoked wheels, and with the lower rear radius-rods anchored below the hull instead of on its flanks to form true wishbone geometry with the lower rear links, and so minimize toe-steer. Steering geometry was altered to accommodate the 13-inch wheel set-up, but in later events the original 'B' R6 was put back on to 15-inch wheels until development settled down. Simplified gear-linkage appeared on the ZF transaxles, which were still preferred, while at Monaco both Clark and his new teammate Peter Arundell — fresh from dominating Formula Junior — were fielded in a pair of modified 25s, respectively R6 and R4. Jimmy, in what was to become his renowned 'Old Faithful' R6, was using the latest 1964 type 33 13-inch wheels and tyres, uprights,

gearbox, driveshafts and rear suspension, which had the top radius-rod relocated on the hub-carrier on the same level as the lateral link, whereas formerly it had mounted at hub-height. This move distributed braking torques and motive power more evenly between the two rods and offered improved control. Arundell's R4 retained the earlier suspension geometry with 13-inch wheels and tyres, type 33 uprights and modified gearbox. Journalists dubbed these variants the 25D and 25C, but to Lotus they were still 25Bs. In Holland, 25C R4 came closer to 'D-spec' with late-model drive-shafts and steering-arms, but it still retained low top-radius-rod rear suspension. Later in the year further modifications to the ageing but still-successful '25D' included the adoption of modified Mercedes-Benz 220S-derived sliding-spline half-shafts. Meanwhile, the Parnell team, managed by Tim (son of Reg) Parnell, had acquired two ex-works 25s, R3 and R7, which they modified in line with the Team cars, though using BRM V8 power and Hewland transmission, and they also subsequently acquired R4, which had first been loaned to them for the 1964 Austrian GP. By that time, poor Peter Arundell had suffered severe injuries in the Reims F2 race, which effectively put paid to his GP career; although he was to reappear as Jimmy's teammate in 1966 he could never reproduce his brilliant early-F1 form with these Lotus 25 variants.

During their long career the Team Lotus 25s won no less than 14 World Championship GPs, including the 1965 French race with old R6, and 11 non-championship F1 events, including the 1965 Goodwood race, which fell, inevitably, to Jimmy in R6 — a true classic among classic racing cars.

LOTUS 29

Breaking into the 'Brickyard' (1963)

'I was sceptical. Here was some Englishman who'd never raced there (at Indy) and he said all he wanted was 350 horsepower and gasoline when all the others were getting 400 on methanol and nitromethane . . .'

Bill Gay (Ford engineer)

When the Lotus 25 made its debut at Zandvoort in May, 1962, Porsche driver Dan Gurney took one look and exclaimed: 'My God, if someone took a car like this to Indianapolis they could win with it!'. He asked Colin if he would like to see what the world's richest motor race was like, and the Lotus chief readily agreed. Dan was driving a mid-engined Buick Special that year for Mickey Thompson. A year earlier John Cooper and Jack Brabham had shaken the front-engined Indy establishment by tackling the race with an F1-derived 2.7-litre Cooper-Climax, and the World Champion had brought it home an honourable ninth amongst the 4.2-litre Offenhauser-engined roadsters. The 500-Miles race purse in 1961 had totalled $400,000, of which the winner pocketed $117,975. Evidently mid-engined chassis had a future in such company, but Gurney found that Mickey Thompson was not the man to prove it.

Dan paid Chapman's air-fare to the mid-west Speedway city, and he could not believe his eyes: 'I thought I'd gone back 15 years... I could imagine this was what it must have been like to watch the Mercedes and Auto Unions pre-war at Tripoli. I thought, well — all you've got to do is to get an engine with about half the power of these great lumps of junk, build a decent chassis and you've won the race...'

Coincidentally, Ford Detroit had their eyes on Indy. Engineers Don Frey and Dave Evans were there that day, and while Colin and Dan (who had been placed 20th) returned to Europe pondering their plans, Frey proposed a Ford engine for the '500' based on existing experimental alloy blocks for the Falcon sedan. Evans approached leading USAC chassis men, but back in Cheshunt Colin Chapman was scheming a Lotus proposal to Ford.

On July 23 he and Gurney presented themselves at Ford's front door. Frey and Bill Innes — Ford's foundry and engine division chief — listened sceptically as the Englishman proposed in essence a low-powered economy car which would complete the race with only one pit-stop instead of two or more as had been usual. Stops cost about 30 seconds, but the greatest winning margin in the previous five events had been only 27.6 seconds, and in 1961 it had been barely eight. The elimination of a refuelling stop could therefore win the race. Chapman went away with approval to develop the basic idea further, but Ford hedged their bet. A similarly tentative overture was made to A.J.Watson, whose roadster chassis had won the previous four '500s'. Ford vacillated. Their previous Indianapolis dabble of 1935 had been the PR catastrophe of the century...until the Edsel came along. They arranged a survey of the Speedway, and an Offy engine was acquired for comparative testing. It produced 407bhp at 6,000rpm on alcohol, and when their V8 produced 351bhp on gasoline and 400 on methanol they felt they had the power for whichever approach they should choose — Watson or Chapman.

Then Jimmy Clark won the US GP with his Lotus 25, and subsequent tests with the 1½-litre car at Indianapolis rocked everyone back on their heels. Ford wanted to buy a 25 to test, but there was nobody available with experience to drive it. Instead, they dropped an engine into Nelson Stacy's Galaxie stocker for tests at Daytona that November. He lapped at 154.8mph on methanol and 146.7mph on gasoline. On fuel the engine returned 2.2mpg, but on petrol its economy improved to 6.41mpg. A computer run predicted Indy lap speeds of 150mph for a mid-engined Lotus-Ford, and the decision was taken to 'go gasoline'.

Senior engineer Bill Gay flew to Europe to finalize designs with Colin Chapman, then to order special 58mm Weber carburettors from Italy. Colin had suggested carburation for simplicity and economy, despite fuel-injection being universal on the Offies. And so the stage was set.

Len Terry detailed the Lotus 29 from Colin's

Clark tries the prototype Lotus 29-Ford for size at its press showing at Cheshunt in March 1963. Standing behind are (left to right) Len Terry, Colin Chapman, Steve Sanville, Dick Scammell, David Lazenby, Ted Woodley, Ced Selzer and Bob Dance (back as chief mechanic for the second time in 1977-78) while Jim Endruweit (chief at the time) squats alongside the most potent Lotus yet built.

The prototype 4.2 Ford Fairlane-derived Indy V8 nestling in the monocoque chassis of '29/1', showing the stack exhausts used for simplicity's sake in the initial build. Note the right-hand gearshift for the Colotti four-speed transaxle, 25-style suspension and massive sliding-spline halfshafts.

The clincher — Clark's pace in the 1½-litre 25-Climax during Indianapolis tests after the 1962 US GP finally decided Ford of America to attack the 500-miles race Chapman's way. Here Colin and Jimmy pose for the Speedway photographer with their funny little green car — actually 'R3'.

careful schemes. The bathtub monocoque mirrored the 25's, though with a regulation minimum wheelbase of 96 inches. This was 5 inches greater than the 25's, and Colin reckoned to allow 2½ inches each for the lengthy assemblies of Ford's power pack and Dan Gurney's lofty frame. The tub was wider and deeper than the 25 for improved tank space and rigidity. It was further stiffened by the engine, rigidly mounted at eight points. A special dispensation was obtained from USAC to allow the use of rubber fuel bags when fibre-sheathed metal tanks had been mandatory. Six cells were used, with two in each side pontoon, a fifth behind the seat bulkhead and the sixth a fibre-sheathed aluminium scuttle tank above the driver's legs. All six were interconnected, and refuelled under pressure through a Demon inlet valve on the hull's left side. Closing the airvent cap on the scuttle triggered automatic shut-off. Non-return valves between the tanks prevented fuel surge from left to right through the anti-clockwise turns, or forward under braking. They opened to allow rearward flow into the collectors under acceleration.

Suspension was similar to the 25's, but larger diameters or heavier gauges appeared throughout. Uprights were cast in high-tensile magnesium-zirconium alloy. Rear-wheel bearings were larger, and massive half-shafts used Saginaw recirculating-ballsplines and Hooke joints. Track width was pure 25, but alternative pick-ups allowed the hull to be suspended either symmetrically between the wheels or with a 2.875-inch offset towards the left. Two wheel sets were considered, using knock-off Dunlop wheels with specially wide rims. They could carry either 6.00-15 front and 7.00-16 rear offset-tread Dunlop tyres developed for the Cooper-Climax of 1961, or Firestone's 6.50-15 and 8.25-15 combination which the Americans had evolved for the race.

Ford's V8 was founded on the 4,260cc Fairlane pushrod unit, but with alloy crankcase, block and heads. Bore size was reduced very slightly, and mechanically operated valves replaced stock hydraulic tappets. The bare unit scaled 70lb in alloy as against 150lb stock, and fully assembled with all

First tests at Snetterton with Clark running '29/1' with unpainted aluminium bodywork prior to its press presentation. The symmetrical suspension was replaced by an assymmetrical layout once serious testing began in the USA.

accessories the prototype race V8 scaled 360lb and was expected to produce 370bhp at 7,000rpm. A three-plate Borg & Beck clutch fed a four-speed Type 37A Colotti transaxle. Only two speeds would be used for most running.

Dearborn had also developed a quad-cam fuel-injected methanol V8 — though heeding Chapman's protests that a reliable 350 horsepower was sufficient and a rampant 500 might well prove an embarrassment. Their Offy engine had a bore approximately the same as the V8 and a Chinese copy of the head design was made for the 'full-race Fairlane'...apparently overlooking the vast disparity in stroke between four-cylinder and V8. Consequently, the quad-cam's ports and valves were enormously oversize and gas velocities were hopelessly low.

The prototype 29, with symmetrical suspension and separate stack exhausts, was tested at Snetterton in March 1963 before being flown to the USA for evaluation at Ford's Kingman, Arizona, test track. There it lapped at 165mph, but the V8 proved unreliable. A final shakedown was arranged at Indy. Bill Gay specially prepared an engine, but it snapped a camshaft on the test bed and was wrecked. A replacement was hastily built-up and flown to Indianapolis, where it was turned into a runner with wiring looms and parts cannibalized from a pair of hired Fairlanes! Few realised what a makeshift effort this Lotus-Ford Indy debut had become — especially when the car performed to order.

Jim Clark drove first on March 24. Next day he was lapping happily at 146mph, against Parnelli

Jones' 1962 race lap record of 150.729. The final-drive ratio was lowered, and on Dunlop tyres Dan Gurney lapped next day at 150.501mph — second-fastest-ever Speedway lap and just as the computer had predicted. The car covered 457 trouble-free miles and two weeks later the gasoline engine design was frozen as Ford Project AX230-2.

Indy qualifying and practice occupies the whole month of May. When the 29s proved consistently fast on Firestone's new 15-inch tyres the roadster establishment screamed. They claimed they were being 'forced' to run obsolete 16-inch wheels and tyres. Firestone should withdraw the 15-inchers or make them available to all. Strangely there was no such protest against Mickey Thompson's 12-inch Sears Allstate special tyres, which were uncompetitive. The furore was a compliment to the 29s' sheer pace.

Firestone agreed to make the tyres available to all. That began a scramble to find sufficient 15-inch wheels. Ted Halibrand, the Indy wheel-king, forced through a hasty batch of castings, but there were not enough to meet demand. Lotus' Dunlop wheels then cracked across their perforations and only one set of Halibrands could be obtained — on loan from Smokey Yunick, whose car had been wrecked by Curtis Turner. The plan was to share the set between the two cars for qualifying, but on May 18 Gurney crashed at Turn One, wiped-out his 29's right-side and ruined the wheels. Jimmy had to qualify on Dunlop wheels while crew chief David Lazenby and his men prepared the 'Mule' prototype car for Dan to

'Rookie' driver James Clark of Scotland poses his 29 race car at Indy prior to the 1963 '500' in which he was a sensational — and possibly 'robbed' — second. Note the Dunlop perforated disc wheels with knock-off hubs, Firestone track tyres, and the immaculate preparation.

race. Jimmy's four-lap average of 149.750mph placed him fifth on the grid, and next day Dan put his 'Mule' on row four with 149.019mph.

Final pre-race panic was to find a pit crew experienced in high-speed wheel-changes and refuelling. Bill Stroppe's Mercury stock-car team was enlisted from Atlanta, while Pete Weisman (later a celebrated transmission designer) was to handle the hoses.

Meanwhile, the first Saturday in May saw an excellent omen as Lloyd Ruby shook the USAC faithful by setting a 106mph record lap and leading all the roadsters for 40 laps at Trenton, NJ, in his ex-F1 Lotus-Climax type 18...

Parnelli Jones led the '500's, early stages in J.C. Agajanian's Watson-Offy Willard Battery Special. He had to build a time cushion from the Lotus-Fords to make his extra pit-stop(s), lapped at 151mph and stopped on schedule at 62-laps. As the other roadsters pitted, the 29s strode forward. On lap 67 Jimmy led with Dan Gurney second, and Jones was third by 17 seconds. At 70-laps Clark's average was a record 141.793mph and at 80-laps (200-miles) it was 142.566. On lap 92 Gurney lost 42.2 seconds for three wheels and refilled tanks. Jones took second place. On lap 95 Clark rushed in — and out again after 32 seconds. He rejoined third, and Jones was in the lead. At 100-laps (half-distance) Clark was second trailing Jones by 40 seconds. At 116-laps the yellow caution lights came on — under which the field must maintain station at reduced speed — and Jones made his second stop and rejoined still in the lead. At 130-laps his record average was 142.

495mph; Jimmy was second and Dan Gurney was running sixth. While the 29s could not close on Jones he could not pull away from them — and his inevitable third stop was drawing closer. Gurney was up to fourth, then, under another yellow, Parnelli made his stop. He rejoined 21 seconds later, 11 seconds ahead of Clark, with Gurney now third. It was Jones-versus-the Revolution and the enormous Speedway crowd was going wild.

Lap 172 — Jimmy only 10 seconds behind Jones. Lap 173 — 7 seconds. By lap 177 only 5 seconds split the Lotus from the lead. But now, as Jones backed-off into the turns, his Offy was blowing smoke. Oil was reported on the car's left side and simultaneously Jimmy fell away. Dan lost third place in a stop for tyres and fuel, did two more laps then returned for the rear wheels to be tightened. Jones' car was clearly dropping oil and the lightweight Lotus-Fords were difficult to control on the treacherously narrow Indy 'line' — although they were not so confined to it as the unwieldy roadsters. Chief Steward Harlan Fengler had warned in his race briefing that any car dropping oil would be black-flagged, so Clark sat back and awaited what he believed to be inevitable. It never happened.

Johnny Poulsen, Agajanian's crew chief, was in animated discussion with Fengler. Then it was Chapman's turn. Fengler fixed his binoculars on Jones' car; he thought the spray looked like water. On lap 189 Eddie Sachs spun on the 'fluid' and kissed the south-west wall. Next lap he lost a wheel and crashed properly. The yellow came out, and

Unlucky Dan — Gurney's 'race' 29 is dragged back towards Gasoline Alley after his qualifying crash at Indy in 1963. One of the valuable Halibrand wheels lies shattered at the rear while the torn-off front wheel left emphatic evidence of its departure in the side of the monocoque. This car was subsequently rebuilt and sold to USAC entrant Lindsey Hopkins to become Bobby Marshman's first Pure Oil Firebird Lotus for 1964. It is owned by Jim Toensing in California, 1978.

Jimmy found himself slowed right down by roadsters ahead and could just see Jones' tail disappearing in the distance. After several laps of this he passed the baulking cars, but the stewards didn't react. With seven laps remaining the green blinked on and Jimmy was now 22 seconds behind Jones. On the slick Speedway he could do no better than win back 3 seconds of that gap, and Jones thundered thankfully past the flag to win this truly classic race by 19 seconds. The Lotus-Ford and its 'Rooky' driver was second, Gurney's sister car seventh after its delay. Clark paid tribute (typically) to Jones saying '...he did a damn fine job', while Benson Ford told Fengler 'We are delighted with the race outcome and I believe that was the finest decision you could have made'. No way did Ford want to win by disqualification.

Jimmy's second-place money was $55,000. Colin's deal with Ford yielded another $20,000 bonus for qualifying both cars, and $25,000 more for second place...and all expenses paid.

Later that year the 29s ran at Milwaukee. Clark qualified his car on pole at 109.307mph and led from start to finish, lapping all but Foyt's second-place roadster. Dan was third, while Jimmy set a new lap record and averaged 104.48mph for the 200 miles. In September the Trenton '200' saw Clark qualify with

32-second laps, Gurney with 33-seconds and the quickest roadsters at 35! The 29s left the rest for dead in the race, until an over-age oil line parted in Jimmy's car and then Dan's engine swallowed a piece of piston which blocked its oil scavenge uptake — his V8 literally drowned in its own oil. Foyt inherited the $11,000 first place — but the Lotus-Ford had made its mark. The message was that mid-engined is best...

At the end of 1963 the 29 which Dan had crashed in Indy qualifying was sold through Ford to Lindsey Hopkins, a long-time USAC entrant who had assisted with track-racing know-how early in Ford's researches. Through that winter Hopkins, crew chief Jack Beckley and driver Bobby Marshman tested the car with Ford's new quad-cam engines. At Indy in 1964 their Pure Oil Firebird 29 was at a fine pitch of preparation. Marshman lapped at a record 157.178mph, then broke the 158mph barrier. The American driver qualified his car second-quickest to Clark's 1964 Lotus-Ford, and he led the '500' until a transmission oil leak killed his hopes at 33-laps. Jerry Alderman Ford bought the car for Al Miller to drive in the 1965 and 1966 '500's — the old veteran coming home fourth and being demolished in the startline multiple pile-up, respectively. Meanwhile, the unhappy saga of the Lotus 34 had unravelled...

The Hopkins crew with Bobby Marshman and their modified 29 which led the opening laps at Indy in 1964, running Halibrand wheels and Firestone tyres. The full-race centre-exhaust quad-cam Ford V8 engine is now in use. Marshman was killed that November while testing Hopkins' replacement Lotus 34 Firebird — a tragic fate for such obvious talent and potential.

One 29 lived on very actively — veteran Al Miller, seated here in Jerry Alderman's ex-Hopkins Firebird, was soon to finish fourth behind Clark's works 38 and Parnelli Jones' Kuzma-modified 34 in the 1965 Indy '500'. Miller averaged 146.581mph for the 200 laps, while Clark's 29 had averaged 142.752mph in its run to second place two years before.

73

LOTUS 33

The ultimate '25' (1964-65)

'It was really a logical development of the 25 — it was stronger,
stiffer, lighter, simpler and it used the latest wider wheels and tyres.
Oh yes, it was going to be a lot quicker, too . . .'

Len Terry

Len Terry's prime responsibility during the 1½-litre years at Lotus was development of the type 25 family under Colin Chapman's direction, plus growing involvement with the Indianapolis programme, which culminated in his 500 Miles-winning Lotus 38 of 1965. The Formula 1 type 33 crystalized 25 development around the new generation of 13-inch diameter broad-tread Dunlop tyres introduced in 1964. Its monocoque was simpler to construct than that of the earlier 25s. Their cockpit skins had run parallel from seat-back to dash panel, and had then kinked inwards to converge towards the pedal box. The 33's were straight, converging all the way from seat-back to pedals, and probably made a stiffer tub. The suspension modifications and alterations were as described in the preceding chapter where 25B-25D variants were concerned. Apart from its myriad detail changes, the Lotus 33 featured a ¾-inch longer wheelbase to accommodate the latest flat-plane-crank Climax V8 engine and in prototype form the first 33, R8, was intended to save all the excess weight which lengthy development had built into the type 25s.

Cheshunt's weight-saving programme was extensive, but not always successful...

Terry and car-builder John Lambert both recalled R8's test debut, when it had been fitted with ultra-lightweight suspension components using very thin, larger-diameter high-tensile steel wishbones, links and radius-rods. Colin had long since adopted a programme for 'making the cars look smart' with brilliantly polished green-and-yellow paintwork and chromed suspension parts. Ted Woodley vividly recalls chrome-plating valve caps. The new type 33 lightweight suspension was accordingly chromed, but as Len Terry ruefully recalls, '...we didn't know much then about hydrogen embrittlement'. Jim Clark took R8 out on test and a suspension component failed. He tried to spin the car to a stop, and as side-load came on the new suspension so it literally

shattered like so much glass-crystal, Jimmy ending up on the infield sitting in a bathtub bereft of all four wheels and surrounded by bounding fragments of ultra-lightweight tubing. 'I'm never going to drive another car with that suspension...' he remarked, and he meant it.

The car was rebuilt with a more conventional suspension set, and Clark drove it at its debut in the Aintree '200'. After practice troubles he started from row two, and he was battling with Jack Brabham for the race lead when a back-marker shut him off through the tricky ess-bend at Melling Crossing and R8 was suddenly on the grass, then cartwheeling off a straw-bale barrier. Len Terry had binoculars on the car at the time, and as it reared up on two wheels he saw a vivid demonstration of Clark's reflexes as the World Champion grabbed forward to knock the switches off. The new Lotus 33 was badly crumpled about the front and left-side, it lost one wheel and it finally reappeared in practice for the Belgian GP at Spa almost two months later. Evidently R8 was never the same after its rebuild, and Jimmy was always happier in his Old Faithful 25 R6 until the later 33s came along.

The first of these later models, R9, made its debut at the 1964 German GP, followed by R10 in the South African GP on New Year's Day, 1965. This car was written-off in Clark's uncharacteristic Race of Champions crash at Brands Hatch when, under pressure from Dan Gurney's Brabham, he under-steered on to the grass out of Bottom Bend and was deflected by ruts into the earth bank protecting the rear of the pits. The unsatisfactory R8 was sold to Dickie Stoop for Paul Hawkins to drive as a private entry during 1965, its season including immersion in Monte Carlo harbour, while R11 emerged as Clark's new first-string car at Spa, yet in certain circumstances he still preferred old R6. The one-off type 39 described later took the number R12, while R13 was used by Parnell for a rebuild of one of his

Minor divertissement in the Rouen paddock before the 1964 French GP with Scotland's reigning World Champion involved in a little tartan fashion photography (unusually for him). He is seated in the prototype 33 '8', rebuilt after its Aintree '200' disaster. Note the high-radius-rod rear suspension with far more beefy chassis pick-ups than on the earlier 25s, the new six-spoke wide-rim cast-alloy wheels and a very much abbreviated engine cover. Peter Arundell is behind in his 25B 'R4', while Jimmy's spare car, 'Old Faithful R6', which he actually raced, is third in line. Behind photographer Mike Cooper on the left is Cedric Selzer (owner of the toolkit), with Jim Endruweit and Dick Scammell behind Arundell. On the right, Ferrari driver Lorenzo Bandini shows interest in the model. 'R8', incidentally, is the car which Paul Hawkins dropped into Monte Carlo harbour the following year.

75

Spirit of '65 — Jimmy Clark winning his fourth consecutive Belgian GP (in treacherous rain) at the wheel of his new 33 'R11'. The low-level exhaust system identifies the engine as a flat-crank Climax V8, and its pronounced megaphones show it to be the rare 32-valve version. The knock-off hub nuts and parasol injection-trumpet gauze were very typical of Lotus that season.

A win for Mike Spence at the 1965 Brands Hatch Race of Champions, an unusual success for a Lotus number-two. Spence intelligently made much more of the drive than others had managed, and also won the non-championship South African GP for Team in January 1966. The car here is 33 'R9'.

76

'Old Faithful R6' in 25/33 form during the French GP at Clermont-Ferrand in 1965. Clark used an early 90-degree-crank Climax V8, identifiable by the high exhaust system, and 'Motor Sport' reported 'It almost goes without saying that Clark took the lead' — from pole — 'on the first corner and ran away from everyone . . . '. He led all the way and set a record fastest lap — perfection.

Champion in trouble. Jimmy won his fourth consecutive British GP for Lotus at Silverstone in 1965, but was desperately nursing his 32-valve Climax engine through the turns during the closing stages as its oil level had dropped dangerously low. Here he coasts 'R11' through one of the corners late in the race, using power only along the straights when remaining oil surged back to cover the pump intakes.

Championship clinched. Clark and 'R11' on their way to Team's fifth consecutive GP victory of 1965 at the Nurburgring, where the German GP result assured both driver and constructor of their second world titles.

Champion's prerogative. Clark trying both his cars during practice for the Italian GP at Monza, in 1965. Number 24 is 'R11', the true type 33 with 32-valve Climax engine, which Jimmy raced, while number 28 is 'R6', with older 90-degree-crank 16-valve engine, which was raced by the Italian Giacomo 'Geki' Russo in the GP itself.

continually updated private 25/33s, in this case R4, which had been effectively destroyed by Dick Attwood at Spa.

At that Belgian GP meeting, Team's cars were converted to knock-off centrelock wheel fixings using similar-pattern wide-rim cast-alloy spoked wheels to those formerly bolt-attached to the 25B series and 33 cars.

In 1966, the first season of the new 3-litre formula, one final type 33 was constructed, embodying all the experience of this 25-based family's long and distinguished career. This was R14, completed in time for the British GP at Brands Hatch, and built to carry the second of the two very special 2-litre Climax V8 engines built for Colin by Leonard Lee's men. It was handled by Clark, Peter Arundell (on his return to the team) and Pedro Rodriguez during 1966, while the following season saw Jimmy campaigning the car to win the Tasman

Championship 'down under' before driving it along-side Graham Hill's R11 (which used 2.1-litre BRM V8 power) in Team's 25-family farewell race at Monaco, 1967.

During this period, the Lotus 33s amassed a lion's share of success in Jimmy's 1965 World Championship season, carrying him to five of his six GP victories, plus wins in three non-championship races, including teammate Mike Spence's unique victory at Brands Hatch, which in some measure compensated for the loss there of R10.

The Lotus 33s in Team's immaculate green-and-yellow livery dominated 'the great years' of a generally unpopular Formula.

The ultimate 33, 'R14', with 2-litre 32-valve Climax power, driven by the reigning World Champion in the 1966 Dutch GP, where he indulged in an heroic struggle with the two 3-litre works Repco Brabhams before the engine's crankshaft vibration damper broke up and bits punctured the water-pump casing. After a stop to add water (losing two laps) Clark rejoined and finished third. This car was presented by Colin Chapman to Leonard Lee, of Coventry Climax 'for services rendered', and is cared for today by the Donington Collection near Derby.

LOTUS 34

The year the tyres failed (1964)

'Ooh yes, the 34 . . . do we have to talk about that one? I got into terrible trouble with Ford over that . . .'

Colin Chapman

After the excitement of 1963 the Lotus-Ford Indy contract went ahead for 1964. The new year's cars were little more than developed type 29s, carrying the full-race quad-cam Ford V8s with Hilborn-derived fuel-injection in place of carburettors, and ZF transmission in place of the clumsy Colotti. Straight pump gasoline was still used, and the cars were given a new type number — Lotus 34 — perhaps to keep Ford happy...

After the 29s' practice speed in 1963 on makeshift Dunlop rubber, the company moulded proper racing tyres for the 1964 Lotus-Fords. In turn, Ford's V8 was now available to many USAC entrants, but Indy's two top-ranking drivers, Parnelli Jones and A.J.Foyt, remained faithful to the Offenhauser-engined roadsters. Ford wanted Foyt to run the works team's spare 34, but Colin wanted it in hand in case the 1963 practice crash should be repeated. Dunlop's tyres were another contentious issue, for Ford's competition chief Jacque Passino suspected they were too soft to last the race — and he favoured the harder, less grippy, Firestones.

Clark and Gurney were delighted with the Dunlops' speed and neither was keen to change despite Marshman's pace for Firestone. Still the Hopkins 29 had spent months in preparation, while the 34s were slowly reaching their peak through May. Colin, silver-tongued as ever, converted Ford's hierarchy to his view on both spare car and tyres; Foyt was left to run his Offy and the 34s stayed on Dunlop.

On May 18 Jimmy qualified on pole with Marshman second, Rodger Ward (whose suggestion it had been for Cooper to tackle the '500' in 1961) third in a mid-engined Watson-Offy, and Jones, Foyt and Gurney on row two. Then Dan tried full-load runs and his Dunlops began to 'chunk' — scattering overheated lumps of tread. Dunlop frantically revised their moulds with shallower and more stable tread patterning. New tyres were made in a deserted factory over the Whitsun holiday and were flown post-haste to Indiana.

On Memorial Day the '500' was red-flagged to a halt after one lap when a grisly fireball collision claimed seven cars and two drivers' lives. After 1¾ hours the restart was taken in single-file order with Clark leading the way for five laps until Marshman went by, and his Pure Oil Firebird 29 led until lap 33. Jimmy inherited the lead, but seven laps later he sensed a peculiar tremor from his car's rear-end and as he slowed it rapidly intensified into a shattering vibration, then came a terrific thump and lurch as the 34's left-rear suspension collapsed and its wheel fell inwards at the top. Jimmy held the car as it slithered crazily to rest. The hastily-rebuilt Dunlop tyres had shed great sections of tread and the resultant imbalance vibration had collapsed the suspension. Dan's car was called in as a safety measure at 110-laps and the Lotus-Ford assault had failed...too publicly. Foyt, the man not allowed to drive a Lotus-Ford, won in his Sheraton-Thompson Offy and trousered $153,650 as against Clark's $2,100 lap-leader money. Foyt took the rise out of Ford in his victory speech. Ford Vice-President Charles Patterson was furious, as on his way to Victory Circle Foyt had treated him to a hand-signal which might have meant 'second-best'. More grimly, Ford had brought gasoline to Indy, and the fireball accidents were a result of its greater volatility compared with methanol. And weren't these mid-engined funny cars more flimsy anyway than the traditional roadster? For Ford, Indy 1964 was a PR nightmare.

Next day Lee Iacocca (General Manager, Ford Division) ordered a post-mortem. Andrew Ferguson, Lotus team manager: 'When we went to Dearborn the day after the race Colin said to me "You've never been to one of these meetings before, have you? Ooh, they really know how to look after you". I knew there was something wrong as soon as we

Dan Gurney, who always had most of the bad luck going at Indy where the Lotus-Fords were concerned, in his type 34 prior to the 1964 race. The car has a 'live' pressure refuelling nozzle mounted in its hull side unlike Clark's 29 pictured on page 71, while the new-style four-spoke Lotus cast wheels and specially moulded Dunlop tyres are prominent features. Otherwise there is little difference between 29 and 34, apart from the centre-exhaust Ford V8 engine and its new ZF transmission.

were shown into the conference room, because there were two chairs on their own — with a ring of chairs facing them...'

The Lotus men were confronted by Leo Beebe and Frank Zimmerman of Special Vehicles, Don Frey and PR man Bob Hefty. Colin apologised for his Dunlop choice and its failure. Frey explained that Ford were determined to retrieve their image, and wanted Lotus to sell Ford the cars immediately. The 'Old Man' agreed, much to Andrew's amazement: 'I think he was dog-tired...and he just couldn't fight them'. Ford were not convinced they should dispense with Lotus altogether, but would consider Colin's plans for Trenton and Milwaukee if he presented them on paper. The group walked from Frey's office to Beebe's to finalize the sale, and with time to think the old Colin Chapman emerged. He claimed he had not realised that the cars were to be sold immediately. The Ford men were dumbstruck, but Colin was into his stride and he talked them round — a new set of terms were agreed for the later-season races.

In July, testing at Trenton, sports car pilot Walt Hansgen crashed one of the works 34s, and in August at Milwaukee he crashed again. Clark and Gurney were anxiously chasing World Championship F1 points in Austria that weekend, and in the USAC race Parnelli Jones was joined by Foyt — his rift with Ford having been healed. Jones' drive was co-sponsored by J.C.Agajanian, and he topped Clark's 1963 qualifying record for Milwaukee, as did Ward's Watson-Ford and Foyt's 34. Colin was there to supervise the cars and Jones led all the way to win. Foyt was not so fortunate as a gear-shift bracket failed after two laps and he was out. That morning Lazenby's crew had fuelled Jones' car unaware it stood on rising ground, front wheels higher than the rear. Fuel flowed back through its injection system and flooded a cylinder. As Laz tried to fire it up with

the trolley starter on the grid it coughed, started then died. Puzzled, he tried again. This time the engine caught, gasped, there was a shattering bang — a glittering fireball blasted past his right ear, mushrooming into the sky — and the V8 settled down to run cleanly. 'That really excited the crowd — and me too!'

At Trenton, Jones and Clark drove the cars, Parnelli setting a new record to take pole and win untroubled. Jimmy's engines were off-song throughout, he qualified only seventh and was out after 96-miles.

Hopkins acquired Jones' Trenton winner for Marshman at the end of the year. They had Ford and Goodyear test contracts, and at Indy Marshman lapped at a staggering 161.4mph. Then he hit 191mph on the straights to lap at 163, and moved to Ford's test track to set a new closed-course world record. Testing is a lonely, self-extending business, and Bobby Marshman had never been blessed with good luck. On November 27, at Phoenix, the Pure Oil Firebird Lotus 34 slammed into the wall, and its immensely talented young driver suffered fatal burns.

The surviving 34s were taken over by Jones and Foyt for 1965 and they contributed to the Lotus triumph at Indy, when five of the cars set the first five qualifying speeds, Foyt actually on pole and Jones fourth. Then Jones had an upright fail on his 34 and hit the wall. It was his second failure of this type, and USAC's Safety Committee grounded all Lotuses until new uprights could be made. Colin responded angrily that the failures were on an old car out of works hands, but the officials insisted and the new Lotus 38s had also to be modified. Foyt led the race very briefly before his transmission failed at 115-laps, and Jones' 34 ran very well to a nail-biting low-on-fuel second place behind Jimmy Clark's victorious new car.

Bitter failure. Jimmy Clark, his face taped as a protection against flying grit and stones, fights his 34 to a halt at Indy in 1964 after the left-rear Dunlop tyre had stripped its tread and vibration had wrecked the suspension. As he walked disconsolately back to the pits a shaken bystander told him how shocked he had felt when he saw the collapse. 'You should have been where I was, mate . . .' was the Scot's response. Meanwhile, passing in the background, Rodger Ward took his mid-engined Watson-Offy on to second place behind Foyt's winning front-engined Watson. It was Ward who first suggested that Jack Brabham should take the Cooper to Indy, in 1961, which started the whole road-racing-style revolution there.

Foyt joined the revolution in 1965, driving this ex-works type 34 which Parnelli Jones had driven to victory at Milwaukee late the preceding year. He qualified on pole at a shattering 161.233mph, but was classified 15th in the '500' after transmission failure.

LOTUS 38

Mission accomplished (1965-67)

'When . . . the last majorette had pranced off the race track, Tony Hulman quavered "Gentlemen, start your engines" in a voice choked with emotion and the effects of a bad microphone connection . . . It was a one-man motor race, and that man was Jim Clark . . .'

Car & Driver, 1965

After the Indianapolis fiasco of 1964 Ford were extremely circumspect in their negotiations with Colin and Lotus for 1965. Leo Beebe did the deal on a lump-sum basis — no bonuses, no extra fees for drivers. Len Terry was briefed to produce a new Indy design to match revised USAC regulations — the revisions having followed the Turn Four disaster of 1964 — and he did the job while Chapman was away with Clark pursuing the Tasman Championship.

Len's revision of the monocoque theme was itself to become a trendsetter, and it brought Lotus-Ford their ultimate Indy success. Now two pit stops were mandatory during the '500', gravity towers replaced pressure refuelling and fuel carriage within the cars was strictly proscribed. The 38 appeared with a 'full' Terry monocoque structure to form a stressed-skin tube into which the driver inserted himself through a cockpit opening, as distinct from the preceding 25/29/33/34-style 'bathtub' in which he lay. Stressed panelling formed a 360-degree section around his legs and behind his shoulders. The old six-tank interconnected fuel system had to go, since there simply would not be the pressure available to fill it quickly enough. Three cells replaced it, two large ones on either side extending way back beside the engine, and one centrally behind the seat. The wheelbase was unchanged at the regulation 96-inch minimum, but the track was extended to 60 inches and the fuselage's offset to the left was now 3 inches. Weight was 1,250lb — just on the limit. Power came from Ford's latest quad-cam V8 retuned to run on dope and offering 500bhp. A ZF two-speed transaxle was retained. The nose-section was longer and more elegant than the earlier cars' bluff beaks, and with ram-pods over the inductions, centralized exhausts and neatly-cowled transmissions the latest Lotus-Fords looked 'right'.

David Lazenby and his crew flew out with the new 38s in April for their scheduled early-season debut at Trenton. Clark and Roger McCluskey were to test

the cars there, but the American totalled his against the wall when its throttle jammed open. John Lambert, the car builder, recalled, 'I think we saved the pedals from that car, but not much else'. Rather than risk the survivor at Trenton, the team headed straight to Indy.

Ford's history attributes the McCluskey crash to 'a dangerous modification of the throttle-control lever...' by Lotus. Actually it seems the linkage should have been assembled with a 60-thou end-float to allow for expansion as the engine heated-up while running. Lazenby is adamant that this end-float had been omitted in Ford's engine assembly, and as the V8 worked up temperature in McCluskey's first few laps so the spindle seized; unfortunately, with the throttles wide open.

After his disappointments at Indy with the Lotus team Dan Gurney — whose idea the whole thing had been after all — decided to go it alone in 1965. He took a new type 38 with him, backed by Yamaha and entered by his new All-American Racers team. Parnelli Jones became prime candidate for Jimmy's number-two, but Agajanian wanted too big a share of the glory for Ford's liking. Jones fell back on his updated Agajanian 34 and Colin signed instead the stock-car veteran Bobby Johns.

Pre-qualifying in the Indiana sun went well. The Lotus garage doors would open in the evening cool, and Jimmy would appear and drive his car faster every day. Foyt became increasingly 'psyched' by the Scotsman's speed. The first qualifying day saw each runner going ever faster. At 12.51 Jimmy made his attempt, and smashed all records at 160.729mph. At 1.04 a visibly quivering Foyt unleashed his older car, turned 161.958 on his opening lap and secured pole position at 161.233. A year previously his pole speed had been a mere 154...

Then Ford decided that their 18 engines should all be torn down before the race. Clark's engine was tested on pure methanol pre-race at 505bhp on the

Dearborn bed. Foyt's achieved 495; in qualifying both had run 20 per cent nitromethane additive.

Just before the race the legendary Wood Brothers stock car pit crew flew into town to service the works team's stops. The '500' was run one day after Monaco, and Team Lotus gave Monte Carlo a miss as they concentrated on the Speedway classic. Jimmy Clark led from the start, Foyt steamed by for lap 2 and was repassed by the Scot's glittering green-and-yellow Lotus on lap 3. Jimmy then led all the way save nine laps after scheduled fuel and tyre stops. The Wood Brothers — Glen, Leonard, Delano and Clay with their cousins Ken Martin and Ralph Edwards — made stunning use of their Ford-improved gravity gear. They loaded Clark's 38 with 50 US gallons in a searing 19.8-second first stop. On his second they loaded 58 gallons in 24.7 seconds. Nobody could live with that, not when matched to his pace around the Speedway.

Gurney's Yamaha 38 duelled with Jones' 34 until its engine failed after breakage of an improperly heat-treated cam-drive gear. Jones was second, and Al Miller fourth in the wonderful old ex-Firebird 29. Johns ran coolly home in seventh place.

Jimmy's 40-lap average speed was 149.334mph. The 50-lap mark was passed at a record 152.153mph and the 100-lap average was 152.185mph (5mph up on the old record). He won at 150.686mph, compared with Foyt's 147.350 in 1964. Team Lotus collected over $150,000 for his day's work. Next morning Clark — who had been doubtful about tackling the 1965 race because it worried his mother so deeply — 'phoned Leo Beebe from his motel and thanked the Ford executive for having talked him into doing it.

Later that summer Team took one 38 on a European exhibition tour, and Clark drove it in the Swiss hill-climb at Ste Ursanne-Les Rangiers — in the wet. Fitted with symmetrical suspension and a five-speed ZF gearbox the car made six climbs, the quickest being 3.6 seconds slower than Siffert's FTD in Rob Walker's F1 Brabham-BRM.

After three years the Ford deal with Lotus expired as they put their backing behind Gurney's AAR team for 1966. Colin found new support from Andy Granatelli's STP Additives division of the Studebaker Corporation, and new type 42 cars were planned with 4.2-litre BRM H16 power. This remarkable power-pack was never to become raceworthy, so before the 1966 '500' Clark and his new teammate Al Unser were switched to 38s.

Lotus Components had sold a pair of customer 38s to Foyt and to Mario Andretti's sponsors for $22,500 each. Since the new Lotus works at Hethel Airfield, Norfolk, was heavily committed, the two car's tubs were built by Abbey Panels of Coventry. When delivered they were found to be in ordinary soft-aluminium instead of the high-tensile alloy sheet used by Team. Extensive reworking was vital to make them anywhere near raceworthy, but their

Len Terry's new-style full-monocoque 38-Ford in two guises, when Clark won at Indianapolis in 1965 (number 82) and when he was second in 1966 (number 19). The stressed fuselage structure loops over the driver's legs in the scuttle area and forms a deep tank section behind his shoulders, with horns extending rearwards on either side to support the engine. Since pressure refuelling was now outlawed only three tanks were used, one either side extending from the forward filler necks away back into the engine horns, and a central seat cell. Note the air-deflector screens, and the Halibrand rear wheels featured in 1966. The STP crew behind Clark include Andy Granatelli on Chapman's right and Dave Lazenby on his left, while Maurice Phillippe is second from the right, beside Alan McCall — later with McLaren and then manufacturer of the Tui racing cars.

rigidity was never up to scratch. They were dubbed the 'Soft-Alloy Specials' and the Badcock records show them to have been numbers 38/5 and 38/6. With three cars nominally built for 1965 this would suggest that McCluskey's written-off prototype at Trenton had been replaced by a renumbered car, rather than just 'rebuilt'.

Dealings with these cars were confused, and there may have been a third 'Soft-Alloy Special' as David Lazenby believes that Al Unser drove one for STP in 1966. Andretti qualified his Brabham-Brawner rather than the flexi-Lotus for that year's '500', but Foyt ran his 38. Gurney was driving his own Len Terry-designed Eagle (son of Lotus 38) while Foyt's

Suspension assymmetry as seen on the prototype 38 at Cheshunt in March 1965. The Ford V8 passed a great deal of gas . . . Below, a mock-up quad-cam Ford engine and ZF transaxle in a 38 under construction at Cheshunt and, on the opposite page, the tub itself awaiting external skinning.

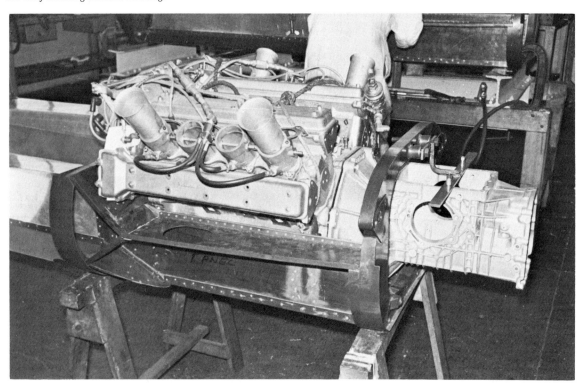

Sheraton-Thompson teammate George Snider had a Coyote, which was the Lotus 38's spit-image.

Early in the month of May, STP's cars suffered a string of engine failures. ZF had made their gearbox quill-shafts too long, and as Lazenby's crew bolted-up gearbox to engine so the crankshaft bearings became end-loaded; bellhousing spacers were fitted once detective work revealed the fault. Then the cars understeered too much. Colin and Maurice Phillippe (Terry's replacement) were on hand and the suspensions were modified front and rear to add front-end adhesion. Jimmy put 'Granatelli Green' (STP's vicious dayglo vermilion) on the centre of row one at 164.144mph and Foyt's 38 was the fastest second-weekend qualifier on row six, with Unser right behind.

Foyt's car was demolished in the infamous start-line pile-up that year, as was Miller's 29, and after 1 hour and 23 minutes delay the race was restarted. Clark's 'Old Nail' 38 led after Andretti's engine failed at 27-laps. With oil down the 38 was oversteering wildly as it then had too much front-end grip. On lap 62, slowing for his first stop, Jimmy spun out of Turn Four. He regained 'the lead' on lap 76 when Ruby's leading Eagle stopped, but nine laps later he spun on to the back straight and glanced the wall. He stopped briefly to check for damage then rejoined 'third'. On lap 132, when Ruby and Stewart's leading Lola both stopped, Clark was 'leading' yet again. Actually, Graham Hill's Lola had passed Clark during the confusion of his early spin, and as

Stewart's car broke to lose him the lead and Ruby was black-flagged for dropping oil (remember 1963?) Graham Hill actually took the chequered flag 44 seconds ahead of Jimmy. A confused Clark drove into Victory Circle thinking he had won again, but the timekeepers located the STP lap chart's error, and second place — with its $76,992 purse — was accepted. After the race the 'Old Nail' was sold to Foyt, but it was not the Texan's year for soon afterwards he slammed it into the Milwaukee wall and suffered nasty burns to face and hands.

In mid-October the cars were taken to Japan for the Mount Fuji USAC-style race. Bobby Unser's STP 38 was placed second to Jackie Stewart's Lola, but Clark couldn't start after engine failure during practice.

In 1967 the H16s still proved unraceworthy, and new Indy chief mechanic Mike Underwood had a desperate time to prepare competitive machinery. Clark was out again in a 38, qualified slower than in 1966 on the first day and ran 18th when rain stopped the race after only 18 laps. Next day the restart was taken, and after 36 laps Jimmy's car streamed smoke and retired with 'seriously oiled plugs' — a piston had collapsed. He was classified 31st. Larry Dickson was classified 15th after spinning out Gordon van Liew's Vita Fresh Orange Juice 38 at 18-laps, while the 38-derived Coyotes of Foyt and Joe Leonard started from row two and were placed first and second. The Len Terry Lotus 38 was a most significant motor car...

Lotus-Ford 38s reappeared at Indy in 1967 for their third '500' Speedway classic, but Clark's 'Old Nail' suffered an early engine failure and was classified a meagre 31st. It was modified with extra left-side bias in the form of a pannier oil tank. Lotus four-spoke cast-alloy wheels reappeared all round that year . . . The same year Larry Dickson's much-modified duck-tail 38 (number 22) owned by Gordon van Liew qualified 21st and was classified 15th after spinning out at 180-laps. Added left-hand bias was clearly the 'In' tweak for 1967 . . .

LOTUS 42F

The most obscure Lotus (1966-67)

'It was a real old cobble-up, but the thing was that it went so well and handled so nicely that we realised the value of weight distribution and how you could gain more than you might lose by playing with wheelbases and tracks . . .'

Colin Chapman

For 1966 BRM were building new 3-litre engines with 16 cylinders arranged in H-formation, as described in the next section, and 4.2-litre variants were put in hand for sale to customers interested in Indianapolis. The whole scheme was very ambitious, and over-optimistic, and the engines never became anywhere near raceworthy.

Len Terry had left Team Lotus to work on Dan Gurney's Eagle F1 and Indy projects. His contract was due to expire in September 1965, but he wanted to leave in May, and Colin agreed to let him go if he could replace himself. He introduced an ex-De Havilland, ex-Ford engineer named Maurice Phillippe, whose aeronautical background had

'You always learn far more from your mistakes than you ever do from your successes' — Colin Chapman. This is the remarkable Lotus-Ford 42F which Mike Underwood's men hastily cobbled together for Graham Hill to drive in the 1967 '500'. The monocoque fuselage was intended originally for BRM H16 power, hence the enlarged tank section behind the driver's shoulders. However, the 4.2-litre H16 was stillborn and a tubular spaceframe was added to carry a trusty Ford V8. The result was a wheelbase 10-inches too long and quite remarkably good handling . . . which was food for profitable future thought.

majored on wing structures and who had built himself a monocoque-chassis 1172 Formula sports car (named the MPS) as early as 1955.

Maurice became Chapman's detail designer, and after producing the engine support framework which made the type 39 into a Tasman Formula car for the new year he plunged into the type 42/43 monocoques intended to carry BRM's complex H16-cylinder engine.

To carry them, since they would accept rear-suspension chassis loadings through the crankcase, Maurice designed an all-new truncated monocoque nacelle very similar to the successful type 38's, but which terminated behind the cockpit in a flat closing panel. Rigid attachment points were provided here to pick-up the engine-cum-gearbox-cum rear-suspension assembly, but they were never to match a raceworthy BRM 'live round' — merely the mock-up assembly and prototype engines.

When the H16s were late for 1966's '500-Miles' the STP Lotus team simply fell back on their existing 38s, and they did well, placing second, running third (Unser's car) and very nearly winning for the second consecutive year. Cars were in short supply for 1967

and Jimmy Clark was to drive an ancient 38 modified with an outrigged left-hand oil tank, and one of the 42 tubs was hastily cobbled-up with a tubular space-frame engine bay to accommodate a Ford V8. Since the truncated monocoque already lacked engine-mounting legs in which fuel could be accommodated, its centre seat-back tank was much larger than the 38's. The hefty Ford V8 was much longer than the H16, and so the car emerged with a wheelbase around 106 inches — ten whole inches more than the 38 standard to which it had originally been designed.

This ungainly special was dubbed the Lotus '42F', and Graham Hill qualified it on the second Indy weekend at 163.317mph (quicker than Clark's 38 the previous weekend) but 31st on the grid. In the race a piston failed at 23-laps and Graham was classified 32nd. With Jimmy 31st it was a crushing Lotus defeat, but there was light in all this darkness, for the unlikely 42F had handled extremely well. Formerly Colin had designed his cars as short and narrow as possible — now the 42F proved that longer wheelbases and curious weight distributions had some good things to offer.

A complicated box of tricks. BRM's H16 engine was a masterpiece of packaging, but it was beset with reliability problems in Formula 1 guise and was destined never to appear in 4.2-litre Indianapolis form. This is one of the later lighter-weight 3-litre versions, which faced formidable opposition in the form of the Cosworth Ford V8, an engine which Lotus helped to get off the ground and which was to dominate Grand Prix racing for the next decade.

LOTUS 43

H16 and a single success (1966)

'It was rather ironic that for my first race in the Lotus it was powered
by a BRM engine — my old friend the H16 . . .'

Graham Hill

As the first season of the new 3-litre Grand Prix formula, 1966 was regarded as an interim year by all concerned, but more so by those who had engines forthcoming but not yet ready. Team Lotus were in this unhappy situation with their World Championship to defend. Keith Duckworth was designing his Cosworth DFV V8 engine for 1967 with Ford finance and Chapman encouragement, while for 1966 Colin had ordered BRM 3-litre H16 motive power, with 2.1-litre V8s and a very special 2-litre 32-valve Climax V8 in ex-1½ litre cars as a temporary, pre-H16, expedient.

This unit was in effect two BRM 1½-litre V8s, with their included angle within the vee opened-out to 180 degrees, mounted one above the other with their crankshafts geared together. It was a compact package for such complexity, and its crankcase was stressed to act as a chassis member extending from the rear panel of a truncated forward monocoque nacelle which simply terminated behind the cockpit seat-tank. Major rear-suspension loads were fed into the engine and gearbox, while double radius-rods on either side fed direct into pick-ups on the monocoque's flanks.

Driving like fury — Clark at Monza in 1967 with the 43-BRM H16, lifting its inside front wheel through sheer cornering effort and a touch too much front roll-stiffness. He started the Italian GP badly, climbed from second-last to fifth, then suffered a puncture. He charged very hard thereafter, only for the BRM transmission to jam in gear and put him out.

This bulkhead engine mounting was similar to that used by Ferrari with their hardly less complex flat-12 1½-litre engine in 1965, and was also used by BRM for their own H16 cars. The type 39 built for the stillborn 1½-litre flat-16 Climax FWMW engine approached this type of mounting, though it would have supported its power unit on aviation-style perforated angle-beams on either side.

The monocoque which Phillippe drew featured a Terry-style (see the Lotus 38) 360-degree stressed section enclosing the driver's legs, plus an enclosed tank section behind his shoulders. In comparison to BRM's contemporary P83 it offered a lower frontal area about the cockpit and was smoother and sleeker. Front suspension was 33-derived, with the now familiar chrome-plated fabricated top rocker arms actuating inboard coil/damper units, high-mounted rack-and-pinion steering and a wide-based lower wishbone with all-inboard anti-roll control. At the rear a reversed lower wishbone picked-up beneath the BRM gearbox, while tall vertical extensions of the cast hub-carriers met single lateral top links which pivoted inboard on supports bolted to the cylinder-heads. BRD sliding-spline half-shafts were used, and the raked outboard coil/dampers were mounted ahead of the axle-line.

In Team's rich green-and-yellow colours the prototype 43 looked stunning when Peter Arundell gave it its first serious run in practice for the Belgian GP at Spa; its mechanism failed after three slow laps. At Reims, in July, the car made its race debut in the French GP. Arundell was in gear-selection troubles from the start, survived three troubled laps, made two pit stops and retired 43/1 with its second sheared distributor drive of the meeting. BRM redesigned their transmission during that summer, and frantic development work wrung improved reliability from the 16-cylinder engine. At Monza, 43/1 reappeared for Clark to make his 3-litre-powered F1 debut and it behaved itself in practice; he started on the front row, and after making a terrible start he tore through the field to run fifth before suffering a puncture and later troubles, which finally retired the car after 59 laps. Both works BRM H16s had failed during the opening two laps...

The next GP was at Watkins Glen, in the USA, where Jimmy inherited the lead in 43/1 and actually nursed it to the finish to score the H16 engine's only race victory. In Mexico he suffered a painful engine-breakage in practice, which gushed hot oil and water on to the back of his neck, and he retired from the race with a deranged gear-change. For 1967 Graham Hill returned to Lotus to become 'joint number-one' with Clark in a powerful Ford-supported team, and they began their season in South Africa with a pair of 43s, Jimmy taking the new 43/2. In the race Graham bent his car's front suspension, which allowed it to bottom and wear a hole in an oil-pipe. Clark's car overheated, continued after a pit stop to remove the nose cone, and retired when the metering-unit diaphragm failed.

That was the end of Team Lotus' efforts with the H16 engine, and both cars were subsequently sold to private owners to have Ford V8 engines fitted in tubular rear bays for Formula 5000 racing. For Team, much better things were on the way...

The season's victory — Watkins Glen, 1966, saw Jimmy's 43-BRM H16 win his and Team's third United States Grand Prix, using the BRM works team's spare engine. The type 43's Indy heritage is evident in this shot, as are the wide-splayed rear radius-rods to clear the side induction boxes and the individual exhaust clusters for each cylinder bank.

LOTUS 49

The Cosworth Ford classic (1967-70)

'I just wanted a simple car which wouldn't give us any problems,
so we could sort-out the engine . . .'

Colin Chapman

'I was tickled pink to be sitting in front of this very modern Grand
Prix engine . . . it really had some squirt . . .'

Graham Hill

'The Lotus 49' has set new standards for Grand Prix cars . . .'

Denis Jenkinson ('Motor Sport')

During the years 1967-1969 Team Lotus built, rebuilt (and rebuilt again) nine type 49s powered by the quite remarkable Cosworth-Ford DFV V8 engine. Those nine, in ever-changing form, scored 12 World Championship GP victories during this period, which was a creditable performance, though not one which mirrored the cars' stature at that time. The Lotus 49 introduced the DFV to Formula 1 in a victorious debut at Zandvoort, where Graham Hill led the race in his prototype car before retirement, and then left Jimmy Clark to smash the lap record and win handsomely in his 'second-off'. The integrated design of car and engine set a trend which others were to follow, and the power unit itself was to win seven consecutive World Championship titles until toppled by Ferrari in 1975. The DFV was Champion once more in 1976, while Ferrari fought back in 1977. The Cosworth engine became the first ever to win over 100 Grand Prix races, and four of its Manufacturers' titles were taken by Lotus cars.

Some say the engine made the car, for the 49 of itself was by no means faultless. It was a blemished gem, but a gem proven by four gruelling seasons of front-line service.

To study the car, one must first study the engine. Cosworth Engineering was seeded at Lotus in Hornsey. Primarily a partnership between Mike Costin and Keith Duckworth, who met at Lotus Engineering in 1957-58, Cosworth was founded to prepare Lotus cars and tune Climax engines. Duckworth, the graduate engineer, worked full-time for his new company. Costin, the gifted engineer-driver and tireless worker, contributed little for the first three years, as shortly after Cosworth's formation he signed an exclusive contract for that period as Technical Director of Lotus. Duckworth operated from Friern Barnet in those early days, and Frank Coltman recalls some graffiti above the Cosworth parts hatch, where someone kept waiting had inscribed the unkind and overly critical — 'Cosbodge

& Duckfudge Ltd'...

Duckworth made his name as a builder of racing engines with the Formula Junior Ford 105E variant which he produced late in 1959. Two prototype units were ready for Boxing Day at Brands Hatch, and one made its debut in Alan Stacey's first-off FJ Lotus 18. Cosworth engines in Lotus cars were to dominate FJ for much of its existence, and the company grew with Bill Brown and Benny Rood joining Costin and Duckworth in partnership. In February 1965 Leonard Lee announced Coventry-Climax's final decision to cease F1 engine production. They had won 86 International F1 events since 1958 and had powered every successful GP Lotus.

Colin Chapman was left to search for a new engine for the forthcoming 3-litre formula, beginning in 1966. BRM provided immediate help, but his close and long-lasting relationship with Cosworth offered greater potential. He asked Keith if he thought he could produce a Grand Prix engine. He said he did, so Colin searched out the money to finance it.

Duckworth's estimate of initial costs was £100,000. Ford had backed Cosworth in producing the successful 1-litre F2-type SCA engine on a Cortina base in 1964, but on first approach they were not interested in Formula 1. Chapman: '...we then had meetings with David Brown of Aston Martin... he was very interested but...virtually wanted to buy Cosworth. Then we tried Macdonald of the British Sound Recording Company, and there were several other interested parties. We'd virtually made our minds up to go back to Brown when I was invited to dinner one night with Harley Copp' (Ford of Britain's Vice-President, Engineering).'I said ''Look, you're missing out on the best investment you've ever made...for £100,000 you can't go wrong''. He thought that was nothing like enough to get the initial work done, but I managed to convince him it was and that Keith was really someone special. Harley went back to Walter Hayes' (Director of

The Lotus 49s complete their first racing lap during the Dutch GP at Zandvoort, in 1967. Graham Hill has streaked into a rapidly growing lead from pole position in '49/1', with Clark's '49/2' running sixth behind Brabham, Rindt, Gurney and Amon.

Public Affairs) 'and within a few days it was all under way...'

Never before had Duckworth designed a complete engine from scratch, so an intermediate step was made by Ford funding £25,000 for a 116E production-based F2 engine for the new 1,600cc formula of 1967. This would provide a 16-valve twin-cam 4-cylinder from which the Formula 1 engine — which Keith was evolving as a V8 — could effectively be doubled-up, using the balance of £75,000. Ford of Dagenham also offered specialist facilities, such as their foundry, to extend their contribution far beyond 'mere money'.

The Formula 2 'Four-Valve A-series' Cosworth FVA engine was proven in *Libre* racing during 1966 with Mike Costin driving, and the 'Double Four-Valve' DFV followed smartly in its wake. Duckworth's engineering approach is logical and forthright to a fault. He produced a simple 90-degree V8 of minimal complication but considerable sophistication. He aimed for minimum frontal area within the restrictions of this layout. Exhaust clusters and head-width made it impossible to carry much fuel on either side, so he decided to make it instead as short as possible so the front would mate with a monocoque's rear bulkhead without wasting any space. The stressed crankcase would then accept

suspension loads to act as the rear part of the chassis. Ancillaries like water and oil pumps and distributor, which normally appear at the front of an engine, were therefore slung low beside the crankcase beneath the exhausts. Chassis-mounts were provided in the form of strap-plates attached to the cam-cover front-ends, with lower mounts on the forward corners of the sump. All shear was taken out through these lower mounts, with the relatively thin strap-plates allowing the engine to expand around 15-thou when hot without stretching the monocoque to which it was attached.

This concept was evolved in partnership with the chassis designers — Chapman and Phillippe — and the resultant Lotus-Ford 49 was to emerge as a beautifully integrated entity. The bulkhead engine mounting mirrored that of the BRM-powered types 42 and 43, while the extremely compact Cosworth package allowed a large fuel load to be concentrated well back between driver and engine, where it would encourage consistent handling with little effective change between full and empty.

The 49 monocoque fuselage was skinned in 18-gauge L72 Alclad aluminium-alloy sheet shaped over mild-steel bulkheads. The tub formed 360-degree stressed sections around the driver's legs and behind his back. Its side boxes housed 15-gallon fuel

After Hill's retirement from the Dutch GP Clark moved smoothly into the lead, set fastest lap and won going away in the 49's fairytale debut.

bags, draining through non-return valves into a 10-gallon centre tank behind the inclined seat-support plate. Fuel pick-up was from the centre tank, which topped-up from the side cells as the car accelerated and surge washed open the non-return valves. Mike Costin recalled how the system passed sediment, causing persistent misfiring problems in early races, and how the problem was side-stepped by fitting 1965 Climax-style filter gauzes. In 1978 designers were still suffering DFV fuel-feed troubles, '...and all because they won't use systems we recommend' Mike fumed.

An access plate on top of the forward monocoque section opened on to the pedal assembly hung from the fabricated front bulkhead while ahead of this structure was a vee-shaped oil tank and lightweight subframe supporting the dual-purpose oil/water radiator. A detachable glass-fibre nose-cone clothed this area, and was the only 'bodywork' on the car. All oil and water pipes were internal, apart from the water return pipe to the radiator.

Suspension was familiar, with top rocker-arms actuating inboard coil/damper units and an anti-roll bar, with a fabricated lower link jointed to a radius-rod leading from an inboard pick-up well back on the hull. New cast uprights supported thick ventilated brake discs well inboard of the Lotus cast-magnesium

wheels, and so exposed to direct air-flow. Anti-dive geometry was built-in.

At the rear, triangulated tubular frames provided inboard pick-ups on the cylinder-heads, with a cross-frame providing lower mounts below the very light but uprated ZF 5DS12 five-speed-and-reverse transmission. This incorporated sliding-spline joints within its output-shafts, Colin considering '...ZF did us a beautiful job on those...'. Suspension location included the usual single top links, reversed lower wishbones with twin radius-rods feeding drive and braking loads into the monocoque flanks, and an anti-roll bar. The inclined outboard-mounting coil/damper units were ahead of the axle, and massive brake calipers behind it, front and rear.

Ford were wary of bad publicity from over-publicized F1 projects failing early on, so the DFV received a muted introduction. The first of the five engines for 1967 was handed to Team Lotus on April 25, 1967, two days after completion and five months after commencement under a contract effective from March 1, 1966. The original target debut of Monaco was postponed, and instead the Team Lotus 49s, resplendent in green-and-yellow livery, made their fairytale first appearance in the Dutch GP at Zandvoort.

They were to take pole position for the next 11

The age of aerodynamic aids dawns modestly for Team Lotus at Spa-Francorchamps for the 1967 Belgian GP, where in practice both 49s wore bib spoilers like this one seen on Clark's '49/1'. Without any balancing download on the rear of the chassis they induced unpleasant instability and were removed for the race.

consecutive Grand Prix races, and while Graham Hill often led events in his car it was always Jim Clark's which would survive to win four GPs and the Spanish non-championship race at Jarama to close the 1967 season.

During the year there were no fundamental engine problems, although its rather savage characteristic of producing power with a bang from 6,500rpm demanded wariness from the drivers. Smoother-acting throttle and clutch linkages were devised, while on the stop-go Bugatti circuit at Le Mans, for the French GP, continued torque-reversals distorted the ZF transaxle case and caused the final-drives to fail. Massive cross-bolted side-plates were fitted as a temporary (British GP-winning) expedient, while ZF rapidly redesigned the casings.

These transmissions had always featured fixed intermediate ratios and final-drives, which could be altered only by complete strip-down and replacement. During their ZF years Team had taken a choice of complete transmissions with them to each race, changing whole assemblies rather than strip and reassemble a gearbox to change ratios 'in the field'. With the DFV's characteristics this was unworkable, and early in 1968 the easily-gutted, omni-adjustable Hewland gearbox was to be adopted.

Brakes were altered early in 1967 as the original ventilated discs cooled so effectively they glazed their pads. Softer pads were tried before solid discs were substituted. Front suspension rocker-arms proved suspect, and were uprated twice, after the British and German GPs. Graham Hill lost the lead of the British GP when a rear-suspension Allen screw worked loose. This top-link mount was twice modified to

prevent any recurrence, and at the end of the year more beefy suspension frames were adopted.

Meanwhile, Team had suffered a major blow as, at the London Motor Show, Esso confirmed rumours that they were pulling out of racing. Esso had supported Lotus for many years. Now team manager Andrew Ferguson contacted Britain's top 200 companies in search of sponsorship. Replies were sparse, but coincidentally David Lazenby — then running Lotus Components — was hunting for backers to support a projected two-car team of Lotus 47GTs. He heard that John Player, of tobacco fame, were interested in promotion, and contacted Sales Link, their PR agency. The reaction was enthusiastic, Ferguson was given the tip and he provided Player with a proposal to sponsor Lotus F1, F2 and GT teams with projections of cost and possible return. A visit was arranged to Player's Nottingham headquarters and within two hours Colin Chapman and Geoffrey Kent (Player's Managing Director) had done the deal. Gold Leaf Team Lotus had been born, and later, as John Player Team Lotus, it was to flourish into 1978.

But most bitter tragedy soon rocked the infant team as, after winning the 1968 South African GP (to score his 25th Championship race win and so break Fangio's record of 24) Jimmy Clark died in a piffling Formula 2 race at Hockenheim that April.

Graham Hill picked them up in splendid style by winning the Spanish and Monaco GPs in quick succession, and he went on to take Lotus' third World Championship title with a victory in Mexico to close the season.

That year saw the Lotus 49 develop beneath its

British GP, 1967, with Team Lotus running first and second — Hill leading in the hastily-assembled '49/3' (using a type 33 nosecone) from Clark's faithful '49/2', which won handsomely. Graham had severely damaged his regular '49/1' in a practice accident caused by a rear-suspension pick-up point failure, and the new race car had been built-up for him at Hethel overnight. It lost the lead when a rear-suspension bolt came adrift, and after repairs it suffered a major engine failure.

The greatest drive — Jimmy Clark led the Italian GP briefly in 1967 before '49/2's right-rear tyre deflated. He stopped to change the wheel on lap 13, rejoining 100-yards behind the leaders on the road but actually one lap down and in 15th place. Helped to a small extent by retirements, Clark tore back through the field to regain the lead, only to suffer fuel starvation in the final laps and drop back to third at the finish after leading into the final lap. Surtees' Honda beat Brabham's Repco Brabham to the line by 0.2-second — it was quite a race!

After Clark nursed his crippled '49/2' over the finish line to win yet another US GP at Watkins Glen in 1967 one headline read 'The Ultimate Race Car — It Breaks at the Finish Line'. The right-rear suspension top link had failed, allowing the wheel to lean inwards. Graham Hill was 6.3-seconds behind in second place with '49/3', troubled by clutch slip in the race he was meant to win.

new red-white-and-gold livery first applied half-way through Jimmy's successful Tasman tour in New Zealand. Experience with Firestone tyres indicated that a more rearward weight bias would improve behaviour. Experiments were made with 49/5 at Race of Champions time, where the car ran with a huge oil tank wrapped saddle-fashion over the gearbox with a small cooler perched on top. Wider deep-cone wheels were used, and the car was then torn down to be rebuilt as the prototype 49B. Progressive growth in tyre size had rendered futile Lotus exercises in reduced frontal area. Vestigial sports-car-style spoilers and wings had appeared on the GP cars at Spa in 1967, and these were to proliferate during the new season. Maximum downforce was the target, to load tyres with a dynamic mass which did not in turn add extra weight to be accelerated and braked. The type 56 turbine cars had evolved for Indianapolis with their wedge profile, and the prototype 49B

inherited a semi-wedge format.

Colin adopted a longer wheelbase to help remove weight from the front wheels, achieving it by raking the front suspension arms 3 inches forward. To limit rear-wheel toe-steer, tunnels were hollowed out beneath the fuselage's belly, and the lower radius-rod inboard pick-ups were placed forward in them and well inboard. A more substantial subframe supported the rear suspension, oil tank and the latest Hewland FG400 gearbox, and the DFV cylinder-heads were relieved of carrying direct suspension loads. The reprofiled nose-cowl carried adjustable airfoil-section vanes on either side, while the engine disappeared beneath an upswept glass-fibre cowl into which a NACA duct was sunk to feed cooling air into the resited oil radiator. The deep-cone cast-magnesium Lotus wheels had grown from 8-inch to 10-inch wide front rims for the last two races of 1967, and now 12-inch wide fronts became standard with 15-inch

The last victory — South African GP, Kyalami, 1968, with Clark storming away to win in the new '49/4' from Stewart's new Tyrrell-entered Matra-DFV and the Repco Brabhams of Rindt and 'Black Jack' himself. This was Jimmy's 25th World Championship GP win, breaking Fangio's record of 24 which had stood for ten years. It was also the last Formula 1 appearance of Team's honoured green-and-yellow colours — the end of an era.

Triumph in adversity. Graham Hill brought Team bouncing back after Jimmy Clark's death by winning the Spanish GP, opening the 1968 European-centred World Championship season. Here at Jarama he raced '49/1', fresh from its Tasman tour. This splendid Geoff Goddard study clearly shows the classic type 49 in its final pre-49B form with the tall rear hub-carriers, high rear anti-roll bar, solid front brake discs and slender nose cone with side ducts releasing hot air from behind the radiator.

Ringing the bell yet again — Graham Hill on his winning way during the 1968 Monaco GP, where he added another Monte Carlo laurel to his hat-trick for BRM in 1963-65. His car is the prototype long-wheelbase, Hewland-gearbox 49B '49B/5' with deep-cone wheels, extended lower rear radius-rod tunnelled into the monocoque, nose fins, upswept engine cowl with NACA duct to feed the gearbox oil-cooler and swept-forward front suspension rocker-arms.

diameters. At Monaco, Hill was — as usual — supreme to win his fourth Monte Carlo classic, while new teammate Jack Oliver made an inauspicious debut by severely damaging 49/1.

The damaged car was salvaged and stripped, then as many parts as possible were used in the construction of a replacement 49B/9. This 'salvage and restore' policy was to become common practice, and accounts for the nine type 49 development entities producing in their time 12 individual chassis numbers...

In the high-speed Belgian GP at Spa both Team 49s suffered constant-velocity half-shaft joint failures, and the following Dutch GP was the last in which the semi-wedge 49Bs appeared as more ambitious aerodynamic aids were on the way.

At Spa, strutted airfoils reacting on the rear-end of the chassis had been introduced by Ferrari and Brabham, their effect being trimmed-out by balance vanes on the nose. Chapman was to become a vociferous advocate of this innovation. For the French GP, at Rouen, Team's 49Bs appeared with strutted rear 'foils acting directly upon the rear suspension uprights to convert maximum download into traction. Team calculated downthrust approaching 400lb at 150mph, but in practice Jack Oliver's car demonstrated the dangers of losing such download at speed. He ventured innocently into the slipstream of another car approaching the pits straight and 49B/6 slithered out from under him and slammed into a brick gate-post beside the track at around 140mph. It was a tribute to the monocoque's strength that Jack escaped unhurt.

This wing period had increased drive-line loads like never before.

This wing period had increased drive-line loads like never before. Improved rear-wheel traction pounded joints and gearbox alike and failures constantly occurred, while the introduction of Firestone's improved YB11 tyre aggravated the problem. Heavier half-shafts were fitted, Mercedes-splined on the first 49Bs, and a succession of BRD and Hardy-Spicer constant-velocity and Hooke joints appeared. Finally, for the US and Mexican GPs ending 1968, the first Lohr & Bromkamp 'Lobro' plunging CV joints were adopted. They proved capable of accepting engine torque and the extremes of suspension movement and formed the basis of the Lobro joints still used in 1978.

The inauspicious start to the Lotus 'wing era' left their development unhindered. Strutted airfoils grew higher, wider and finally were doubled-up fore-and-aft in South Africa in March 1969. Passive mounts, preset in the pits, were normal, but a feathering rear wing was used on Hill's car in Mexico, in 1968, employing a fourth pedal to the left of the clutch to feather the wing along the straights. As the driver's left foot moved across to the clutch, bungee cords in tension increased the wing's incidence angle, added download and increased drag to slow and steady the

Graham Hill was always an honest and dedicated plodder as a driver rather than a man of instinctive genius. Often he would cover more than race distance during practice, grinding round and round to set-up his car the way he liked. Here, during one such session, is Graham in '49B/5', the front access panel removed and showing-off its shallower rear uprights, Firestone tyres, relatively massive coil/damper units and oil-cooler atop the tail tank. Colin Chapman gazes unamused at the back of his number-one driver's head while mechanic Bob Sparshott peers at the Hewland gearbox.

car more effectively in the turn. At Barcelona, for the 1969 Spanish GP, the 49Bs carried outsize wings which 'topped out' over the very fast hump after the pit-straight. Their struts had been stressed to accept compression loads from the wings, but not to withstand negative loading as the chassis 'fell away' from them over the hump. Both Hill's and Rindt's cars suffered wing collapses which sparked enormous accidents. Graham's rebuilt 49B/6 was to be rebuilt again, but Jochen's 49B/9 was twisted into a fuel-gushing write-off, from which very few components were salvaged.

In the middle of practice at Monaco (where Dick Attwood stood-in for the injured Rindt as Hill's teammate) the CSI abruptly announced a peremptory wing ban pending proper definition of permissible aerodynamic aids. The teams fudged temporary

49s in '68. On the opposite page, the Hewland FG400 gearbox buried beneath its welded aluminium oil-tank and oil-cooler, 49B uprights, the much-troubled half-shafts with their joints which took such a pounding when wings were adopted, the massive top cross-beam to pick-up springs and top links, and the hydraulic brake circuitry clipped along the top radius-rods. The oil-tanks (lower picture) were black-crackle-finished later in the year, and the beauty of the stressed engine mounting was often demonstrated as the DFV and transaxle were unbolted and lifted away from monocoque, leaving the rear suspension totally independent, as shown here at Monza. Note the beefed-up late-season, half-shafts. Top-duct exits (above) for expended radiator air appeared at the 1969 Italian GP after a public debut in a FordSport Day demonstration at Mallory park a few days previously.

expedients, such as semi-wedge-style gearbox covers in the Lotus case, while nose-vanes remained unaffected. Graham Hill notched his glorious fifth Monaco victory, Jo Siffert was third in the Walker 49B/7 and Attwood an admirable fourth — all on the same lap at the finish. For those who said Lotus cars were fragile, Monaco in 1969 proved otherwise.

At Zandvoort, the prototype Lotus 63 four-wheel-drive car appeared, and this experimentation was to deflect the team for the rest of the season. Wing rulings had opted for limits of 80cm height above road level and 110cm width, mounted behind the rear axle. Thus the appearance of the 49Bs changed for the later races of 1969, which saw internecine warfare between Rindt and Hill at Zandvoort, and some titanic battles between the Austrian — rapidly establishing himself as the faster of the two — and his great friend Jackie Stewart in the Tyrrell Matra. Jochen was an abrasive, outspoken character, who had fitted well into the Brabham team the previous year, but with Chapman the driver/team chief

relationship was always strained. Colin found it difficult to exchange shades of opinion with his new charger, whose English was good, but not that good — and very blunt indeed. As Rindt tended to be critical of the team and of Chapman, as well as of his cars, Team Lotus was not a happy band that season.

Before the British GP the problem was persuading the drivers to take the new type 63s seriously, and stop concentrating on the proven 49Bs in order to accumulate championship points. So 49Bs 8 and 9 were sold (to Jo Bonnier and John Love, who already had 49/3), leaving Team with only 49B/6 — resurrected once more — and the two 63s. As the joint number-one drivers grumbled, so Bonnier's car was taken back for Hill, Rindt drove number 6, while Bonnier handled one 63 'on loan' and John Miles was a cadet driver in the other 63. The Love sale was rescinded as the 63s did not prove their potential. Mario Andretti — who had produced a sensational pole position in his first Grand Prix race, driving a Team 49B at Watkins Glen in 1968 — was brought

Remarkable shot of Hill's '49B/5' during practice for the 1968 French GP at Rouen, running for the first time with a strutted rear aerofoil mounted directly on the rear uprights. Here, under power, the car is squatting so violently its front suspension is near full-droop and the right-front tyre is barely contacting the roadway . . . despite the front fins' pronounced incidence.

The effect of having the rear wing's downforce abruptly reduced was promptly discovered by the unlucky Jack Oliver during practice at Rouen. Here he surveys all that remained of '49B/6' after hitting a brick gate-pillar at around 140mph. His survival uninjured testified to the monocoque's strength.

Here we are again — '49B/6' reconstructed and racing once more with Graham Hill aboard for the 1968 Italian GP at Monza. This classical planview from the tower on entry to the Curva Parabolica shows-off the 49B's swept-forward front-suspension rockers, new top-duct nose, square cut-off on the outer deflector screen transparency, incredibly compact DFV engine configuration and the wing area in use.

Jo Siffert scoring an immensely popular British GP victory for Rob Walker Racing in their replacement (and brand-new) '49B/7', having had their original '49/4' destroyed in a workshop fire after a Brands practice crash beginning the season and the loan from Team of '49/2'. Colours were Scots dark blue and white, and 'Seppi's helmet was red with two stripes and the Helvetic cross in white.

And they went forth and multiplied. South African GP, 1969, with Graham (above) practising '49B/6' with same-level wings front and rear, mounted directly on to the wheel uprights and with cable actuation to feather them against 'bungee-pressure' along the straights. John Love's private Team Gunston '49/3' ran his own South African concoction (right) with hydraulic wing-actuation cylinders on each strut. Note the much more robust regulation roll-over bars of 1969, and wider front fins extending to the inner wheel-rim faces.

Death-knell for strutted wings was sounded as Graham Hill's '49B/6' thumped into the guardrails at Barcelona's Montjuich Park during the Spanish GP of 1969. The accident was caused by load reversal on the strutted rear wing over the hump in the background finally causing wing failure and collapse. Below, a front wheel bounds away as Graham protects his face and the car comes to rest having bounced back across the track. Within minutes the wreck was struck by Jochen Rindt's sister '49B/9', which suffered an identical collapse while leading. 'R6' was to be rebuilt yet again, but 'R9' was beyond salvage.

back to handle the 63 while Hill and Rindt concentrated on their trusty 49Bs. Graham was now driving as a shadow of his former self, while Rindt was knocking on the door of success without achieving it until finally he scored his maiden GP victory at 'The Glen' in 1969. Sadly, Hill crashed 49B/10 mightily when a tyre deflated. He had push-started the car after spinning a lap earlier and, unable to refasten his seat belts, was thrown out to suffer severe leg injuries as the car cartwheeled. Team Lotus' third season with the type 49s ended with two first places to their credit, but they had lost their world titles to Stewart, Tyrrell and the Matras.

Colin's original aim with the 49 had been to produce a simple car which could exploit the new Cosworth-Ford engine and allow its race development without chassis problems to side-track the team. During these three seasons of 1967-1969 the model had run over-life as the intended replacement 63s had proved a failure. The 49Bs were notorious

for their fuel-system troubles — repeatedly failing to scavenge the last few gallons from their tanks — and for roasting their drivers with hot air from the radiator in the nose. They pitched and wandered under braking, a trait which Siffert especially enjoyed exploiting to the Nth degree when in close company, and which earned the Swiss charger the title of 'Last of the Late-Brakers'. The 49 was far from perfect, but it was to see yet another season...

Early in 1970 development of the two-wheel-drive 49 replacement was slow, and the old cars proved themselves still admirable in their old age. Firestone developed a new 13-inch front tyre and four 49Bs (6-8 and 10) were modified accordingly with new front uprights, revised geometry and 13-inch wheels to carry them, and were redesignated 49C.

Dave Charlton, in South Africa, had acquired the ex-Bonnier car (which Jo had crashed heavily in practice for the Oulton Park Gold Cup late the previous year), while Miles joined Rindt as Team's

Rindt and Hill were not exactly the best of teammates, as seen here during the early stages of the 1969 Dutch GP, with Jochen chopping across Graham's bows in the Tarzan Curve. The cars are '49B/6' rebuilt and '49B/10', respectively, wearing their new regulation-height-and-width rear wings.

'Last of the Late Brakers'. Siffert charging '49B/7' hard towards second place at Zandvoort in 1969 with the car's nose almost scraping the roadway. The Walker car was notable during 1969 and 1970 for its highly polished cam-covers, and often it wore the supplementary pannier fuel tank seen here. The makeshift rear spoiler-cum-engine cowl and extinguisher-bottle mounting were in temporary response to the new regulations.

109

Doing a Siffert. Jochen Rindt brakes '49B/6' desperately hard during his great battle with Jackie Stewart's Matra in the 1969 British GP at Silverstone. Such pitch-down during braking produced marked geometry changes, which made the 49s far from stable. It also altered their aerodynamic profile, and made accurate brake-balancing exceptionally difficult. Note the centre duct added to feed cool air into the cockpit.

Graham Hill locks over '49B/10' into the Parabolica at Monza during his last GP drive in Europe for Team Lotus. The car is running without wings for minimum aerodynamic drag on this super-fast course. The lower rear radius-rod mount tunnelled into the tub is clearly visible, and the extinguisher bottle is on the oil tank. This car was effectively written-off in Graham's US GP accident the following month, but was rebuilt.

Victory at last for Rindt as he took '49B/6' to first place in the 1969 US GP at Watkins Glen. It was Jochen's 49th GP, and the first of his six Championship-qualifying victories for Team Lotus. That nose-top spoiler is there again . . .

Sheer Tiger. Jochen Rindt woke up half-way through the 1970 Monaco GP, driving 49C 'R6' rather than the new type 72, and hurtled into second place behind a confident Jack Brabham. When the Australian slithered off on the very last corner, the Austrian and his veteran Lotus were through to victory. The car carries a triple-tier type 72 rear wing and has twin oil-coolers mounted beneath it.

number-two and Graham Hill — still not fully recovered from his US GP injuries — was staging a remarkably heroic comeback in Walker's veteran car, now in 49C form.

The cars proved remarkably competitive until the new type 72 appeared, with development, to become the prototype for the Grand Prix car of the early-'seventies. Rindt's Monaco victory against all odds, and in triumph over his own mentality as until half-distance he had merely stroked sulkily around,

was the highnote of the 49-family's final front-line season. In April 1971, Tony Trimmer drove 49C/6 in the Good Friday International at Oulton Park, and after a practice crash the old car was repaired with parts cannibalized from 49C/10 (on display at a garage in Bradford) and the English club driver survived a pit stop and brought it home to finish sixth, four laps behind Rodriguez's winning BRM. It was Team's type 49 swansong — the postscript to a classical career.

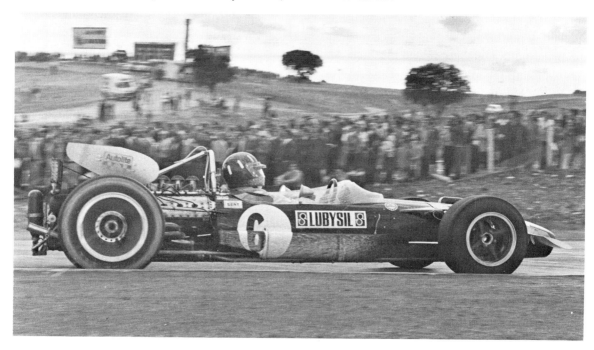

Rob Walker's hard-raced '49B/7' in uncharacteristically scruffy state during the 1970 Spanish GP when a fiery first-lap accident caused foam extinguishant to plaster most of the surviving cars. Here the car is in 49C form, with 13-inch four-spoke cast-alloy front wheels, and Graham brought it home fourth. In the previous race at Kyalami, the first of the year, he had been placed sixth yet was still barely able to walk due to his US GP leg injuries. This shot emphasizes the type 49's compactness.

A new era dawns. Emerson Fittipaldi driving a rebuilt '49B/10' in his first Formula 1 race — the 1970 GP at Brands Hatch. The car is again in 49C trim, with small front wheels and Team's type 72 rear wing. Emerson drove with supreme intelligence to finish eighth, in Germany he was fourth, in Austria a troubled 15th, and then his new type 72 became available for Monza.

LOTUS 16-49T

The Tasman interludes (1960-69)

"Doing the Tasman races was always great but — Cor — you needed
a strong constitution with somebody like Innes taking you round
all the parties and barbecues . . . the racing was almost
incidental . . ."

Dick Scammell

Some of the world's most enthusiastic motor race followers are found in New Zealand and Australia, and both nations have long motor racing histories. Through the 'fifties an Antipodean summer series of International *Formule Libre* races became increasingly significant, as some European drivers and one or two works teams took cars south of the equator. In 1954, BRM actually ran a V16 in New Zealand, and behind these major events lay a healthy national calendar. The market for sports Lotuses and single-seater Coopers was quite strong, and after David Piper took his two Lotus 16s to New Zealand in 1960 and did rather well, Team Lotus themselves headed 'down-under' in January 1961. They ran type 18s with full 2.5-litre Coventry Climax engines for Ireland, Clark and Surtees — with Jim Endruweit and a youthful Dick Scammell looking after the cars. Quite a battering was handed out by the local circuits, and the poor old Lotus 'queerbox' transmissions had a dreadful time. Dick went to Australia on his own to care for Ireland's lone Warwick Farm entry — and gained a lifelong impression of 'Ireland abroad'. They had a marvellous time, which was partly what the Tasman series was all about. In the 'Farm' race, track temperature was 148 degrees Fahrenheit, and Innes was cooking in his car on the grid when Rob Walker's mechanics under Alf Francis calmly unlatched the side panels on Moss' similar car, retained the top panel on catches they had made up specially, and left the maestro to drive in the cool. With a minute to go before the start there was no time to modify Innes' mount. Still he finished second, but forethought like that was what made the Walker/Moss combination so formidable.

In 1962 Moss did well with Walker's new Lotus 21, and Team's only entry of the series came at Melbourne's Sandown Park with a 21 for Jimmy Clark. During 1963, when Indy-derived 2.7-litre Climax engines were confirmed as the power plant to use, New Zealander Tony Shelly flew the Lotus flag

in his ex-Parnell 18/21. When the Tasman Championship evolved for 1964 a 2.5-litre limit was applied, but still the old Climax FPF 'four-banger' ruled the roost. Team Lotus returned to the fray in 1965 with Clark driving a singleton type 32B special, based on a Formula 2 forward monocoque chassis with its rear legs removed and replaced by a tubular subframe to support the larger Climax engine. Jimmy enjoyed a superb 'summer' season's racing, clinched his first Tasman Championship title and returned to Europe bronzed and sharp, and with his pilot's licence in his pocket — having qualified down-under.

For the 1966 Championship, BRM fielded a brace of 2-litre V8s and Jackie Stewart was simply unstoppable. Clark was there once again to defend his title, but his hefty Climax FPF could not combat the multi-cylinder BRMs. His car was the Lotus 39, originally intended for the stillborn flat-16 Coventry Climax 1½-litre F1 engine, but modified for Tasman racing with a Phillippe-devised multi-tubular rear bay. Still, the series was of value, for the 39 ran Firestone rubber and the races effectively provided an extended tyre-testing prelude to the World Championship season.

In 1967 Lotus went the multi-cylinder way by shipping the last type 33, R14, south with its two 2-litre Climax engines, and Jimmy humbled BRM and took his second Tasman title. In 1968, with 2.5-litre DFW versions of the Cosworth F1 V8, Jimmy's so-called Lotus '49T' took the Championship yet again — and his last GP victory in the Australian event at Sandown Park.

In 1969 Team returned with a pair of DFW-powered 49 variants for Graham Hill and Jochen Rindt, and after a turbulent beginning to the series in which the pair pushed and shoved each other they slowly settled down. But the title fell to Chris Amon's more nimble 2.4-litre Ferrari Dino, with Rindt second in the championship and Graham fifth.

David Piper took both his Lotus 16s to New Zealand for the 1960 Tasman races, and is seen here in the ex-Hill '368' or '16/1', with its 'big bump' radiator fairings beneath the nose, letter-box cockpit air intake and egg-shaped exhaust aperture. David ran very well, fielding the earlier '363' once for Frank Shuter to drive in the New Zealand GP at Ardmore only for the hapless Kiwi to collapse with appendicitis during practice and his place to be taken by a cautious Arnold Stafford.

Roy Salvadori driving Yeoman Credit's type 18 into second place at Invercargill's Teretonga Trophy race in 1961. Team's own 18s had a torrid time in this series with 'queerbox' failures on the bumpy circuits. Note the abbreviated windscreen with its side panels cut away — it was hot...

Walker beauty — the 2.5-litre Lotus 21 which Rob entered for Stirling Moss in the 1962 New Zealand races, shown here on its winning way at Christchurch to take the Lady Wigram Trophy. Moss ran soft Dunlop D12 tyres against the company's advice, and although they were almost through to the canvas at the finish they gave him a useful grip advantage; as so often a Moss gamble paid off. Earlier he had won the New Zealand GP in this car. It was subsequently sold to John Mecom Jr, in the USA.

Tony Shelly's black-painted Parnell-assembled 18/21 performed nobly in Tasman events, running Climax engines 1-litre larger than those originally intended for it. Shelly was the son of the Wellington Jaguar distributor and drove reliably to some worthy results in a rather uncompetitive car. He later replaced it with a Lola, John Riley taking over the Lotus.

After a three-year absence Team Lotus returned to New Zealand for a full Tasman Championship programme extending into Australia in 1965, using this F2-derived 32B with 2.5-litre Climax engine in a tubular rear frame. The 2.5 limit had been fixed for the 1964 Tasman Championship replacing the Formule Libre of the previous year. Here at Longford, Tasmania, for the Australian GP, Jimmy Clark had already clinched the title, but a down-on-power engine prevented him finishing this race better than fifth. For 1966 the 32B was sold to Jimmy Palmer, the talented son of a Hamilton (NZ) motor trader who had been racing Lotus sports cars in International Tasman events at 17 and later shone in re-engined Lotus Juniors. In 1968 the old 32B reappeared at Longford, driven by Mel McEwin.

A 1.5-litre Tasman class saw all manner of smaller Lotuses running during this period, such as Leo Geoghegan's twin-cam Ford-powered type 32 seen here. In 1964 Rex Flowers and Roly Levis shone in the small Tasman class in New Zealand with Lotus FJs, while in Australia Geoghegan, Glyn Scott and Arnold Glass campaigned type 27s. In 1967 Dene Hollier did well with a 27 in New Zealand . . . the smaller cars invariably gave a good account of themselves.

116

Engine bay of the Lotus 39 Tasman car originally intended to carry the still-born Coventry Climax 1½-litre flat-16 engine in Formula 1. The tube-bay conversion was Maurice Phillippe's first job on joining Team Lotus; the original perforated-angle booms intended for the 16-cylinder are visible low down. The 2.5-litre FPF 4-cylinder engine was not man enough to combat the 2-litre V8 BRMs during the 1966 Tasman Championship, and Jackie Stewart won the title from Clark.

Australia's Leo Geoghegan bought the 39 and in 1968 fitted a 2.5-litre Repco V8 engine. In 1969 this tall strutted wing was added, seen here at Warwick Farm — where it poured.

Following the precedent set by BRM, Team Lotus took a 2-litre V8 down-under in 1967 in the form of Jimmy's ultimate 33, 'R14'. Here he leaves the startline for the Lady Wigram Trophy on the airfield at Christchurch, alongside Jackie Stewart's 2.1-litre BRM. The leading Lotus threw-up a marker tyre which shattered Stewart's windscreen and burst an oil-line to put him out, leaving Jimmy to win. He went on to clinch his second Tasman title.

Gold Leaf livery appeared on a Team Lotus car for the first time in the 1968 Lady Wigram Trophy race, on Clark's 49T 'R2'. He immediately won the 11-lap preliminary race, set the first 100mph Wigram lap while leading throughout the main event, and scored GLTL's maiden International victory. As is obvious from this Euan Sarginson shot, he waited for nobody! The following weekend, at Teretonga, a tiny rear aerofoil was tried, mounted over the gearbox, but it was removed after practice and most people regarded it as a leg-pull...

118

49Ts at 'The Farm' as Clark leads Hill towards a second consecutive Lotus 1-2 finish in the Australian section of the 1968 Tasman Championship. Graham joined Jimmy just for the Australian races, running '49/1' alongside '49/2'. Flares ahead of the front suspension cut-outs are very noticeable here, having been added to promote hot-air extraction from the radiator. Chasing hard is Amon's Ferrari 246 and Courage's McLaren M4A. Next race was the Australian GP at Melbourne's Sandown Park, which Clark won by 0.1-second from Amon. It was his last-ever 'GP' victory. He finished the final race of the series at Longford in fifth place to clinch his third Tasman title.

After rolling his original 49T 'R5' at Levin after a torrid battle with his teammate Graham Hill in the main-race preliminary, Jochen Rindt was provided with what was effectively a brand-new '49B/10' to race at Wigram and in the remainder of the 1969 Tasman Championship. This car was reconstructed from the original '49/2' which had been raced by Jo Siffert in Rob Walker colours after Clark's efforts with it in the 1968 Tasman Championship, and had been returned to Team when Rob's mechanics completed his replacement '49B/7'. 'R2' had been raced by Oliver late in 1968 and finally by Moises Solana in GLTL colours in the Mexican GP, then had been torn-down for reconstruction as a full 49B. Here, Jochen is heading for victory in the Wigram Trophy race, while later he won the Warwick Farm '100' in the car. Hill's '49T/8', used throughout the series, had the high wing, but lacked the top-ducted nose and ran the original type 49 ZF 5DS12 transmission. It was the car driven by Attwood in that year's Monaco GP.

LOTUS 56

Gas turbines and four-wheel drive (1968)

'Disconsolate, almost in tears, Andy Granatelli showed more class in losing than most Indy car owners — who still want to ban the turbine — do in winning . . .'

Al Bochroch ('Autocourse 1968-69')

At Indy in 1967 STP's Paxton Turbocar was a sensation as Parnelli Jones led most of the race until a tuppenny gearbox bearing failed with only 10 miles left to run. Turbine cars were new to the Indy race, but had a longish Speedway history. In 1955 a Boeing 502 turbine had powered an ancient Kurtis roadster in tyre tests, and in 1956 a Boeing engineer named Len Williams presented an SAE paper to show how a turbine car could out-drag the Offies away from corners. Car owner John Zink took note, and he had Williams plan a Boeing turbocar for the 1961 '500'. This 'Trackburner' was delayed until 1962, but could not improve on 145mph laps when 146 was required to qualify. Who drove number '52'? Dan Gurney...

That year the Granatelli brothers were struggling to qualify their temperamental 700-plus horsepower Novi V8s and Andy was impressed by the turbine's total reliability. He logged away that impression for a day when 'the turbine problem' would be overcome. The problem was simple, and it was big. With 2WD and hard, narrow tyres wheelspin was the enemy. Turbines provided peak torque at stall, which gave them their advantage out of relatively low-speed turns. Such torque, however, is a wheel-spinner. Turbines had typically slow throttle response, and once the driver summoned full power it was delivered a second later and he was fully committed to its eventual arrival. There was similar lag on backing-off. Runaway wheelspin was often the result.

This very rare shot of a very great racing driver in a car presaging an era he was not to see, shows Jimmy Clark in the prototype Lotus 56 turbine car at Indianapolis in March 1968, shortly before he was killed. The Paxton-STP Turbocar is on the left. The aerodynamic form of the 56, its same-size wheels and front drive shafts are clearly visible.

Pre-race line-up at Indy in 1969 with Joe Leonard (above) in Granatelli's type 56 in which he led the race, and Graham Hill (below) in Team's STP-backed sister car, which might have won had it not thrown a wheel. Provision was made for nose-fins, as can be seen from the mounting and adjusting holes up front. The ducts ahead of the front wheels and beneath the rear suspension fed cool air into the ventilated brake discs. Driver preference in rearview mirrors is interesting.

Lotus 56 details showing, top left, the front suspension, inboard brake with underslung caliper, upright design and coil/damper actuation. The tubular link alongside the coil/damper operated a low-mounted anti-roll bar. It was this corner which tore away in Mike Spence's fatal accident, the wheel striking his head. Note the proximity of the dash panel and steering wheel. Top right, rear suspension; bottom left, driver's view; bottom right, the Morse chain transfer-drive cover and UA Pratt & Whitney turbine motor.

Granatelli had a similar problem with his Novis and their V16 BRM-like centrifugal supercharging. On a visit to the United States late in 1961 Stirling Moss suggested Ferguson four-wheel drive would be the answer, as in his successful Formula 1 Ferguson P99. In August 1963 the old P99 was tested at the Speedway for Granatelli by Jack Fairman and Bobby Marshman. The result was the Ferguson-built P104 Novi 4WD which ran lucklessly at Indy from 1964-67, but which successfully controlled wheelspin and gave Granatelli the gas-turbine bug for 1967. The new car he used was designed by Englishman Ken Wallis and was built by Andy's brothers Joe and Vince and their team at Paxton Products in Santa Monica, California — the turbine was not the most potent available — the brothers had learned from their Novis that too much power could prove embarrassing. They used the Pratt & Whitney ST-6 industrial version of the PT-6 turbine built by United Aircraft of Canada. It had been designed in 1959,

entered production in 1963, and the ST6B-62 as supplied to Granatelli developed 550bhp at 6,230rpm — at sea-level and at 69 degrees F. Power fell to 515bhp at 80 degrees and to 450 at 100 degrees F. Output torque reached 890ft/lb at stall, diminishing with speed. The engine was 5-feet long which dictated a sidecar mounting in the Paxton, but it weighed a mere 260lb bare.

Though the car was too late for its intended entry in 1966, another turbine car took the Indy stage. It was the Jack Adams Aircraft Special packing a GE T58 turbine into the nose of a 1961 Watson roadster frame. The car had 1,350bhp, vicious acceleration, hit 200mph on the straightaways and didn't handle at all! The USAC Rules Committee were aghast, and a formula was drawn up to limit turbine engines to around 600bhp. Ex-driver Henry Banks' committee decided arbitrary limits of 23.999 sq in maximum area for the actual air inlet to the turbine compressor for axial-flow types, and 28.5 sq in for the less efficient centrifugal-flow types. By coincidence this axial-flow limit was just above that of the ST6B-62. In March 1967 both Jones and Clark test-drove the Turbocar at Indy and were impressed, and then its race performance (in temperatures of 59-68 degrees F, which suited it just fine) stood the new, mid-engined USAC piston-power establishment on its ear. On June 26 Banks' committee announced new limits of 15.999 sq in inlet annulus area on all turbine Indy engines. Granatelli took legal action, but lost. He cast around for alternative power, but Lotus were interested in giving the turbine approach another go, the portly STP boss hardened his resolve and poured money into a Chapman-conceived team of Turbocars for 1968. So the Lotus-Pratt & Whitney type 56 came into being.

Granatelli's agreement with United Aircraft for exclusive automotive use of their turbines was in its second and final year. The Canadian concern met the new regulations by removing two of their engine's three original axial compressor stages preceding the main centrifugal compressor. It was like reducing a piston engine's compression from around 6.3:1 to only 4.9:1, and power output fell (t.back) to a 430bhp baseline. Simultaneously, turbocharged Drake-Offenhauser engines were proliferating around the Speedway, and from 2.8-litres they were pounding out anything between 600 and 700 horsepower. Surely the turbines were left with no chance... but Colin and Maurice Phillippe knew that speed through the corners was the key.

During Indy testing with the previous years' conventional cars Lotus had discovered that the lowest they ever sat was when they were stationary! Even on the bankings, with 25-30 per cent extra loading on the cars, they rode above static level, so aerodynamic lift was quite enormous. Relatively small set-up changes had disproportionate effects. Nose lift made it tricky to put the cars into a turn at 160-170mph. The normal weight-transfer effect when the driver changed from acceleration to braking was magnified by the change of attitude (nose-up to nose-down) which of course altered the degree of lift and thus dynamic weight distribution. In wind-tunnel tests the Lotus team researched the effect of pitch and yaw on various body shapes, and concentrated essentially on minimum lift rather than minimum drag, though the two are interrelated. The result was the simple wedge which flew in the face of all preconceived ideas of how a racing car should look, while using aerodynamic effect literally to smear the car down on to the track at speed.

In March tests at Indy the prototype 56 could not improve on 161mph laps, which wouldn't even have made the 1967 race. In mid-April, at Hethel, Graham Hill demonstrated the new Lotus-P&W 56 to a staggered press audience. The lengthy turbine engine was now mounted behind the driver in a car whose overall length was up to 14ft 2in from the 38's 12ft 6in, but all that length offered aerodynamic surface to be downloaded. The monocoque hull formed an enormous 16-gauge aluminium-sheet bathtub which was actually very low and light, with kerosene fuel cells within its side pontoons as before. It was cross-braced by a capacious box structure at the front housing steering, front-drive cross-shaft, brakes and suspension, while at the rear a massive fabricated bridge arched over the rear drive unit and oil tanks. Identical suspension members were used all round, with fabricated double wishbones actuating inboard coil/damper units by top cantilever arms. Massive 10¼-inch-diameter Girling ventilated brake discs were 1⅛-inches thick, and in keeping with Phillippe's brief to maintain the lowest possible centre of gravity, the calipers clasped their discs from underneath. Each disc reacted on the road wheel through the Lotus-Ferguson four-wheel-drive system's half-shafts.

The turbine was flexibly mounted within the hull as it could not withstand chassis loadings, and its air supply entered through NACA ducts sunk into the glass-fibre bodywork alongside the far-forward driver's shoulders. The exhaust was a rear-cranked chimney behind his head. A 3-inch Morse chain transferred drive sideways from the engine output shaft, behind the driver's seat, to a Ferguson compound centre differential on the left-hand side. Steel torsion-shafts then fed ZF spiral-bevel final-drives at either end. The car was very light at 1,350lb in initial form, which was some 400lb less than Paxton's 'Silent Sam'. What's more its C of G was very low indeed, so low that anti-roll bars became virtually redundant.

Four 56s were to be built, one as a spare, the others to be handled for Team Lotus-STP by Clark and Hill, with a US driver in Granatelli's own car in addition to Parnelli Jones in our friend 'Sam'. But after the March Indy test Jimmy Clark was killed, and Jackie Stewart was listed to take his place. Then he damaged his wrist in a Spanish Formula 2 race, and Mike Spence was recruited from BRM to fill the vacancy. STP hired Gred Weld to handle their own new 56 and the month of May began.

On May 3 Jones rejected his Paxton drive as he considered with its weight disadvantage and reduced power it could never be competitive. Next day Spence proved the new Lotus' potential by lapping at 164.239mph, on May 7 he lapped consistently at 169 and his best of 169.555mph was the second-fastest ever at the Speedway at that time. The turbine cars had been super-tuned.

Between tyre tests in March and the qualification period in May, Firestone had developed new tyres which were tailored to the 56s' symmetrical weight distribution and 4WD and added 3-4mph to their lap speeds. Ferguson's Type A centre diff for the car, with 50/50 torque-split, provided too much understeer for some tastes and was replaced to order by a Type B diff with 45/55 bias to the rear. Using gasoline instead of kerosene gave better throttle

After the strict limitation of turbine engine potential for 1969, Granatelli's men at STP modified one of their type 56s to employ turbocharged Offenhauser 4-cylinder power. This is the result, with popular Art Pollard aboard. The nose has been opened and reinforced to accept a radiator, and there is a larger pannier oil tank.

response through increased volatility, and richened mixture boosted power to more than 500bhp. Turbine blade temperature rose in sympathy from 1,650 to 1,850 degrees F, which was acceptable for short periods only. Then Colin decided that the turbine's gas generator-section idle speed should be set very high at 80% of its maximum speed instead of only 60%. Used in qualifying only, this setting allowed the drivers vastly-improved throttle response after braking against 80% of 500bhp. The turbine could hit full torque again only 0.2-second after the driver floored the throttle, as against 0.5-second with a 60% idle speed. The drivers were briefed to take the line which enabled them to run as long as possible at 80% power through the turns.

After his quick laps on May 7 Mike Spence was asked to shakedown Greg Weld's car late that afternoon. He began at 163.1mph and took progressively higher lines into the turns. Then he entered Turn One so high he ran on to some dust, began running wide and tried to tighten his line and drop down the banking. Observers then believe he changed his mind, realising he would spin, and attempted to kiss the wall at as mild an angle as possible. The Lotus struck the wall almost broadside on, lost its right-side wheels but was very little damaged. Tragically the torn-off front wheel hurtled back and struck Mike on the head. He was gravely injured, and died 4½ hours later without regaining consciousness.

A USAC Committee, headed by S.A.Silbermann, immediately inspected the wreck and found no trace of any failure, but Carroll Shelby — whose Wallis-designed, Goodyear-funded turbocars had never even looked competitive, unfortunately chose this moment to withdraw his entries, explaining, '...it is impossible to make a turbine-powered car competitive with a reasonable degree of safety and reliability...', and that looked like an indictment of the Lotuses as well as of his own cars.

Meanwhile, Colin Chapman was more distraught than his men had ever known him. He was to return home and leave the running of his cars to Granatelli: 'I am filled with grief at the loss of my long-time friend and associate Jimmy Clark, and the additional loss, just a month later to the day, of Mike Spence. As an understandable result I want nothing more to do with the 1968 Indianapolis race', he announced, 'I just do not have the heart for it'.

Then Silbermann discovered certain Lotus suspension parts did not comply with regulations. Steering and suspension parts were in wrong material, '...although they might well be equal or even superior in strength to the specified materials', said Silbermann. Dick Scammell recalls Granatelli in tears at this new blow. 'Now look what you've done to me', he raved at USAC officials. But he rode the blow once more, and ordered new parts to be made. 'It got so whenever we saw Andy he had his attorney right behind...'

After so much tragedy and drama all concerned were as teed-up for qualifying as Foyt had been in 1965. Weld stood down, and Joe Leonard and Art Pollard were brought in to drive the cars with Graham Hill. Neither American was an acknowledged ace, but the 56s' fine handling made them so overnight. Through the speed trap in Turn One Andretti held the record at 154mph. In qualifying Graham stormed through the quarter-mile trap twice at 156.5mph and on one occasion — typical Hill inconsistency — at an incredible 158mph. Through the short chutes the 56s were spectacularly brisk, and acceleration on to the longer straightaways was unmatched until they ran out of power and levelled-off at 195mph in race trim. The American drivers shimmered consistently and without effort through the Turn One trap at 154mph, which made Andretti sick...

The result was pole for Joe Leonard at 171.559mph (compared with Andretti's 168 the previous year), Graham was second at 171.208mph and Art Pollard was cheerfully on row four with 166.207mph. Bobby Unser's more powerful Eagle-Offy completed the front row, but he was under 170 for his four-qualifying-laps average. It was chassis power which counted in 1968.

Meanwhile, P&W engineers were aghast at modifications to their turbines. The standard fuel-pump drives were designed as fail-safes, using phosphor-bronze shafts set to shear in aircraft if the unit overheated pre-take-off. Lotus race preparation replaced them with steel shafts, but United Aircraft wouldn't look at that and ordered the fail-safe type to be refitted. STP complied. Lotus' entry for Graham Hill, typically, used the steel shaft they preferred.

The 56s had around 480hp for the race and Leonard led briefly before Unser's raucous Eagle-Offy stole by and led until his first stop. The cars had insufficient power to pass on the straights, but picked-up tremendously through the turns. Graham ran fifth and Pollard tenth, then Hill's race ended suddenly in the only 'steel-shaft' car when the front suspension broke at 111-laps and put him into the Turn Two wall. At 150-laps Unser led Leonard by 10 seconds, then when they stopped Lloyd Ruby led. Unser's gear shift broke as he left the pits, so he was slow away, and when Ruby's Eagle misfired Joe Leonard took the lead. With 25 laps to run the yellow came on and the pack closed on Leonard as they all slowed their pace. After he had crossed the line at 188-laps Pollard's seventh-place 56 died abruptly on the back-stretch, then with nine laps to run, Leonard's turbine shut itself down and he coasted to a silent stop before Turn One — certain victory stolen from him. Under the yellow light the turbines had heated-up, and when accelerated once the green blinked on again their fail-safe fuel-pump drives had simply failed! Graham's car, the one with the steel pump drive, would have survived such treatment, but another Granatelli gremlin had got at that one. Leonard and Pollard were classified 12th and 13th, and Hill was 19th overall.

The National Championship Car Owners Association were then too blind or too simple to see the chassis-power message of that race, and petitioned USAC for a further turbine limitation if not an outright ban, and 4WD itself also came under fire. For 1969 the turbine inlet annulus area was further restricted to 11.999 sq in, making them quite uncompetitive, and it was announced that from 1970 4WD and gas turbines not made purely for automobile use would be illegal for USAC competition.

Granatelli took over the 56s for the remainder of the 1968 USAC season — including the road races at Mosport and Riverside — and then in 1969 a rear-drive '56' appeared at Indy with turbo-Offy power for Art Pollard to drive. He made the race at 167.123mph, had the transmission break at 7 laps and was classified 31st for a $10,816 prize. Gary Bettenhausen attempted to qualify another 56-turbo-Offy, but raced a Gerhardt instead. Meanwhile, the chassis lessons of the Lotus turbocars were to have far-reaching effect in Formula 1...

LOTUS 56B

The tentative Formula 1 gas turbine (1971)

'We had a tremendous fuel tank because of the kerosene . . .
55-gallons I think — was stupid! The weight of the car was like a
prototype . . . I was really watching the race from the cockpit . . .'

Emerson Fittipaldi

In 1968 Graham Hill ran quickest in practice for the
USAC race at Mosport, driving one of the Indianapolis Lotus 56 turbine cars, until he hit a patch of oil
and demolished its front suspension against a bank.
The main problem found on the Canadian road
circuit was reducing the power sufficiently for slow
corners without losing pick-up away from them. The
more Graham backed-off the throttle into the turns
the greater lag he had when he planted his foot back
on the power to accelerate out of them. Therefore he
was standing on the brake without closing the
throttle, and that 'beat hell out of the brakes...'.
Otherwise, Graham's reaction was how fabulous the
smooth-riding 4WD turbine felt for road-racing.

A plan was discussed with United Aircraft's Pratt
& Whitney engineers to produce 3-litre-equivalency
gas turbines for Formula 1, where the Spear-Penney
equivalency formula gave a closer match between
gas turbine and piston engines than USAC's arbitrary rules. Three cars would have been built, but
United had been interested in Indy largely because of
its US publicity value, and to them Formula 1 was an
essentially European activity with little potential
business spin-off. Still work began, low-priority, on
producing a '3-litre' turbine. The months rolled by,
until at Monaco in 1970 Colin had virtually a chance
encounter with his P&W contact from Indy days,
and in conversation it was revealed that the F1
turbine was nearly ready. The fourth Indy type 56
tub was lying unused at Hethel, and the first engine
was received later that year and tested in the autumn.
It was hoped to spring a surprise on the opposition at
Monza, but braking-cum-throttle lag were still
problematic for road-racing, and the car was held
back for 1971.

The Formula 1 Lotus-Pratt & Whitney 56B was
very similar to its USAC predecessors in original
form, using an STN/76 turbine with a single axial
compressor stage and one centrifugal stage feeding an
annular combustion chamber, while the output stage

powered an epicyclic reduction gear and the output drive-shafts. Morse Hy-Vo chain offset the drive to the left, overall ratio changes being made by removing the magnesium chain cover and swopping its sprockets. As at Indy the driver had just two pedals — a throttle and the biggest brake pedal ever seen in Formula 1.

The car's debut was made in the 1971 Race of Champions, Fittipaldi driving. It bottomed very badly, and finally wiped-out its right-rear suspension. Modified to use 2.3-inch-smaller-diameter Firestone tyres for Oulton Park, the car (naturally) had revised bump stops, and new brake cooling ducts. Reine Wisell drove, a tyre burst and damaged the suspension again, but the 56B had run fifth. The car was expected to be more suited to Silverstone, and for the International Trophy Fittipaldi drove it, qualified on the front row (using larger brakes) but then suffered a minor suspension failure on lap 2 of the first heat.

Repaired for heat two, the 56B came home third after inheriting the place.

Its hull was subsequently reworked to accommodate extra fuel tank bulges on either side. At Hockenheim, for the Rindt Memorial race in June, Dave Walker was to drive. High inter-turbine temperatures had been observed at Silverstone, and now the turbine engine was fresh from a rebuild in Canada. During practice at Hockenheim it suddenly broke-up internally — apparently due to a reassembly fault — and the entry was scratched. A replacement unit appeared just in time for the Dutch GP, to be held in the wet at Zandvoort, where Walker stood a real chance of proving something. He was up into 10th place from the back of the grid by lap 5, only to miss his braking mark into Tarzan Corner and crash into the fencing. Wisell drove in the British GP, lost power and was unclassified. Ramifications from the Rindt crash at Monza in 1970 were still developing,

Dave Walker whooshes away from the Hunzerug turn at Zandvoort in '56B/1' during the 1971 Dutch GP. In wet conditions the turbine car's throttle lag should have been minimized and its four-wheel drive might have given a real chance of success, but while soaring through the field the Australian driver dropped his car into the catchfencing.

The first-ever Formula 1 gas turbine car unclothed, showing off its Indy parentage, the outrigged battery and extinguisher mounts up front, and the cross-tube beneath which the driver had to thread his feet to reach the pedals. Firestone deep-groove rain tyres are worn here, while for GP-distance races the tub sides were later bulged to provide additional fuel capacity.

and the 56B, painted gold and black, was the lone 'Lotus' entry in the Italian GP, under the World Wide Racing banner. Fittipaldi drove, ambient temperatures were too high for the turbine to produce its peak power, and he soldiered home eighth. Then in the *Preis der Nationen* Formula 5000 race at Hockenheim, one week later, Emerson put the 56B on the front row and finished second after setting fastest lap. End of experiment — the car was then retired, on that 'highish' note.

LOTUS 63

Four-wheel drive and failure (1969)

'The real trouble with four-wheel drive was that the first time the driver got near the limit he terrified himself so much he never went near it again!'

Colin Chapman

Four-wheel drive has held a long-lasting fascination for racing car designers. Many had been attracted by its potential before 1960 when Harry Ferguson Research began to build their front-engined P99 which Stirling Moss eventually drove in Walker colours to win the 1961 Oulton Park Gold Cup. At that time it looked as though 4WD was about to become 'the thing', but with a 1½-litre Formula 1 there wasn't sufficient spare power available to cope with the inevitable weight penalty.

By 1964, the new 3-litre formula regulations for 1966 were known. With the much-publicized return of power 4WD looked interesting once again, and BRM cobbled-up an experimental vehicle which proved to them that wheels all-driven were virtually undrivable.

Ferguson re-emerged with an Indianapolis project, matching one of their advanced 'FF' 4WD systems to the fearsome supercharged Novi V8 engine. It showed some promise. Then, in 1967, the Granatelli brothers' STP Corporation rang the bell by combining smooth gas-turbine power with 4WD in their Ken Wallis-designed Turbocar and they very nearly won the 500-miles classic to the horror of the Indy establishment.

At Hethel, work began on the 1968 type 56 Indy cars, combining turbine power and Ferguson 4WD, and again the 500 rocked and nearly fell. Prospects looked bright for a 4WD Formula 1 replacement for the 'short-life' Lotus 49s, and so the Lotus 63 evolved.

Colin recalled: 'Our Indy experience with four-wheel drive was good, we had all the sophisticated and complicated lumps of stuff laid in, and since we had the bits we thought, OK, we'll have a go. At the time tyres were relatively lousy, we didn't have much download and we had a problem handling 3-litre power, so putting it down through all four wheels seemed to be the way to go. The front-engined Ferguson had been heavy and the experi-

mental BRM was cobbled-up, and although BRM said it wasn't the way to go we were conceited enough to think they hadn't done it right...and everybody else seemed to follow us!'

To do it right Phillippe's staff produced a complex bathtub monocoque similar to that used in the Lotus 56 and in the latest Indy type 64, with the engine mounted about-face behind the driver but well forward between low-cut monocoque pontoons. Its clutch assembly faced the driver's seat-back, and the drive was stepped through a five-speed Lotus-Hewland gearbox to the left-side, where a central torque-split device fed propellor shafts driving offset ZF final-drives on either axle. The offset was inherited from left-turn-only Indy practice, was mirrored in McLaren's 4WD car, but reversed by Cosworth and Matra, who built their 4WD cars with a right-hand transmission offset to be on the inside of most right-turn road-racing circuits.

As much mass as possible was concentrated within the 63's wheelbase. The seat-tank space was occupied by the transmission, so fuel cells lined the pontoon side-boxes, extending along either side of the engine. The driver's seat was forced far forward by the transmission bay, and to reach his pedals he had to wriggle his feet beneath the front axle tube. Hill wasn't keen on that feature and Rindt hated it, loudly.

Suspension was by massive fabricated-sheet wishbones and links, front and rear, with inboard cranks actuating upright coil/damper units in chassis mounts. Tubular subframes provided pick-ups and pivots at either end. Huge ventilated Girling disc brakes were mounted inboard front and rear, reacting through the half-shafts. Wheels were 13-inch all round, and to obtain adequate lock a remarkable double-crank swinging drag-link system had to be adopted, actuated by one end of a conventional Lotus/Cam Gears rack-and-pinion.

Due to his joint-number-one drivers' opposition to

Mario Andretti had seen the possibilities of 4WD at Indy, but they did not apply to road-racing. Here the gifted Italian-born American hustles '63/2' into the first turn at Nurburgring during practice for the 1969 German GP. Unfortunately, it crashed heavily on the opening lap of the race.

the experimental 63 Chapman commissioned John Miles to drive the prototype in its first race, the 1969 French GP at Clermont-Ferrand. With no preconceptions of F1 car behaviour Miles drove nobly in practice, only to retire on the second race lap. At Silverstone, John brought his car home ninth, having spent 30 laps jammed in third gear, then Colin brought in Andretti — a 4WD enthusiast — for the German GP at Nurburgring. Mario was well up on the opening lap when 63/2 grounded under full tanks, bounded off the road and crashed. The damage was severe, the new tub needing re-skinning.

At Nurburgring, Colin and Rindt had a heart-to-heart, which helped clear the air at Team Lotus, and the Austrian appeared in 63/1 two weeks later for the Oulton Park Gold Cup. He started from row two, 3.2 seconds slower than Stewart's Matra on pole, and lay consistently second to score 4WD's greatest 1969 success. At Monza, Miles retired with camshaft failure after four laps, and for the North American races 63/2 reappeared, rebuilt. Rindt tried it and spun in practice, while Miles left the race with gearbox seizure. At Watkins Glen, Andretti was to handle the car at the scene of his sensational 1968 debut, and when it rained in practice the 4WD cars were expected to show their mettle. They were just as slow in relative terms as they were in the dry. Mario retired after a first-lap shunt bent 63/2's

suspension, and after three misfiring laps of the Mexican GP John Miles retired to spell *finis*.

Colin realised that while at Indy four-wheel drive was a big advantage it was only because the torque tyre-to-ground was low because the cars never dropped below about 150mph. 'When we started putting a lot of torque through four-wheel drive we were in trouble because the driver couldn't balance the car properly. With two driven wheels on the back he could balance his car with steering against throttle, but with four-wheel drive every time he went on and off the throttle he affected the cornering power of both ends simultaneously. With the torque-split fixed front to rear, there was only one precise speed at which he could go through corners tidily. If he lifted off he reduced the cornering power of his tyres and flew off the road — and if he stood on the throttle he reduced the cornering power of his tyres and also flew off the road! It limited his options.'

Chronic power understeer, heavy steering, lack of feel with the power on and a hefty weight penalty killed the Lotus 63s. Their drivers were happiest with the torque-split adjusted to feed its total power through the rear wheels, and then one might as well have driven a 49...it was lighter.

While the 63 was expensive, Team suffered more in terms of wasted effort for many parts were ex-Indy. Others lost more money in their 4WD experiments.

Four-wheel-drive complexity shown in this front-end shot of '63/1' on test during the 1969 Dutch GP meeting at Zandvoort. The tubular frames providing pivots for the front-suspension rockers are clearly visible, together with the Indy bottom-clasped ventilated discs, unusual steering arrangement, foot pedals and the front-drive cross-tube with its left-side-offset final-drive.

Midships engine bay of the Lotus 63, with its DFV turned about-face to place its output end behind the driver's seat. The 63s were seen with both under and over exhausts on their debut, but Lotus settled on the low-level system in racing. French journalist Jabby Crombac — a great friend of Lotus and former Mark 6 racer — ponders the works . . .

131

LOTUS 64

The most complex Lotus ever built (1969)

'I guess we were doing around 150 . . . suddenly I saw the wheel come off Mario's car and hit the wall first a good hundred yards before his car did. Then other parts began to fly . . . it looked as though four or five cars had been involved there was so much wreckage flying around.'

Art Pollard

Turbine power for Indianapolis in 1969 could never hope to match the new turbo-Fords and Offies under the latest set of vested-interest regulations, which for those who enjoy the noise of pure-bred piston racing engines was a wondrous thing. Andy Granatelli's STP Corporation instead acquired the latest turbo-charged Ford V8s and Lotus built four-wheel-drive type 64s to carry them. After the initial ban on 4WD for 1969 the regulations had been eased to permit its use with rim-widths limited to 10 inches as against the 14 inches permissible with two-wheel drive. The 64s drew heavily on type 56 monocoque configur-ation and running gear, though with the wedge nose-cones opened-out to admit air to conventional radiators, while the Lotus-designed, ZF- and Hewland-made transmission system shared many components with the Formula 1 type 63.

After his US GP ride with Team Lotus Andretti ordered a 64, but Firestone unexpectedly cut-back and he was left out on a limb. Granatelli took over his car, though it was to be prepared by Mario's own crew. In early tests at Hanford the prototype proved 'a pig', Andretti's job-sheet listing 95 items. But for the '500' the chassis was to become 'the most sanitary in which I had ever ridden'.

The usual three race cars and one spare were assembled, and in early Indy practice Mario wound up to lap at 170.197mph, then hit 171.657mph! Graham Hill was hard-pressed to improve on 160mph and Jochen Rindt was even slower and spun his car spectacularly. Huge duck-tail rear spoilers were fitted, but the rear hubs then began to over-heat and so new finned components were made and fitted. The first qualifying weekend was rained-out and the following Wednesday Mario survived an enormous accident when his car's right-rear hub failed, threw the wheel and put him into the wall when he was set for a 174mph lap. 'Super-Wop' emerged with facial burns and later qualified his old Hawk-Ford for the race — and won.

Investigation of the failure revealed poor heat-treatment. There was insufficient time for the hubs to be remade and properly tested — and so the surviving Lotus-Ford 64s were withdrawn from the race. This was a traumatic moment in a tense season for Lotus, and many past frustrations now bubbled to the surface. The sale of the cars and spares to Granatelli after Indianapolis had been something of a haggling match in the previous three years. Before the first failure the 64s had looked on paper to have the legs of their opposition. Ten minutes before the public announcement of the cars' withdrawal, Andy Granatelli gave his verbal agreement to buy them anyway, at a price of $95,000. Soon afterwards the STP and Lotus men were to meet in the Speedway Motel to finalize the deal and sign over the cars. Andrew Ferguson was late by a couple of minutes and as he walked into the Motel car park he was nearly flattened by a white-faced Chapman furiously reversing out. 'We're not selling the cars!' he roared. 'Hide them, take them away and don't let Granatelli have them. Don't let him find them!' He then floored the throttle and screamed away to the airport and home.

Andrew, bemused, walked into the Motel and found the STP hierarchy similarly open-mouthed. He was told that Granatelli had agreed to take the cars for the quoted price, but then queried the cost of spares from Lotus, which had been 'high' in the past. Colin, smarting from the withdrawal, took this as an immediate slight and after a furious but brief inter-change stormed out. Fergie left politely, and rushed off to hide the cars — not wanting STP to slap an injunction on them.

The Ford engines had to be craned-out and returned to Ford so Andrew had to find somewhere quiet to do the job. Eventually he contacted the secretary of Lotus' shipping agent at Indianapolis Airport and she 'phoned her husband, who cleared the family cars out of his home garage, 40 miles

The most complex Lotus ever built, and never raced — the Indianapolis type 64 of 1969 with turbocharged 2.6 Ford V8 engine and four-wheel drive. Four were built and three were driven at the Speedway by Mario Andretti, Graham Hill and Jochen Rindt.

or more outside the city.

Andrew then acquired a single-car trailer, coupled it to his hire car and with a 64 under wraps on the back he took-off. Mechanics Arthur Birchall, Dale Porteus and Hywel Absalom made a string of return trips until the makeshift garage was bulging at the seams. Ford, meanwhile, had gained the impression that their engines had been stolen, and sent a sheriff after Andrew to find out just what was going on! One by one the V8s were removed and filtered back to Dearborn via devious cross-country routes. Ferguson was under orders to beat out some arrangement with STP and he was there for ten weeks or so while the now stripped chassis were shifted from hide-out to hide-out, including one with no proper roof, which left them nicely rusted. Andrew had thought the rent was cheap when he hired it. Eventually the whole deal collapsed, Granatelli told Andrew as a parting shot that he'd known all the time where the cars were kept, and Colin passed sentence on the most complex cars his company had ever made, with one of his favourite expressions: 'Andrew, bring the cars back to Hethel, where I will personally put a hacksaw through them, I will personally dig a hole, and I will

Andretti's 64 at the Indy pits during pre-qualifying showing off its far-forward driving position, slabby monocoque and added duck-tail spoiler. Opposite page: soon afterwards rear-hub failure sent Mario's car slamming into the wall, producing this scene. What appears to be an Offy-engined Lotus 56 on the right of the upper picture is actually Carl Williams' rear-drive Gerhardt with outboard coil-spring front suspension; the Lotus influence is obvious. The rear-end of Andretti's 64 was torn away and the tub twisted like a skinned banana, leaving ruptured fuel bags to feed a brief but fierce fire.

personally bury them!'

In fact the three surviving hulls lay mouldering in Hethel's hangers for eight years. London dealer Rob Lamplough had bought them, as he thought, in the early-'seventies, but Colin vetoed the price. This case went to court and ended in a finding against Lotus, who were ordered to make the cars over or pay substantial forfeits. The 64s were jinxed right from the start of their lustreless careers. They marked the end of Lotus interest in Indianapolis, but by this time its specialized form of racing had contributed enormously to Formula 1 design in terms of structures, systems and aerodynamic development.

LOTUS 72

Colin's third trend-setter (1970-75)

'Just you wait until I get my new Lotus — it will make this lot look a load of junk . . .'

Jochen Rindt

'The 72 went through unbelievable variations. By the end of its six seasons it was a totally different car to what had begun; you could write a book about that one alone . . .'

Colin Chapman

After the expensive lesson of the Lotus 63, change was imminent for 1970 and it came in the sensational form of the wedge-profiled Lotus 72. During the 49s' three-season life Colin had become increasingly frustrated with their simplicity's inevitable short-comings. He was particularly niggled by Graham Hill's habit of grinding round mile after mile in race practice, trying to sort-out his car's bump-stops: 'My big dream of a car for Graham', he laughed, '...was one with rising-rate suspension so he could never ever get on a bump stop! Then he couldn't play around with it, and that alone would have made my season...'

Planning the 1970 car began as soon as the type 63 approach proved to be a blind alley. Colin and Maurice Phillippe discussed their approach interminably and 'The Old Man' drew up his specification. While the 49 project had begun integrally with its engine, the 72 was to form an integrated project with Firestone's development of a new very light-construction tyre. Very low unsprung weight, near-the-limit all-up weight and smooth pitch-free characteristics would allow the new car to employ softer (faster) rubber compounds than the opposition, without the overloading and tyre destruction seen when such tyres had been used by vehicles not specifically designed for them. The Lotus 72 was to give 'qualifying tyres' race-distance life.

To achieve this aim the new car was to use rising rate suspension, which would provide very soft springing without the lack of control which could allow bottoming under full tanks. Torsion bars would make the simplest system, and 'compound' torsion bars would place the least demand on space. Indianapolis experience had proved the wedge shape very successful at producing negative lift, or downforce, and to employ that shape Colin and Maurice opted for side-mounted radiators, which in turn removed the heat-source which had roasted so many drivers in the 49s. Shifting the oil tank to the rear also helped in

this respect, and contributed towards an increased rearward weight bias, which extended the 49B philosophy. Inboard brake mounts at front as well as rear enabled Firestone to hone their tyres to a new pitch, and the whole package was rounded off with a new-design three-tier wing to provide a better lift: drag ratio.

The compound torsion bars consisted of an outer sleeve internally-jointed at one end to a solid inner bar, which passed back through the middle of the sleeve. While this outer tubular section was rigidly mounted to the chassis structure at its open end, the inner bar protruded to pick-up a linkage attached to the wheel upright. The geometry of this linkage was such that the more the wheel deflected so the greater the rate of twist on the torsion bar, so producing more twist for less wheel movement near the limit of its travel. In practice this provided suspension which adjusted automatically to maintain constant handling characteristics as the car's fuel load burned off and it ran progressively lighter.

Compound torsion bars had been adopted as they were half the length of conventional bars of similar rate. They were machined with extreme accuracy on equipment normally used for making gun barrels, and used crowded roller-races at the bar's business end to maintain clearance between the two parts.

Suspension location was by conventional upper and lower wishbones, exquisitely fabricated from nickel-chrome-molybdenum sheet at the front and from steel tube at the rear. At the front they were mounted on a subframe at a sharply downswept angle towards the nose to provide anti-dive. At the rear the forward pick-ups were higher than the rearward to give pronounced anti-squat to prevent the car burying its tail under power. This arrangement was hoped to provide the required smooth-riding, low-pitch characteristics, but it is interesting to note that in 25/33 days pro-squat rear suspension had once been adopted to improve traction...

The 1970 Dutch GP with Jochen Rindt dominant in his revamped Lotus '72/2' with revised and stiffened monocoque fuselage and all-parallel suspension. Here the car sits up over the hump away from the Hunzerug, showing-off its door-stop profile perfectly, with clean underside, nose-top spoiler to break-up lift, inboard front brake air-intake and exhaust ducts and the modified triple-tier rear wing with extended tips on either side achieving maximum width without threatening to foul the Firestone tyre shoulders.

The inboard-mounted brakes reacted on the wheels through the half-shafts at the rear and through specially-made Lotus brake-shafts at the front. Hardy-Spicer and Lobro drive-shaft joints were used. The brake discs were solid, cooled through flush NACA ducts in the nose cowl up front, with chimneys formed above them to expel 'used' air.

The monocoque itself was fabricated from multi-curvature panels shaped over steel bulkheads. To achieve the complex shapes necessary, soft 18-gauge NS4 alloy sheet was used for the outer skins, with thinner but stiffer inner panels of 20-gauge L72 Alclad. The whole monocoque tapered gently forward in a semi-wedge shape, and the outer surfaces were flush-rivetted aviation-style and were waisted towards the radiator ducts to provide optimum airflow. The inner panels sloped sharply

inwards in the cockpit to accommodate the necessary fuel tankage, which was housed in FPT rubber bags in the side-boxes and fed a collector tank residing beneath the sloping seat-back. The front end of the monocoque was formed around a 5/8-inch square-section steel tube structure, which carried the suspension and a spidery front subframe carrying the battery and body supports. At the rear the DFV engine was bolted rigidly to the monocoque closing panel, and suspension loads were fed through sandwich plates on the Hewland FG transaxle. Since the suspension was relieved of major braking torques with the discs mounted inboard, only upper radius-rods were fitted at the rear.

The new three-tier rear wing, with its aerofoil slats said to be set at 10, 20 and 30-degrees incidence from bottom to top, was mounted above a three-

Communication between Rindt and Chapman was never easy, and the ever-present media microphones didn't help. This shot of the Austrian ace's regular '72/2' shows the 'hair-driers' used to draw hot air from the inboard solid front disc brakes after a run (to prevent heat-soak boiling the fluid). The front suspension and brake shafts are clearly visible, as is the right-side radiator-duct extension spacer fitted at Jarama and found to be illegal at Osterreichring! The Firestone tyres used by the original 72s were developed specially for the car.

John Miles' full potential as a Grand Prix driver was probably never realised. Here, in '72/1', he leads Regazzoni, Beltoise and the ill-fated Piers Courage at Zandvoort, in 1970. His 72 is carrying far more 'wing' than Rindt's pictured on the previous page. Note the more acute front-fin angle.

The ends of the matter — Lotus 72 front and rear, early in 1970, showing the original anti-dive front subframes, inboard brakes with double-jointed shafts coupling them to the road wheels, central pedal box and forward subframe supporting battery and extinguisher bottle. At the rear the suspension linkage may be seen, with compound torsion-bars protruding low down, 'nerf bar' behind the Hewland gearbox, inboard damper just visible above the left-hand exhaust and inboard brake caliper on the right below the oil-tank.

gallon oil tank wrapped over the gearbox. The upper 'foils were adjustable, the system allowing the effective wing incidence to be set at a greater attack angle than was possible with one-piece wings. The necessary balance was provided by the wedge nose-cone with its additional side vanes.

In this form two 72s appeared for the type's debut in the Spanish GP at Jarama. Rindt had an early fright as an insulating spacer, clamped between one front brake-shaft and the disc to prevent heat melting UJ lubricant, overheated and broke-up, allowing the fixing bolts to fidget and stretch until they broke, so leaving braking on only three wheels. Ventilated discs promptly replaced solid discs on this car — 72/2. Ambient heat proved too much for the hip radiators, whose ducts were enlarged by the fitting of spacers between pod and hull. Standard wheels were as for the 49C, 15-inch rear and 13-inch front with

Jochen on his way to winning the 1970 German GP very narrowly from Ickx's Ferrari at Hockenheim, with '72/2' sporting the eared engine airbox introduced at Brands Hatch two weeks previously. The car is diving under heavy braking, though nowhere near as much as did the 49s before it. The hip radiator duct and single-radius-rod rear suspension show clearly.

Tragedy at Monza — the sorry remains of '72/2' are removed from the site of Rindt's fatal accident during practice for the 1970 Italian GP. After protracted legal wrangling an Italian court decided that the right-front brake-shaft snapped to precipitate the accident, but that the driver's injuries were inflicted by improperly installed crash barriers — the responsibility of the Monza authorities. The whole front-end of the car was ripped out when a barrier joint parted, allowing the car to strike a floodlight standard.

15-inch and 10-inch rim widths. Experimental 17-inch-wide rears were tried by Jochen, but understeer became excessive and 15s were used thereafter.

In this Spanish GP and the following Silverstone International Trophy race the 72s handled poorly, apparently rolling excessively and lifting the inside rear wheel in corners. Wet Silverstone practice showed the 72s to be finding grip in conditions which didn't offer any — and that characteristic remained

with the type throughout its life.

After Silverstone, frantic rethinking went on, and only 72/1 went to Monaco — as a spare car. Rindt's 72/2, meanwhile, was torn down and reconstructed by Colin Knight's team of fabricators at Hethel. They had been under tremendous pressure in the original build programme and now had to scrap much of their recent work, revise their monocoques and make new parts all over again. Removing anti-squat

Emerson Fittipaldi driving '72/5' to his maiden Grand Prix victory at Watkins Glen in 1970 to put Jochen Rindt's World Championship points total for the season beyond the reach of Jacky Ickx and Ferrari. This clinched the World titles for both Rindt (posthumously) and Team Lotus and was a magnificent comeback for Lotus in their first race since the Monza catastrophe.

Reine Wisell, Team's likeable Swedish second driver from the 1970 US GP examines his '72/3' during the 1971 season. Rearward weight bias is very evident in this shot of the Lotus 'wedge', emphasizing its rear-mounted oil-coolers with their intake cowls, the new-style in-line oil-tank and the slim and tapering front-end. Torsion-bar tips protrude beneath the coolers and truly slick dry-weather tyres have arrived, these low-profile Firestones allowing the adoption of a wider one-piece rear wing extending over the tyre shoulders without fear of fouling them.

Tall airboxes first appeared on the 72s in the 1971 British GP, as seen here on Fittipaldi's '72/5'. Brake-cooling NACA ducts on the nose have disappeared with the adoption of very large ventilated discs, though the hot-air exhaust chimnies survive. At the rear the outboard-mounted damper barrel is visible behind the radiator duct, the original well-inboard location having proved too hot. A change to Koni dampers had been made at Barcelona earlier in the season and according to the drivers it 'transformed the car'. At Monaco twin-radius-rod rear suspension appeared to form the so-called 72D variant. Emerson drove a fine race at Silverstone to finish third.

1972 was a season of triumph for Fittipaldi and his JPS Lotus 72, seen here in the British GP at Brands Hatch. Only one exhaust primary remains between the twin radius-rods, the rest curling away underneath, while the cantilevered centre-strut rear-wing mount and sleek new airbox are further modifications. The Melmag disc wheels were very light, but manufacturing problems were to cause too many failures.

from the rear suspension — which seemed to induce a diagonal jacking effect across the car — was relatively simple, requiring new subframes to provide parallel pick-ups for the double-wishbone system. Removing anti-dive from the front, where it tended to render the already light steering feelingless as the suspension stiffened under braking, was much more tricky because once the front subframe and pick-ups had been altered the shaped monocoque skins would not fit. In effect, therefore, 72/2 was virtually new without anti-dive and anti-squat, using a new and stiffer monocoque built forward from the original rear cockpit bulkhead and the four engine mounts! John Miles' 72/1 retained anti-dive, but lost its anti-squat. For the German GP, at Hockenheim, a new parallel-suspension car — 72/3 — appeared for John while 72/1 was reduced and rebuilt as new to become Rob Walker's late-delivered 72/4 for the indomitable Graham Hill.

After his amazing drive to snatch victory at Monaco in the 49 as Jack Brabham slithered off on the very last corner, Jochen had won on merit at Zandvoort in 72/2, and with luck at Clermont-Ferrand. There, the 72 chassis had been further stiffened with cross-bracing within the tub behind the driver's shoulders and with strengthened suspension pick-ups. The dampers had also been repositioned at the rear, where they had been thoroughly cooked by hot air exhausting from the radiators. For the British GP, at Brands Hatch, the Austrian's 72 appeared with a neat air-collector box above its fuel-injection system, gulping air through ducts on either side of the driver's helmet. This was to be another trend-setter. Luck smiled once more, and Brabham ran out of fuel on the last lap to provide a beaten Rindt and the Lotus 72 with another victory. A marvellous race on the awful circuit at Hockenheim saw Jochen win on merit by 0.7-second from Jacky Ickx's Ferrari, and then the 72s hit trouble in the Austrian GP at Osterreichring.

There, the scrutineers spotted that the Jarama radiator-pod extension took the 72s' hulls beyond the 110cm maximum width. The pods were drawn in accordingly and Colin found his drivers pulling 200rpm more along the straights! Rindt lost fourth place after a spin when his engine tightened, while Miles suffered a front brake-shaft fracture but fought his car safely to a halt. This failure was caused by a central drilling imperfection, the shafts being drilled to provide some driveline 'spring' and to save a little weight. The drill had been run in from either end but had not met properly in the middle and so provided a stress-raiser from which the shaft fatigued. At Oulton Park, for the Gold Cup, stop-gap solid shafts were fitted to Jochen's 72/2 while the dark-blue Walker 72/4 made its inauspicious debut. Rindt won the second heat, and then came Monza and the Italian GP, with the Austrian set to clinch his World Championship.

Rindt and Miles had their usual cars there, while Team's newcomer, Emerson Fittipaldi, had a new 72/5 to replace his former 49C. The Brazilian promptly crashed his new car to put a ripple in its tub, which stayed there for many months until it was completely rebuilt. Then came Saturday morning and Rindt's fatal accident, when 72/2 was running experimentally without wings, with standard braking ratios and on new unscrubbed tyres. Investigations ran for seven years until an Italian court ruled that a front brake-shaft failure had precipitated loss of control, but that improperly installed safety barriers had actually caused the World Champion-elect's fatal injuries.

Gold Leaf Team Lotus cancelled their Canadian GP entries, allowing Ickx and Ferrari to stride closer to Rindt's points total, but at Watkins Glen Fittipaldi won, with his new Swedish teammate Reine Wisell third, and this clinched a posthumous title for Jochen Rindt and a fourth Constructors' Championship for Lotus.

Team Lotus had won Formula 1 races in every season since 1960, but in 1971 they were to fail for the first time in twelve seasons. Their youthful drivers lacked experience, and Emerson injured himself in a mid-season road accident and its after-effects lingered longer than he was perhaps willing to admit.

Winter changes for 1971 included a redesigned oil system and tank, and a return to drilled torsional brake-shafts in place of the thicker solid shafts used for the US and Mexican GPs of 1970, which had tended to overload the transmission because they would not twist, and which made the cars' behaviour changes very sudden and sensitive to throttle.

Firestone introduced new low-profile tyres in South Africa, and fabricated steel uprights were produced to accommodate the different centre-line heights for the shafts. The original magnesium uprights were suspected of twisting, and as cast-mag uprights strong enough to resist twist would be heavier than a fabricated steel component the change was made. For the Good Friday Oulton Park meeting 72/5 appeared with a new one-piece rear wing and in-line oil tank replacing the saddle type to clean up the car's slipstream.

All these were detail changes amongst scores of more minor modifications not warranting any change in type number. While the 1970 change to remove anti-squat was considered as 72B-spec, the further change, removing anti-dive as well, produced the 72C. The 72D appeared at Monaco in 1971 as

Fittipaldi's regular 72/5 with revised rear suspension to employ the new low-profile Firestones more efficiently. Twin radius-rods appeared on either side, with parallel lower links replacing the bottom wishbones to restrict toe-steer. New upper links appeared, and the gearbox sandwich plate which had originally provided suspension pick-ups was replaced by an upper crossbeam and a lower subframe beneath the gearbox, as on the 49s. These changes tamed the sudden transition from understeer to oversteer which had been suffered early in the year.

At Silverstone, for the British GP, a tall single-scoop airbox replaced the lop-ear used previously. Maurice Phillippe left that autumn to design USAC and eventually F1 cars for the American Vel's Parnelli Jones team, and the 72s' next major modification came prior to the US GP, when rising-rate was removed from the rear suspension. At The Glen (on 13-inch rear wheels and higher-profile tyres) Emerson qualified a whiskery 0.017-second off Stewart's pole time in the Tyrrell, only for terrible race problems to drop him to 19th at the finish...

The new black-and-gold John Player Special livery was applied for 1972, when Dave Walker joined Fittipaldi from the GLTL F3 team, and the unlucky Wisell was dropped. The tubs were re-skinned with 16-gauge sheet, and winter testing before the Argentine GP produced a third-generation rear wing for the cars' third season, but the year was to see a long succession of oil tank, wing mount and wing revisions made by Team's designers, Martin Waide and Ralph Bellamy. Wheel sizes stabilized at 15-inch rear and 13-inch front once more, exhaust systems were revised to weave their differing ways through the new suspension, and Emerson Fittipaldi showed his full potential.

Pole position at Monaco in 1972 was taken by Emerson Fittipaldi with his '72/7' seen here. He finished third in the race

JPS Lotus 72 front and rear showing the later parallel-suspension front subframe adopted very early in the type's career, with ventilated brake discs, inclined inboard dampers, forward anti-roll bar and different brake-shaft joints and gaiters, plus disc-type wheels. Note the conventional rivetting in this late 72 monocoque compared with the flush rivetting of the earlier numbers. Later-model details are very apparent at the rear.

This triumphant season for Team produced wins in Spain, Belgium, Britain, Austria and Italy, plus four non-championship events — the Race of Champions, International Trophy, Republic GP at Vallelunga (Rome) and the 312-miles *Formule Libre* Rothmans 50,000 at Brands Hatch. By Monza, in September, either Hulme or Stewart had to win all three remaining GPs with Emerson's Lotus not even placing fourth to deny him the Championship, but he won in Italy, and the world titles were secure for the Brazilian and for Team Lotus.

For 1973 the cars set out in 1972 trim, with Ronnie Peterson joining Fittipaldi as joint-number-one driver, and due to Firestone's dithering about whether to stay in racing Colin took a Goodyear tyre contract. This necessitated suspension retuning to match, but Emerson won the season's first two races, troublefree, in Argentina and Brazil. At Interlagos, the two veteran 72s were over a second faster in practice than their fastest competitor — they were faster even with full tanks so great was their advantage. Colin returned home and briefed Ralph Bellamy to lay down a replacement car: 'All we need is a 72 100lb lighter...'. It was going to be as easy as

An historic moment, not only for Emerson, winning his eighth GP, but for Lotus, winning their 50th! The scene is Montjuich Park, Barcelona, and the 1973 Spanish GP, with '72/5' limping across the line with the left-rear tyre deflated and almost off its rim. Charging up behind is Clay Regazzoni's BRM — out of contention.

The end of the road for Emerson's noble '72/5', which had served so well, came during practice for the Dutch GP at Zandvoort, in 1973, when wheel failure sent the car off at very high speed into the barriers. A virtually all-new car was built to take the '72/5' identity.

146

It happened at last — Ronnie Peterson was provided with a 72 sufficiently strong to carry him to the finish in what was by 1973 his rightful first place. The venue was Ricard-Castellet, for the French GP, Ronnie's 40th Championship race. The car is '72/6', with deformable-structure side-panels integral with the radiator pods, all exhausts below the radius-rods, and well-outboard cantilevered rear wing.

Once he had found the key to winning Peterson made it a habit, and here at Monza in 1973 he upset teammate Fittipaldi by beating him into second place and ending the Brazilian's last hopes of retaining his World title. Now '72/6' has the late-season enlarged engine airbox, and one of the largest cantilevered rear wings yet seen.

After the evident failure of the type 76 to produce a worthy successor to the faithful old 72s Ronnie proved they could still win in 1974, at Monaco, Dijon and Monza. Above, he waves a wheel at Monte Carlo with a touch of opposite-lock, and below he howls round Dijon on the way to his second successive French GP victory. The car in both cases is '72/8'.

'Kerbs? What kerbs?' Typical Peterson in action at Monaco in 1975 with his specially-made '72/9', which fitted into the series after 'JPS/9' and 'JPS/10' had been produced and had failed. Here Ronnie was placed fourth, but the tyres the 72 required were becoming obsolete. The integral radiator-pods of the deformable-structure cars (mandatory after the 1973 Spanish GP) are particularly well-shown.

that...or at least, so it was thought.

New deformable-structure tank protection was to become mandatory from the Spanish GP, and Martin Waide drew the 72s' conversion. The ageing tubs were unstitched, rejigged and reappeared for the Race of Champions with double-skinned crush pads on either side formed into integral radiator ducts in place of the separate pods used previously. New undertrays projected beyond the original tub side to attach the additional structures. The fabricated steel uprights had grown through progressive development until they were heavier than comparable cast-magnesium components, and just as new castings were being made Goodyear changed their tyre sizes and a stopgap upright appeared which was large, ugly, and worked rather well. During the year a series of airboxes and extended wing-mounts appeared, while Ronnie's cars were progressively strengthened to withstand his driving — and at last, in the French GP, he survived to score his maiden win. There was considerable rivalry between the quiet, instinctive Swede and the cool, scheming Fittipaldi. The reigning Champion's cause suffered at Zandvoort, however, when a wheel failure during practice effectively destroyed his faithful 72/5 and a virtually all-new car had to be built-up — slowly — to replace it.

Wide-track experiments were made, which necessitated stiffer torsion-bars, which took ages to

make, and as magnesium rear uprights proved over-weight yet again, another bite was made at the fabricated steel type.

Early in 1974 Goodyear reverted to 28-inch-diameter rear tyres, and in Brazil the 72s, now being driven by Peterson and Ickx, were fitted with year-old uprights to match. Ickx won the Race of Champions driving the revived 72/5 brilliantly in a downpour, and as the new Lotus 76 failed to offer any advantage, so the existing 72s raced on at Monaco, and Peterson won! He was to win twice more in the 'obsolete' old 'R8' on two more widely divergent circuits — Dijon and Monza. So effective did the 72 still prove that a brand-new car, 72/9, was slowly built-up at Hethel, but parts were cannibalized from it to repair 'R8' after a practice crash at Nurburgring, and it was badly delayed. The wider front track (just over 1-inch on either side) appeared at Dijon, and drilled brake discs were adopted for the British GP at Brands Hatch. Narrow-track form reappeared at Monza and continued into the North American races where, at Watkins Glen, the 72s ran into a massive understeer problem on new Goodyear tyres, and the writing was on the wall for the grand old cars...

Their 1975 season was catastrophically bad. The 'lightweight R9' was still not ready for Ronnie to drive in Argentina, and in Brazil his 'R8' and Ickx's faithful 'R5' appeared with new rear uprights offer-

The end — Brian Henton in the revived '72/5' at Silverstone during the 1975 British GP, the car running in the type's ultimate '72F' guise with engine spaced away from the tub to extend the wheelbase, and coil-springs around the damper in place of torsion-bars at the rear. Henton finished 12th in the US GP, the 72's last race.

ing changed geometry to correct the handling, and both had larger front-brake discs. Ronnie's 72/9 appeared for the Race of Champions (and was third), but he was restless, and then Jim Crawford was brought in to drive Ickx's car in the Silverstone International Trophy, but twice crashed mightily in pre-race testing and practice. Steel-cable torsion-bar actuation was being tried, operating only under tension (on bump).

The cars tumbled down the grids as Goodyear tyres (particularly fronts) were standardized around Ferrari, McLaren, Tyrrell and Brabham — all cars very different in concept from the Lotus 72s. The new tyres' radial-rate characteristics demanded the heavier loadings of more conventionally-suspended cars to achieve adequate working temperatures, and Team Lotus suffered badly.

At Ricard, for the French GP, Ronnie's spare 'R8' carried helper coils wrapped around the front damper barrels to assist the torsion-bars. Its weight distribution was also altered drastically by out-rigging the engine some 5-inches back from the tub on a tubular frame and enclosing a new oil tank to replace that over the gearbox. Ickx's 'R5' was in similar long-wheelbase form, but lacked the helper

coils. Ronnie raced his regular short 'R9' with helpers fitted and finished tenth, but Ickx retired. It was the Belgian's last race for Lotus.

In the British GP, Brian Henton and Jim Crawford joined Ronnie, driving 72s 'R5' and 'R8' with pure coil-spring rear suspension in place of torsion-bars. Peterson's 'R9' was in 1973 trim, and that didn't work, either! Henton crashed heavily and Team were lost, as their results show. John Watson had a one-off drive at Nurburgring as 'R9' continued in standard form, with 'R8' retaining its long wheel-base and coil-spring rear suspension. In the 1975 United States GP, at Watkins Glen, Peterson drove 72/9 and Henton 72/5, starting 14th and 19th on the grid and finishing the race fifth and 12th, respectively. That spelled *finis* to Team's story of the Lotus 72 after a desperately troubled final season — yet Ronnie had still picked-up two Championship points on his car's swansong, six seasons after the prototypes' introduction. In that period the classic 'wedge' had won 20 World Championship-qualifying GPs and had brought Lotus three Formula 1 Constructors' titles. Building a worthy replacement had proved difficult, but it was not to prove impossible...in the long run.

LOTUS 76

'Lighter 72' proves a failure (1974)

*'It just made the drivers so impatient Ronnie finally said "drag out
the old one — I'll race that" . . .'*

Colin Chapman

After that fateful Brazilian GP performance early in 1973, when the old Lotus 72s were so incredibly fast on their new Goodyear tyres, Ralph Bellamy set to work laying out a '100lb lighter 72'. Colin specified that its suspensions and geometries should be identical in principle to the old cars', but attached to an updated tub.

This was a 16-gauge L72 alloy-sheet fabrication, shallow and slightly wedged, with a flat stressed panel covering the driver's shins. The separate front

subframe of the 72 was deleted, but torsion-bar springing was retained all round with fabricated double-wishbone wheel location at the front and an inverted system at the rear with twin parallel top links, a single lower link and twin radius-rods. Anti-dive and rising-rate geometry appeared at the front. Ventilated disc brakes, 10.1-inches in diameter, were mounted inboard front and rear. The tub and body design involved a series of delta forms, the cockpit surround and engine cowl-cum-airbox being

The new London Theatre was the venue for an extravagant John Player press launch of the first Grand Prix car to bear the tobacco company's name from new. More knew it as the Lotus 76 despite their protestations (and Chapman's appeals to determined journalists).

Jacky Ickx retires from his home GP at Nivelles-Baulers with 'JPS/10' (76/2), running with a conventional rear wing in place of the biplane-type shown at its launching. The type's career was miserable — for a Grand Prix Lotus.

as narrow as possible to feed clean air on to a biplane (in original form) rear wing.

The real novelty was the 76's use of four foot pedals and a gear-knob button to operate a new electronic clutch. The far left-foot pedal was to be used for leaving the line, after which the clutch could be withdrawn by using the gear-shift button. The left foot could then be used for braking, balancing the car smoothly into turns and minimizing its pitch-change. The right foot controlled the throttle as usual, while the remaining pedal (actually sharing a vee-arm with the left-foot brake control) offered alternative right-foot braking. Clutch withdrawal was achieved by a hydraulic system operating at 800psi and fed by a pump driven from the starter motor, which was reversible and controlled by two relays. The motor ran in the conventional direction to turn the engine, and backwards to drive the hydraulic-system pump. The gear-knob button began the motor spinning in reverse while opening the control valve — an hydraulic accumulator smoothing operation while providing sufficient pressure storage to release the clutch at least once without the starter's help. Transmission was then via the conventional Hewland FG400 five-speed gearbox. The Lotus 76 was the first F1 car to be designed and built entirely under the John Player Special regime, and so took the 'Mark I' chassis type, with the prototype individually numbered 'JPS/9' since the latest type

72 was at that stage 72/8, or 'JPS/8' according to its chassis-plate inscription.

Ronnie Peterson was particularly enthusiastic about two-pedal, left-foot braking possibilities with the new car, and Lotus effectively had exclusive use of the automatic clutch release mechanism for a year as Automotive Products' manufacturing capacity for the parts was fully extended with Lotus orders! Unfortunately, it was unsuccessful...

Tests with JPS/9 and its sister JPS/10 (76/1 and 76/2) in Britain and South Africa were reasonably satisfactory. Then for the South African GP Ickx's newer car was without electro/hydraulic clutch actuation, while Ronnie's had the pedals rearranged; right-to-left they were throttle, brake, clutch, brake — and footrest. In practice the starter motor failed when used to purge the hydraulic system, and once replaced a short circuit killed the engine whenever Ronnie pressed the gear-knob button. In the race the Swede's throttle jammed into the first corner and he swept-up Ickx and both new Lotuses — sorry, JPSes — were damaged.

Peterson led the non-championship Silverstone race with his 76 in conventional three-pedal form, but a rear tyre blistered and then his engine seized to put him out. The car's handling had never impressed, Ronnie leading in spite of the car. In Spain, the troublesome auto-clutch had disappeared from both cars 'for further development' and both quali-

'JPS/10' again, this time in its very special form with coolers faired-in behind the front wheels, cut-down type 72 nosecone and 72 rear-end sheltering beneath a 76 airbox, as hastily cobbled-up overnight for Peterson to drive in the 1974 German GP. He had crashed his regular '72/8' heavily in practice, but he finished fourth in this 'bitsa' in the race.

fied very well. Ronnie led in the early rain, with Ickx fourth, before engine failure and brake trouble retired both. In Belgium, the 76s suffered further troubles, and as development lagged so Peterson persuaded Colin that the proven old 72s would be more effective for Monaco. The 76s were relegated to spare-car role there, and in Sweden, and on the way home from Anderstorp Team stopped at Zandvoort for some development testing. Some experimental brake pads gave trouble in 76/1 and Ronnie crashed very heavily, knocking himself unconscious for a while and badly damaging the car.

For the Dutch GP at that circuit Ickx's spare car, 76/2, appeared with revised weight distribution. achieved by moving its water radiators far forward behind the rear wheels and shrouding them in new side panelling. Still the 72s were preferred, and raced.

Colin recalled: 'When we got the 76s the trouble was that their systems didn't work — fuel, oil, cooling and brakes didn't work — and the steering wasn't very good. Nothing very serious...! We got stuck-in and did an awful lot of work until Ronnie got impatient and said "drag the old ones out". Halfway through the programme neither would drive them and then we put one on the scales and it weighed the same as the old 72! Its rear hubs were cracking and I

had this terrible fear of a wheel coming off. I just couldn't live with that so I said to Ralph, "Look, there's no point in sorting it all out; if we do, all we've got is a car the same weight as the 72 with 50 new problems...".'

Team didn't even take a car as spare to the British GP, but in Germany they were glad to have the revamped 76/2 on hand, for Peterson had a wheel break on 72/8 and the resultant shunt damaged it severely. Overnight Team's mechanics assembled a 'special' for Ronnie to race, using JPS/10's tub, radiators and front suspension, mated to the 72's engine-and-rear-suspension set. It finished fourth. Both 76s were complete with 72-type rear-ends in Austria, where Ickx raced his car hard but collided with Depailler's Tyrrell, and he retired again at Monza where the Swede won in the Lotus 72. One car, 76/1, made the trip to Canada and the USA as spare. Tim Schenken drove it as a third Team entry at Watkins Glen, qualified as second alternate and took off after the grid — being disqualified on lap 6 — and that was the end of the luckless Lotus 76's Formula 1 story. One car was subsequently loaned to British sprint driver David Render, while the trusty old 72s raced on through 1975 — and fell from the tightrope of competitiveness which they had trodden so well.

LOTUS 77

Lessons from the vital link (1976)

'It taught us that if the big things aren't right you can "mess about" with the small things 'til the cows come home and you are never going to make it . . .'

Colin Chapman

After the near-catastrophe of the Lotus 76 and the final obsolescence of the 72s, Team Lotus fortunes were low and a new car was absolutely vital for 1976. Early in 1975 a new design team had been set-up under Peter Warr at Hethel, consisting of Mike Cooke, Geoff Aldridge and Martin Ogilvie. They were to translate Colin's latest chassis concept into

the metal, while in parallel Ralph Bellamy had been diverted into another new project. He was to revive the dreaded Lotus 'queerbox'. Colin's frustration with Hewland's practical but hefty short-life transmissions had finally brimmed over, and typically he had some new ideas as well. He contacted Richard Ansdale, assembled a set of original transmission

drawings, dropped the lot into Ralph's lap and said 'Here you are, see if you can make this lot work...' twenty years on!

Meanwhile, as Colin tells it, '...the 72 had worked fine as long as we could obtain the tyres designed for it. Once we found ourselves building-up cars to suit what tyres we could get we were in trouble. Now I wanted to find out all over again what made racing cars work...'.

In recent years great changes had occurred, not only in Formula 1 but also within the Lotus empire. The majestic true road circuits of the 'sixties were fast being replaced by shorter, tighter, autodromes. Silverstone had once been merely medium-fast. Now it was rapidly becoming Europe's fastest Formula 1 circuit. During the Clark era Lotus had been a small specialized company assembling its road cars mainly from proprietary parts. Team Lotus had been a relatively large part of the business, staffed by a devoted band of men. Now Colin's empire included a car company which produced far more of its own cars' components than many much larger manufacturers, plus two boat-building concerns and a plastics company as well as Team. Demands upon his time were intense, and perhaps that had its effect on Lotus' dismal racing record of 1975. Still the ambition to regain lost Lotus racing fortunes was intense. One research project immediately produced

Colin's Confusacar — 'The Old Man' shows off his adjustable type 77 in the Heathrow Hotel car park after its press launch in October 1975. The car featured near-linear (as opposed to rising-rate) front suspension hung on new Lockheed-Lotus brake calipers and an extremely slim fuselage. Tests proved the adjustable front structure to be flexible and the massive brakes were thought to impair straight-line speed. Consequently, Len Terry was commissioned to produce the outboard-front-brake conversion seen here, which helped heat the front tyres more effectively. A mid-season tweak was the driver-adjustable rear anti-roll bar, the flexible 'blade' linked to the anti-roll bar giving 'soft' response in the position shown, stiffening as it rotated to place its broad surfaces vertical to the road. The cockpit cable control was lettered 'H-M-S' — hard, medium, soft — as it slid forward.

155

Achievement. With help from the type 78 R&D group, Team Lotus made their 77s truly competitive by the end of the 1976 season. Running with swept-back front suspension and 4-inch-shorter-than-standard wheelbase, Mario Andretti qualified 'JPS/11' on pole for the Japanese GP at Mt Fuji and won a rainswept race. Here, in practice, his car shows off its nose-mounted oil-cooler ducting, extended radiator pods, eared engine airbox and under-chassis aerodynamic skirts. Very few teams had ever climbed back on to the Formula 1 tightrope after being as down-and-out as were Team Lotus in 1975.

the type 77 — and another was to evolve the epochal type 78.

Keynote of the first design was adjustability. It was evident how well short-wheelbase cars reacted on short tight-corner circuits, while long-wheelbase cars were more at home on faster curves. Narrow-track cars often showed an advantage in straight-line speed, yet wide-tracks gained on bite when turning-in. Formula 1 cars differed widely in design, yet their lap times might differ by mere hundredths rather than tenths of a second. The 77 was to explore all these permutations in form and weight distribution, while Ralph's new gearbox should have added another dimension, but its development was slow and it missed the boat.

Before the 77 was unveiled it was realised that to test all possible combinations of geometry, track, wheelbase and weight distribution — plus all the peripheral variables involving wings, springs, dampers, brake balances, etc — might take something like two years' daily running without entering a single race. The car was to provide a vital link in new development, but it could not provide the answer. A research-and-development team was established separate from Team Lotus, and the 77 was to adopt hardware from their researches as it became available.

The new Lotus 77, or John Player Special Mark II, was shown to the press at Heathrow in late-September 1975. Aldridge's slimline monocoque chassis included a structural pyramid top panel above the driver's legs and housed 38 gallons of fuel in two side and one central rubberized cells. A 2½-gallon oil tank resided on a shelf behind the monocoque nacelle, with short pipe runs linking engine and oil coolers, these being fitted behind sharply angled radiators in detachable glass-fibre hip ducts. Naturally, the car's suspension was its most interesting feature. To combine freedom of adjustability with a requirement for all-inboard brakes, Martin Ogilvie had pencilled a system in which two brake calipers per disc doubled as structural suspension supports. The cast-magnesium calipers were developed in conjunction with Lockheed and clasped their discs one ahead and one behind the axle. At the front they were mounted on tubular subframes, which could be substituted to vary both track-width and anti-dive degree. At the rear, the calipers were mounted on special transmission side-plates, which could be rotated to adjust anti-squat. The car was typically Chapman in the way every possible component performed at least double-duty. The right-hand side-plate, for example, also housed an integral clutch slave-cylinder.

The brake discs were enormous, 11½in x 13/16in, in fact over-braked in anticipation of one feature of the new Lotus gearbox which will be described later. Double front wishbones were beautifully fabricated,

156

with a link in tension anchored on the upper wishbone and drawing on a pivotted bottom spring mount to compress a coil/damper unit against its top pickup on the trailing front brake caliper. Rear suspension used inverted parallel links, as on the 76, with twin parallel radius-rods on either side beautifully formed by the French SARMA concern in light-alloy. Here the coil/dampers were inclined, outboard-style, with their feet on fabricated uprights and their top mounts on the inboard brake-caliper castings. Exquisitely compact front hub-carriers contained new RHP/Lobro CV joints-cum-wheel bearings-cum-hubs, while similar units appeared at the rear. Wings were foam-filled alloy-skinned 'foils front and rear, the latter being mounted on a neat pillar housing the gearbox oil-cooler and ducts, rear light (now mandatory) and auxiliary battery socket. Glass-fibre body panels included the radiator ducts, detachable slimline nose-cone and cockpit surround-cum-engine cover, which itself incorporated an integral engine airbox. Transmission was by the old faithful Hewland five-speed FG400...

Early tests with the new car proved disappointing. Its brakes were extremely powerful, but its straight-line speed was poor and there was an evident lack of rigidity about the whole adjustable structure. Ronnie Peterson and Jim Crawford drove in early tests, and all too soon the 1976 season had begun and the cars — JPS/11 and JPS/12 — were racing.

Brazil opened the Championship series and Ronnie drove JPS/12 (77/2) with Mario Andretti engaged for this race only in JPS/11 (77/1). Ronnie crashed his car after coolant sprayed on to a rear tyre, and after an overnight rebuild it developed a steering-system fault. In the race the two new Lotuses collided — shades of the ill-fated 76s' debut. Was it all going to happen again?

Peterson thought so, and left Team Lotus for March. The inexperienced pair of Bob Evans and Gunnar Nilsson were engaged for South Africa, Brands Hatch and Long Beach, and the Swedish new-boy drove alone at Silverstone. The 77 was failing to heat its front tyres adequately, as had the 72 before it, and with Team's staff under pressure Len Terry's Design Auto concern down in Dorset was asked to produce a quick outboard-front-brake conversion. Len found Ralt F2/F3 uprights would do the job, fell back on conventional 10½-inch disc brakes to fit within the wheels and pencilled a suspension comprising a new bottom wishbone, top rocker-arm and coil/damper unit alongside the narrow tub. A 'one-off' set was fitted to 72/2, which Evans had failed to qualify after heroic practice efforts at Long Beach. Gunnar's own 77/1 had been demolished after a suspension failure in that race, but at Silverstone he qualified the revised model fourth and finished sixth. 'Terry conversions' were subsequently standard on 77s.

For the Spanish GP, opening the European season,

Mario Andretti appeared as number-one with Nilsson his teammate, both cars using outboard front brakes. An eared engine airbox complying with new regulations appeared here, but in mid-season the cars used their Brazil-style cockpit-side air intakes, then later returned to the eared-style airbox. In pre-race testing at Sweden's Anderstorp circuit the new JPS/14 (77/3 — there was no '13' for obvious reasons) crashed heavily, but for the GP Mario qualified on the front row and many watches made him fastest. Then the race starter considered he had anticipated the flag, but Mario led the field for 45 laps until his engine exploded. Nilsson spun into the pitwall early on, right under Colin's stoney gaze, but Lotus were clearly clambering back on to that tightrope.

After the Spanish GP Tony Southgate had joined Team as chief engineer and trouble-shooter in the field. He had served formerly with Eagle, BRM and Shadow, and was to help build reliability and consistency into the cars. He had been introduced by Tony Rudd, who was then running the 78 R&D team. They had built themselves a test rig to simulate chassis loads, and Team had used it to investigate their current 77. There is a difference between strength and stiffness, and while the 77's structures proved sufficiently strong in early form their stiffness was deficient. As 'goodies' destined for the 78 became available, so they were race-proven on the 77...and its improvement continued.

The latest car, JPS/14, was rebuilt after its Swedish adventure, only to break its bottom engine mounts in French GP practice at Ricard and sag in the middle. It became a development chassis, appearing with one oil cooler sunk in the nose (like Southgate's Shadows) to add forward bias to the weight distribution, instead of two at the rear, and later added a cockpit-adjustable rear anti-roll bar and compressed-air starter allowing the use of a very small ultra-lightweight battery. These features became standard on the race cars. Revised front-suspension geometry appeared at Monza, as did deeper aerodynamic skirts to contain airflow beneath the hull, and for the North American races a 4-inch-shorter wheelbase was adopted and the cars ran brush-skirts. At Mosport, Mario's practice car broke a stub-axle and threw a wheel. Inevitably, it was '14'. Then to the final race in Japan, which would decide the World Drivers' Championship between James Hunt and Niki Lauda, but it was Andretti who shone. He qualified on pole, splashed round second in Mount Fuji's foggy downpour, fell back as he consciously conserved his tyres on a moderately drying track, then took the lead as those ahead stopped to change wheels. Mario drove home to win by one clear lap, with Gunnar sixth in the second car, and Team Lotus were back in business. The vital link had served its purpose...and better was to come.

LOTUS 78

The 'Wing Car' arrives (1977)

*'The 78? Well I'll tell ya — it's just beautiful. It feels like it's
painted to the road . . .'*

Mario Andretti

In the summer of 1975 Lotus Formula 1 cars were in
deep trouble. Colin related how '...I sat down and
thought really seriously about what we wanted, and
decided the answer was a wing car...'. He compiled a
27-page concept document specifying his requirements and he presented it to his engineering director,
Tony Rudd, who was to establish a new research-
and-development group within the Lotus empire. As
Tony told the story, that brief was far more than an
outline for a new car design, it was a measure of
Chapman's greatness. 'He realised that in racing we
were down and out, and that we'd got it all wrong by
the latest standards. And he made the right long-
range strategic decisions while still involved in racing
day-to-day. In his famous 27-page brief not only did
he suggest the way to go, but he also listed all the

things he didn't know, and then he left it to an old
has-been like me and to a bunch of new boys to tell
him all the answers...'

Rudd might have been rather older than his
colleagues, but he wasn't quite a has-been. He had
trained at Rolls-Royce and had served with BRM
from 1951 to 1969. He had been chief engineer
responsible for the 1½-litre cars which had given
Lotus so much trouble, and had joined Chapman in
1969 with ultimate responsibility for all Lotus
engineering. He was not, however, closely involved
with the racing cars until 1975, when R&D work
began at Ketteringham Hall. This rambling country
house lay folded in the woodlands close to Hethel.
During the war it was a Bombardment Group HQ for
US 8th Air Force bases like Hethel itself, and it later

*'Fawlty Towers' really looks
the part. Ketteringham Hall,
where Tony Rudd set-up the
Lotus research-and-
development group which
brought 'wing cars' and
'ground-effects vehicles' to
Formula 1.*

158

Mario Andretti winning his naturalized home GP at Long Beach, in 1977, with 'JPS/17', his brand-new third-off Lotus 78. It was quite a lucky win as Scheckter's Wolf suffered a puncture in the closing stages, but Mario and Niki Lauda in the Ferrari had been battling wheel-to-wheel with Scheckter for many laps. Note the nose oil-cooler, wide front track and side panniers of the type 78.

became a boarding school before falling virtually derelict. Lotus acquired it and Ralph Bellamy became one of its first inmates with his gearbox project. Tony's Esprit production-car team arrived soon after, and with that project's completion Colin put him in charge of long-range Formula 1 research. His new group was to operate independent of Team's everyday race commitments. They were to supply the answers Colin needed and to test the feasibility of the type of car his brief outlined. Those 27 pages were dated August 1975, one month before the 77's release. Ralph Bellamy was one early member of the group, and Peter Wright another. He had been with Tony Rudd at BRM in 1969 — when they had actually been developing a wing car! After a spell in charge of Specialised Mouldings' wind-tunnel (he had a degree in aerodynamics) he joined Lotus to run their plastics company's research, and since that was now complete he joined Rudd and Bellamy at Ketteringham Hall — or 'Fawlty Towers' as it was known.

During the autumn of 1975 this trio discussed with Chapman myriad questions of principle. The philosophy was simple in essentials — to use the car's own form to produce worthwhile aerodynamic effect instead of simply loading an aerodynamically redundant hull by relatively tiny wings at front and rear. Many further refinements were to be tested before the best ingredients would combine within the finished mix.

Charlie Prior, a first-class model and pattern maker from the Esprit team, was retained to build quarter-scale cars and aerodynamic devices for wind-tunnel testing. Questions were pursued in depth. If either bluff or chisel noses could be used then both would be tested. If the chisel then promised better they would consider why, if it worked so well up front, should not other chisel sections be used to gain some more elsewhere? Tests and questions continued into the winter until a general concept hardened. Radiator siting is vital to racing car design, and the De Havilland Mosquito aircraft's inner wing section with its buried leading-edge coolers came to mind. A mimic section was made and tested upside-down to provide negative lift. Maximum lift with minimum drag was the target, and Tony recalled the message he received from the tunnel testers that Christmas — it read simply, 'The Mosquito flies...'

With concept, shape and principles decided Ralph sat down to draw the car while Peter Wright perfected its aerodynamics. Mike Cooke then set-up and ran a test rig, simulating racing loads on every component as it was made. Unacceptable deflection brought immediate redesign until stiffness was adequate. This rig, loading parts with weights (actually concrete-filled oil drums) via wires and pulleys, proved invaluable in building reliability into the car. It also served to pinpoint the 77's early deficiencies and helped make that car competitive.

Left, Andretti makes it two-in-a-row by winning the 1977 Spanish GP in his type 78 with Nicholson-McLaren DFV engine. Above, Gunnar Nilsson driving an excellent wet-weather race to win the same year's Belgian GP at Zolder in his 78 after over-enthusiasm had put out Andretti's pole-position car in a first-lap collision. The very popular Swede opted to prove his ability in a car other than the Lotus for 1978, but tragically he fell victim to ill-health. Engine failures robbed Andretti and Team Lotus of just reward for their 1977 potential, as below at Silverstone, in the British GP, where a Government restriction on tobacco advertising saw the JPS logos removed. The aerodynamic skirts extending to the road surface were important in isolating the airflow regimes around and beneath the car. The pannier leading-edge air-intakes are visible between the front-suspension members.

161

Andretti locks over '17', as Team knew the car, into the Old Station Hairpin at Monaco on his way to a troubled fifth place, showing-off the 'Mosquito' leading-edge top-ducted panniers and very-wide-track front suspension of the 78. Below, the type 78 'office' with right-hand gearshift, left-hand notched selector sliding fore-and-aft to adjust the rear anti-roll bar, and almost hidden by it the fuel cock to select tanks. Note the dash-panel roll-over protection hoop (mandatory since 1976), minimal padding, perforated bulkhead and clearance bulge in the cockpit surround for the gearshift hand.

Once Bellamy had finalized his layouts Martin Ogilvie moved up from Team at Potash Lane to R&D at Fawlty Towers. He detailed the new 78's suspensions and 'bits that moved' while Ralph completed the chassis, and then they combined to do the body.

The prototype Lotus 78 — JPS/15 — emerged in August 1976 and was driven first time out at Hethel by Eddie Dennis, Ketteringham's shop foreman. To limit unknowns on the car it used a Hewland transmission rather than the new Lotus gearbox, which had taken second priority to the car. Nigel Bennett — a former tyre engineer who had joined Team on Firestone's retirement from racing at the close of 1974 — conducted onboard instrumentation tests with loaned Goodyear recording equipment, while Andretti and Nilsson drove in extended circuit testing. When Colin decided to race the new invention his R&D group had amassed 2.2 miles of circuit-test recording tape, had completed over 150 individual investigations, 54 rig tests and 400 hours of wind-tunnel time. The statistics were impressive, but did the car really work?

Tests indicated that it did, although aerodynamic values were only some 75 per cent of those predicted from wind-tunnel tests of models.

On December 21, 1976, the new John Player Special Mark III as it was known was unveiled to the press at London's Royal Garden Hotel. Andretti enthused about its 'boulevard ride' and it certainly looked different.

Its monocoque fuselage was slim like the 77's, but had broad panniers on either side. The tub formed into a stressed tank section behind the driver's shoulders, and had a structural top panel at the front which enclosed his legs. It was light and extremely stiff (rig-testing had seen to that) and used Cellite sandwich material in its front bulkhead and side skins. This material consisted of two thin dural sheets enclosing aluminium honeycomb. It was extremely strong and stiff, though light, and came direct from aviation, where it was used for Trident airliner flooring in Lotus' particular section. It had also appeared in the Cosworth 4WD car of 1969. Swept-back front rocker-arms and wide-based fabricated lower wishbones located the front hubs and their 77-style twin-caliper disc brakes, while inboard coil/damper units resided in neat niches within the tub sides. Massive fairings streamlined the tubular top rocker-arm pivot support where on the 77 it had been exposed. At the rear the Cosworth/Hewland assembly matched the 77's in all save two major details, complete with parallel-top-link suspension pick-up by Lotus inboard double calipers. Where the 77 had used a single bottom link, the 78 substituted a massive fabricated wishbone, though the geometry was identical. A neat change on JPS/16 on show was the oil tank, which now wrapped round the bellhousing spacer between engine and gearbox; on JPS/15 oil had been carried in a 4-inch-longer rear section of the tub. All subsequent 78s were to use the shorter tub and bellhousing tank with a 107-inch wheelbase instead of JPS/15's 110-inch.

Still the car's secrets lay largely within its box-like panniers. They housed water radiators, Mosquito-style, within the leading-edge intakes, with hot air exhausting through top ducts. Duct ramps were provided by the upper face of fuel tanks outrigged from the tub. Their undersides curved upwards towards the rear, stopping short in line with the front engine mounts to provide an inverted wing section. It was closed-off by a Cellite end-plate extending virtually the full distance between the wheels on either side. The pannier's upper surface similarly ran alongside the engine to flick-up above the exhausts ahead of each rear wheel. Beneath the end-plate a bristle skirt (later changed many times) extended to ground level. It was required to separate two distinct airflow regimes, one beneath the car and the other one around it. In effect, a depression would be formed beneath the car which would literally suck it down on to the road. Conventional front fins and rear wing supplied added trim, but still there was more.

Its weight distribution had been given extra forward bias by its side radiators just behind the front suspension, its nose oil-cooler and the forward driving position. All three fuel cells lay in perfect line across the car around its centre of gravity to achieve Colin's requirement for 'minimum change in handling and response as the fuel load lightened'. After testing permutations with his 77s he found that only one thing really matters, '...how long it is, how wide it is and where the weight is! We'd tried seven different rear-suspension geometries on one occasion and the drivers were hard-pressed to notice any difference. But when we increased the front track by an inch they raved "That is just fantastic!"...'.

Accordingly the 78's front track approached the Formula 1 width limit, wider than the 77 so that the longer lever-arm would virtually stick out a paw as the driver applied steering lock and give him terrific 'bite'. With Goodyear's front tyres now loaded to working temperature (though heating was well-controlled by the car's dynamic weight distribution) front-end grip became enormous. In turn that allowed the use of near-zero-slip differentials to limit wheelspin, which in a more conventional design would merely induce enormous understeer. Then the USAC-style adjustable rear anti-roll bar was adopted, as promoted by Andretti, plus a preferential fuel-drainage system from the same source. This allowed the driver to select which tank he emptied first in order to maintain a weight bias on the 'inside' of the car — thus the left-hand tank would be emptied first on most essentially right-handed circuits. Equally, the driver could juggle his fuel load as it burned down and Andretti in particular was so sensitive to fine tuning that he could trim his car out of trouble and into optimum balance on the fuel tap and anti-roll adjustment. Mario had developed a working rapport with Chapman unmatched since Jimmy Clark, and

78 secrets, showing the rear suspension with its massive fabricated uprights, inboard ventilated brakes, tiny gearbox oil-cooler, adjustable-stay rear wing, inclined coil/dampers and the anti-roll bar with its adjuster blade visible by the top of the right-hand wheel upright. In the workshop at Ketteringham, below, we see the 78's effective 'wing section' pannier fuel tank, with ramp forward face behind the radiator matrix and upswept underside. The section was not as effective as had been hoped, but could not easily be changed. The nose oil-cooler is clearly visible, while three spare DFVs sit on the bench behind.

The Prodigal Son came home in 1978 and went well, as expected. Ronnie Peterson in his 78 'JPS/16' during the US GP West at Long Beach early in 1978, clearly showing the latest rigid side-skirts. SuperSwede was shown the 'fuel change' signal so many times to ensure he noticed it that finally he tugged the tap control right out of his car and threw it at his crew!

he worked unceasingly during 1977 to set-up his 78s to an unprecedented pitch. In USAC left-turn-only track racing, 'stagger' — the use of unequal-circumference tyres — and 'cross-weighting' — diagonal stiffness in the car adjusted in the spring platforms — were normal adjustments to be made, and the Italianborn American was highly attuned to both and to their effects. For road-racing the 78s he would carefully match his tyres, and with Chapman, Bennett and (briefly) Southgate all working in the field, even lateral tyre stabilities would be juggled by altering wheel offsets with their adjustable Speedline rims. The result was Mario leading more World Championship race laps than any other driver. He won four GPs, Gunnar Nilsson won a fifth in Belgium in the rain, but a string of five engine failures and three other mechanical faults kept Andretti, Lotus and the world titles apart. Three new Cosworth development engines failed and alternative Nicholson-McLaren DFVs broke twice. Mario won with luck and Nicholson power in his adopted home GP at Long Beach, and again on merit with the same engines in Spain. Luck shone again at Dijon, where he won the French GP on the last lap, and the sweetest victory came at Monza before an Italian crowd, where a revised development engine with less radical valving survived to the flag. An aeration problem was suspected with the bellhousing oil tank but never proven, though alterations were made. In Argentine practice Mario's 78/2 had its front-end blown-out by an exploding extinguisher bottle, and

in Brazilian practice the car caught fire. Race retirements in both events were mechanical, caused by RHP/Lobro joint failure and a battery solenoid malfunction. Then in Sweden, after leading 68 of the GP's 72 laps, Mario's car ran low on fuel due to its Nicholson engine's metering unit having vibrated itself on to full-rich. These failures brought frustration, but two driver errors caused more irritation. Mario seemed determined to win his races from the first lap, and early accidents at Zolder and Mount Fuji didn't help his cause.

At the end of the year Lotus-JPS were second to Ferrari in the Constructors' Championship, Andretti third and Nilsson eighth amongst the drivers, but still Mario had won four qualifying GPs while World Champion Lauda and runner-up Scheckter had only won three each. It was a Championship system which rewarded consistency, not winning, and Colin considered 'merely driving for points just isn't the name of the game as far as I'm concerned....'. His Lotus 78 had been the car of the season, and if it had a fault the opposition believed it was its restricted straight-line speed. Team thought that was not quite true, for other problems had intruded on the faster circuits, and in any case the car offered so much downforce its drivers liked to use it all, and didn't care to compromise by trimming-out even a little of its adhesion in favour of straight-line speed. Above all, the 78 excelled on bite into corners and traction out, and so the 'wing car' had arrived — a triumph for Chapman and for Rudd's development team.

Standard-setter of his time – Ronnie Peterson in the Lotus 78, here on his way to winning the 1978 South African GP after a torrid closing-laps duel with Patrick Depailler's Tyrrell. Tragically, both would die behind the wheel of Formula 1 cars, Ronnie at Monza in old 78/3.

Of course, not everything had been rosy. It was clear that the protruding wing tanks, exhausts and outboard rear suspension on each side restricted underwing floor area and obstructed airflow through the sidepod tunnels. Because the underwing sections were well forward, that's where the 78s centred their download pressure, and that's why they displayed such enormous turn-in grip on their wide-track front ends. In fact front-end performance could always overwhelm the rear if drivers pressed too hard.

Nonetheless, by the time the much improved Type 79s came on stream in 1978, these earlier 'wing cars' had accumulated more success, and were clearly still the cars to beat. Tragically, poor Gunnar Nilsson had developed a terminal cancer, and with Count 'Googie' Zanon's financial backing Ronnie Peterson rejoined Team as Andretti's partner, not altogether to the American's great comfort. . .

Mario had raced 78/3 and Peterson 78/2 in each of the first five new-season races from Argentina in January to Monaco in May. Their 10 starts yielded two wins – in Argentina and South Africa – one second, two fourths, one fifth, a seventh (after leading), an 11th and two retirements, only one of them mechanical, the other due to a collision in Brazil which broke the Peterson car's suspension.

At Zolder in his revised 79/2, Andretti dominated totally while Ronnie's 78 was delayed by a stop to change tyres, but raced back into second place for Team's fourth 1-2 *Grande Epreuve* result.

From the Spanish GP at Jarama, Peterson's new 79/3 replaced his faithful 78. Mexican privateer

Hector Rebaque had meanwhile bought old 78/1 and drove it sensibly before retiring. In Germany, Rebaque drove his second 78, chassis '4, into sixth place to score his first Championship point, but he then crashed in the cloudburst in Austria which also claimed Andretti's 79. Then came the Italian GP at Monza. . .

In race morning warm-up Peterson crashed his regular 79/2 following brake problems. No spare 79 was available so he fell back on his veteran 78/3 spare car for the race. After a fudged start procedure, the grid packed together funnelling down at high speed from the wide start-area into the relatively narrow road-circuit. Hunt's McLaren nudged Ronnie's car's right-rear wheel, sending it careering into a right-handed slide head-on into a guardrail protecting the entrance to the high-speed banked circuit.

The massive impact crushed the 78's single-skin forward monocoque and broke both poor Peterson's legs. The chassis was demolished, its fuel system ruptured and the wreck caught fire, although Peterson was quickly pulled clear, notably by Hunt. He was seriously injured, but alive and in no apparent danger, only to die that night in hospital due to complications following fracture surgery.

After the 79's introduction into Championship racing at Zolder, the works 78s had made only two more starts – that in Belgium yielding second place and fastest lap for Peterson in 78/2, while the type's tragic swansong was at Monza, where Ronnie's 78/3 was of course utterly destroyed in that tragic accident.

LOTUS 79

'Black Beauty' (1978)

'You could call the 78 a 'wing car' while the 79 takes the whole idea one stage further — it's more a true 'ground effects vehicle' . . . and it's legal!'

Tony Rudd

None could challenge Lotus' redemption after that remarkable season of 1977. The existing John Player Special Mark IIIs raced on into the new year with Ronnie Peterson rejoining the team alongside Andretti. Mario began the year in style by winning at Buenos Aires, while Ronnie stole a last-lap victory in a going-slow race in South Africa after Andretti's car ran low on fuel and lost the lead.

Meanwhile, a much-refined JPS Mark IV, or Lotus 79, was on the way to capitalize on experience with the Mark III. While the type 78 had used reasonably simple inverted side wings for its downthrust the 79 went much further towards being a true ground-effects vehicle — and recognizable side wing sections were dispensed with. It was now hoped to find the extra '25 per cent' of aerodynamic effect somehow misplaced between the original windtunnel models and the type 78. It had been claimed that the 78s began heavy and shed weight with development, but still they were not light enough. One interesting item in Colin's original concept had been provision of onboard jacking to save time when testing and in race-qualification. The original cars had been too heavy to dare install it, but the 79 was to come a little closer.

Meanwhile, the R&D group had become diluted. Tony Southgate had returned to Shadow in mid-1977, and now Ralph Bellamy moved to Copersucar. Both embarked on wing-car designs, but Chapman had foreseen a braindrain and had compartmentalized his team to prevent individuals copying Lotus practice too quickly. In effect, Bellamy, Southgate and Wright were each reckoned to know about 30 per cent of the 78's ingredients, Rudd knew some more, but Chapman held the key to their successful mixture...

Under Colin's usual beady-eyed direction the new type 79 was drawn and detailed by Geoff Aldridge and Martin Ogilvie. One major objective was to improve airflow through the side panniers, and to do

this the outboard fuel tanks and rear-suspension springs were deleted. F1 regulations had set an 80-litre maximum size for individual fuel cells, but this was changed and the 79 accommodated all its fuel in a single tank between the driver and engine. Two tanks had been drawn here in an early scheme, but one replaced them, sending the driver further forward. The tub was extremely slender and was stiffened by a fabricated stress-panel bulkhead around the dash area, like the 77/78 and so reminiscent of much earlier Lotus cars. An arched top panel enclosed the driver's legs and tapered down to the shallow and narrow nose. A single large water radiator hung, raked forward, on the tub's right side, with a smaller oil-cooler on the left. Front suspension was now squared-up rather than raked back as on the 78, and its inboard coil-springs were now buried within the hull sides. The wide-apart top rocker-arms and lower wishbones offered minimal interference to airflow entering the side pods, and exit from them was vastly improved with inboard coil/dampers at the rear and up-and-over exhausts like those sometimes used in the bad-old 4WD days of 1969. The now familiar double-caliper disc brakes reappeared, outboard front and inboard rear. Without its bodywork the 79 looked gawky and spare, but with its panelling in place it was transformed into the most beautiful of modern Formula 1 cars — Black Beauty indeed.

When Ralph Bellamy had moved to 78 design his gearbox project was presented to Brian Spooner for completion. Little more than a basic concept was in existence, and Brian was to detail and draw it more or less alone. Colin wanted a smaller, lighter gearbox than a Hewland, with longer internal life. The old 'queerbox' gearwheels would last forever, but the six hapless dogs used to engage all ratios took a fearful beating and they were its downfall. Now the simple 'stack of five drop gears' (only as long as your index finger) was to be revived, but with improved selection — and some new and subtle attributes.

This time the input shaft was a fixed hollow sleeve with the gearwheels free to rotate around it. Within the hub of each gear lay four balls, and engagement was effected by a 'bobbin' which slid inside the shaft, knocked-up the balls into engagement with their individual gearwheel and so locked it to the shaft. This in itself offered a pure sequential change rather like the queerbox, but with individual engagement mechanism for each ratio instead of one mechanism being expected to engage them all. As Colin told the story: 'We got cold feet on the latest version and used two bobbins so the change could be non-sequential and we could use a conventional gate'. One bobbin now selected second and third, the other picked-up fourth and fifth, and there was provision for a third so the 'box could run to sixth and seventh. First was engaged by a simple muff-coupling and spline. So, power entered on the bottom selector shaft, the fixed gears were on the top shaft, and 'son of queerbox' had arrived.

The German ZF company, who had made the original Lotus 'box, supplied their limited-slip diffs for the new one, but were too committed to help further. Getrag — another well-known German transmission company — was approached and became extremely interested for they had used similar ball-engagement in an ancient bubble-car gearbox; they were intrigued with the idea of feeding 500hp through such a system and agreed to help. Spooner modified his design from their experience, and the project developed well — though slowly — with Getrag making most components to Lotus' designs, ZF providing almost complete differentials, and Oerlikon in Switzerland cutting the crown-wheels-and-pinions. An early scheme had been to use 4WD final-drives from the type 56s. These were beautifully made by ZF, with extra nose-bearings on the pinions to resist bending loads. In the new transmission these extra bearings were tricky to accommodate and so were deleted early on. How-

168

The prototype 79 'ground-effects' car on test at Ricard-Castellet in December 1977, showing its rigid skirts, end-plate-supported rear wing, enclosed engine bay and far-forward driving position, containing Andretti. The 'aerial' is actually an air-speed pitot head. The lower picture shows Mario practising '20' for its first race, the 1978 Silverstone International Trophy, which it led before spinning out on a flooded Abbey Curve. The rear bodywork is cut lower than on the prototype '19', and flick-up fairings have been added around the rear tyres. The filler has also been removed from the roll-over bar skinning.

ever, an early Oerlikon evaluation had shown that pinions supported in this way would only just about withstand Formula 1-type torque. Simple overhung pinions of this same size were to have a very rough time, and early problems with the new transmission involved its very conventional final-drive, while the experimental bits were virtually troublefree...

Of course there was more to the new Lotus gearbox than merely a longer-lived and lighter method of swopping cogs. Since its gear engagement involved neither dogs nor meshing there was no need to declutch. Now the driver could merely back-off the throttle when changing-up, flick the lever through a gear and go back on the power...if he could time it right with the fearsome responsiveness of a DFV behind his shoulders. A free-wheel mechanism could be applied which would allow the same clutchless trick for down-changes...if the driver could time it right with the fearsome, etc, etc. The clutch pedal could be forgotten once the car had left the startline, and therefore provision was made to use a right-foot throttle, left-foot brake and central clutch pedal, and for the driver to race two-pedal.

Chapman : 'We learned at Indy the only quick way was to honk into corners on the power and the brakes at the same time to minimize pitch-change, then

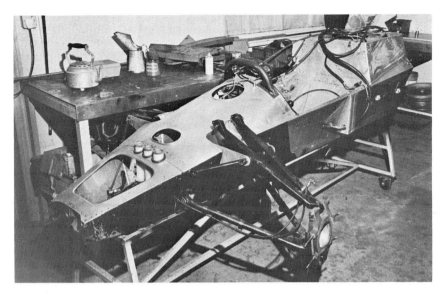

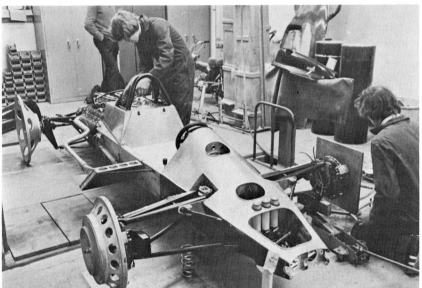

The derelict hulk of '19' — the Ricard prototype 79 — lying at Ketteringham in May 1978 awaiting rebuild as a gearbox test vehicle. The single fuel-tank section is clearly visible behind the cockpit, as is the original low-arch scuttle structure which cramped Peterson's knees. The centre picture shows '20' being checked after repairs to its Silverstone damage, revealing the type 79's astonishingly gawky frame hidden by that beautiful bodywork. Note the raised scuttle structure. Bottom, the guts of the Lotus gearbox, 1978-style, showing the tiny gear cluster and the two-part bobbin mechanism which slides within the input shaft and knocks-out engagement balls to lock-on the desired gear. The 'box was used on the 78s in practice in South America and South Africa, 1978.

come off the brake and leave the corner smoothly under power. On faster road circuits you sometimes have to just dab the brakes to check the car, and that unsettles it. If our drivers could left-foot brake with the power still on they could damp-out pitch, the nose wouldn't fall and then by rolling off the brakes away they'd go. Two-pedal control simply offers a quicker way of driving. Then, with a freewheel installed, there's no engine braking, and that can help because engine braking varies dependent on what gear you're in and what revs you're using, and that means you can't be precise when balancing the brakes. Remove engine braking and you can brake more accurately. Having this freewheel under development is the reason for the 77s, 78s and 79s being basically over-braked.'

The prototype 79 — JPS/19 — was tested at Ricard in December 1977, when various improvements were suggested. It used the new Lotus gearbox with similar result, and after limited running it was returned to Ketteringham and was dismantled. It was later to be built-up as a gearbox development hack — replacing an old 77 in that role — and eventually as a show car. Meanwhile, JPS/20 (79/2) was built-up effectively as a 'Mark 2 Mark IV'. Its monocoque was stiffer, with stronger cockpit sides, and a raised dash hoop and front panel which also gave Ronnie Peterson more knee-room. Rear suspension was modified with a deeper upright and a longer lower wishbone picking-up on the centreline beneath the gearbox. The bolt-on glass-fibre side pods retained carefully-shaped top-exit cooler ducts, and were shaped underneath with a rearward-expanding venturi section to offer improved depression.

The new 79 used its side pods effectively as venturis in which air entering up front was accelerated to exit cleanly at the rear. Skirts sealed this U-section air chamber against the road surface to enclose the low-pressure area sucking the chassis down. It was 'ground effect' in a most elegant manner. These new internal 'effect sections' terminated at the front engine mounts on the Ricard car, but in 79/2 extended rearwards alongside the engine. The body tray around the induction system was lowered and flick-ups were added to fair-in the rear wheels. Airflow on to the rear wing was improved.

In this form Andretti gave the car its race debut in the non-championship Silverstone International Trophy. The car's sleek beauty immediately impressed, but after 58 practice laps the Lotus gearbox's pinion failed. A sister transmission on Peterson's 78 failed at precisely the same distance. Still, the Swede qualified on pole, with Andretti third fastest and loving every lap in his new car. It rained furiously on race day, Ronnie crashed during the warm-up and Andretti led until 79/2 aquaplaned wildly off-course on the flooded Abbey Curve and crashed heavily into an earlier victim of the puddles.

Damage was quite severe, but the car was rebuilt while JPS/21 (79/3) was being completed and both

Assembly of a Lotus gearbox at Ketteringham in 1978, the gearbox section itself lying within his hands, while the rest of the casing is actually the final-drive housing, with the input shaft from engine to gearbox visible where it passes the differential mechanism.

were to emerge in a revised 'Mark 3' form. The rebuild was a massive refinement. Now the 'mangle-gears' reappeared in the cars' rear-ends, and over-the-gearbox exhausts were adopted to pull their profile within the rear cross-section of the tub. 'Clapper board' aerodynamic skirts were used, formed from rigid Cellite sheet with a lower rubbing edge, riding in channels beneath the panniers. The rebuilt JPS/20's second race and the type 79's first GP came at Zolder in Belgium in mid-May. Mario qualified as he had done the year before with the 78, over a second faster than the rest of the field! He led with little apparent effort from start-to-finish — the Lotus running perfectly in a class of its own. Ronnie's sister 78 was delayed by a pit stop to change tyres, but soared back through the field to finish second and so bring Team and Colin Chapman — two days after his 50th birthday — their fourth 1-2 GP result. Team Lotus had pulled hard on their own bootstraps, and were once more dominating that tightrope.

The strongest partnerships are often those which have taken many years to form. Colin Chapman and Mario Andretti looked on top of the World as their 1978 season developed; not since the days of Jimmy Clark had Colin found such empathy with his leading driver . . . and the results flowed similarly.

After the Zolder triumph Peterson took over 79/2 while Andretti had a brand-new 79/3 completed for him as a race car in time for the Spanish GP at Jarama, and they took another imperious 1-2, Mario ahead again.

In the Swedish GP at Anderstorp the hastily-completed Brabham answer to Lotus ground-effects emerged as the controversial BT46B fan-car. Lauda won with it after Andretti had started from pole and retired, and Peterson was third, after being blatantly baulked by Patrese's Arrows in second place. Andretti's failure was put down to titanium valve spring caps dishing under load, allowing the retainers to fall out in three cylinders, whereupon a valve had finally broken.

The fan-car was ruled out of competition thereafter, and the 79 was reinstated as the only pure ground-effects car of the season, though Wolf made a valiant attempt to close the gap. The third Type 79 1-2 in four races came in the French GP, while at Brands Hatch Peterson qualified his car on pole but both 79s failed after leading in the early stages. Andretti won the German race from pole, and Peterson started alongside him on the front row, led and set fastest lap before retiring with gearbox failure.

Ever since whumping 79/3 over a kerb during

qualifying at Ricard — losing pole there to Watson's Brabham-Alfa Romeo — Andretti had felt sure his chassis was somehow out of true, despite its having been back on the jig at Ketteringham, but Hockenheim dispelled his fears. Until then he had doubted the 79's straightline speed on such a fast circuit: 'Any doubts I had about the car were gone now. Really fast tracks I'd got to dread with the 78 but the 79 could run with anybody. . .'

The prototype 79/1 had been extensively rebuilt to the latest standard as a spare car for these late-season races, while Andretti regularly used chassis '3 and Peterson chassis '2. In Austria the 79s qualified 1-2 on the grid for the third consecutive time — setting totally new performance standards — but not without problems. Andretti's car ran new aerodynamic-section wishbones in practice and with the rear wing eased-off to 2-degrees incidence for high speed the car felt 'really spooky through the quick turns'. The wishbones were the only new thing on the car, so they were replaced by the normal types, and it all came back as good as ever, so sensitive were these new-era cars. . .

Torrential rain then saw the GP red-flagged after only 7 laps had been completed, by which time Andretti — typically pressing too hard, too soon — and Rebaque in his private 78 had both crashed.

172

Peterson then won the restarted 47-lap second part from pole in 79/2, setting fastest lap on the way.

In the Dutch GP at Zandvoort the 79s again qualified fastest in team order and achieved their fourth 1-2 of the season, Andretti winning from pole in new car JPS/22 — 79/4 — using salvage from his wrecked Austrian 79/3 on a replacement tub.

The Italian GP followed at Monza. Andretti qualified gaily on pole in 79/4, but Peterson shunted 79/2 after brake problems in practice and had to fall back on the old Type 78 spare. As mentioned in the previous chapter, he was victim of a starting procedure muddle which sparked a horrifying multiple collision on the charge into the first corner, and he was badly injured, dying that night after surgical complications.

Meanwhile the race had been restarted, Andretti won on the road, but was docked a minute for jumping the restart and classified sixth. He had still set fastest lap and clinched his World title, but any joy that he and Team might have felt was nothing against their loss.

They were committed to run two cars in the US and Canadian GPs ending the season and Frenchman Jean-Pierre Jarier was taken on to accompany Andretti. At Watkins Glen, Mario qualified 79/4 on pole while Jarier drove 79/3, now rebuilt since its Austrian crash. In race morning warm-up Andretti's car broke its right-rear stub-axle and threw a wheel. He took over 79/3 for the race, guessing at correct adjustments to suit his needs, while Jarier was strapped into old 79/1 — which had arrived from the UK only that morning — for its race debut.

Andretti led initially in the spare 79, which oversteered viciously as well as suffering spongey brakes, and after falling back, an engine failure finally put paid to the car's misery.

Jarier meanwhile was plagued by tyre and fuel problems, but after an early stop to replace a left-front tyre burned out by his inducing too much understeer under full tanks, he simply soared through the field to challenge for second place until his tank ran dry with just three laps remaining. He had set fastest lap, emphasizing the 79's superiority, and now the feeling was that with a 79 any halfway decent driver could make his mark, you did not need to be someone as special as an Andretti or a Peterson. Peter Wright's and Team Lotus' point had been made in quite indelible terms.

Jarier rubbed it in at Montreal, where he took pole position for the Canadian GP in 79/3, built a huge 30-second lead by half-distance, and only then had to drop back on lap 49 as brake fluid leaked from a ruptured line and he was forced to retire.

Meanwhile, the frustrated World Champion's 79/4 handled poorly throughout and its monocoque was found subsequently to have been twisted by the Watkins Glen incident. Andretti could not use his spare car in this long race because its fuel capacity was too restricted. After a minor collision early in the race he could only finish a distant and disappointing 10th to end Lotus' trendsetting but ultimately so bitter-sweet season.

The 79s had made 20 starts in 11 GPs, winning six times, with four seconds, a third, a sixth, one 10th and a 15th — Jarier at Watkins Glen — and there were six retirements. They took 10 pole positions, the last seven in consecutive races — eight to Andretti, one to Peterson and one to Jarier. Only the French GP broke their run, where Watson's Brabham-Alfa Romeo had bettered Andretti's front-row time by a quarter-second while the kerb-damaged Lotus was being checked.

The cars also set five fastest race laps — two each to Andretti and Peterson, one to Jarier. When they were beaten for fastest lap they still set second and third fastest times — behind the Brabham fan-car — in Sweden; third and fourth at Ricard; second and third at Zandvoort — by 0.01 second — behind Lauda's Brabham — and fourth fastest (by Jarier) in Canada at season's end.

These results combined with the 78s' good season-start saw Team Lotus take the Formula 1 Constructors' title by 86 points from Ferrari's 58, while Andretti took the Drivers' title from Peterson's tragically posthumous second place.

The 79s would run on into 1979 while the intended replacement Type 80 was being developed, and it was immediately clear that Lotus' ground-effects lead had been overtaken. . .

John Player had ended their 11-season sponsorship of Team and were replaced by Martini for 1979, the cars running in British Racing Green livery, blazoned in the famous red-and-blue Martini stripes. The prototype Lotus 80 would carry the chassis number ML23 following on from the John Player Special 'JPS' number system, which had just reached 22 in 79/4, and it was actually old 79s '2-3-4' which began the season, with a brand-new 79, chassis '5', ready for Andretti at the third race, in South Africa.

Gerard Ducarouge's new Ligier-Cosworth JS11 design proved a far more effective ground-effects car than the reigning Constructors' Champion. Heftily, indeed rather crudely, constructed, Ligier nonetheless appreciated the magnitude of ground-effects downloads and Ducarouge's Matra-Simca endurance racing experience built-in rigidity and strength to accommodate such loads reliably. While these cars dominated the Argentine and Brazilian GPs, Team's new driver Carlos Reutemann finished second in Buenos Aires and Andretti fifth — in 79s '2 and '4 respectively — then in Brazil they qualified 3-4 behind the two new Ligiers, and Reutemann finished third behind them in 79/3. The Lotus 79 had become 'the best of the rest'. . .

At Kyalami, the 79s finished 4-5 with Andretti able to set third fastest race lap in his new 79/5, and at Long Beach Reutemann could qualify on the

The Type 79 in its final Martini Racing-liveried form is demonstrated here at Zolder during the 1979 Belgian GP by Carlos Reutemann. The enigmatic Argentinian would have nothing to do with the Type 80 from early on, and concentrated solely and relatively unsuccessfully upon the 79. But the class car of 1978 had been found out by others' progress. . .

front row while Andretti finished fourth and set fastest lap.

The new Lotus 80 then made the first of its only three race appearances in Spain, placing third, while Reutemann inherited another second place in old 79/2 — but it was a distant second and suddenly the 79 was unable to match the race pace.

In Belgium, the new 80 was set aside and Andretti returned to 79/5 for the race, retiring with brake trouble, while Reutemann finished fourth, and in Monaco Reutemann drove 79/4 into a reliable third place after Andretti qualified slowly in the 80 and left the race with rear suspension failure.

At this point, with seven races run and eight to go, that epitome of the efficient ground-effects car, the Williams FW07, came on song, the latest 312T4 Ferraris were showing the value of sheer power and reliability, and the Ligiers were still very quick, despite having lost their South American edge. Now Team Lotus toppled from the tightrope as surely as they had in 1975 with the old Type 72s. . .

In those first seven 1979 races, Team had made 14 starts, finishing 11 times in the points. In sharp contrast, their last eight races would see them make 16 starts and return only four finishes, just one of them in the points – Andretti's fifth at Monza, where he also set sixth fastest race lap and Reutemann finished seventh.

There were also two starts in non-Championship races, where against meagre opposition at Brands Hatch, Andretti had actually qualified 79/3 on pole and finished third, while at Imola, in September, Reutemann qualified 79/2 third and inherited second place in a sparse field; a rare late-season highlight.

The 80 had made its last race appearance in the French GP where its brakes, suspension and general aerodynamic misbehaviour caused Andretti terminal despair, and thereafter Team had been forced to do as well as it could with 79s which were now just being run ragged by the opposition.

Team's nadir came in Austria, where Andretti's clutch failed at the start and Reutemann eventually just surrendered to 'handling problems'. After his third-place finish in Monaco he seemed to have given up completely and was not in contention for the rest of the year. Some of Team's people nicknamed him 'Doris'. . . yes, it got that bad.

Andretti did his determined best, but it was now clear that where the Lotus 79 had been in a class of its own the previous year, times had now changed and it could not perform under pressure.

Peter Wright: 'In its day the 79 had been very effective, but then it had been the only proper ground-effects car around, and a lot had been compromised to make it effective. . . Now, in 1979, it was up against second-generation ground-effects cars which showed-up its deficiencies in cooling, brakes and also in structural stiffness, I am afraid. The 80 had been our second-generation car which had all the right capabilities in braking, cooling and structural rigidity, but while we tried to find out what was wrong with its aerodynamic behaviour we had to go back to the 79 and with the pressures of the calendar preventing proper test and development it was no longer adequate into the second half of the season. . .'

The one-time epochal Lotus 79s' front-line racing career ended at Watkins Glen on October 7, 1979, with Reutemann qualifying remarkably well sixth fastest in 79/3 and running third in the rain-swept opening laps before being distracted by the fire extinguisher sensing unit which had come adrift and was bouncing around inside the cockpit. He lost control and spun off. Andretti meanwhile had 79/5's gearbox progressively strip teeth before jamming in fourth to cause his retirement on the 16th lap.

The Lotus 79 represented both the pinnacle of Lotus' middle period at the top of the pile, and the beginning of their grotesque slump towards the early-eighties. But it is properly remembered as the last of Colin Chapman's blinding flashes of brilliance which — as developed by Peter Wright, Ralph Bellamy, Martin Ogilvie *et al* — sent his team off in a most singularly profitable direction, and one which simply revolutionized all racing car design. . .

LOTUS 80

A wing too far (1979)

'We've opened up a new field of ideas with the 80. I believe in the
principle — we've just got to develop it . . .'

Colin Chapman

During 1978 Team Lotus had ruled the Formula 1
world with their ground-effects 'magic ingredient'.
Forced on by the need, somehow, to match the pace
of the Lotus 79s, the opposition had actually forged
ahead of Team in production of robust, rigid and
reliable chassis with adequate brakes and cooling.
Only when the 79s were pushed hard by rival cars
matching their magic ingredient in 1979 would the
handsome Lotuses' shortcomings surface.

Aerodynamic concentration proved to be a two-
edged sword where Team was concerned. In 1979 it
seemed as if the Type 79s' former aerodynamic
superiority had made Team forget some of the basics
of effective Formula 1 design, and when Colin's
second-generation ground-effects Lotus 80 flopped,
so Team was exposed, wrong-footed, the 79s'
chassis integrity was found out and the Norfolk
team fell hard from the tightrope. . .

The Type 80 had emerged as an attempt to
produce a low-drag ground-effects car developed
from the 79 which was quicker in a straight line, and
which would generate its download by use of
longer, lower-drag underwings.

While Team were still building this car, Gordon
Murray had anticipated their thinking in his
Brabham BT48 design which he introduced at
Buenos Aires in the season-opening Argentine GP.
The object of both cars was to provide an
aerodynamic shape which could run stably without
the need for drag-inducing separate nose 'foils and
tall rear wing. The Brabham BT48 stole a march on
Lotus with its rear wing reduced merely to a broad
trim-flap attached to the rearmost top edge of its
body-panelling, and it also carried full-length
underwing sidepod sections extending from just
behind the front suspensions right back along each
side to the extreme tail.

First time out in practice at BA, this new
Brabham displayed the uncontrollable fore-and-aft
pitching motion which would become known as

'porpoising'. Initially, as the car pitched naturally
on its springs under acceleration or braking, so its
sliding skirts on each side — which were designed to
seal off the underwing low-pressure area against
aerodynamic infill — broke contact with the road
surface.

As they lifted they allowed ambient-pressure air
to leak into the underwing areas, killing ground-
effect download and allowing that end of the car to
bounce free as it stopped 'sucking'. As the car then
came down again its skirt seal would be renewed,
download would suddenly soar, and the car would
instantly suck down, its aerodynamic centre of
pressure rushing forward. At this point natural
suspension spring rebound could then spark
another oscillation cycle, the CoP rushed from nose
to tail like a frenzied ferret, this porpoising became
self-exciting and the car would simply pass beyond
all suspension control.

During one such porpoising cycle in Argentine
practice Niki Lauda found his Brabham's front
wheels bounding along clear of the road. . . Back in
the pits its full-length underwing floors were
promptly torn out and the car was reworked
overnight with much shorter and far more
conservative aerodynamic aids. Team's personnel
quite enjoyed that sight, knowing that Murray
relied upon aerodynamic intuition in his designs,
not the moving-ground wind-tunnel which Peter
Wright used. Team remained confident that their
Type 80 with its full-length venturi tunnels would
do the job properly. But their confidence was also
misplaced.

At Kyalami, the BT48s ran with conventional
high-set rear wings trimming out a far-forward
underwing CoP which allowed them to dispense
with their conventional nose 'foils. Two weeks later,
the non-Championship Race of Champions was
due to be run at Brands Hatch in England, but the
weekend saw Kent blanketed in snow, and the race

The hapless and unloved Lotus 80 had its brief moment of glory in the 1979 Spanish GP at Jarama where Andretti finished well and the new car showed apparent promise. Here, head-on, it demonstrates its curved-planform sliding skirts beneath the sidepods and the separate sealing skirts either side of the shark's-mouth air intake under its nose, replaced by side-fins for the race.

was postponed although the public announcement of the Martini Racing-sponsored Lotus 80 went ahead in Brands' Kentagon functions building.

Few Grand Prix cars since the streamlined Mercedes-Benz W196 and Connaught B-Type of 1954-55 have looked so sensational first time out.

Colin explained his new 'wingless' Lotus like this: 'Our basic idea was to produce the same amount of negative lift as the 79 but with all the downforce coming from the underbody profile. There is no point in producing more and more downforce. What we need is less drag. If our calculations are right the underbody shape of the new car should give us as much downforce as we had from the 79 with wings. Consequently the 80 should need no conventional wing system.'

It was based on a 79-derived aluminium monocoque chassis lightened by extensive use of titanium in areas where formerly mild-steel had been used, skinned both inside and out largely in aluminium honeycomb sheet. Front and rear top-rocker-arm suspension was used, actuating inboard coil/damper units and the hefty rockers themselves were fabricated in titanium, which material — while much lighter than steel — is also far less stiff. These Ti arms were consequently designed deeper-section than comparable steel components to compensate, but they still represented another mistake, because welding titanium successfully and reliably is a highly-specialized and extremely critical procedure.

Team had a sub-contractor confident of his skill in this area, but they would find his confidence was exaggerated.

Titanium needs to be welded in a purge chamber, in an atmosphere painstakingly purged of oxygen, on a brass or copper table, not steel, otherwise oxygen spoils the process, the weld oxydizes, becomes brittle and the finished components crack, split and fail.

The Type 80's arms were compromised in this way, oxydization attacking them unseen within the box-section. Their first failure struck in a demonstration at Donington Park; subsequent inspection of the burst rocker revealed suspect welding, so the whole batch of arms was then scrapped and Team subsequently fell back on heavier but well-understood steel fabrications.

Meanwhile, the new car carried twin-caliper balanced brakes mounted outboard at the front, initially inboard at the rear where provision had been made to mount them outboard on the uprights. This would clear airflow through the underbody venturis which extended right to the extreme tail. There the Lotus-cased Hewland FGA-based transaxle was shrouded in a smooth moulded faring reminiscent of a flying-boat's hull. The venturi tunnels on each side were fared throughout in this way, with only the wide-based lower rear wishbones intruding. Even they used an elliptical streamlined section in order to minimize airflow disturbance.

Where the conventional Hewland gearbox casing was split longitudinally, the new Lotus 80 casing split crosswise on the rear-axle centre-line, leaving the gearbox complete in a rear half, the integral oil tank and clutch housing in the forepart. Type 79 features such as driver-adjustable front and rear anti-roll bars, low-percentage limited-slip diff, and thinking on wheel movement, suspension geometry and weight distribution were carried forward into the new design.

In overall length, the long-nosed new car was right out to the F1 limit, 8 inches longer than the 79. Wheelbase was 274.8cm (108.2 inches), fractionally longer than the 79's, while front track was 3cm (1.2 inches) narrower and the rear 1cm (0.4 inch) wider. The 80's long nose incorporated a shark-mouth top-exit air duct with a simple but steeply-cambered 'foil flap introduced there to control the airstream through the duct. At the release function Colin insisted this flap did not affect distribution of download fore-and-aft, only the total amount of download generated beneath the entire car.

To ensure that the long nose section would generate worthwhile download it carried its own side-skirt system, extending from nose-tip rearwards to front suspension area. The main skirt system then extended from just behind the front suspension, straight past the rear suspension to the extreme tail where vertical end-plates supported that single low-level rear trim-flap. The entire underside of the car was cowled-in with only those lower rear suspension arms out in the airflow.

A single radiator core in each sidepod cooled water (right-side) and oil respectively, while the single fuel cell between driver and engine contained

39 gallons, one more than the 79.

Sponsorship was by Martini, Essex — which was Monaco-based publicity-hungry American David Thieme's spot-market oil-broking company — and Tissot Watches.

Once testing began, one demon in the 80 design was recognized early on. Its lazy-ess curved skirts inevitably stuck in their skirt-boxes if one end should lift significantly relative to the other. When they stuck up, they lost download as became clear in initial tests at Jarama, Spain. These skirt-boards were moulded in carbon-fibre/foam sandwich material. Without a rear wing the car was totally reliant upon them and the sidepod underwings for download; a front wing was fitted to the car but at no stage in those initial tests — with Andretti driving — did a rear wing go on.

Revised skirts and nose 'foils were then tested by Reutemann two weeks later at Donington, but Colin agreed with Nigel Bennett and the other engineers not to take the still-unsorted car to Long Beach, as had originally been planned. After further tests at Zolder the 80 went back to Brands Hatch for the postponed Race of Champions on April 15. In race morning warm-up it wore a conventional rear wing above its body-top-height trim-flap, but its skirts still gave trouble, there were leaks of oil and brake fluid, so Mario raced his 79 instead, starting on pole.

Testing revealed in particular that any pitch in the car would quickly wear away its under-nose skirts, while the curved planform of the car's midship section still created headaches when the main skirts there skewed, one end high, the other low.

The Spanish GP at Jarama on April 29 finally saw the 80's race debut. In practice Andretti ran it

At Zolder Mario bent the 80, by this time shorn of its under-nose sliding skirts and fitted instead with the conventional-style canard fins seen here. The adjustable trim-vane in the nose duct is clearly visible, as are the car's troublesome welded-up top rocker-arms in the front suspension which were badly fabricated from titanium.

without under-nose skirts, carrying conventional nose 'foils, and he qualified fourth fastest on row 2, only 0.57 second slower than Laffite's Ligier on pole, and he finished third minus one nose 'foil.

But while Jarama is a stop-go circuit with only one decent straight and a succession of slow corners, Zolder for the Belgian GP on May 13 was quicker with a number of fast curves. There Andretti's 80/1 appeared with a shorter unskirted nosepiece and revised 'midship sections. A Lotus 80 Mark 2 was under development, with a further-forward CoG and shorter side pods. Inaccessibility made the 80 difficult to work on and practice problems and the time spent fixing them saw Mario qualify fifth fastest, 0.7 second slower than Laffite again, before practice ended in a collision between Mario and Jochen Mass' Arrows, in which the Lotus' left-front corner was crushed, ripping the bottom front wishbone pick-up out of the tub and breaking the outboard end of the top rocker-arm. The damage was repaired overnight, but Mario wasn't happy so raced his back-up 79 instead.

At Monaco the 80 was all at sea, Mario qualifying only 13th — over 1.5 seconds slower that Scheckter's Ferrari T4 on pole. It broke its rear suspension in the race.

Then in testing on the very much faster circuit at Dijon-Prenois, Peter Wright recalls: 'We suddenly encountered the most dreadful bouncing problems' and stiffening the suspension to control this pitch then made the car skittish and again uncontrollable in an agonizing descending spiral of failure and frustration. Two 80s were taken to the French GP there, the prototype 80/1 now accompanied by the Mark 2 80/2, with reshaped underwing mouldings, the suspension raked back to move the CoG forward, a revised nose and the upper rear wing section now removed. The sides of this car still retained their lazy-ess form, but while Andretti as always was happy to continue with development work, his team-mate Reutemann was entirely disillusioned and concentrated on his proven though rapidly-ageing 79.

Team had split itself into two camps, one operating the Reutemann 79, the other Andretti's 80s and results suffered badly. In Dijon practice, Mario was very unhappy with the 80 Mark 2. It wore away its new nose-piece in pitch and Mario fell back on 80/1, which also misbehaved. He got nowhere and retired on lap 52 complaining of brake and handling problems.

Three 80 tubs had been built at that time, but after this pathetic outing Colin cut his losses and agreed with Reutemann – and Andretti by this time – to make the best of the old 79s. So the 'wingless dream' Type 80s were ditched.

LOTUS 81

Zorro's blunt-edged sword (1980)

'This is a very simple car, a lot more simple than the 80 . . . to sum up, the 81 is an ideal car — for last year'
Mario Andretti

After Team's bitterly disappointing 1979 season, Martini & Rossi withdrew their sponsorship and David Thieme's extravagant Essex Petroleum concern became major sponsor for 1980 in their place. By this time Lotus R&D was heavily involved in development work for the ill-fated De Lorean project. Colin had seen his Type 80 fail so publicly, Lotus Cars — the Group's production company — had fallen on desperately hard times and although Team was completely independent of Group, being a private company owned jointly by Colin and by his old friend and Group Finance Director Fred Bushell, money generally was short and as commitments elsewhere in Colin's business empire demanded more of his time so Team began to drift in Formula 1. . .

A conventional 79-development car known as the Type 81 was produced for the new season, carrying Essex's garish blue, red and chromium-tape livery. It was unveiled at a bewilderingly over-the-top December '79 reception in the glitzy *Paradiso Latin* night-club in Paris, the prototype car being lowered from the club's ceiling amidst deafening razzmatazz, punctuated by a conspicuously out-of-place rendition of *God Save the Queen*. . .

The last Type 79, chassis 79/5, had run at Ricard as a test-bed for this new Type 81 project, nicknamed the '79X'. Back at Ketteringham Hall at that time far more exotic ideas were evolving which embraced just the kind of 'magic ingredient' which could be guaranteed to hold Colin's attention and pump up his enthusiasm once more.

But short-term the new Type 81 would prevail, which, being a conventional development of 79-cum-79X thinking, simply would not set Formula 1 alight. Its aluminium honeycomb tub was essentially Lotus 80, using new suspensions with two-element fabricated top rocker-arms at the front, raked back as on the '80 Mark 2' to shorten the wheelbase some 5cm (2 inches). The sidepods were very robust, strong enough for the crew to sit on — as Colin often would in the pitlane, talking to his drivers. They were Andretti again, starting his fifth season with Lotus, joined now by the wealthy young Italian Elio de Angelis, fresh from his maiden Formula 1 season with Shadow and at 22 the youngest driver in the class. In fact his move had breached a Shadow contract option on his services, and he had to settle out of court with Shadow proprietor Don Nichols when the American sought an injunction against him.

The entire upper part of the 81's body was moulded in one piece, and the sidepod design was straight-sided and razor-edged amidships with straight skirts replacing the troublesome lazy-ess shape of the failed 80. Essential improvement came in the rear-end design where new uprights were sunk virtually flush into the wheels to cause as little aerodynamic interference as possible in that vital underwing tunnel area. It was also planned to use narrower 17-inch rear wheels to improve airflow there even more. The laterally-divided 80 gearbox was retained, while all brakes were outboard of course, and all coil/damper suspension units inboard.

With the change of sponsorship the 'ML' — Martini-Lotus — prefixes of 1979 had become 'EL' — Essex-Lotus — for 1980 and two of the new Type 81s, chassis EL81/1 and EL81/2, ran in Argentina to open the new season's campaign, driven by de Angelis and Andretti respectively. Three more Type 81s would emerge during that season, '3 new as a spare at Kyalami before being crashed very heavily by de Angelis at Long Beach. It was then completely rebuilt under the same number, while chassis '4 emerged new in Monaco as spare only, to be written-off almost immediately by Andretti in practice. It was completely rebuilt incorporating a half-season's development work to emerge as the ultimate Type 81B, finished-off in the Hockenheimring paddock in August.

Nigel Bennett had left Team to join Ralph Bellamy at Ensign, his place being taken at Ketteringham by another former tyre-engineer, this time Malcolm Jones, who was ex-Goodyear at Wolverhampton. Unfortunately he did not really develop as a race-engineer and moved on, Nigel Stroud and, later on, Steve Hallam and Tim Densham becoming the extremely capable race-engineers who would care for Team's regular two-car entries into the mid-'eighties.

In Argentina, Andretti suffered a practice brake failure, de Angelis crashed but qualified fifth fastest on the Saturday, just ahead of his team-leader, and so Team had bounced back. But the race story then told otherwise. Andretti's metering unit failed and de Angelis had his prototype 81's suspension bent in a collision.

For the rugged Interlagos course at Sao Paulo, Brazil, the 81s' damper mounts were reinforced, de Angelis again out-qualified Mario and ran throughout with the leaders, to finish a rather distant but nonetheless rousing second! Mario spun off on the opening lap. . .

After the failures of 1979 this was progress indeed. The flashy Mr Thieme — nicknamed *Zorro* by the racing press after his broad-brimmed black hat — wanted the fuel funnels highly-polished for Kyalami and when that polishing set up a reaction between the polish and the welds, metal particles were released into the 81s' fuel systems which caused three seized engines there in three hours. . .

Kyalami revealed the 81s to be desperately slow on a long straight. Mario tried running without a rear wing, but his 81 was still slow, 'just flat-ass uncompetitive' he said. Elio again out-qualified him, but after his engine refused to fire when required on race day he had to start the race from the back of the grid and in trying to make up ground he immediately spun off at Leeukop. Mario finished a distant 12th, losing power as his 81's exhaust system broke up.

New gearbox casings appeared at Long Beach carrying revised rear suspension, extending the wheelbase 3 inches. Elio was second fastest in first practice before falling back down the field, and Mario emerged over a second quicker than his young team-mate in the unmodified spare car, but the race was a disaster, both 81s crashing early on.

Elio's 81/3 was severely damaged and was totally rebuilt for the Belgian GP opening the European season at Zolder. He still drove his spare short-wheelbase car in the race, qualifying on row 4, while Mario preferred his regular SWB car after back-to-back tests against the LWB version proved it a second quicker. De Angelis crashed again, but was classified 10th, while Mario's gearchange went awry.

With Essex Petroleum based in Monte Carlo, the

Nigel Mansell trying hard in the otherwise little-loved Type 81 in the 1981 Belgian GP, at Zolder, on his way to that fine third place which compensated so much for all Team's early-season trials and tribulations with the intended 81-replacement Type 88 'twin-chassis' cars. The knife-edge bodylines were very much a Chapman fad at this time.

place was plastered with Essex advertising for the Grand Prix. Team ran four 81s, each plagued by oversteer and lack of grip. Mario wrote-off his new chassis '4 in qualifying, but looked set to score points until a late-race pit-stop with the gear linkage again astray dropped him to seventh. De Angelis was ninth after spinning, pushing the car to restart, then coming in to have his seat-belt tightened.

The leading *Grande Costruttore* teams boycotted the following Spanish GP at Jarama, where three 81s arrived with strengthened rear rocker-arms. Mario qualified his on the fourth row, Elio five places further back, his car lacking grip at both ends, but he finished third in a race subsequently denied Championship status, while Mario's engine failed.

The 81s had thus showed patchy form, but form

nonetheless, yet neither driver had much to smile about in France where gearbox and clutch failure ended runs started from the sixth and seventh rows.

A serious test session followed at Snetterton, and for the British GP the 81 tubs were stiffened with raised cockpit sides. Yet in practice at Silverstone wholesale changes of springs and roll-bars were still needed before Andretti showed any progress, while de Angelis crashed in the final session when a sidepod collapsed. In the race he stopped to change tyres, then had a rear suspension cross-member break; Mario ran sixth, then fifth . . . then his gearbox failed yet again.

Massive testing preceded the German GP at Hockenheim, where the 81s were still slow on the straight; Mario finished seventh, while Elio had a

wheel bearing break up and was classified 16th.

Colin had taken on young Formula 2 and 3 driver Nigel Mansell on a testing contract, and at Osterreichring he drove the longer-wheelbase 81B which had been completed new in the paddock at Hockenheim, then qualified in Elio's discarded 81/ 3, bumping Lammers' Ensign off the grid. In qualifying, Mario spun then ran out of fuel, while Elio crashed mildly. In the race, none of the Lotuses shone, and although Elio finished sixth, both Andretti and Mansell suffered engine failures, the determined English novice after a respectable debut made agonizing for him by fuel seeping into the cockpit and soaking through his overalls to his skin.

At Zandvoort, reprofiled sidepods were tried on the spare car. They worked well so were quickly grafted onto Mario's race chassis, but he could only classify eighth, out of fuel, while de Angelis collided with Pironi's Ligier on lap 2, and Mansell suffered a frightening brake failure in the 81B, which he managed to spin to a safe halt.

The Italian GP followed at Imola, where the cars' handling proved unpredictable throughout; Mario's engine failed early in the race and Elio finished 10th after damaging a skirt.

Suspension movement was increased for the bumpy Watkins Glen US GP course where Team arrived with only two 81s and Andretti crashed his in Friday practice. De Angelis was on fine form and qualified very well, fourth-fastest overall. Andretti, in uncomfortable contrast, was seven places behind him, but in the race both 81s behaved and the young Italian finished fourth and Mario sixth — scoring his first point since the previous year's Italian GP!

By the end of the race he had used-up his 81's brakes, but Arnoux's Renault ahead of him was in even more trouble with its tyres burned out, so Mario could claw ahead before the flag.

The three surviving 81s continued in service into early 1981, chassis 81/1 performing spare-car duties at Kyalami, where 81/2 and 81/3 were raced respectively by Nigel Mansell — who had become a fully-fledged number 2 to de Angelis following Andretti's move to Alfa Romeo — and Elio himself.

The South African GP was run to FOCA sliding-skirt regulations in defiance of the FISA governing body, which had banned such devices. The *Grande Costruttore* teams of Ferrari, Renault, Alfa Romeo and Talbot-Ligier consequently boycotted this 'pirate' race, leaving the 19-strong Cosworth-only field to race in half-wet conditions with de Angelis finishing third and a troubled Mansell 10th three laps behind. FISA deprived the event of its World Championship status, then the Maranello-signed Concord Agreement brought peace to Formula 1, reconciling FOCA and FISA — temporarily — and the fixed-skirt 6cm ground-clearance regulations were accepted.

The new allegedly twin-chassis Lotus 88 was completed in time for Long Beach and it was entered there and at Rio and Buenos Aires for de Angelis, but it was ruled illegal each time, forcing him to fall back on 81/3. Mansell raced 81/2 at Long Beach and in South America, 81/1 at Zolder.

At Long Beach he tigered his obsolescent car into seventh spot on the grid before crashing in the race, possibly as a result of suspension failure sparked by hitting a wall in morning warm-up. De Angelis also hit a wall, but then at Rio he managed fifth place for 2 points in the wet, Mansell finishing 11th, and in Argentina — in Colin's huffy absence — the Italian finished sixth for another point while Mansell's engine failed.

Team scratched its Imola entries and arrived at Zolder for the Belgian GP relying upon its now decidedly elderly, heavy and persistently understeering 81s. Nigel was quicker, qualifying 10th, and in the race he got his head down and charged hard, juggling his anti-roll bar adjustment to trim the handling as the old car's skirts progressively wore away and he ran strongly in third place for 34 of the 54 laps to finish in that position behind Reutemann's winning Williams and Laffite's Ligier-Matra V12.

This was quite an extraordinary result, and as de Angelis inherited fifth place for Team's best performance for more than two years, Colin was beside himself with elation after all the Type 88 frustrations he had been through. 'You're now a star!' he told Nigel Mansell, who believed him. The incredibly determined young Englishman — very much a latter-day Graham Hill — would indeed make the grade, but not just yet, and not with Lotus. . .

The new Type 88-chassised conventional-spec Type 87s were then made ready in time for the next GP at Monaco, where they replaced the old 81s, although chassis '2 performed spare-car duties for Mansell three times – at Monte Carlo, Jarama and Dijon.

LOTUS 86

'Twin-chassis' test car (1980)

'It only ran three times, enabling us to establish its capabilities,
before the rules were changed . . .'

Peter Wright

After the failure of the Lotus 80 in 1979 and on into
1980 while Essex Team Lotus were floundering in
Formula 1 with their lacklustre Type 81s, Colin and
his engineers at Ketteringham Hall were hunting
eagerly for the new magic ingredient which would
put them back on top of the pile, where they had
been only some 18 months before.

The degrees to which aerodynamic loads had
increased in the opposition's second-generation
ground-effects cars of 1979 had demanded more
rugged chassis and suspensions than ever before.
Team's cars had been found out in this area, and
thoughts turned towards some system which would
isolate aerodynamic downloads from the chassis
itself.

While the driver had a more comfortable time and
could feel far more from a chassis which dived under
brakes, squatted under power, and rolled under
cornering load, every such change of attitude was
anathema to consistent generation of ground-effects
aerodynamic download. As the available space
between the sidepod underwing floors and the road
surface varied so the centre of pressure would chase
about the car and make it become aerodynamically
unstable.

What Colin and Peter Wright discussed was a plot
to produce a car which behaved pretty much like an
old-time 49, running inside a rigidly-suspended,
pitch and roll-free aerodynamic body. In effect they
wanted to return to the old days of 1968-69 when
strutted wing loadings on the 49Bs had been fed
direct into the unsprung part of the car, the wheel
uprights in this case, through which tyre contact
patches could be loaded direct, enhancing traction
and cornering power without affecting the sprung
part of the car — its chassis and the driver within.

An ingenious scheme to do this was conceived at
Ketteringham Hall as early as October 1979, but the
short-term requirements of the conventional Type
81 — and problems with it — delayed proper

development for a year.

That 1980 season, in fact, witnessed an
increasingly bitter dispute between the British-
dominated Formula One Constructors Association
— FOCA — and the French-dominated governing
body of the sport, the *Federation International du
Sport Automobile* — FISA — under its autocratic
new President, Jean-Marie Balestre.

The era of sliding-skirted ground-effects
aerodynamics had seen Formula 1 lap times
plummet and cornering speeds soar. The British
Cosworth-Ford teams like Williams and Brabham
had proved most effective in this new Lotus-
initiated aerodynamic age, and it was as well for the
competitiveness of Formula 1 that this was so, for
the turbocharged power of the French Renault
factory team was now threatening to overwhelm all
3-litre naturally-aspirated engines like the
Cosworth DFV, and all the teams whose only
source of power it had become.

The leading British teams had compensated for
their power deficit by sophisticated aerodynamic
chassis development. Renault notably had the
power to pull far larger add-on wings through the
air than the Cosworth brigade could contemplate,
but their grasp of Formula 1 car aerodynamics was
demonstrably inferior to that of the most effective
British teams — which short-list no longer included
Team Lotus. . .

FISA moves to ban sliding skirts were viewed
with intense suspicion by FOCA, whose member
teams generally considered this to be merely a
subterfuge to cripple their chassis performance and
so clear the stage for Renault's turbocharged cars,
and for the Ferrari and Alfa Romeo turbo engines
soon to appear. Brabham hedged its bets by having
a BMW turbo engine under development, but the
row over the sliding-skirts ban simmered through
1980 then raged that winter into '81.

FISA indeed banned sliding skirts and applied a

These two views of the unraced Type 86 'twin-chassis' test car are the original design registration prints shot for Team Lotus at Ketteringham Hall upon the car's completion late in 1980. The enveloping outer bodywork carries sliding-skirt boxes and side-radiator ducting, its sideplates supporting the highly-cambered rear wing section which has a centreline oil-cooler duct above the gearbox. Note swept-back twin-element top rocker-arm front suspension.

6cm ground clearance rule for the new season. The team engineers had discussed this clearance rule with FISA's technical committee and had pointed out that it would be unpoliceable. While a 6cm clearance could be measured when stationary in the scrutineering bay, how could it possibly be enforced out on a circuit at speed? Gordon Murray and David North of Brabham led the way in adopting hydraulic lowering suspension systems which maintained the car at a legal height when necessary, and then allowed it to settle down at speed. As it lowered at speed, its legal fixed-length skirts came back into ground contact — thereby reintroducing ground-effects download generation beneath the shaped sidepod underwing floors, which themselves were still permitted by FISA.

As the 1981 season developed FISA backed itself into a corner, effectively admitted the 6cm clearance regulation was impossible to police, and so confined itself to restrictions upon the structure of the fixed-length skirts permitted. With their flexibility reduced by this new move, designers had to reduce suspension movement still further to ensure consistent, relatively pitch-free ride control.

So Formula 1 entered an era of near go-kart solid-sprung cars which were quickly recognized as some of the most dangerous ever built, wheel travel slashed from around 5 inches to less than an inch, exposing both car structure and driver to enormous

jounce loads and destructive vibration.

Meanwhile, at Ketteringham, the Team Lotus engineers had foreseen FISA's victory in the battle to ban sliding skirts, and had been encouraged to develop their scheme to insulate aerodynamic downloads from conventional chassis behaviour. Their new rule-bending device would in fact still be legal within contemporary regulations. Rather than have separate sliding skirts moving up and down relative to bodywork which was attached rigidly to a sprung chassis, why not spring-mount the entire body structure on the wheel uprights to transmit aerodynamic loads direct to the tyre contact patches, while leaving the conventionally sprung chassis to ride free within the movable body, giving both structure and driver a far more comfortable time insulated from download effects? The floating body would still have sliding skirts to ensure an efficient aerodynamic seal against the road; the vital point was that its download would be insulated from conventional chassis and driver.

A test car, the Lotus 86, was built up around a suitably-modified aluminium-honeycomb 81-type tub, supporting quite conventional rocker-arm suspensions front and rear. The body top was like the 81s' moulded in one piece, but here it was attached to the sidepods and underbodies rather than to the monocoque tub structure. The entire body top/sidepod/underbody assembly was then supported by its own sketchy frame, which featured three cross-members, one passing through slots in the tub sides under the driver's legs, one between tub and outrigged engine and the third over the top of the gearbox at the rear.

The conventional monocoque chassis used soft, reasonably long-travel suspension, while the 'floating' body structure was mounted on spring-loaded pick-ups at the end of the lower front wishbones and at the feet of the rear wheel uprights.

Oil and water radiators hung in the body structure, with flexible hoses connecting them to the DFV engine on the back of the tub. As road speed and aerodynamic download rose so the body, complete with its fixed side-panels and their lower-edged skirt seals, would contact the road surface to provide the necessary pressure seal and exploit the ground-effects download available from each sidepod's shaped underwing floors.

What we might describe as the conventional 'primary chassis' now simply coped with normal road surface bumps while the 'secondary chassis', comprising the separate all-floating bodywork assembly, loaded-up the road wheels and tyres. But with an eye on arguing this concept through predictable protests that it somehow breached the regulations, Colin would find it expedient to turn that order around and call the floating body unit the 'primary chassis', and the inner monocoque with its road-wheel suspension system the 'secondary chassis'. The new car would emerge in a highly-charged atmosphere of protest, appeal and litigation and barrack-room lawyer semantics became very much the order of the day.

Meanwhile, as Peter Wright recalled: 'The first concept of the twin-chassis prototype Type 86 started in October 1979, but it was delayed by problems with the 81. It ran fully-skirted in November 1980, but only three times, enabling us to establish its capabilities before the rules were changed. . .'

Team had taken it to Jarama, in Spain, where Nigel Mansell did virtually all the test-driving apart from a few laps by Elio de Angelis. But as news broke of this revolutionary concept, so Balestre of FISA reacted vigorously to protect his pet sliding-skirt ban decree which he had applied 'on safety grounds'. This permitted him to side-step the stability clause in the regulations which had been included specifically to prevent authority applying expensive rule-changes at short notice which could render costly team hardware obsolescent overnight.

As first news of the Type 86 broke, FISA issued a 'Clarification of Article 3, Clause 7', adding the following wording: 'Any specific part of the car influencing its aerodynamic performance: must comply with the rules relating to bodywork; must be rigidly secured to the entirely sprung part of the car (rigidly secured means not having any degree of freedom); must remain immobile in relation to the sprung part of the car. . .'

Until that moment there had been little doubt that the 86 concept was legal within the regulations as then applied. *Autosport* magazine's Christmas-issue editorial commented: 'The new regulations are described by FISA as clarifications of existing rules. We reject this description. The addition of a clause, specifically stating that any part of a Formula 1 car influencing its aerodynamic performance must be rigidly secured and immobile in relation to the sprung part of the car, cannot be described as a clarification. This is an entirely new rule. It has been established with total disregard of FISA's own discipline which demands that there must be two-year stability of the technical regulations. . .

'We have no doubt that the Lotus 86 has been built to comply with the rules as written; little doubt that an attempt will be made to get those rules rewritten to render it illegal, probably again on safety grounds. That is not simply shortsighted; it is criminally stupid. . .'

And so it would prove to be, eventually.

Despite this move, Colin was convinced he could still argue a race version of the 86-based twin-chassis concept around FISA's regulations, on the basis that they had no power to break their own just-agreed two-year stability clause, and so he gave Team the go-ahead to press-on with manufacture of the developed Type 88 model for 1981.

Meanwhile, the one-off 86 test hack had done its job, and it was retired into store in 'The Piggeries' behind Colin's palatial East Carleton Manor. . .

LOTUS 87

The alternative — legal — 88 (1981)

'It's a bit of a handful everywhere, quite honestly, but all I could do
was give it my best shot . . . if it just had the turn-in ability of
the 81 . . .'

Nigel Mansell

At the time that the Lotus 88 was being drawn it was anticipated that there could be problems regarding its legality. Consequently, an alternative conventional-layout Type 87 was sketched-out, based around the same new carbon/Kevlar — see next chapter — monocoque tub. When the 88 row erupted and it became clear that Team would be very lucky to win its fight, the Type 87 drawings were quickly finalized and parts rushed through to convert what had been intended as the second 88 into 87/1, which was tested by Mansell at Donington Park while the rest of the Formula 1 circus was racing at Imola in the San Marino GP. Mansell then handled this prototype at Monaco, by which time a second 88-series tub had been rigged in conventional Type 87 trim for de Angelis.

These new Lotus 87s were rigged with rather spare and gawky bodywork in broad Type 81 style, and as short-wheelbase, narrow-track, relatively softly-sprung cars they shone on tight street-type circuits.

This happy attribute made for an auspicious debut at Monaco, where Mansell got on with the job in hand and concentrated hard upon 87/1, while de Angelis dickered about between 87/2 and his spare 81/2 and made little progress, developing his new car along a very different route to Mansell before finally being prevailed upon to follow the Englishman's lead as he was setting some very quick times.

In fact Nigel qualified, quite sensationally, third on the grid, only 0.1 second slower than Piquet's Brabham on pole, despite understeer so severe that it had his hands visibly shuddering on the wheel in the tight street circuit's corners.

This was an enormous fillip for the team, boosted further with Elio sixth quickest. But in the race Mansell lost third place on lap 15 to investigate odd handling and eventually retired with a broken rear top link pick-up. De Angelis climbed to fourth

before his engine failed.

Two weeks later, perhaps the most significant Team Lotus development of 1981 was announced at a function at Brands Hatch. Colin had negotiated a renewed John Player Special sponsorship deal with Imperial Tobacco, both the 87s and the freshly-announced 88B appearing in the familiar black livery with Essex's co-sponsor logos still on the sidepods, but now very much subsidiary; *Zorro* was in eclipse.

At Jarama, the confidence engendered by Monaco and newfound secure sponsorship evaporated in practice problems, but de Angelis and Mansell then finished 5-6 in the race, Elio in the nose-to-tail queue behind Villeneuve's baulking turbo Ferrari which won outright, by just 0.24 second from the *fifth*-placed Lotus 87! Mansell was sixth, 27 seconds adrift.

Lotus practice for the French GP at Dijon was also fraught, but the 87s inherited a 6-7 finish, Elio ahead.

Team's British GP at Silverstone was then riven by the 88B dramas, which left Mansell no chance to qualify for his home race, though Elio scraped onto the grid, third-slowest in his 87, now back on Goodyear tyres after Team's brief Michelin period, and all at sea as the race engineers learned anew. During the race Elio's car was right and he put up a storming drive, sixth and closing on Patrese's fifth place when he overtook Laffite under the yellow flag at Beckett's and nearly collected an ambulance carrying Nelson Piquet after the Brazilian's Brabham had crashed.

The Beckett's observer reported this incident to race control, who black-flagged de Angelis. He had been black-flagged so often in the 88 he now stopped, in no mood to accept a ticking-off, assumed he had been disqualified again and erupted from his car and flounced away, finished for the day.

Nigel Mansell, Colin Chapman and Elio de Angelis pose for this 1981 publicity picture outside Ketteringham Hall with the quick-fix Type 87. This was a stopgap conventional-layout car intended to use the new carbon-Kevlar composite Type 88 monocoque chassis in case the governing body should cut up rough on the 88's 'twin-chassis' concept, as they had. Note blade nose-top wing, side-exit ducts from exhausted radiator air and moulded-tub upper section exposed to form outer bodywork surface. Incidentally, in restoring the Hall, Colin insisted upon all its internal window sills being angled sharply downwards 'to prevent you untidy lot stacking books and papers on them!'.

The original 88/1 had been present as spare, while 87/2 had been rigged as 88B/2 for Mansell's use in practice, being hastily re-converted to 87 trim for second practice, in which he was unable to qualify. Chassis 87/3 had been brought across from Hethel brand-new for de Angelis to race, while his new 88B/4 used in practice was subsequently torn down and rigged as the latest 87/4 for Mansell's use in the next race at Hockenheim. There was thus no 88/3, although there was an 88/2 and an 88/4. Still with me?

At this stage in the season the faster circuits packed the calendar, and they found out the 87s' unsuitability. Neither car showed much form in Germany, where the Essex stickers on Team's vehicles were masked-out with black tape, reflecting non-payment of dues, until race morning when they were uncovered amongst some ironic ceremony. Mansell first hit a March in the race, then flurried into the pits after smashing his car's nose-cone on Villeneuve's Ferrari. He struggled out of the cockpit and began tearing off his overalls, calling for water to be poured over his body, petrol having leaked into the cockpit, causing painful chemical burns. De Angelis, meanwhile, went on to finish a lapped seventh.

Austria saw Mansell's sheer determination as he fought his evil-handling 87 round in qualifying, and in the race he ran seventh until his engine blew, having led his team-mate, who finally finished seventh again. The Essex stickers again played peep-bo at this meeting, and again at Zandvoort, where Mansell suffered a catalogue of problems in yet another fraught practice period, then had his electrics cut out after one lap, while de Angelis finished a lapped fifth.

A new car, 87/5, was completed in the Monza paddock garage as spare for the Italian GP, where Team's cars qualified together on row 6, Elio marginally faster, and on his home soil the Roman inherited a distant fourth place, while Nigel retired with evil handling after 87/4's skirts had worn away in the early fuel-heavy laps.

The Canadian GP was run in bitterly cold wet weather and Mansell impressed observers with his bravery in practice in a visibly difficult car, and he survived a frightening incident when a rocker-arm broke while he was in fifth gear on the fast back leg — he spun at high speed, without hitting anything hard. De Angelis inherited sixth place and another point in the race, despite a minor collision and spin involving Villeneuve's Ferrari at the hairpin. Mansell, meanwhile, struggled against diabolical handling, spun after a tyre change and limped back to the pits with his rear wing deranged. He was almost at the pits when he was rammed from behind by Prost's Renault, both cars being disabled and retiring on the spot.

Las Vegas hosted the final round of the 1981 Championship, where Mansell qualified on row 5, de Angelis on row 8, the Italian stopping on lap 3 to investigate impossible handling and finding an incurable water leak instead, while the Englishman produced a typically vigorous and determined drive to finish fourth.

Team started 1982 with modified 87Bs featuring wider sidepods and a spacer between engine and gearbox to lengthen the wheelbase. They behaved poorly. At Kyalami, de Angelis and Mansell qualified 15th and 18th respectively, Elio finishing a distant eighth while Nigel's car died on the opening lap with electrical failure, Jarier crashing his Osella in avoidance. This lacklustre performance ended the Type 87s' career.

Mansell at Monza in 87/4, showing off the model's later-season cleaned-up nose section and separate canard wings, plus the eared induction air intakes added to the Cosworth engine cover. This car began life as the 'twin-chassis' Silverstone car 88B/4, being converted to 87 configuration for Nigel's use at Hockenheim.

LOTUS 88

Genius' final fling (1981)

'I'm not fighting just for the car's sake as much as to defend technical freedom in Formula 1 . . .'

Colin Chapman

'The irony of it all was that the car just didn't handle. The drivers said it was a load of junk . . .'

Martin Ogilvie

'People were afraid the 88 might be quick and they jumped on it . . . The 88 was a very clever idea, but it was so complicated. Too complicated . . .'

Nigel Mansell

Having decided that the so-called twin-chassis concept of the Type 86 possessed real potential, work had begun late in 1980 on the definitive Type 88 race car design. Not only would the new model embody the twin-chassis idea, it would also have a share in introducing an entirely new form of monocoque structure to the racing world.

Ultra-light, ultra-stiff carbon-fibre composite materials had been introduced into the aerospace industry during the mid-'sixties. Extremely high stiffness for minimal weight was the new composite's greatest single attribute. Carbon fibres were produced industrially by a process developed at Britain's Royal Aircraft Establishment at Farnborough, in which polyacrylonitrile (PAN) fibres — basis of the dress fabric Courtelle — were carburized under special conditions to produce a very practical fibre possessed of extreme stiffness and substantial tensile strength.

Individually, these fibres were a little weaker than familiar glass fibres, but for their weight they were something like a staggering eight times stiffer than both glass and conventional engineering metals.

Meanwhile, another new man-made material known as Kevlar had been developed by Du Pont Chemicals of America. It could be made much more simply without the special conditions and intense heat necessary to manufacture carbon-fibre. It was based on an organic polymer, similar to a high-grade cellulose like flax, but Kevlar was four times stonger, it could not rot like flax and was about a third as stiff as carbon and much cheaper.

Now both carbon and Kevlar fibres could be spun into thread, and then woven into cloth, and in the application which Peter Wright with Colin Chapman's blessing dreamed-up for them, the properties of both materials would be combined. This combination cloth could then be moulded and cured into a rigid shape by either of two main methods. The more primitive was to use it in familiar glass-fibre style, laid-up with epoxy resin brushed on by hand, then rolled-in to ensure even distribution throughout the mat. The piece made this way could then be left to cure chemically as the epoxy matrix hardened, which could take 48 hours or more.

A more sophisticated method involved use of fibre-cloth pre-saturated in epoxy resin as 'pre-preg'. It could then be shaped over or within a mould and cured into very complex shapes if necessary either by application of a chemical catalyst — as above — or by exposure to heat and pressure within an autoclave pressurized oven.

In both processes the resin-saturated cloth workpiece could be encased in a vacuum bag from which all the air would be evacuated to ensure even, bubble-free distribution of the resin throughout the matrix, and to prevent contamination by airborne agents.

Thus the moulding technique at its simplest was similar to glass-fibre lay-up, but in carbon or Kevlar the finished moulding was far stronger, it could be lighter and was also very much stiffer per unit weight. The key was the resin matrix which, when cured, locked the cloth fibres relative to one another. Fibre orientation within the finished piece could be aligned to take maximum advantage of their individual tensile strength and great stiffness, while minimizing the fibres' brittle behaviour under compression, for the strength of composite materials of this type is extremely directional.

Once set within a well-cured resin matrix, individual fibres could fracture without significant reduction in component strength because the resin matrix spread loads throughout the cloth fibres. Should one fracture, there would always be another right alongside which would not. Unlike in sheet metal panels, fractures seldom propagated as extensive cracks because the plastic matrix did not transmit cracks, and fibres — usually the Kevlar —

could in any case be aligned as 'crack stoppers'.

Wing endplates and other carbon and Kevlar-composite body parts had been used in Formula 1 since the mid-'seventies. Gordon Murray of Brabham had made the first significant use of carbon as a structural component in the top tub scuttle panel of his 1978 Brabham BT46. Into 1981 the recent era of ultra-slim monocoque chassis necessary in underwing sidepod ground-effects cars had placed great demands upon structural rigidity to harness and resist the aerodynamic downloads being applied. The more slender the chassis, the less stiff it became because it represented a thinner beam.

The 88 twin-chassis concept would now, of course, sidestep part of this problem, but the car would be heavy unless weight could be saved, and extra chassis stiffness is always valuable. Consequently, plastics boffin Peter Wright counselled construction of a carbon/Kevlar-composite monocoque tub. He specified a design which would exploit the stiffness of carbon combined with the impact resistance of Kevlar.

Peter developed a construction method which was simple and effective as the dawn of such technology — in racing terms — and which with minimum plant enabled good quality control of the panels being made. The composites shop at Ketteringham Hall produced a basic flat sheet of carbon/Kevlar-skinned sandwich, stabilized internally by a light but rigid Nomex paper-foil honeycomb filling. The sheet was about 8ft square. The carbon/Kevlar fibre cloths were laid-up 'by hand and the bucket-and-brush wet-resin method'. To roll the epoxy resin hard into the middle of such a large panel involved rigging-up a gantry to suspend the composite shop lads in mid-air over the workpiece so they could reach it without leaning on the vulnerable edges.

The sheet was then left to cure chemically, but before the epoxy had gone off absolutely hard a large template could be placed over it defining the required peripheral shape and enabling the various access holes to be cut and drillings to be made to take mounting strongpoint bobbins which would pick-up the bolted-in aluminium bulkheads, engine mounts, sidepod attachments etc.

Towards the end of the curing process, with the flat sheet shaped and still just flexible, 'fold-lines' could be routed out of it and the sheet then folded-up along those lines 'like a Kellogg's box' to match an inserted male former. This shaped the sheet accurately into the enclosed tubular shape of a monocoque chassis. The sheet's mating edges had been feathered and were now bonded together, these edges then being secured under bonded-on fibre tape. Once finally cured the male former inside the tub could be dismantled and drawn out backwards.

This Wright/Ogilvie/Chapman concept then called for aluminium bulkheads machined from the solid to be inserted and bolted into place to stiffen the tub structure and provide strong-points for suspension and engine mountings. This system would pay enormous dividends in later years as it minimized damage to the composite chassis moulding in accidental suspension-tweaking impacts, and also enabled some freedom in precise bulkhead positioning. They could easily be detached, if necessary redesigned, and resited to pick-up alternative suspension geometry if required, without dictating a complete remake of the chassis moulding itself.

Coincidentally with Team's developments in this new technology, John Barnard of McLaren International was well advanced along a similar road, in his case taking a pure carbon-composite — sans Kevlar — moulded tub design to the aerospace Hercules Corporation in America where they had the massive and costly plant necessary to mould it for him in basically five large prefabricated sections. Not for them any bucket-and-brush wet-resin techniques. They used pre-preg cloth cured to a precise programme by pressure-cooking within their immense aerospace autoclave ovens.

In fact Barnard's McLaren MP4/1 was unveiled first to public gaze — by just two days — on Thursday March 5, 1981, Colin launching his carbon/Kevlar Type 88 that Saturday at London's Heathrow Hotel and causing great hilarity by referring to the 'space-age' McLaren as 'a little bit out of date I'm afraid' . . .

The slender carbon/Kevlar monocoque of the Type 88 carried driver, fuel and Cosworth DFV engine, while a fully-floating body unit based on a triple-cross-member ladder frame provided radiator and cooler mounts and underwing sidepod structures and sat on very short spring units acting direct through each wheel upright. Because the front uprights had to steer, the floating-body spring mounts picked-up there on the outboard extremity of the lower wishbones, but at the rear they located direct on the uprights. The road-wheel suspensions were provided by conventional top rocking-arm systems at front and rear with inboard coil/dampers.

Colin explained how the body unit, which he now called the 'primary chassis', could be very stiffly sprung, while the internal 'secondary chassis' could be softly sprung to give the driver a comfortable time, enabling him to give of his best while also protecting the relatively delicate engine and transmission mechanism from jounce loads.

The body and its aerodynamic ancillaries — with fixed not sliding skirts now, following FISA's ban — needed to be very stiffly sprung to reduce pitch, download on the 88 in fact compressing those tiny springs until they became coil-bound and so transmitted the immense download generated by both overbody and underbody airflow direct into the wheel uprights and so to the tyres.

Elio de Angelis in 88/1, Baixada de Jacarepagua, Brazilian GP practice, 1981. Here we can see its inner-chassis folded-up carbon-Kevlar composite monocoque with its integral racer-taped windscreen deflector and the mounting-point insert bobbins betraying the location of internal bolt-in bulkheads. The outer-chassis side panels and rear wing are carried on those delicate little separate coil-spring units visible within the front suspension bays. Right, the upper body panel is lifted over Elio's head and (below) all dressed-up . . . but nowhere to go. Peter Wright takes notes while Colin Chapman is in intercom-contact with his Italian driver. Chief mechanic Bob Dance is behind the car.

Two of the three cross-beams uniting its side panels actually passed right through the monocoque/engine assembly, that at the front being fed through slots in the composite moulding to pass through the extinguisher-bottle bay under the driver's knees where there was some height available to allow vertical movement. The 'midship beam passed between the tub's rear bulkhead and the front face of the DFV engine, which was spaced back from the tub to give it room. The rearmost beam arched up over the gearbox.

'During the past two seasons', Colin explained, 'we have been dogged by pitch-sensitivity in our cars whenever we tried to use full-length ground-effects undersurfaces. To resist such pitch we had progressively to stiffen the springs until only half the suspension movement was being controlled by the dampers and the rest came from actual deflection within the top rocker-arms! In spite of this, there was still enough angular variation between acceleration and braking to start the dreaded porpoising on occasion, and such hard suspension could shake the driver until his feet actually left the pedals . . .

'Very hard suspension is not ideal for roadholding and handling, so we now have the driver's pod sprung for optimum behaviour in both these areas, while the primary chassis has very restricted suspension movement to avoid angular deflection of the body in the pitching sense . . .'

This strangely whale-like Essex and Tissot-liveried car carried its water and oil radiators in the 'primary chassis' right and left sidepods respectively, cooled by air fed from between the front suspension links and discharged laterally through 'midship side ducts. Nose trim 'foils were available if required while a rear adjustable flap sat at body-top level between the flaring Batmobile-style sideplates.

Goodyear had recently bowed out of Formula 1 racing, partly in protest at the public dogfighting of the FISA/FOCA winter battles which had just been

settled by FOCA's acceptance of the sliding skirt ban in return, effectively, for FISA keeping its nose out of FOCA's Formula 1 financial control. Consequently, the new 88 was on Michelin tyres which would be used by all major teams until Goodyear returned to the fray in mid-summer, although at that time the fear was that they were out for good.

From its unveiling, the new 88 was flown straight out to California for its debut in the US GP (West) at Long Beach. Colin had gone to great pains at Heathrow to explain the car's legality, with its visible bodywork forming the 'primary chassis', thereby falling in line with the new regulation which demanded that 'any specific part of the car influencing its aerodynamic performance . . . must be rigidly secured to the entirely sprung part of the car . . . must remain immobile in relation to the sprung part of the car'. Since only this 'primary chassis' was 'entirely sprung', being suspended on those tiny spring units at each corner, and obviously remained immobile in relation to itself, the 88 *must* have been legal.

But another way of looking at it was that the floating body merely formed a massive aerodynamic surface acting in effect like a hugely overgrown and merged front and rear strutted aerofoil, clearly illegal as a 'movable aerodynamic device' and very much free to move relative to what most people considered to be the car's chassis 'within the spirit of the regulations'. Since 1969 all aerodynamic effects had had to transmit their download to the tyres through 'the entirely sprung parts of the car', prohibiting direct attachment of 'foils and fins to the wheel uprights. 'Entirely sprung part of the car . . .' was interpreted as meaning 'the chassis', which most construed as that load-bearing section of the car supporting the road-wheel suspension. Colin insisted his car had two chassis, but the opposition would not accept that, and insisted it was illegal to transmit download direct to the wheel uprights. And was the word 'chassis' singular or plural?

Clearly, Colin's careful wordplay was intended to avoid breach of the revised new FISA regulations which had been amended following the Type 86's test appearances the previous winter. And it just didn't wash . . .

Although the car passed scrutineering at Long Beach and Elio de Angelis drove it in Friday practice there, it was against a chorus of protest from the opposition teams. The stewards then issued a statement at 6pm that evening.

It read: 'In the matter of the protest against the Lotus 88, the Stewards of the Meeting, after consideration of the rules and hearing all the parties to the protest decided to uphold the protest. In addition, the times taken (for the Lotus 88) in the qualifying session shall not stand.'

Chairman of the stewards, John Bornholdt, added: 'We are dealing with a very innovative car. If the rules were clear it wouldn't have taken so much time to come to a decision . . .'

Of course Colin instantly appealed and was allowed to run the car in the remainder of practice and the race on the understanding that any points it might score would be forfeit if the protest was confirmed. But then when Elio drove in Saturday morning practice, the 88 was black-flagged, and Colin reacted to this second affront by calling an immediate press conference.

'We are still convinced that the car complies to the regulations and we would like to see a written statement as to why it is breaking the rules. The stewards spent nine hours and upheld the protests without consulting the scrutineer who passed the car in the first place. These days I don't think people are very receptive to innovative ideas, but I'd be interested to know precisely on which grounds these protesting teams object to my car. The fact that they haven't specified their objections suggests to me they're not really sure why they think it's illegal . . .'

Bornholdt subsequently explained that statements on illegality were not required under FISA rules, but in searching the rules further after permitting the car to practice while under protest the stewards had found that they were in error and that this was not allowed, hence the black-flag incident.

On track the untried 88 had in any case misbehaved, breaking its fuel pump drive after a few laps on Friday, while Elio had been flagged-off before he could do any serious lappery on the Saturday. He fell back, relatively thankfully, to his old 81 and qualified 13th . . .

Phase One of the great Lotus 88 saga was then completed by Colin's Long Beach appeal against the car's exclusion being heard before an ACCUS Court of Appeal convened in Atlanta, Georgia, on March 19. They cleared the car and Team took it optimistically to Rio for Phase Two — the Brazilian GP on March 29.

Pre-Rio, FISA announced that the ACCUS decision carried authority 'on American territory only and concerns the Long Beach Grand Prix alone . . .' The 88 passed through scrutineering at Rio's Jacarepagua Autodrome, but at least six teams including Williams and Ferrari immediately protested its legality.

Midway through Friday morning practice the stewards came to the Lotus pit asking to examine the car again. They particularly wanted to check its conformity with a regulation which required that even with both tyres deflated on one side the body should not touch the ground. The mechanics did their stuff; the body did not touch the ground. The officials then wheeled the car to and fro; the bodywork still did not touch the ground. One hefty official then leaned hard on the bodywork — and it touched the ground.

The Brazilians walked away, saying no more.

Nigel Mansell failed to qualify for the 1981 British GP as his 88B – seen here – was ruled illegal and his replacement 87 was completed too late to give him any chance at all. The 88B has more components mounted on its outer chassis, including the windscreen, radiators and engine induction ears.

Then, when the 88 was rolled out for the afternoon practice session it was immediately black-flagged and proclaimed illegal, because its bodywork had touched the ground . . . De Angelis drove his 81 again in the race.

Colin was implacably determined by this time to prove his point, and the 88 saga progressed to Phase Three in Buenos Aires for the Argentine GP on April 12. This time the scrutineers just rejected it out of hand and Colin stormed away to the airport and out of Argentina before practice had even begun, having briefed his long-time friend, Swiss-born French journalist Jabby Crombac, to distribute the following statement:

'For the last four weeks, we have been trying to get the new Essex-Lotus 88 to take part in a Grand Prix, to no avail.

'Twice it was accepted by the scrutineers, twice it was turned down by the stewards under pressure of lobbies. The USA national Court of Appeal ruled this new car eligible and gave a firm recommendation it should be allowed to race; it was still forced off the track by protesters and the black flag.

'And now we have been turned down again from participating in the Argentine Grand Prix even though the Argentine Automobile Club's technical commission commented on the innovative design it features and the worthiness of its technological advances.

'At no time throughout this ordeal has any steward or scrutineer come up with a valid reason for the exclusion consistent with the content and intention of the rule.

'It is a particular disappointment for this to have happened at the Argentine Grand Prix which has marked more pleasant points in the history of Team Lotus. It was here, in 1960, that we were welcomed into the band of sportsmen competitors with our first full Formula 1 car, which was as innovative then in its way as the Essex-Lotus 88 is today. It was also here in 1977 that we ran the first ground-effects car ever in motor racing, a principle which every Formula 1 car has since copied.

'Throughout these years we have witnessed the changes which have taken place in Grand Prix racing, and unfortunately seen what was fair competition between sportsmen degenerate into power struggles and political manoeuvrings between manipulators and money men attempting to take more out of the sport than they put into it.

'We have a responsibility to the public of the

Grand Prix and to our drivers and this has stopped us from withdrawing our cars from this event. But for the first time since I started Grand Prix racing, 22 years ago, I shall not be in the Team Lotus pit during a race for this reason. During this period no team has won more races or more championships than we have, nobody has influenced the design of racing cars the way we did through innovations which are already finding their way into everyday motor cars for the benefit of increased safety and energy conservation. And yet we are being put under unbearable pressure by our rival competitors, who are frightened that once again we are setting a trend they may all have to follow.

'The matter shall go to its next stage at the FIA Court of Appeal in two weeks' time. We shall defend our case with all the arguments we can muster for the defence of a cause we consider worthy.

'When this will be over I shall seriously reconsider with my good friend and sponsor David Thieme of Essex Motorsport whether Grand Prix racing is still what it purports to be; the pinnacle of sport and technological achievement. Unfortunately this appears to be no longer the case and, if one does not clean it up, Formula 1 will end up in a quagmire of plagiarism, chicanery and petty rule interpretation forced by lobbies manipulated by people for whom the word sport has no meaning.

> Colin Chapman
> Team Essex Lotus
> Buenos Aires
> April 10, 1981   9am

PS: When you read this, I shall be on my way to watch the progress of the US Space Shuttle, an achievement of human mankind which will refresh my mind from what I have been subjected to in the last four weeks.'

This not altogether carefully-considered statement triggered a tough riposte from J-M Balestre at BA, who stated that Chapman was in breach of the recently-signed Concord Agreement and added that his statement had discredited the Formula 1 World Championship. Consequently, Balestre added, FISA was imposing a $100,000 fine on Team Essex Lotus. Now while the Formula 1 family might squabble within itself, it would always close ranks against an external threat, and Balestre promptly found himself faced with a joint statement from representatives of 13 Formula 1 teams expressing concern at his handling of the Lotus press release incident — particularly with regard to that gratuitous fine. Ten days later it was rescinded.

Peter Wright meanwhile spared a thought for 88 mechanics Geoff Hardacre and Nigel Stepney '. . . who had run the build of the prototype car and who were beavering away all hours to get it running . . .'

The Lotus appeal to the FIA Court in Paris was then heard on April 23, when Team's submissions were rejected on two counts. Firstly, the so-called 'primary chassis' did not conform to the definition in the FIA Yellow Book; the chassis was referred to as a body/chassis, which terminology was judged to mean that the bodywork has to be integral with the chassis.

Under 'Definitions, Article 252' the regulations read: 'Mechanical components include all parts for the propulsion, suspension, steering and braking and all accessories whether moving or not which are necessary for their normal functioning'. The rule book continued: 'Chassis: Structure of the car which holds mechanical components and coachwork together', coachwork having been defined as 'All entirely sprung parts of the car licked by the external air stream, except the safety roll-over structures and the parts definitely associated with the mechanical functioning of the engine, transmission and running gear'.

Colin and Peter Wright submitted that the only definition which counted in Formula 1 was that as laid down in the new Concord Agreement, not the Yellow Book. Nowhere did it state that you could not have the coachwork on one chassis and the mechanical components on another. And meanwhile, the 6cm ground clearance regulation was being openly flouted by every other team, purely because it had been so poorly framed and was unpoliceable.

Commenting on his future plans, Colin said: 'I've got no cars now. Two 88s are built and a third is being built — and I don't know about my sponsor's future . . .' In fact, David Thieme had fallen foul of the Credit Suisse bank for alleged malpractice and had been arrested in Zurich and was held in jail for two weeks without charges being preferred . . .

It's an exciting life at the top.

An Essex sponsorship payment was apparently pending, and Team finances looked frail without it, especially since the expensive 88s were now ruled illegal. At 2.30pm on Tuesday, April 28, Colin announced his decision to cancel Team's entries for the San Marino Grand Prix on May 3, as there had been insufficient time to prepare alternate raceworthy cars following the 88 ban. It was to be the first Grand Prix missed by Team Lotus since they had entered Formula 1 in 1958 . . .

The 88 tubs were rigged with conventional bodywork and radiator mounts in time for the Monaco GP, emerging as Type 87s there, but meanwhile Colin still harboured ambitions for the twin-chassis 88. He knew instinctively it was the way to go, and was not averse to continuing to play with words.

He had a mildly revised 88B-spec developed in which as Martin Ogilvie recalls 'we hung more bits on the bodywork to add weight to our claim that this was actually the main part of the car'. The gearbox oil cooler, brake ducts and a large new screen were all now on that unit, and Colin presented it for examination to the British Royal

Another view of the car which, given a more favourable political reception, could so easily have transformed the future of racing car design. This is the 88 in its original form, as prepared for Elio de Angelis to drive (all too briefly) in practice in Brazil.

Automobile Club Motor Sports Association — RACMSA — in June, prior to their British GP at Silverstone. Now the original descriptions of 'primary' and 'secondary' chassis had been amended.

Now Colin pleaded that his 88B featured 'two sprung structures' which RACMSA officials accepted as a definition meeting the letter of FISA's law, rendering the 88B legal and accepting Lotus' two entries for the cars in the British GP on July 18.

RACMSA issued a statement saying: 'The scrutineers of the British Grand Prix, the RAC Technical Commission, have unanimously decided that the new Lotus 88B racing car does not breach the Formula 1 technical regulations. That means, assuming identical cars are presented to the scrutineers at Silverstone, that unless the decision of the scrutineers is successfully challenged before the Stewards of the Meeting, the Lotus 88B will be competitively raced.'

From Paris, Balestre promptly rocketed the RACMSA with the unequivocal statement that FISA considered the Lotus 88 *and all its derivatives* to be in breach of the regulations. Any organization accepting such cars would be in breach of the Concord Agreement and such a breach would strip

their race of its World Championship status.

RACMSA stuck to their guns, and obtained tacit agreement from the bulk of FOCA teams not to rock the boat further by protesting the 88Bs at Silverstone. The goodwill of the so-called 'Grandee' teams like Ferrari could not, however, be secured. Sure enough, when on the Wednesday evening prior to the Silverstone race three 88Bs, the two sometime 87s and one new car, were passed by the British scrutineers, Ferrari, Alfa Romeo and Talbot-Ligier immediately protested.

De Angelis and Mansell practised the cars on the Thursday morning while the stewards discussed this latest imbroglio. Balestre issued a FISA statement after practice had begun, repeating their view that the 88Bs did not comply with the regulations and that RACMSA should enforce this decision of the International governing body. It was implicit that if they did not do so, the British GP could be stripped of its Championship status.

After studying their book of rules, the stewards regretfully concluded that FISA did have the power to inflict such a severe penalty so the 88Bs were excluded and their Thursday practice times declared void.

Mansell had qualified his 88B on the Thursday,

but after it was stripped out overnight and rebuilt as an 87 he failed to make the grid. Goodyear had just returned to Formula 1, Team was struggling to set-up its cars on their latest rubber and with so many changes from 88B back to 87 concentrated into two days they ended-up all at sea. Another 87 was brought from Hethel for de Angelis, who qualified with one heroic lap, and that was the end of the 88 saga.

At last the model's coffin lid had been nailed down tight, and they would run no more in anger, being retired to occasional display duties, never once having raced, but having generated more heat and more column inches of print than most racing cars could ever achieve.

Colin's interminable battle with authority to bring the 88 to the starting line had been for him totally a battle of principle, but a principle which the contemporary specialist media had tended to misunderstand.

He was not fighting a short-term battle with FISA merely to allow him to race *that* car *that* season. His obsession was not with the 88, but with the Formula 1 designer's freedom to introduce and race-develop an *entirely* new idea. That was the principle for which he had fought so hard, and that was the unwritten, unstated, almost sub-conscious principle which had first drawn him towards motor racing over 30 years before.

As Peter Wright explained: 'The bitterest disappointments were FISA never allowing us to prove that the 88 twin-chassis concept *would* work. It was the logical engineering answer to a well-defined problem and their response to it was completely irrational and illogical in engineering terms. Every time we tried to run the car they just waggled a black flag at it, and I sat beside Colin through innumerable court hearings in the attempt to prove our case.

'He told me time after time: "I'm not just fighting for the 88, I'm fighting for the Formula 1 designer's right to do development like this and to prove it in competition. When every advanced or adventurous or unproven new idea gets jumped upon by the law-makers before it's even been tried in anger, that's not the kind of Formula 1 racing which interests me. I've never been in Formula 1 just because it promotes the name or because there's good money to be made in it. As far as I'm concerned the whole point of going Formula 1 racing is to advance the principles of automotive engineering far quicker than they could possibly advance without the stimulus of competition."

'He said that, and he meant it. And when despite all our arguments they still wouldn't let the 88 race his disenchantment with Formula 1 was very deep, and *very* genuine, believe me.'

One irony of Colin's bullish faith in the car was that, in chief designer Martin Ogilvie's words: 'It just didn't handle. The drivers said it was a load of junk. In theory it really was the way to go, but like so many new approaches it needed the driver to adjust to a whole new set of inputs and to find a new way of describing to the engineers what was going on . . . that's never easy. . .'

And then the tragedy of it all was that through this saga the Brabham-introduced lowering suspension ploy had gone through challenged but unhindered by FISA, until their efforts to restrict such systems then triggered an era of ultra-low-ride-height racing cars with effectively zero suspension travel. Their solid suspensions depended mainly on tyre sidewall squidge and suspension arm flexion, they battered their structures, components and drivers alike, and though blindingly fast they triggered a number of terrifying accidents.

Jochen Mass' March hurdled the barriers to penetrate a spectator area at Ricard — happily without causing serious injury in what could easily have been a massacre. More seriously, two Ferrari accidents which could be blamed on that genre of regulation-engendered cars — though admittedly as modified for 1982 — killed Gilles Villeneuve and ended Didier Pironi's potentially brilliant driving career.

Such tragedy *could* have been averted had drivers been able to ride in comfortable, softly-suspended cockpit pods, divorced from the massive-download, rigid suspension requirements of floating aerodynamic bodyshells loading the wheel uprights direct.

Colin Chapman's reliance upon semantics may have fudged the issue, and as Peter Wright recalls in retrospect: 'The idea was absolutely legal when originally conceived, but once they'd changed the rules I think it quite probably was not.'

Considering what followed, it now looks like a safe, sensible and logical development which agonizingly fell foul of a regulation introduced by ignorant and unqualified authority 'on safety grounds'. It was actually a safe and sensible way ahead, but they could not recognize it as such, while rival teams protested it to protect their own interests.

As Will Rogers once said: 'I don't tell jokes, I just watch the Government and report the facts. . .'

Above all, the Lotus 88 saga destroyed much of Colin's surviving interest and faith in Formula 1 as an interesting and valuable crucible for engineering progress, and it would not be rekindled until the prospect of running a turbocharged engine became a reality, late the following year . . .

LOTUS 91

The 10 per cent lighter 87 won a race! (1982)

*'That Lotus is nothing special at all, but when de Angelis beat me in
Austria it shows what can be done with a bit of luck and an
ordinary car . . .'*

Keke Rosberg

Through 1981 it had become increasingly clear that Team Lotus had lost its way. The controversial failure of the 88 had cost money and time. Team found itself trailing behind the opposition in development of lowering-suspension devices to sidestep the download-limiting 6cm ground clearance requirement. Colin was quite embittered by his team's treatment at the hands of its rivals, and his interest in Formula 1 had taken a heavy blow from which it would never really recover. . .

In retrospect, some of the engineers who worked with him in what would prove to be the last year of his life recall how his distate for the way Formula I had gone, combined with demands and pressures from Group Lotus and shockwaves from the De Lorean project's collapse, served to distract and dissipate his genius.

One recalled how: 'Colin seemed to have lost his grip on what made a racing car handle. In the Lotus 72 days if you made its front end softer it went round corners better, whereas in the ground-effects era the cars did just the opposite . . . towards the end it was as though the Old Man was just too over-committed and perhaps too old to be mentally alert enough to keep his grip on what Formula 1 needed. All the other top designers and team people had only their racing and racing cars to worry about. The Old Man had so much on his plate it wasn't surprising he'd lost touch . . . especially after all that business over the 88 which came closest to turning him off completely. . .'

Colin had made Peter Wright chief engineer and eventually a director of Team Lotus, but he was never formally an employee of the company, he was always a self-employed consultant, and with Colin's enthusiastic blessing he could pursue in effect what ideas or projects interested him. An undeniably brilliant, innovative thinker, his influence tended to favour the theoretical over the practical and if a theory was perhaps slower on circuit than Team's

more practical rivals, Peter might still prove that Team were the only ones in step, on paper. In his defence, R & D, which was his forte, was all about taking a theory and developing it until it could perform in practice . . .

For 1982, Formula 1 regulations were amended to permit the use of fixed skirts with protective bottom-edge rubbing strips. Such rubbing strips had been expressly forbidden the previous season. Without such strips the skirts had been terribly vulnerable; as soon as they touched the ground they were damaged and that was why the cars had been run with such restricted suspension travel — to keep the skirts off the ground at all costs while still maintaining an adequate airflow seal, and those solid suspensions had punished both car structures and driver alike.

During 1981, when most teams had run inward-facing skirts with their unprotected lower edges rolled-under and riding on an air-bearing as ambient-pressure air bled in from around the car to fill-in the low-pressure regime beneath the underwing venturis, Team's technical direction had favoured outward-facing skirts.

The thinking was that since the depression beneath the underwings would suck the skirts inwards as well as sucking the car downwards, it was more sensible to start with skirts set in a splayed-out static attitude so that they would draw in towards the vertical under load. Unfortunately, what happened in practice was that these plastic skirts proved even more liable to touch the ground, when instantaneously they would be damaged and their seal spoiled. With the skirt system ruined, ground-effect download would be first compromised and then lost.

For some time during this period while thrashing around to find their next magic ingredient, Team even went through the stage of studying photographs of the opposition's cars and features

199

and learning what they could from them, rather than leading the pack as had been their proper role in the past.

The new John Player-liveried Lotus 91 for 1982, built to the modified regulations, might have been stubby-nosed and bulbous-podded, but it was also the prettiest Formula 1 Lotus since the Type 79.

Martin Ogilvie was primarily responsible for its design, which with its softly rolled body lines broke away from Colin's preferred crisp razor-edged shapes. Peter Warr had just returned to the fold to replace Peter Collins as team manager, and he recalls how: 'The Old Man I think was rather irritated that Martin rather than he himself had produced such a pretty little car. This was an odd facet to his otherwise so generous character. . .'

Peter Wright described the 91s as 'effectively a much tidied-up version of the wide-track 87B. We tried to take 10 per cent weight off *everything*'. The 91s used similar wet-resin lay-up carbon/Kevlar tubs to the preceding 87/88 series, though without the front-end slots demanded by the 88s' 'primary chassis' cross-beams.

The Type 91 tub weighed only 40lb, 'about half the weight of one made in aluminium', Colin declared, 'and about three times stronger'. He added: 'Ten years ago you had a 1,500lb car with about 1,500lb of download on it. Now, with ground-effects, you have a 1,500lb car with around 4,500lb download on it. The forces that go through these cars are almost *unimaginable*!

In consequence the 91 featured stiffer cast-magnesium front uprights and hubs than its predecessor, stiffer twin-element top rocker-arms at the front and a reinforced gearbox casing. The bodylines induced less drag than the preceding 87 shape in the wind-tunnel, and the side-pod coolers were now top- instead of side-ducted. Rear suspension featured machined rockers and fabricated steel uprights. A range of alternative wheelbase and track suspension components was provided for easy adjustability and to allow easy weight distribution changes to match tyre development. The doubter took this as evidence — as with the old Type 77 adjustacar — that Team had lost its way.

Brakes were outboard front and rear and like the anti-roll bars were driver-adjustable by lever and cable from the cockpit.

All the British Cosworth-engined teams were at that time adopting a new ploy to compensate for their power deficit against the turbo teams, in this case using onboard water tanks piped-up ostensibly to cool the brakes by total loss. The point was that replenishing of coolants was permitted within the regulations before post-race scrutineering. In this way the cars could actually run a Grand Prix with the brake-cooling reservoir empty so leaving the car below the regulation minimum weight. Coolant could then legitimately be replenished, including the

big 'brake-cooling' water bottle in the sidepod, before post-race scrutineering, and the extra weight of that water would then bring the cars up to the legal minimum limit. Since there was nothing in the regulations expressly forbidding such antics this ploy was perfectly legitimate. A legal Formula 1 car was merely one which complied with the regulation at the moment of scrutineering, whenever that might be, and weight-wise that meant before qualifying and after the race had ended. . .

Dimensionally, the new 91's overall length was quoted as 430cm (169.3 inches), overall width the regulation maximum 215cm (84.6 inches). Three 'quick-change' wheelbases were available — 108.2, 110.2 and 112.2 inches. Front track was 70.25 inches and rear track 65.87 inches.

Chassis numbers of the new 91-series followed on after the 87 sequence which had ended in 87/5, thus the prototype was 91/6 and was new for de Angelis at Rio, where 91/7 was available for Mansell. Chassis '8 would follow new at Zolder as a spare car, subsequently raced late-season by Elio, while chassis '9 was new as the spare at Monaco, and was to be raced only once that season — by de Angelis — at Detroit. It was an unsuccessful moulding, Team's 'Flexi-Flyer'. Chassis '10 was new for Nigel's use at Las Vegas, while the spare car through the height of the season from Brands Hatch to Osterreichring was 91/5, a conversion of the last Type 87.

The easily-variable track and wheelbase dimensions had reflected the unsuitability of the SWB 87s on the faster circuits the previous year. On their debut at Rio both new cars were damaged in minor practice incidents, de Angelis then being rammed by Baldi's Arrows in the race, while Mansell drove hard and well to finish fifth.

Prior to Long Beach, Team tested at the small Willow Springs track where Mansell crashed heavily, but he bounced back as always for the GP itself and in short-wheelbase form the black 91s finished 5-7, Elio ahead. All FOCA teams then boycotted the San Marino GP at Imola as part of their continuing battle with FISA, but returned at Zolder where a high attrition rate helped Elio finish fourth with Nigel in clutch trouble two laps behind but fifth after Lauda's McLaren had been disqualified for being under-weight in post-race scrutineering.

Tight-circuit tests at the small Croix-en-Ternois circuit in northern France preceded Monaco, where Mansell always shone, and this time he led his team-mate home 4-5.

The North American tour followed, taking in Detroit and Montreal, both cars retiring in Motown without making much impression, then Nigel crashing over Giacomelli's stricken Alfa on the first lap in Canada, damaging his wrist which was caught in the whirling steering wheel spokes when his car's front wheels smashed onto lock in the impact. Elio finished fourth there, one lap down, but confirming

Buxom beauty – Martin Ogilvie pencilled a very attractive Formula 1 shape in this Lotus 91, so attractive in its rolled edges and gentle curves that Colin Chapman seemed rather put out by it all and insisted upon a more razor-edged and ugly form in the subsequent 92/93T cars, which would be The Guv'nor's last Formula 1 fling before his premature death. Here is Mansell in 91/7 (Brazilian GP, Rio, 1982), the 91-series chassis numbers taking up where the 87-series had ended.

his ever-growing reputation for staunch reliability. . .

Mansell's injury was quite serious, the arm was splinted, but he was unfit to drive at Zandvoort. Pre-race testing there looked extremely promising, but the 91s disappointed at the GP where Roberto Moreno was enlisted to deputize for Nigel, but looked completely out of his depth and failed to qualify. Elio could only qualify 15th and then retired after a skirt change had failed to control terrible porpoising.

The 91s were quick again in tyre testing prior to the British GP at Brands Hatch, and one of the four Lotuses present featured pull-rod front suspension replacing the hefty top rocker-arm layout. Nigel was determined to drive despite pain from his Montreal injury, but it was a wasted gesture as he had to give up, his car misbehaving and leaving him in agony. Elio meanwhile ran third towards the end only to be pushed back to fourth by misfiring.

Geoff Lees deputized for Mansell in the French GP, from which de Angelis retired with fuel pressure problems, the newcomer finishing 12th.

Hockenheim again saw the 91s quick in testing, but agonizingly slow for the race. Mansell finished ninth with his wrist improved but still splinted, and de Angelis retired with transmission trouble.

Peter Warr's turbocharged V6 engine deal with Renault for '83 was announced at the following Austrian GP, and at that same meeting Elio de Angelis signed a new Team contract for the coming year. He qualified seventh fastest and on race morning a cracked rear rocker-arm was replaced on his 91.

Early in the race he settled into fifth place, inherited fourth when Arnoux's Renault stopped, and when Nelson Piquet's Brabham made its scheduled refuelling stop — introducing this kind of race tactic to modern Formula 1 — the capable Italian found himself running third. Patrese's Brabham then blew-up while leading, which left Alain Prost's Renault turbo well in the lead with Elio's John Player Lotus in second place and Keke Rosberg's Williams chasing hard on its tail. The drama became electrifying on lap 48 of the scheduled 53 when Prost's fuel injection abruptly faltered, stranding the Renault and leaving Elio in the lead of the Austrian GP. . .

The meteoric Rosberg piled on the pressure in second place and on the last lap stormed up onto the

Chapman's last victory, and Cosworth-Ford's 150th for the DFV series of V8 engines, came here at Österreichring in the 1982 Austrian GP, won by Elio de Angelis in his regular 91, seen here running without nose wings.

91's tail. Out of the last curve he ducked out of Elio's slipstream and lunged for the line, but the Italian just hung on to beat the Williams by 0.05 second, about half a car's length. . .

It was de Angelis' maiden *Grande Epreuve* victory and Team's first win since the 1978 Dutch GP, four years previously. Colin was beside himself with delight, vaulting the pit barrier as the cars finished and hurling his cap high into the air, just like the old days. . .

Nobody suspected it was to be the last race win of his glittering career.

Nigel Mansell, meanwhile, had qualifed 12th on the grid, but retired before half-distance with engine failure.

After such excitement the final three races at Dijon, Monza and Las Vegas were anti-climactic; the Lotus twins 6-8 in Dijon's 'Swiss GP', Nigel seventh and Elio retiring with a sticking throttle after running nowhere in Italy, then collision damage and engine failure respectively putting them out at Las Vegas.

Peter Wright described that season to me as 'desperately frustrating'. It had been characterized by de Angelis' fine testing performances, spoiled by a corporate inability to reproduce such times in qualifying, after which Elio would often come good again in the race when he was already too far down the grid to stage much of a worthwhile recovery.

For much of the year the cars suffered from two main problems — porpoising over bumps and understeering on the slower circuits. After the brief pull-rod front suspension experiment they raced rocker-arms to the end of the year. Contrary to the 87s, the 91s were more effective on the faster circuits, but it took incredible effort to set them up, many miles of testing before they were 'right there'. In a race between full tanks and empty it was difficult to maintain the car within its competitive 'working area'. The year saw progressively more weight biased towards the front of the cars, and they ended it with Team placing sixth in the Constructors' Championship.

At least now their long marriage to the latterly-uncompetitive 3-litre naturally-aspirated Cosworth-Ford V8 engine was nearly over, and the banns were up for the new era with the 1,500cc turbocharged Renault V6. . .

LOTUS 92

Computerized Lotus-Ford swansong (1983)

'Since the 92 was our last Cosworth car and everyone else who mattered had turbos, Colin decided it had to have something special . . .'

Peter Wright

In November 1982, FISA abruptly banned the use of ground-effects underwing tunnels by announcing a new regulation which would take effect for the forthcoming 1983 season, stipulating a flat bottom extending the full width of the car and running from a point in line with the trailing edge of the front tyres back to a point in line with the leading edge of the rear tyres.

Some form of underside ground-effects venturi or aerodynamic diffuser surface would still be permissible both ahead of and behind this 'midships flat-bottomed area, but effectively the aerodynamic shenanigans which had kept the British teams on a par with the turbocharged brigade for so long had now been buried.

Team had Renault turbo V6 engines on the way, but initially at least Viry-Châtillon could only provide sufficient for de Angelis' new 93T car, and his number 2, Nigel Mansell, would have to rely upon naturally-aspirated Cosworth-Ford power until mid-season.

Of course there was no point in developing a new Cosworth car for this pilot turbo year, but the existing hardware had to be updated to flat-bottom form and the two cars converted in this way for Nigel Mansell's use were classified Lotus Type 92s.

His regular early-season car was old 91/10, which he raced regularly from the Brazilian to the Canadian GPs, while his spare car used the monocoque of 91/5, *nee* 87/5, during that same period.

Colin was anxious that even this last-gasp Cosworth car should have some magic ingredient which would make it more effective than the rest of the depleted Cosworth field and consequently it adopted Lotus R&D's new computer-controlled active suspension system along with the latest short-stroke 'DFY Mark 1' revised Cosworth-Ford engine, which offered a little more power.

The active suspension system was heavy for Formula 1. It featured hydraulic rams on each suspension corner piped to reservoirs pressurized by a small engine-driven pump. The rams were intended to replace conventional springs, dampers and anti-roll bars, and their reactions were controlled from a central micro-processing computer unit which was fed with electronic information from load sensors and transducers on each ram plus various accelerometers to form an electronic picture of the car's movements and attitudes and the movement of the road surface beneath its wheels.

The computer was programmed to analyze all these inputs and to react virtually instantaneously by extending or retracting the suspension rams as required to optimize chassis attitude, suspension bump or rebound and anti-roll control. In theory wheel movement could be greatly reduced, giving more consistent ride height, hence improved aerodynamic performance while also minimizing handling changes between full and light fuel loads.

The first active-suspension Type 92 was tested at Snetterton on December 16, 1982, driven by youthful cadet Team driver Dave Scott, who had just recently been recruited by Colin from Formula 3. During the test an ashen Peter Warr drove into the paddock to break the news of Colin's death in the small hours of that morning. . .

Unfortunately, the weight of the active system at that time was a handicap, matched by its poor reaction times and operating efficiency in Formula 1 terms. It was run only at Rio and Long Beach, where during qualifying Mansell had a real fight on his hands after the car landed heavily over a yump which metaphorically sent all the system's sensors clean off the clock, the jacks reacted violently, and the car bounded and swerved along wildly for many a yard before it all settled down again.

Thereafter the system was stripped off and Lotus R&D's active suspension unit at Hethel buckled

The Cosworth-engined Type 92 '10' in Mansell's hands at Monaco during the 1983 GP marked the end of the long line of British V8-engined Lotus Formula 1 cars, which had been founded in 1961 with the first Climax units in Lotus 21 chassis-frames, and in 3-litre terms in 1967 with the debut of the epochal Type 49s. Here, first lap at Mirabeau, is Nigel trying everything to get past one more car – in this case Chico Serra's Arrows – in the damp early stages before his wet tyres 'went off'. The 92 could be differentiated from its 91 predecessor by the more rearward engine intake siting and angular body-lines.

down to intensive further development for road car use, attracting worldwide major-manufacturer interest, but facing several more years' work to get it right.

Meanwhile, Nigel's only worthwhile finish with the 92 was sixth in Detroit, otherwise being classified 12th three times, at Rio, Long Beach and Imola. The two flat-bottomed 92s were then torn

down, one composite tub went back into store, while it seems probable that after its Montreal swansong 91/10's was cannibalized to form the third of the new-era Ducarouge-designed 94Ts which would bring Team back towards the top. Meanwhile, the Type 92 had ended Team's 17-year association with the Cosworth-Ford V8 engine. It had served them well. . .

LOTUS 93T

Team's turbo age dawns — but slowly (1983)

'The first turbo car was just a testbed to teach us what we didn't
know about that kind of technology . . . because we were starting
from scratch in so many ways, it taught us that we had an awful lot
to learn . . .'

Peter Warr

The basic thinking behind the new turbocharged Renault V6-engined design for 1983 was to produce a simple and straightforward car which would introduce Team to this new era of racing and allow them to learn what 650-700bhp road-racing needed without too many trick features to trip them up. One joker in the pack, however, was FISA's November 1982 imposition of flat-bottom rules — banning ground-effects sidepod tunnels — for the new year, as described in the preceding chapter.

The Renault engine itself was a 90-degree 1,491.6cc V6 with twin belt-driven overhead camshafts per bank actuating four valves per cylinder. Renault Sport at Viry-Châtillon, south of Paris, were just then changing over from their original thinwall cast-iron Type EF1-series blocks to a lighter aluminium type, considering that 'if Ferrari can get away with turbocharging an aluminium-block engine, so can we'. Their engines used German-made KKK turbochargers and Renix — Renault Electronics — engine management systems which continuously monitored and computer-matched electronic ignition and fuel injection to demand and to pre-set mapping programmes. Like their rival turbocharged engines, the Renault V6s demanded voluminous ancillaries known as intercoolers which were simply radiators through which the hot pressurized induction charge passed on its way from the turbocharger to be cooled and hence made more dense before entering the induction logs on top of the engine. These turbo engines also demanded larger-capacity water radiators than had been customary with naturally-aspirated 3-litre engines. So there was not a lot to carry.

Martin Ogilvie had laid out this first-ever turbocharged Formula 1 Lotus, which has since gone into legend as being vastly over-large, over-weight and ungainly. It was certainly something of a disaster, but it is not true that it was unduly large.

In fact its frontal cross-section was smaller and its all-up weight lighter than that of the hastily-made 94T hybrid which would replace it in mid-season.

Team had been given details of predicted fuel consumption by Renault Sport, which of course were considerably higher over a GP distance than they had become accustomed to with the Cosworth engines. In fact Formula 1 tank capacity at that time was restricted to a maximum of 250 litres, but other turbo teams led by Brabham had adopted pit-stop strategy to fit fresh soft-compound sticky tyres and to refuel mid-race. They found this allowed them to run faster throughout the race than would have been possible non-stop, and to take this strategy to its logical conclusion cars had then been built with small-capacity fuel tanks, so they were incapable of running most complete races non-stop, but were always close to the minimum weight limit.

Another advantage of this pit-stop strategy was that it enabled teams to cascade fuel through their turbocharged engines to help cool them internally and so make them survive higher boost pressures than would otherwise have been possible, thus releasing still more horsepower.

As turbo engine tyros, Team were not into all this, and their simple 93T initiate design was based around a reshaped new carbon/Kevlar folded-up monocoque with a flat, sloping scuttle section replacing the arched type of earlier designs.

Team's composite-chassis technology had advanced since its early dawn. At last a proper curing oven had been installed at Ketteringham Hall, big enough to swallow the whole car-sized basic composite building sheet and body panels, and to bake them at around 125 degrees C. Now the bucket-and-brush wet-resin lay-up method had also been superseded for the 93T and its successors by use of pre-preg cloth which demanded less resin.

The new Renault engine mounted virtually fully-stressed on the back of the new tub, but unlike the

Team's first turbocharged Formula 1 car, 93T/1, on test at Rio during the winter of 1982/83 with Elio de Angelis coming to grips for the first time with Renault V6 power. The Ogilvie-designed car was a tentative entry into this new performance world, and suffered accordingly. Note evidence of the new Pirelli tyre contract, pull-rod front suspension, cut-short sidepod rear-ends and angular nose-top treatment.

DFV/DFY V8s it needed some tubular braces to help.

The new tub's tank section could accommodate 45 gallons of fuel compared to the 91-Cosworth's 38 gallons, which made the tub large, while attention to providing a full driver safety cell and extensive footbox protection then made it larger still. Despite the adoption of abbreviated sidepod structures by most rival teams for the new flat-bottom regulations, Martin retained the familiar full-length type to accommodate all the extra coolers which Renault's V6 engine demanded. Combined water/oil radiators and water/air intercoolers were mounted symmetrically in each pod. The car featured bigger twin-caliper outboard brakes than its Cosworth-engined predecessor to cope with its greater performance and reduced engine overrun braking effect.

Front suspension was now by pull-rod system, obviating the clumsy and aerodynamically-intrusive top rocker-arms which Team had retained for so long. Under flat-bottom rules some ground effects could still be achieved by running highly-cambered nose foils and a rear diffuser ramp beyond each end of the regulation flat undersurface. But to make these unskirted devices work adequately would entail running them close to the road surface, which would mean limiting suspension movement if inefficient pitch and underbody damage was to be avoided.

In 1981, leading teams had found to their cost that rocker-arms became undamped springs in such stiff suspension systems, and to make them stiff enough they became even deeper and heavier and more costly in aerodynamic terms, so by mid-1982 pull-rod suspension systems had largely replaced them.

In a pull-rod system the inboard coil-spring/damper stood on a pivoted actuating arm, which was attached to a link rod passing diagonally up to the outboard pivot between top wishbone and front upright. As the road wheel went onto bump, so the suspension arms rose, yanking on the pull-rod, which pivoted up the actuating arm to react against the foot of the coil/damper unit.

Compared to an adequately stiff rocker-arm the frontal area and aerodynamic disturbance caused by the new system's top wishbone and the pull-rod itself was minimal, and overall the system gave a great increase in front-end rigidity.

Front uprights were as usual cast-magnesium, rears in fabricated steel, where the top rocker-arms were machined from solid aluminium. As before, Lotus used their own tailored-case gearbox with Hewland internals.

But Colin, 'The Guv', 'The Old Man', suffered his fatal heart-attack on December 16, 1982, just after seeing the first 93T completed, and it would take Team a long time to get back onto an even keel without his mercurial influence chivvying them along.

And in addition to that inevitable feeling of emptiness and loss following his death, and to the unknown quantity of the new turbocharged engine, Peter Warr had also completed a chancy if extremely lucrative deal to use Pirelli tyres as the Italian firm's development partner through 1983.

The reason for this was that Michelin radials had proved generally superior to Goodyear's bias-plies in 1981-82, and since it was necessary to run consistent ride heights for aerodynamic reasons the radial-ply tyre's more consistently-controlled rolling diameter offered real performance advantages which bias-ply tyres could not match. This was because they tended to 'throw out' at high speed, their diameter growing due to the effect of centrifugal force. The race-engineers had returned to Ketteringham after several fast-circuit races, saying: 'We've just gotta have radials', and with Colin's say-so Peter had gone after Pirelli, who were looking for an association with a major team, and he had landed what was financially 'possibly the biggest race-tyre contract in history.'

Unfortunately, Pirelli radial-ply racing tyres would not be very competitive.

Thus, through that winter of 1982-83, Team had not only lost its guiding light — irrespective of whatever recent handicaps Colin might have suffered relative to the time he could spare them — they had coincidentally gained all the problems related to an unfamiliar new engine and unfamiliar new tyres. In fact Pirelli proved to be well off the pace for much of the season, and when they did at least develop qualifying tyres which worked well,

they only *just* saved Team's future by the skin of their teeth. . .

Only two 93Ts were built, the prototype 93T/1 making its bow in de Angelis' hands at Rio and being raced by him seven times to Detroit, performing spare-car duties thereafter at Silverstone, Hockenheim (where it was raced by Mansell) and Osterreichring.

The second car, 93T/2, was new for Mansell at the Race of Champions, the spare for Elio thereafter and was raced by him at Imola. It was retired after appearing as Nigel's spare car at Silverstone.

De Angelis, in fact, simply gave up on the cars early in their brief career and at Imola he just plain walked away from the race in disgust. His only finish was ninth at Spa. Nigel Mansell, meanwhile, only raced the 93T in the non-Championship Brands Hatch event, which he exited after only six laps with appalling handling problems, before his second-lap retirement of the spare 93T in Germany. . .

Gerard Ducarouge joined Team immediately after the Belgian GP, studied the unloved 93Ts and told Peter Warr quietly that he thought it was better he should start again from scratch. The two cars — without engines — were eventually sold-off as a job lot with Team's inventory of old Cosworth engines to racing car dealer Bob Howlings via his connection with the John Bull Shipping freight company.

Historically they join the Type 42 as perhaps Team's most unlamented Lotuses. . . but then the 42 handled so much better . . .

Bye-bye 93T — Nigel Mansell's unloved spare car, 93T/2, is hauled out of the firing line at Silverstone during qualifying for the 1983 British GP, as Ducarouge's new 94T replacement cars begin to prove their worth. See the top-ducted radiator mountings, upswept exhaust and wastegate pipes ahead of the rear wheels, and note the absence of any under-gearbox aerodynamic diffuser surfaces to achieve some measure of ground-effects download — the 94Ts had them. . .

LOTUS 94T

Ducarouge does the trick (1983)

'It's a pity the Old Man is not here. He would have loved this —
both for myself and for him, especially after the problems we have
had this year . . .'

Elio de Angelis

'Gerard's new chassis and Pirelli's new qualifying tyres coincided to .
save our bacon . . .'

Peter Warr

French engineer Gerard Ducarouge joined Team ex-Alfa Romeo, Ligier and Matra after the 1983 Belgian GP at Spa. There, on May 22, Elio de Angelis had qualified 13th and Mansell 19th in the 93T and 92 cars respectively. In the race they had then finished ninth and retired, having never featured on the leader-board. Peter Warr had to sit there with Imperial Tobacco's marketing director, Brian Wray, put his hand on his heart and guarantee to the sponsor that Team's form would improve in time for the British GP on their mutual home soil.

The contemporary John Player sponsorship deal was up for renewal that July, and Peter asked Wray to allow the team Silverstone and Hockenheim to prove that they could still handle it, despite the loss of the Old Man. Imperial's executive could only allow them Silverstone because the scheduled review meeting would fall between the British and German races. Having had the requirement for improved performance spelled-out, this was a tense time; John Player Team Lotus' entire future hung in jeopardy.

Ducarouge was a carefully-groomed, extremely charming and vastly-experienced engineer specializing in aerodynamic and suspension design and theory. His racing career had been founded with Matra Sports' single-seater and endurance racing team, followed by Ligier, then Alfa Romeo. He had enormous experience of what not to do, and brought with him to Ketteringham Hall what he called his 'Golden Rules' on basic F1 car design parameters, suspension geometry, camber change, castor angles, spring rates and so on.

As he got to know the Ketteringham crew and examined their facilities and existing hardware, Team's people rapidly grew to both like and respect the newcomer. He studied all aspects of the bulky, lumbering 93T which by general consent 'handled like a pig' and as he expounded his Golden Rules the team engineers realized how far out of bed they had

fallen. Gerard painted a new beginning for them, but did he know what he was talking about . . . ? Would fortunes improve?

Having acquired a feel for Team's contemporary state, Gerard spent 24 hours pondering what to do. Finally he took his thoughts to Peter Warr and told him: 'I think it is best that we forget the 93T, set it aside and start again . . . I'd like to do a new car which means new bodywork, new suspension, gearbox, everything'.

Peter swallowed hard, said: 'Just make sure you've got two cars ready for Silverstone', and authorized a crash programme to do just that. Success was vital — everyone knew it — and a frantic design and rebuild period began at the Hall . . .

There was not time to design and build an all-new chassis from scratch and in fact Gerard decided this was unnecessary. 'In the store were the old Type 91 chassis which were nice and small, it was relatively easy to convert them to our new requirements and so we used them in the new cars . . .'

It was at this point that the Team Lotus concept of bolt-in aluminium bulkheads within their composite monocoque moulded tubs really paid off. The old 91 tubs' bulkheads could be extracted and replaced by new, tailor-made to pick-up Gerard's preferred new suspension geometry. The rearmost bulkhead would provide mounts for the new Renault V6 turbo engine instead of the old Cosworth DFV, while the tank bay in the old tubs — which was some 7 gallons smaller than the 93T's since it was tailored to DFV consumption — was cut about to accommodate the new pit-stop strategy filler-neck and breather.

Martin Ogilvie led a bodywork study: 'We made up a wooden chassis and dolloped plaster onto it to build up the shape, but Gerard didn't like it; at that time we didn't know his thinking, and he went back to Paris one weekend and returned with a quarter-

Team back near the top – European GP, Brands Hatch, in 1983. Elio de Angelis' full-liveried 94T/1 took a brilliant pole position during qualifying, but spun early in the race when disputing the lead with Patrese's Brabham-BMW, and later retired with engine trouble.

scale bodylines drawing he'd done . . . it's the only time I recall him drawing anything!'

Essentially Ducarouge was a conceptual thinker, and his natural charm quickly moulded the tiny four-strong Ketteringham Hall drawing office staff to his way of thinking; and they did the drawing for him.

Whereas the hapless 93T had featured pull-rod front suspension, the old 91 tubs had the scuttle apertures for a top rocker-arm, so Gerard adopted this layout in an apparently retrograde — but under these fraught circumstances perfectly practical — step. Team's manufacturing staff laid into the project with their customary energy, Gerard recalling that 94T programme as 'the most beautiful and efficient effort I had ever seen'.

The two new cars were ready in time for Silverstone, and ever since various enthusiasts, myself included, have wondered just which 91 tubs were cannibalized to create them. Club Team Lotus' indefatigable Secretary Andrew Ferguson has his office in the old Chapel at Ketteringham Hall and he

asked himself the same question and drew-up complicated charts to trace the carbon/Kevlar composite chassis series' various incestuous relationships between 87s and 88s, 91s, 93Ts and 94Ts. Since chassis plates had been juggled and swopped around, and hard-pressed mechanics' memories were understandably hazy, little was concrete, nothing was certain, but best evidence at the time of writing suggests that the outer shell of chassis 91/7 became 94T/1 while 91/8 was used for 94T/2. The faithful 91/10 last raced in Type 92 form at Montreal was then torn down as the basis of 94T/3, new for de Angelis at Zandvoort.

The 94Ts' weight distribution was different from the 93Ts' and this in combination with 1982-style stiffer-sidewall Pirelli tyres worked well at Silverstone. De Angelis was wildly enthusiastic there about the feel of his new car, but meanwhile poor Mansell — as usual — was suffering. His 94T had only been completed the day before practice began and it was plagued from first firing-up by an electrical short-circuit. The engine and its ancillaries

Nigel Mansell's 94T/2 carries 'TL'-lettered race livery during the European GP in deference to British anti-tobacco advertising restrictions. Having qualified the car third, Mansell finished in the same position. With Ducarouge's input, Team Lotus was back in business.

were changed overnight, Team's mechanics finishing the job at 6am Friday morning.

Nigel was sleeping in a caravan at the circuit and was awoken at 7am to try the car up and down the runway paddock. The engine seemed sweet, but his first serious practice lap saw the misfire return and despair reign . . .

He qualified 18th in the spare 93T that afternoon while Elio made excellent use of the best Pirelli qualifying tyres so far that season to slam Ducarouge's first Lotus straight onto fourth place on the grid, albeit 1.3 seconds slower than Arnoux's Ferrari on pole.

By this time Mansell's mechanics had changed everything that could be changed on his 94T apart from its wiring loom, so Friday evening saw a new loom ordered from Team's supplier at Diss in Norfolk, who made it up overnight. Elio was quickest in race morning warm-up to barely suppressed excitement within the team. Nigel's re-loomed car ran cleanly as he learned at last how Ducarouge's new creation felt.

The race developed with de Angelis nosing into sixth place at the end of lap 1, but two corners later his engine died and he was out. Team's elation evaporated, but Mansell was still running, ever faster . . . the exhausted mechanics brightened up again. Nigel had gained eight places on the first lap before challenging Warwick's Toleman on lap 5. But then a 40gm balance weight flew-off the 94T's left-front wheel, unbalancing the steering. The car also began to oversteer, wearing its Pirellis, but it now lay eighth and still felt relatively good — after the 93T.

On lap 17 he displaced Warwick for seventh, the team then gave him a merely-average refuelling stop, but he rejoined fifth and was able to press Arnoux, who had worn out his fresh Goodyear tyres. Nigel tried for the inside at Stowe Corner, but the Ferrari driver slammed the door. Then at Club, where the 94T felt ideal, Nigel staged a run up the outside before the ultra-quick Abbey Curve left-hander, but Arnoux blocked him again. Next time round the Lotus aimed right, Arnoux moved across

and Nigel darted left and through, embarrassing the French Ferrari driver into surrendering the corner . . .

Past the pits the black number 12 was fourth, chasing hard after Tambay's third-placed Ferrari, but its tyres were in better shape than its team-mate's, so the first of the Ducarouge-era Lotuses finished fourth upon its debut, and Mansell's drive was the talk of the town.

Imperial were thrilled to bits with the publicity received, and their sponsorship of Team Lotus was reconfirmed at the review meeting. For all concerned it was just reward for a truly heroic effort.

Disappointment then followed in a fraught practice at Hockenheim which left Mansell's 94T misfiring and saw him racing the unloved 93T again. Its engine failed on the opening lap while de Angelis' 94T overheated its way into retirement on lap 10.

Mansell's car at least was on better form in Austria, where he qualified third amongst the real *glitterati*, while Elio had all the problems including

a minor qualifying shunt. Nigel finished fifth on raceday, Elio crashing at the start.

A third 94T was ready for him at Zandvoort, where both Lotus drivers headed the qualifying list at various times, Elio fetching up third-quickest on the grid, Nigel fifth. Both cars went out in the race, Mansell spinning off in a wild challenge for sixth place at Tarzan Hairpin immediately after being signalled to make his pit stop.

The inconsistency of Pirelli qualifying tyres upset Team's progress at Monza. Elio preferred his spare car 94T/1 to the new 94T/3 there, but by their new standards both drivers qualified poorly, before de Angelis then ran fourth and finished fifth in the race, Mansell eighth.

This season saw for the first time a second Championship F1 race on British soil, the so-called European GP hastily organized at Brands Hatch to replace a cancelled New York City event. This was a second golden opportunity for Team to sparkle on home soil in a John Player-sponsored race and they did just that, cementing their new post-Chapman

1983 European GP pit-stop. Team's flame-proof overalled crew go to work on Mansell's 94T/2 and put it back onto the Brands Hatch track in a sensational 9.62 secs, helping him well on his way to finish third and so preserve his place with Team Lotus into 1984. Note the pipe man wearing a de Angelis helmet – surely not Elio himself inside there after his early retirement; a disappointing end for him after qualifying superbly and claiming pole.

relationship with their sponsor.

Elio de Angelis took his first Formula 1 pole position. He said: 'It's a pity the Old Man is not here. He would have loved this — both for myself and for him, especially after the problems we have had this year.'

The Italian had simply dominated proceedings, setting fastest time in three of the four sessions. He crashed his spare 94T/3 mildly on the Saturday morning, but improved his best time in 94T/1 and never needed to use his second set of qualifying tyres, such was the Lotus-Renault's superiority. The car/tyre combination's class was proved as Mansell qualified third in Elio's wake, his chances of getting onto the front row spoiled by spinning cars and debris on the track whenever he tried for a clear run in 94T/2.

Sadly, the race then saw Elio challenging fellow-Italian Patrese's Brabham-BMW for the lead early on; they touched and spun, Elio's engine later failing. Still Mansell was able to repeat his Silverstone performance, this time beavering his way home into third place and setting the fastest lap.

The season's finale came at Kyalami in the South African GP where neither Lotus qualified particularly well — Nigel seventh, Elio 11th — after multiple problems which pursued the cars into the race itself.

Nevertheless, what had started out as a season of sorrow and near-despair had found real direction with Gerard Ducarouge's arrival and had seen a massive and stirring revival in Team Lotus fortunes which none begrudged them . . .

LOTUS 95T

Team back to front (1984)

'We started from a new beginning, with a new chassis, new aerodynamics, revised suspension, virtually everything, at least 90 per cent new . . .'

Gerard Ducarouge

For 1984, Gerard Ducarouge was able to build upon the heartening success of the stopgap 94T cars. With their success he had suddenly assumed the image of a magician. His results with Alfa Romeo had suggested no such stature, but with Team's people, facilities and reaction times behind him, needing only to be guided firmly in the right direction, both parties had struck gold. Gerard had rapidly built an excellent rapport with the long-serving staff at Ketteringham Hall, respect was mutual and the atmosphere there was bright, dynamic and rarin' to go again.

There were some problems. The Pirelli tyre deal had been extremely lucrative, but had undoubtedly handicapped Team's performance. Consequently, for the new year Peter Warr negotiated an alternative agreement with Goodyear who were working rapidly to close the gap on Michelin in radial-ply racing tyre technology. It had become clear that neither of Team's drivers was out of the top drawer. De Angelis could be remarkably consistent and was able to nurse a car as well as any when points were at stake, but if he was trailing behind he could lose heart too easily. Mansell would never give up, he combined immense self-belief with determination, but he made too many mistakes and unfortunately tended to rub almost everyone in the Team up the wrong way.

Comments from some, like: 'It's one thing to have a driver who whinges, but a driver who whinges in a Birmingham accent is *impossible!*', might have been amusing at the time to those not involved, but they demonstrated a situation which was hardly helpful. After Colin's death Mansell would only blossom by leaving Team, which he did in 1985.

Neither driver had reacted well to press criticism of them both being 'good number 2s', and while Team's management would have preferred to take on Derek Warwick for '84 in Mansell's place, the former Toleman driver opted to join Renault instead. Nigel's good European GP following his Silverstone performance had also won him staunch John Player support. The drivers were joint number 1s, Team beholden to prepare competitive and reliable race and spare cars for each of them.

On the car front, as Gerard recalled: 'We started from a new beginning, with a new chassis, new aerodynamics, revised suspension, virtually everything, at least 90 per cent new.' The Lotus-Renault 95T was another good-looking car, four being built. The prototype was very quick in wintertime Rio testing with de Angelis driving, and as the season developed the cars would be in the forefront of every Grand Prix.

Chassis 95T/1 was used in initial pre-season testing before serving as early-season spare until Monaco, being raced only once, by Mansell at Imola. Chassis 94T/2 was his new race car at Rio and was used by him throughout the season. De Angelis' regular race car was 95T/3, but he opted to race his spare car 95T/4 at Montreal, Detroit and Estoril.

However, 1984 was very much the year of the TAG Turbo-by-Porsche-engined McLaren MP4/2s driven by Niki Lauda and Alain Prost, who won a staggering 12 of the 16 GPs. Team proved that Gerard's latest 95T chassis was superb, arguably the best-handling in the business, but a Renault engine was not as potent as a TAG, nor Goodyear as consistently competitive as McLaren's Michelins, and that was enough to make all the difference between merely accumulating points and winning races.

Race distance fuel allowance had now been cut to 220 litres, and in-race refuelling was now banned, although tyre-change stops would still make sense — a non-stop race on hard tyres taking longer than an interrupted run on softer, stickier rubber. Engine fuel economy now became a crucial factor, and

Gerard Ducarouge's first ground-up design for Team Lotus emerged in 1984 as this neat, light, efficient and extremely competitive Type 95T, Mansell in this case driving the prototype chassis '1 on test. Note the additional side-step winglets, added to the wing structure to increase its effective area, just ahead of the rear axle centreline, the 'McLaren tail' fashionable waisting down below, cut-back sidepods and large-area front 'foils.

Another day like Monday – well in the lead of the 1984 Monaco GP, Nigel Mansell kept the hammer down until he lost control over the now infamous 'white line' on the rainswept ascent leading towards the Casino Square. Michael R. Hewett, Monaco GP enthusiast and gifted amateur photographer, was on hand to record the happy scene as Nigel loses his battle to keep the sliding 95T/2 away from that unyielding barrier. . .

214

TAG did the job more efficiently than Renault.

Elio had almost decided to quit just four laps into the Brazilian GP with poor throttle response, but he hung on, looked capable of winning, and finally finished third. He went on to finish the first 10 races, scoring points in no less than nine of them, then he led the German GP going away, only for his Renault engine to break . . .

Elio's finishing record in consecutive outings ran 3-7-5-3-5-5-4-2-3-4 from Rio to the British GP at Brands Hatch, he then retired at both Hockenheim and Osterreichring, finished fourth at Zandvoort, retired from both the Monza and Nurburgring races and ended the season with fifth place in Portugal.

He finished third in the Drivers' Championship behind the untouchable McLaren twins, while Mansell was ninth-equal with Toleman's Formula 1 novice, Ayrton Senna.

Nigel had had a far less reliable and consistent record, his sheer win-or-bust attitude often busting. His first four outings ended in retirement. He then finished third at Dijon, and in the following 11 GPs finished only four times, on each occasion in the points — sixth at Montreal and Dallas, fourth at Hockenheim and third at Zandvoort.

There was a measure of discord within Team with its two drivers racing each other rather than the opposition in both Montreal and Dallas, but on the

215

plus side de Angelis started four times from the front row and Mansell twice; but it was the Englishman who spun off while leading in the rain and pressing unnecessarily hard at Monaco, who became involved in — and was fined for — a multiple startline collision at Detroit and then incensed the rugged Finnish Williams driver Keke Rosberg who accused him of weaving alarmingly while defending his lead at Dallas.

There in the heat on a disintegrating track surface Nigel was trying desperately to retain the lead in a race which could have been stopped at any moment, while at Detroit he tried to nose through a narrowing gap between a Brabham and McLaren off the line, and at Monaco he blamed his loss of control on a white line painted on the road surface over which many far less experienced drivers maintained control in identical conditions. One such in his first Formula 1 season was a Brazilian named Ayrton Senna da Silva, driving a Toleman which thus far had shown little real form. He kept it on the island, and very nearly won . . .

The latest Lotus was really good, in fact arguably *per se* the best-handling Formula 1 chassis of the year. Gerard's practical experience had brought an uncompromisingly methodical and correct way of working to Team, quite unlike Colin Chapman's mercurial approach with its flashes of inspirational brilliance and eruptions of vivid activity. Team provided Ducarouge in turn with an immense human resource free of political pressures and deeply imbued with the Chapman tradition that Nothing Is Impossible.

In the 95Ts Gerard set down his spec at the beginning of the season and Team did not mess with it. Only one of the four 95T tubs was lightly damaged underneath by hitting a kerb. At that time Ketteringham's six-man chassis-build team had produced 17 carbon-composite tubs since 1981, and not one had been lost in action.

The 95Ts were equipped with a basic slow-speed aerodynamic package and an alternative high-speed package and changing from one to another as required was effectively the only change made all year. The philosophy was very much 'put it together and set it up the way it should be, and it will deliver' and within the constraints of its tyre and engine capabilities and those of its drivers it did just that.

Unfortunately, it made more of its drivers than they made of it.

Goodyear gave Team terrific commitment in tyre development as Ferrari and Williams-Honda both lost development time with other problems, but while Akron's race tyres could never match the

Another spectacular Michael Hewett picture from Monaco. Believe-it-or-not, Elio de Angelis didn't hit the armco during this barrier-shaving drive towards the Casino Square on his fastest qualifying lap. Although only 11th on the grid he was to finish sixth in the race.

The slippery profile and the shape of the massive rear wing assembly are seen to good effect in this picture of Nigel Mansell testing the 95T in the sun at Rio. Mansell's best results with this car during his final season with Team Lotus were a pair of third places at Dijon and Zandvoort.

consistent grip of Michelin's, so Lotus could not compete once the race began due partly to this tyre deficiency and partly to the Renault EF4 engine's alarmingly high fuel consumption. Often the drivers had to wind-back turbocharger boost just to conserve sufficient fuel to reach the flag. It was like fighting with one arm tied behind their back.

They completed more than a week's intensive testing mid-season and by the time of the British GP they had already totalled some 26 days' running at race meetings plus an extraordinary 41 days' testing. Renault service was outstanding and the Régie's engineer seconded to Team, Bruno Mauduit, had a splendid time as his cars outperformed the Renault Sport works cars everywhere.

As early as Rio '83 Team had been running alloy-block V6 engines in place of the Régie's original iron-block type, and through 1984 they normally had seven to 10 engines available at any one time. Team Lotus, Ligier and Renault Sport all drew their engines from the same pool, so one weekend's factory engine could conceivably appear in a Lotus the following race weekend and in a Ligier after that. While latest modifications would be proven on one Renault works car it was agreed that they would become available to the clients as soon as they went onto the second works RE50.

Team failed to secure the victory which they seemed poised to score nearly all season. Peter Warr: 'Elio could have won Rio but had a misfire due to the electronics, Nigel could have won Monaco but made an error, at Detroit we had a gearbox failure when Elio was catching up at a second a lap, at Dallas we had more gearbox trouble and another driver error, and then at Hockenheim Elio was just uncatchable before it broke. Elio enjoyed a very good relationship with Gerard and proved himself very mature, he didn't press on hard

when it threatened to destroy his tyres and his finishing record was excellent because of that . . .'

After the Dallas transmission failure a crash programme was started in order to build a new gearbox, while interim stronger gears were obtained from Italy in time for Brands Hatch. The new gearbox casing, new selection system and DGB instead of FGB Hewland internals were running in September tests at Nurburgring, whereas Renault had also initiated a new gearbox programme of their own after Dallas and nothing would be available to them until 1985; clear evidence of the Nothing Is Impossible syndrome, Team's secret weapon.

They tested carbon brakes all season, Mansell racing a set at Rio, where he crashed out of the race while trying to defend his fourth place, and they were then tried again right at the end of the year. Team had done a superb job for Renault and signed-on with them for another three seasons, prompting Régie President Bernard Hanon to 'unlock the door to R&D for us' in recognition.

There was little love lost between the uncompromising Peter Warr and the equally hard Birmingham driver, and latterly the Ketteringham fabrication shop had maintained a wall chart listing this week's Nigel Mansell excuse. Again it was amusing but unproductive, understandable because since moving to live in the Isle of Man the driver was never seen at Team's HQ. Neither did the lads at home base see much of de Angelis. At the end of the season Nigel Mansell moved to Williams in a change which would open up new horizons for both himself and Team Lotus. The driver would always declare that he owed everything to Colin Chapman's faith in him. Since Colin's death, driver and Team had simply grown apart. The association had lasted five seasons, and perhaps that had been at least one too many . . .

LOTUS 96

Team's no-go CART (1984)

'I figure that with a sensible programme, Cosworth doing our
engines and Lotus building the chassis we are looking good. That
Ducarouge, ain't he tasty? . . .'
Roy Winkelmann

During 1984 Team was approached by English-born American businessman Roy Winkelmann with a proposal to build him an American National Championship car for Indianapolis-style CART racing. Roy had set up his own Winkelmann Racing Team during the 1960s with driver Alan Rees. They had graduated from sports and Formula Junior to 1-litre Formula 2 in 1964 using Brabham cars. From 1965 Jochen Rindt joined Rees in the team and the blindingly quick Austrian rapidly established himself as King of Formula 2, running his exquisitely-prepared Winkelmann Racing cars on into 1,600cc Formula 2 from 1967.

Roy's team was most efficiently run, like all his business interests, which included security surveillance and a large bowling centre at Slough, to the west of London. Everything about his Rees-managed racing team spelled care and quality, characteristics which Winkelmann himself demanded in all things.

But in 1969 the team broke up, some of its personnel forming the core of March Engineering, and into 1970 Winkelmann himself was left with no racing interest, other than advising Rindt on business affairs. Then, that September, Jochen was killed in the Lotus 72 at Monza.

Roy stayed away from racing for years thereafter, building up his extraordinary mixture of security, counter-intelligence and night club businesses. But he had the itch to return to racing and he believed he saw his opportunity in the CART racing scene for 1984 in which international interest was blossoming and where the commercial sponsorship potential seemed enormous.

CART racing pivoted upon the 2.65-litre Cosworth DFX turbocharged engine. Roy knew Keith Duckworth and Mike Costin of old and he appreciated that nobody in CART had their engines prepared direct by Cosworth themselves. Rather than buy a proprietary chassis from March or Lola

which would be 'just like any other customer's', he approached Team Lotus International to commission a Gerard Ducarouge-designed car for 1985, and he persuaded Cosworth Engineering to prepare DFX engines for him.

It was an interesting project for the Ketteringham crew and while Winkelmann announced his intentions to return to competition with a three-year CART programme as Winkelmann Team Lotus running Lotus chassis, Cosworth engines and supported by as-yet unspecified commercial sponsorship, he had people touring the US to tie-up suitable big-business backing.

Gerard studied the CART racing scene at New York's new Meadowlands road circuit before setting down a 95T-derived chassis concept complying with the US series' regulations, 'though with the tub built generally to the same method as the 95T but modified, much thicker and stronger because it was possible that the car could hit a concrete wall at 320 kilometres an hour!'.

The basic carbon/Kevlar composite sandwich pre-preg skins were used much as before, but to gain extra shear strength the original void-filling Nomex paper-foil honeycomb was now replaced by lightweight aluminium-foil honeycomb. This material needed to be handled more delicately, but was much stronger in shear when bent. In this respect the 96 marked a new beginning as the succeeding Formula 1 tubs would also employ aluminium honeycomb filling between their carbon/Kevlar sandwich skins in place of the Nomex used in the Types 88 to 95T tubs.

One prototype 96 was built, but even before it was completed it became apparent that poor Winkelmann and his aides were up against an American CART racing establishment which was not too keen to see a Winkelmann Team Lotus break into their kind of racing. A works car and works engines would not be appreciated. Amid

much behind-the-scenes manoeuvring Roy was unable to attract the sponsorship his ambitious scheme demanded, neither could he convince any established driver of the value of his scheme — they all seemed to prefer the known quantities of customer March and Lola chassis and the big buck up front, regardless of competitive prospects and potential winnings ahead. Consequently, the whole Type 96 project stuttered to a halt.

In effect poor Roy Winkelmann retired hurt, while poor Team were left with a very expensive CART racing prototype car standing virgin and forlorn in one corner of their race shop. Into 1986 this handsome green-painted one-off was no longer eligible under altered American regulations, and like the 1969 Type 64s it was fated to become merely a fascinating show car, and an interesting reminder of what might have been . . .

These design-registration photographs of Team's one-off Type 96 CART Indycar show its typically neat and fluent Ducarouge shape, long-chord nose 'foils, neat top-ducted cut-back sidepod form and the F1-derived 'McLaren tail' waisting inboard of the rear wheels . Front suspension features pullrod coil-spring/damper actuation, there's an additional aerodynamic sidetray rigged ahead of the rear wheels, and the moulded monocoque tub beneath that attractive British Racing Green suit of clothes is stiffened with aluminium-foil in place of the earlier-series Team Lotus Kevlar-foil void filling. This feature improved chassis security and rigidity and extended into Formula 1 from the 97Ts for 1985.

LOTUS 97T

Team win at last as Senna shines (1985)

'I won today because my car gave no trouble . . . and I made no mistakes'

Ayrton Senna

For 1985, the young Brazilian Ayrton Senna was signed-on by Peter Warr to join Elio de Angelis. Senna's potential seemed enormous, he had shone as brilliantly as a latter-day Jimmy Clark or Jackie Stewart in Formula Ford and then Formula 3 and had proved very competitive during his maiden Formula 1 season with Toleman the previous year. Peter had actually discussed the possibility of his joining Team for that season, but Imperial had preferred to retain Nigel Mansell's services after his two very good, publicity-promoting drives in the British races of 1983.

By the time of the 1984 Dutch GP Senna's new year deal with Team could be announced and although it caused some problems with Toleman — who insisted they had a continuing option on the Brazilian's services — he was able to buy out that option under a clause in their contract which they seemed to have overlooked.

So Mansell moved to Williams and Senna joined Team Lotus in his place. Warr was so confident of the newcomer's ability that he had actually offered him number 1 status ahead of de Angelis. But Senna, despite his relative inexperience, was sufficiently mature to appreciate that he was still only a new boy in this kind of racing. As upstart number 1 with the established old hand he could find himself the butt of any friction within the team. In effect he told Peter: 'I'd rather be joint number 1 with Elio, that way he won't be afraid of me, he is more likely to share information, and I can learn.' In very short order poor de Angelis would discover just how much of a threat Senna posed to his position, regardless . . .

Gerard's new Type 97T car for the '85 series was another logical development of the previous season's 95T, fitted now with the new regulation deformable-structure crash-protective nose box, and with its rear wing shorn of the add-on side-step winglets which had grown there through 1983-84

and which were now banned. To compensate for this loss of download Gerard adopted two devices, one derived from what he had seen on his visit to a US CART race in preparation for the Type 96 project and the other a completely new device of his own invention.

The CART-derived idea regained some of the over-car download generation lost in the winglet ban, by adding neat little fenced 'foils above the rear end of each sidepod, just ahead of the rear wheels. Gerard's new invention was the addition of curved aerofoil-section vertical deflector vanes on outrigger struts in the area between the front wheels and the tub side, ahead of the sidepod air entry. The idea had been tested and proven in the Imperial College moving-ground wind-tunnel in Kensington, while Gerard also used the full-scale French *soufflérie* at St Cyr, outside Paris.

The precise function of these vanes is still classified at the time of writing, but from their introduction on the 97Ts in Rio opening the 1985 season they were rapidly copied with varying degrees of comprehension and success by most other teams. They certainly cleaned-up turbulent airflow within the front wheels, presumably diminishing drag-inducive vortices in this area, and they also straightened flow through the suspension arms on its way into the sidepod intakes. I believe their lower-tip vortices also produced an effective 'air-skirt' to minimize infill beneath the car, reducing lift and maybe even promoting worthwhile ground-effect. But Gerard specified their use on some circuits, not on others where their effect would be negligible. Some of his imitators tended to run a variety of ever-developing deflector vanes and brake-faring ducts everywhere thereafter, often with little concrete advantage, which caused considerable Gallic amusement in Team's pits.

During the season Senna emerged as a driver of such enormous potential that he became widely disliked in the pit lane. He led at Imola, Monaco, Detroit, Silverstone, the Nurburgring, Brands Hatch and Adelaide and won the Portuguese GP at Estoril and the Belgian GP at Spa.

He took seven pole positions during the season, Elio salvaging one more and inheriting victory at Imola, having never led at any stage on the road, but profiting from Prost's disqualification at post-race scrutineering when his victorious McLaren — which had run out of fuel on the slowing-down lap — was found to be underweight.

Rivals questioned Senna's rugged Formula 3 tactics under pressure as he shut them out into corners and was never averse to banging wheels. But in sheer unhurried car control the newcomer shot straight to the top of the pile, with only Prost possibly as smooth yet quick. Senna showed extraordinary calm in pressure situations at Rio and Estoril, where his driving while leading the race in torrential rain was simply unmatched. He openly disliked Detroit, yet slammed his 97T straight onto pole position there, and after a fraught practice day at Spa he was able to commit himself totally to the race, and to win.

With this cuckoo in the nest, the unfortunate de Angelis found himself relegated *de facto* to number 2. His always fragile Latin temperament often responded to setbacks by retreat rather than a vigorous 'we try harder' approach. Still his ability to bring his car to the finish intact was still extraordinary, and it paid off early in the season, but in the second half that reliability was lost as he perhaps tried to run harder to match the fearsome Senna's pace.

The Italian's first seven GPs in the 97Ts saw him finish 3-4-1-3-5-5-5. He was then unclassified at Silverstone, retired at Nurburgring, and in the next seven outings he finished four times, 5-5-6-5 to score points every time he made it to the line. It was sad and ironic that at Adelaide, in the inaugural World Championship Australian GP ending the season, he should be disqualified for weaving through the grid into his proper qualifying position after being delayed on the parade lap. The stewards had let him run 17 laps before they put out the black flag, and he was in his usual fifth place at the time. It was an unfortunate end to his Team Lotus career after six seasons' faithful service.

Senna, meanwhile, finished seven of his 16 GPs, being classified seventh after dominating at Imola, only to run out of fuel because his Renault EF4 engine — which it was his turn to use instead of the more fuel-efficient new EF15 which went to Elio — burned away the 97T's fuel load before the finish and he ran out. He finished 16th in Montreal and was classified 10th at Silverstone after leading until again his car ran out of fuel, this time due to a broken sensor in his engine's electronic management system, which persuaded the injection to run full-rich on one bank, wrecking Team's pre-race

consumption calculations.

He then finished five of the last seven races, 2-3-3-1-2 in Austria, Holland, Italy, Belgium and at Brands Hatch, before retiring in both South Africa and Australia. He had featured brilliantly every time out and again Gerard had clearly produced a very competitive car, but for Team Lotus 1985 was only satisfying insofar as every year since Colin Chapman's death had seen them do better.

Again a batch of four 97Ts had been built and yet again this tiny car inventory was sufficient, and although some of the tubs were damaged none were written-off. By the end of the season Ketteringham's build crew had produced 21 of the carbon-composite series chassis and still had yet to lose one.

Their mixture of Renault's old EF4 and revised new EF15 V6 engines were serviced by Renault's customer sub-contractor, Mecachrome, in Bourges. The low-compression EF4s could tolerate exceptionally high boost for qualifying, which the new higher-compression consumption-conscious EF15s tailored to the 220-litre fuel restriction would not accept to the same degree. After qualifying on EF4s, the cars would be fitted with EF15s for warm-up and the race, along with new drive-train/rear-end assemblies to replace those freshly-overstressed and compromised by qualifying loads. Essentially the spare car was EF15-powered throughout, being used in practice to calculate appropriate race-tune fuel consumption.

Whereas the EF4 engines required bracing tube support on the rear of the composite chassis, the new EF15s could mount fully-stressed in true DFV style. By the time of Spa, in September, Team had received and fitted fresh engines thus far that season from 87 Mecachrome rebuilds, an average 270 miles going onto each unit before it was returned.

Renault engine designer Bernard Dudot used Lotus as 'the reference to judge the engine. I think we were second to the Honda' he would confess, 'a good compromise between power and fuel consumption'. Interestingly, he found there could be an 80-horsepower spread between outputs (ie, boost level) necessary to achieve the same lap time in Lotus, Renault, Ligier and Tyrrell chassis. Renault Sport's own, now dying, factory team still tried the new tweaks first, but because they had so many other problems results were often inconclusive. They had adopted Garrett AiResearch turbochargers in place of the German KKKs in search of more active co-development, and this R&D work was pursued relentlessly during the season, the 137kg EF15 V6s generally working competitively and well.

Unlike 1984, when the Type 95T spec was set at the start of the year and changed hardly at all during it, the 97T saw more change, partly due to Goodyear tyre developments as they improved rear tyres, then fronts, to-and-fro, but generally

progressing all the time.

It was unfortunate but true that between his victories at Estoril and Spa, Senna's first eight retirements effectively broke down into two due to Team's chassis, five to Renault's engine and its ancillaries, and one driver error.

An electrical fuel pump failure at Rio was caused by a blob of adhesive which caused the motor windings to burn out. Pumps had been in short supply so an old type using internal adhesive had been fitted, which was not used in the new pumps.

Team also accepted the Nurburgring CV joint failure as their fault. But generally there were fewer turbocharger failures than before, which made Renault's change from KKK to Garrett seem wise.

Senna not only impressed everyone with his enormous natural talent, but also with his uncanny mechanical perception. At Monaco he reported that he had over-revved in the morning warm-up. Elio's engine was already being changed in the pit-lane so Team asked Senna if he believed his would be OK for the race. He hadn't buzzed it badly, he felt, but

Elio de Angelis debuts the latest evolutionary Type 97T in the 1985 Brazilian GP at Rio. The beautifully-packaged Ducarouge shape is self-evident – radiators and intercoolers near in-line within the sidepods, expansive rear diffuser section retrieving ground-effects download behind the rear axle and CART-style add-on winglets on top of the sidepod now, just ahead of the rear wheels since the previous season's sidestep mounting on the main wing itself had been banned.

it was still bad enough for it to fail. At Silverstone he had remarked: 'There's something strange about the exhaust gas temperature', and the broken sensor which made him run out of fuel in the race proved him right again . . .

At Zandvoort he warned that the water temperature was a little high and in the race the car lost all but 1.5 litres of its water. Peter Warr admitted: 'We realize we've got to take notice of what he says now . . .', and Dudot laughed: 'With him we don't need telemetry'.

In fact Team had been using onboard recording which could either monitor 10 functions for a limited period, or two functions for race duration. Normally they would elect to record the boost pressure and revs throughout a race, and this equipment laid the anti-Senna stories that he had merely been throwing fuel conservation to the winds and winding-up the boost in fraught race situations. At Silverstone he certainly did not boost himself to a vainglorious dry tank in his battle with Prost; like Fangio, Moss, Clark and Stewart before

225

Ecstatic team chief Peter Warr greets Ayrton Senna as he wheels his victorious 97T/2 into the Estoril pit-road after his superb wet-weather drive to win the 1985 Portuguese GP, his maiden F1 victory and the team's first since the Guv'nor's death in 1982. The vertical deflector vane braced into the front suspension area was an original Ducarouge aerodynamic invention, adding considerable advantage in certain circumstances.

him, he had found extra time within himself without abusing his car.

Then, after the German GP the read-out revealed how he had been running minimum boost and changing-up at only 10,200-10,300rpm while leading comfortably and controlling the race in such

a convincing fashion.

But the vital feature for Team was that after their long drought they had started to win consistently once again . . . the Lotus name was again a serious and consistent contender for World Championship honours.

LOTUS 98T

Going for the Championship (1986)

*'There's no doubt that Lotus' car with wotsisname driving it is stiff
competition, until it runs low on fuel . . .'*
John Barnard (McLaren International)

For the 1986 season FISA's 195-litre race-distance fuel consumption restriction which had been scheduled originally to take effect in 1985, but had been postponed for the season, finally came into effect. It concentrated the minds of all engine and engine management system designers most wonderfully, while enabling the chassis designers to produce slightly smaller cars around smaller fuel cells than the 220-litre type formerly demanded since in-race refuelling had been banned.

Gerard Ducarouge took the opportunity of this change in the regulations to introduce a new manufacturing method for Team's carbon/Kevlar composite chassis. At last they abandoned their old pioneering 'folded-up Kellogg's packet' flat-sheet system which had in fact served them brilliantly well for five full seasons, and now they adopted integral unified moulding of a more fully-formed tub along similar lines to McLaren, Williams and Ferrari.

As in the preceding 96 Indy and 97T Formula 1 tubs, aluminium foil was used as the void-filling sandwich between the moulded composite skins, and again the bulkheads were machined from solid aluminium. Front and rear suspension geometries were revised although the inboard spring/damper units at front and rear were still pull-rod-activated. The smaller fuel cell reduced tub height behind the cockpit, which enabled the engine management system 'black box' microprocesser to be mounted there, partly for easier access and in part to simplify the wiring loom necessary.

Having learned the hard way about fuel consumption problems at Imola and Silverstone '85, another micro-computer was fitted to provide Senna and his new number 2 Johnny Dumfries with an instant continuously-monitoring fuel-state read-out on the dash panel.

Essentially this could be programmed against instantaneous fuel consumption to show how many laps' range remained within the tank. On each lap past the pits, from which the fuel monitor 'brain' could be triggered each lap by radio signal, a 'laps left' readout would be displayed which the driver could compare to the pit signal board being shown to him. If the read-out showed '50' but the signal board '51' he'd know he was using too much fuel and would run dry on the penultimate lap unless he did something about it. On the other hand, if the read-out showed '51' and the signal board '50', he'd have fuel to spare and could press harder or turn-up the boost if necessary.

Other teams had already pioneered this method of driver information with varying degrees of accuracy and success, but with an intelligent driver it provided a very valuable — if sometimes depressing — tactical factor to help him adapt his driving during a race to achieve the best possible result.

The 98T's sidepods carried water/oil radiators and air/air turbo intercooler matrices as before, while its Kevlar one-piece upper body panel now extended right down to the undertray line to permit greatest possible easy access for the mechanics.

The prototype car made its debut in Ricard testing early in February '86, before testing at Rio and then two appearing in the Brazilian GP there, where Ayrton qualified brilliantly for yet another pole position, but then had to conserve his fuel carefully in the race, being well-beaten into second place by Piquet's Williams-Honda.

Renault were now in Formula 1 solely as engine manufacturers, having closed-down their own factory racing team at the end of the 1985 season. Team Lotus was now their quasi-factory team and development partner and its power units were now being prepared and rebuilt by the Régie's Renault Sport R&D unit direct at their Viry-Châtillon HQ, whereas the other client teams — Ligier and Tyrrell — still had to rely for their V6s upon the Mecachrome satellite company's service at Bourges.

The 1986 team – ambitious superstar Ayrton Senna poses pre-season with newcomers Johnny Dumfries and the prototype 98T/1.

For the new season Bernard Dudot's engine development group at Viry-Châtillon had developed a very much modified new version of their 90-degree belt-driven four-cam V6 to form the EF15*bis*. It was available in two forms, standard or DP — which stood for *Distribution Pneumatique* — but inevitably it was reported popularly as the EF15B.

Look into the EF15*bis* DP engine's vee and there beneath all the high-pressure induction gubbins lay a shiny half-litre aluminium 'bomb'. Of course, some of the scandal-mongering Italian press instantly smelled a rat at such a sight and plunged into print head-first, suggesting that Renault were carrying some kind of go-faster fuel infuriator in it for injection at crucial moments . . .

In fact this small pressure vessel was a compressed-gas reservoir for a quite different innovation with future high-performance car potential if it could be developed successfully for long-term reliability, more than 200 miles (or a couple of hours) at a time. This was Renault's ingenious and highly-promising pneumatic valve-closing system.

The old-fashioned but trusty poppet valve-gear, with valves knocked open by a rotating cam and then closed again by some kind of metal spring, had been with us since the very early days of the heat engine.

Within postwar memory two kinds of metal valve-return springs had commonly featured in Formula 1 engines, the coil and the hairpin, with the coil occupying less space and finally supplanting the hairpin-spring. But springs like this were fiddly and heavy, and had always been a source of potential trouble.

Valve-spring breakage was historically the single most common feature in racing engine failures. They inevitably surged and their mass restricted an engine's capacity to rev freely.

Desmodromic, mechanically-closed, valve systems had been used successfully in racing car engines only by Daimler-Benz and OSCA, but otherwise expense and complication had always mitigated against desmodromics, and the coil valve-spring was a well-understood and practical device, despite its known frailties.

Now Renault Sport finalized its experiments with the new pneumatic engines in Lotus chassis, and ran it first in public in Senna's 97T at the December '85 Rio tests. Apart from one or two development-test instances where the compressed gas leaked away and the valves would eventually have met pistons if the engines had not been shut-down in time, I understand publicly, at least, it worked like a dream far into the season which is in progress as I write.

Senna gave the DP engine its race debut at Rio and it seemed that Lotus and Renault and the other

228

customer teams would have kept it all nicely to themselves but for a leak to the French press. There was also a potential technology haemorrhage to the opposition in that Renault Sport engineer Jean-Jacques His, who had been involved during the design and development period, had upped and left after the works team's closure and had joined Ferrari . . .

However, the DP valve-return system was elegantly simple, light and compact, and in conjunction with a brand-new electronic engine management system concept it unlocked the door to several other benefits.

For a start it eliminated the conventional and inevitably suspect valve springs, two per valve — 48 heavy coils in the heads of each V6. In place of each spring Renault used instead a mini piston/cylinder assembly, the piston of which was formed integrally with the valve stem to compress a gas which returned the valve. The in-vee reservoir bottle of compressed gas compensated for any leakage in the system. The trick to making it all work properly was to ensure adequate gas-sealing and valving within the system. Once they persuaded it all to work properly the benefits included considerable weight-saving in the upper engine — simply by elimination of all those springs — consequently lowering the unit's centre of gravity, which was then a great advantage to the chassis designer.

Overall reduction in the mass of the moving parts of this new system reduced problems of mechanical endurance, vibration and valve float as associated with the spring-operated alternative. The risk, which was quite common, of valve-spring breakage was eliminated.

Power could be used more efficiently and with such a great reduction in reciprocating mass of coil-springs and the self-damping effect of the pneumatic 'spring' medium, the maximum engine speed could be increased from 11,000 to 12,500rpm, making the drivers' job easier. The engine had a wider operating range, and could be used with 'shorter gearbox ratios', as Renault put it.

The system also opened new perspectives for the application of more flexible inlet and exhaust valve timing patterns. A new timing system did not involve extensive modification of the cylinder head. Initially most EF15*bis* engines were built with conventional valve-gear, but all would be equipped progressively with the DP system during the season.

In addition to this pneumatic valve system, Renault Sport had also adopted a new ignition system concept in that the EF15*bis* no longer had a distributor to carry the high-tension current to each spark-plug. The entire operation was now controlled by the car's onboard engine management computer. Each cylinder carried its own ignition coil, which located in the spark-plug well. Each of these tiny individual coils was then triggered by a low-voltage signal from the central computer, whereupon it would release the necessary high-energy spark.

The flexi-suspension layout used by Team in qualifying for the 1986 World Championship GPs aroused considerable ire and controversy in a manner which the Old Man would have loved to see. Here at Jerez, Dumfries' 98T/2 sparks its way along on its titanium skid blocks, the minimal ground clearance retrieving valuable ground-effects download . . . or had his undertray come adrift as it did at one stage during these proceedings? Some of Team's rivals suspected this was all part of the ploy!

The advantage with this system was that it provided a power level that was more effectively matched by the management system to the mixture and pressure conditions within the combustion chamber. A new generation of electronic engine management systems had been developed to refine the ignition and injection settings to suit varying operating conditions. The new ignition system could also be tailored more easily to suit each circuit, which under 195-litre fuel restriction was more vital than ever before.

The combination of the DP valve-gear and the revised ignition system saved 2.5Kg (5.51lb) weight in the upper part of these latest V6 engines, while irrespective of which valve-gear system was installed, repositioning the electronics, curving-in the inlet pipes towards each other across the vee, and lowering the plenum chamber induction logs on top had in Renault's words 'reduced the height of the projecting part of the vee by 2cm (nearly ¾in) and narrowed it overall by 4cm (1.57in)', which was a considerable reduction in cross-section, enabling team aerodynamicists to tailor more sleek and compact engine covers, cleaning-up effective airflow considerably around that vital rear end.

The old aluminium-block EF4 engine had originated under 250-litre fuel allowance regulations and had been progressively modified to accommodate 220-litre restrictions in 1984-85. During that latter season, it had come to be used most often in qualifying only. There were two basic EF4 variants available, a low-compression engine which would take a lot of turbocharger boost, and a more lean-burning, less thirsty higher-compression unit which was intended as a 220-litre race engine, running more modest boost.

It represented the ultimate development of the old sports-car-based, well-over-square EF4*bis* (86mm bore x 42.8mm stroke) V6 theme, while the new EF15 which was intended to replace it in '85 had gone to a longer stroke and narrower bore and higher compression in seeking adequate power from

Ayrton Senna's 98T/3 on its way to pole position in qualifying and subsequently second in the race at Rio, Brazilian GP, 1986; note the deflector vanes, just abaft the front suspension arms, and the exquisite finish overall.

lower boost under the 220-litre fuel economy requirements. Its bore seems to have been reduced — if Renault Sport tell us correctly — from 86mm to 80.1mm, while its stroke grew from 42.8mm to 49.4mm (displacing *c*.1,494cc), adding mid-range torque no doubt while also diminishing the vulnerable surface area of piston crown exposed to all that pressure and heat when the turbo blew and the mixture went bang.

The old EF4-series engines had not really mounted happily fully-stressed at the back of a three-quarter-length monocoque in the Cosworth DF-series' manner, on two bolts down below and via strap-plates attached to the cam covers up top. In their Renault-powered cars Team had been worried about them hinging amidships in the vertical plane, so they attached tubular struts which ran from the cam-covers diagonally to the top of the tub, where they linked-in with the roll-over bar braces to make the monocoque/engine union more rigid.

The 1985 new and reheaded EF15 engine had been physically smaller and mounted much more neatly like the DF-series Cosworth V8s. Renault Sport had put all its eggs in one basket and built their RE60 chassis for that season which could only accept the new EF15 engines, whereas Team had expected to start the season running their 97Ts on EF4*bis* V6s before converting to EF15s. Consequently their tubs had included alternative pick-ups bonded-in ready to accept either engine.

Practical experience then quickly showed that the EF4*bis*'s amenability to accepting higher qualifying boost than the EF15 made it a more effective practice proposition, and because Renault had tailored everything to the new engine they were immediately hamstrung, while Team found themselves in the box seat, with tubs ready-made to run EF4*bis* V6s for qualifying then convert easily to the economic EF15 for the race.

Now for 1986, Renault declared: 'The EF4*bis*, often used as a qualification engine during last season, is bigger than the 1986 engine and will no longer find a place in the rear of these new cars. For qualification purposes, only the EF15 unit equipped with water injection and no turbocharger waste-gate, permitting a much higher turbocharging pressure, will be used.'

The fact that Ayrton finished the Rio race with his tank virtually dry whereas Piquet's winning Honda engine had clearly overpowered the EF15*bis* in race-tune as well as finishing with plenty of fuel to spare boded ill for Team's '86 hopes.

But at Jerez, for the Spanish GP, Ayrton slammed the low-set 98T onto another brilliant pole and by reading his fuel state very carefully and fighting a spectacularly hard battle against Mansell's Williams-Honda, which he won by barely a nose on the finish line, he scored Team's first GP victory of the season, again with his tank virtually dry.

Gerard had adopted an ingenious lowering rear suspension device for qualifying which was recognized by FISA as absolutely legal despite some desperate ticking and clucking amongst the other teams, and with the 98T's undertray skid blocks sparking furiously all round the circuit the rear ground-effects diffuser surface worked very efficiently at such low ride levels to enable Ayrton to put all his Renault engine's considerable qualifying-boost power down onto the road. His own skill did the rest.

Sparking spectacularly again, the rich-run engine belching a trailing haze of black fumes, he then put his sleek 98T on pole again at Imola, but there a bad drive-shaft batch wrecked both his and his young team-mate's chances, Johnny Dumfries having done really better than might have been expected at both Rio and Jerez before retirement in both races.

Then at Monaco reigning World Champion Alain Prost found the best of qualifying period traffic to steal pole in the closing moments and despite Ayrton's best efforts in the race the TAG Turbo V6 engine in the McLaren showed vastly superior pick-up to his Renault out of the slow corners, and the McLaren chassis exhibited the traction to use it all. Consequently Lotus' number 1 settled for second place, which became third when Rosberg ripped by in the second McLaren-TAG, and there was nothing Senna could do about it. Poor Dumfries, meanwhile, had failed to qualify after a series of practice traumas.

At Spa-Francorchamps, for safety's sake after the Imola drive-shaft bearing failures, the old rear suspension with larger and stronger uprights and hubs was refitted to the 98Ts, but this tended to unbalance them, not matching the latest front-end set-up. Senna had some hairy moments in qualifying when he could not improve on fourth fastest; he then led the race, but locked-up several times, was caught by Mansell's more powerful Williams-Honda and with an eye on his cockpit fuel read-out settled for second towards the end. Dumfries, meanwhile, qualified in mid-grid, but holed an oil cooler early in the race.

The sixth round of the Championship was at Montreal. Mansell, on top form for Williams, took pole from Senna and early in the race Prost ripped second place from the young Brazilian's grasp with a move which showed the Lotus driver that not everyone was going to be intimidated by his hard-man reputation...

Senna tumbled from second to sixth immediately after this incident, and thereafter, to keep his Renault engine's consumption within limits, he pussy-footed the race, finishing a distant and lapped fifth. Johnny Dumfries had to race the spare car after his own had developed an engine problem in race-morning warm-up. His race ended when he was rammed from behind by Johansson's Ferrari.

The following weekend, on the tight and slow Detroit street circuit, the Renault DP engine's

On top of the world – Senna's win in the Detroit GP of June '86 put him back in the lead of the Driver's Championship. Here he is in his regular 98T/3 during his delayed but impressive run into first place.

consumption would be no problem. Senna out-qualified his on-form rival Mansell — who had now won four GPs with his new team since leaving Lotus — but lost the race lead to the Williams-Honda after two laps when he missed a gear. Ayrton then cut-out Mansell — in gentlemanly style — to regain the lead on the eighth lap, but after 13 of the 63 laps he detected a slow puncture and ducked into the pits for a new set of tyres. He then tigered his way back to what would otherwise have looked such an easy victory, while his teammate Dumfries at last finished a Formula 1 race, seventh and only just out of the points... Team's Brazilian star was once again heading the World Championship table which most mattered to them, while in the Constructors' title-chase they lay third behind Williams-Honda and

McLaren-TAG Turbo. Nearly eight years had passed since, with Mario Andretti's help, Team had linked the Lotus name to the Drivers' World Championship for the sixth time. Now, in 1986, that most coveted of all motor racing titles looked to be once again within their grasp...

But mid-season problems would knock them back, as at Ricard Senna crashed on spilled oil after qualifying on pole and at Brands Hatch he preferred his qualifying-chassis 98T/1 to his brand new 98T/4 for the race and its transmission failed.

Dumfries, meanwhile, continued to develop promisingly, running sixth before engine failure at Ricard, then finishing seventh at Brands Hatch where rumours first surfaced of a Lotus-Honda deal for 1987, Team's 30th season in Formula 1.

COLIN CHAPMAN

'Many a time I've seen Colin talk mechanics into doing what they genuinely think is impossible. Somehow he fires them with his own tremendous enthusiasm, and the job gets done . . . there's no doubt at all he's also an extremely shrewd busineesman — someone would have to get up very early in the morning to put one over on him! . . .'

Jim Clark

'Colin was not your normal Englishman. He was more of a Latin, both in his moments of panic and his moments of genius. He was in tears when I won in Austria and I was in tears when I heard he died. He was a bit of a father to me. A father in racing . . .'

Elio de Angelis

Anthony Colin Bruce Chapman was born on May 19, 1928, in Richmond, Surrey. He was the only child of Stanley Frank Kennedy Chapman and his wife Mary, who ran The Orange Tree pub there. Colin was only two years old when the family moved to Hornsey in North London, where his father took over The Railway Hotel, off Tottenham Lane, right beside the main-line north to Scotland from King's Cross railway station.

Just before the end of World War 2, Stan Chapman moved his family again to a house in Beech Drive, North Finchley, while continuing to run the Hornsey pub. He had great ambitions for his bright young son, and to some extent adopted the airs and graces of upper middle-class life in the London suburbs. When it suited him he would hyphenate the family name to Kennedy-Chapman, and he was certain Colin would go far when he won a place at University College, London, in 1945 to study engineering.

Colin rode to college from Finchley on a 350cc Panther motorcycle until that November, when he hit a taxi and destroyed the bike and bent himself. Thereupon, his parents decided he'd be safer on four wheels than two, so they bought him a maroon-coloured 1937 Morris Eight Tourer for Christmas.

Colin had become wildly enthusiastic about his motoring and about motor racing, avidly reading the specialist press, *The Motor*, *The Autocar* and the monthly *Motor Sport*. At University College he had developed a friendship with a fellow enthusiast named Colin Dare. They formed a loose-knit trading partnership to make a few bob in their spare time, wheeling and dealing in secondhand cars. Colin was shrewd and sharp, and developed his extraordinary open-faced persuasive eloquence by practising profitably on the wicked Warren Street pavement traders.

He learned the ropes of wheeler-dealing very quickly, supposing that ability wasn't actually in-

born, and though he lost on a few deals he seems to have won on more. When it came to dipping into the used-car dealers' biscuit tins of big white fivers he and Colin Dare on average showed a working profit.

Then, in October 1947, the axe fell. HM Government cancelled the basic private petrol ration. Private motoring collapsed virtually overnight and the secondhand motor trade collapsed with it.

At that time the two Colins were holding around £900-worth of severely used cars. Eventually they managed to unload their stock for about £400, but one stuck and could not be moved. It was a 1930 Austin 7 fabric saloon, registered PK 3493.

Colin Chapman decided to cannibalize it to build himself a special. There was a lock-up garage behind his girlfriend Hazel Williams' house in Muswell Hill, which he commandeered to do the job. The old car was stripped, its chassis members boxed for extra rigidity, and with spasmodic assistance from Colin Dare and neighbour Rodney Nuckey — and paintwork by Hazel herself — this first Chapman special was completed with a stresed-skin open body panelled in sheet marine-plywood.

He had a fixation about alloy-bodied Austin 7 specials always losing their separate tails, hence the integrated stressed plywood shell. It mirrored aviation thinking and Colin was indeed as interested in 'planes as in cars and had joined the University of London Air Squadron for basic flight training on Tiger Moth biplanes.

Once complete, the transformed PK 3493 was re-registered OX 9292, and rather than just go the usual dull way and call it an 'Austin Special', its creator chose the name 'Lotus' for 'personal reasons'. And he drove it to achieve early success in mud-plugging trials in the spring of 1948.

During that year he passed his final examinations at London University, emerging from it as

233

A.C.B.Chapman BSc. He had joined the 750 Motor Club and with 35 hours' solo flying behind him in the University Air Squadron he entered the Royal Air Force on a National Service short-term flying engagement, graduating on Harvards at Tern Hill.

He was planning a new special for use in trials, circuit racing and on the open road. This Lotus Mark 2 first ran with a Ford 8 engine which was later replaced by an 1,172cc Ford 10, acquired after a typically confusing but shrewd Chapman deal which saw him finish up with not only a better engine but also a five quid profit!

The new car was registered LJH 702, and after its first competitive outings late in 1949 it was fitted with a shapely alloy nose cowl, enclosing steerable headlights which shone through the grille.

In this car, in June 1950, Colin won a terrific scratch race at Silverstone from Dudley Gahagan's Bugatti Type 37, then for 1951 he sold the Mark 2 to Mike Lawson for trials, running against his first customer in the old Mark 1, which he had retained before it too was sold.

Colin had won his wings as an RAF pilot, but decided against taking a five-year commission, a service life not appealing to his independence. Instead, in April 1950, he took a job with the British Aluminium Company as a structural engineer studying uses of the material to save weight and if possible gain strength in numerous applications. This practical lightweight design experience coupled to his aeronautical knowledge provided the perfect foundation for what would follow.

Colin's round-faced chunky figure and his crisp, clipped theorizing had become a familiar feature of 750 MC 'noggin and natter' gatherings in various London pubs. Occasionally he would roundly criticize some highly-rated Grand Prix design like the Alfetta or the Ferrari V12 or the new V16 BRM or the prewar German cars, and in his better-lubricated moments might declare '*I'm* going to build a Grand Prix car one day'.

'Yes, of course you are', his clubmates would humour him. Most had decent jobs, like his, with a regular income and for them their 750 specials were a consuming hobby, nothing more. But it was different for Colin Chapman; he had ambition, and quite extraordinary dynamism.

To compete in the Club's new Austin 7-based 750 Formula class of racing he bought a 1930 saloon for £15. He stripped it, boxed and stiffened its chassis with tubular cross-members and completed this Lotus Mark 3 special with help from fellow 750 MC members Michael and Nigel Allen.

The brothers began construction of two similar cars for themselves and Colin moved his chassis into their garden workshop in Vallance Road, Wood Green, so all three machines could be progressed together.

But Colin's was furthest-advanced, and since a serious attack upon the 750 Championship was envisaged he soon had the Allens pitching-in to complete his car, forgetting their own. Colin was like that, he had a magnetic way of making people do what he wanted, and liking it . . .

By the end of 1951, in fact, the Allen frames had been completely stripped to keep Colin's Mark 3 running! Its ultra-slim wind-cheating alloy body weighed only 65lb, and its three-main-bearing engine was modified with Colin's famous 'de-siamesed port' cylinder head which stood 750 Formula racing on its ear.

This was typical Chapman ingenuity. He had designed a special inlet manifold welded-up from steel sheet, with each branch split internally by a steel partition which projected into the inlet port cast in the Austin block. This device improved gas-flow, the engine breathed through a big Ford V8 twin-choke Stromberg carburettor and the 95mph Mark 3 — registered LMU 3 — emerged with so much power it became the unbeatable top dog of 750 Formula racing, and frightened many much bigger and more exotic cars in Formule Libre.

'Team Lotus' in those early days saw Colin and the Allens helped by other friends like Derek Wootton, George Beresford and Ken Hawes. To raise funds, one Allen chassis was then completed as the Lotus Mark 3B, registered ONK 408, and after Mark 3's terrific success more 750 MC members wanted Lotus replicas.

In November 1951, Mike Lawson commissioned Colin to build him a new trials car to replace his now outclassed Mark 2. Consequently, Colin set up shop to do the work in the stables behind father Stan's Railway Hotel in Hornsey, Michael Allen became a partner in the venture and they took over the two remaining Mark 3 chassis.

On January 1, 1952, The Lotus Engineering Company Ltd was finally born, with Michael Allen working full-time and Colin — still employed by British Aluminium — part-time. The embryo company made and supplied many 750 Formula parts while Mark 4 was designed and built, using an Austin 7 frame as required and 1,172cc Ford engine, plus road equipment which was soon jettisoned as it became quite normal for trials cars to be trailed to the meetings.

Lawson's new Mark 4 was registered LMU 4, and Colin then designed a Mark 5 which was intended to be the first 100mph 750 Formula car embodying quite radical suspension developments, but it would never be built.

Colin had realized that if Lotus Engineering was to progress it obviously needed a quantity production model, which meant building a frame from scratch, getting away from the secondhand Austin 7 frame base. The Lotus Mark 6 did that.

No longer tied to the 7 frame for 750 Formula competition, Colin set about designing the lightest, strongest chassis structure he could. The result was a multi-tubular frame in welded steel tube with rivetted-on aluminium stress panels to add rigidity. The bare frame weighed just 55lb, rising only to 90lb with all necessary brackets and stress panels. Colin intended to offer the frame plus a kit of modified Ford parts for completion by the enthusiastic special builder. The Ford parts included a front axle beam cut amidships to provide swing-axle independent front suspension. He had schemed out this front-end's geometry with a low roll centre, to provide quite soft long-travel suspension while keeping the wheels as upright as possible during cornering to prevent up-edging of the tyres with consequent loss of adhesion.

The company's first two employees, John Teychenne and Mike Madan, joined Michael Allen at this time, and the Mark 6 prototype with a solid beam front axle and lofty ground clearance was sold to Sinclair Sweeney for trials, registered HEL 46.

The production Mark 6s which followed used the split Ford axle with low centre pivot, and normally the Ford Consul engine pulled below 1,500cc. Unfortunately the prototype with this unit was destroyed in a road accident when Nigel Allen was confronted by a milk float shooting out of a side turning in his path. Suddenly Lotus Engineering faced bankruptcy. The employees had to go . . . finances recovered as the insurers paid up, but Michael Allen had had enough excitement and he pulled out and Colin persuaded him to take the remains of the Mark 6 as his 50 per cent . . .

Colin was sure he could make a success of the 6 in kit form, while also supplying special-building components to like-minded enthusiasts. Hazel loaned him £25, and with £100 from his own account Colin formed the business into a limited company and in February 1953 began invoicing his customers on bold yellow-coloured letter-headings blazoned in green 'Lotus Engineering Co. Ltd', with the names A.C.B. Chapman, B.Sc. (Eng) and H.P. Williams as its directors.

In the early months of that year Colin built-up eight Mark 6 kits virtually single-handed, at a rate of around one every fortnight. His bodybuilders, Williams and Pritchard, moved from Edmonton into a shed in Tottenham Lane to keep pace, and while they bashed their panels by day Colin would come in at night to fabricate the kits. They emerged in customer hands with Ford 10, MG and other engines.

Colin attracted new helpers, two De Havilland aircraft company employees named Peter Ross and 'Mac' Mackintosh, who helped in draughting his ideas. Colin mentioned in passing to them that he wished he had time to build a 6 for himself, their tales at De Havilland about the cars had interested a fellow aviation engineer named Mike Costin, and he went along to the May 1953 750 MC meeting to meet Colin Chapman and look at these Lotus 6s.

Mike was a rugged, blunt character; a sound engineer, totally the practical man. He wanted a 6 of

his own, talked it over with Colin and between them they planned to build chassis number 9. They quickly completed it as 1611 H, with Ford 10 power, and they shared its driving in a series of highly successful club race outings.

Mike Costin: 'Colin had an extraordinary way of making people around him do just what he wanted. I found myself being called Lotus Technical Director. I haven't got very clear memories of those days, apart from being absolutely dog-tired and knackered all the time from working every hour God gave us.

'I do recall first realizing just how sharp Colin could be. I hardly knew him at the time and one night we were screaming back from somewhere in the 6 and somehow we became very conscious of a lot of police activity. I was sitting there thinking about all this when suddenly Colin shot up a side road and slammed on the brakes and before I'd really woken up he was round at my side of the car saying: "Come on, you drive, swop over." So we did, and I drove on, and then a bit later I'd been thinking about all this and I asked: "Why did you want me to drive?", and he said airily: "Oh, I haven't got a licence".'

Colin repaid Hazel's loan with the present of an Austin Chummy which she would drive home late at night from Hornsey to her mother's new home at Cuffley, in Hertfordshire, beyond the suburbs to the north of London.

Another enthusiast named Norman Clarke, better-known to everyone as 'Nobby', walked into the stable workshops behind the Railway Hotel one summer evening, offered to help, and became the new limited company's first formal employee.

The business expanded, Colin charming Costin, Ross and Mackintosh into spending ever more time at Hornsey. Williams and Pritchard took over the rear half of the store shed behind the pub and Stan Chapman finally handed over the rest of the building as well to his son's new company.

In 1954 Colin formed Team Lotus as a separate entity from Lotus Engineering so the fortunes of one could not affect the running or survival of the other. That October Colin and Hazel were married at Northaw Church and set up home in Gothic Cottage — a converted stables — at Monken Hadley, near Barnet.

Mike Costin had brought his aerodynamicist brother Frank Costin into the equation to clothe the latest Mark 8 sports-racing car chassis — which Colin and Mac Mackintosh cooked-up between them — in breathtakingly wind-cheating all-enveloping bodywork, and this new design led to the Lotus Mark 9, 10 and then 11 series upon which the legend would eventually be founded.

As from New Year's Day, 1955, Colin — at 26 — gave up his job with British Aluminium to put all his eggs into the Lotus basket. Mike Costin left De Havilland to run Lotus Developments and the

In 1956 Colin Chapman, the constructor-driver, won the Coupe Delamare-Debouteville sports car race at Rouen-les-Essarts. Back again here in 1957, when the race supported the French GP, Colin was beaten by Alessandro de Tomaso (in tee-shirt), whose OSCA won only after the works Lotus 11 had overheated, forcing Colin to make a pit-stop. He and de Tomaso would later have a short-lived association over a Group 7 Lotus-de Tomaso V8 engine. Colin was always a fine racing driver.

major-formula single-seater side of the rest of the story has already been told in these pages.

Colin was managing director, chief designer, sales manager and number one driver. He was indeed an excellent driver, naturally endowed with the fine eyesight, perception, balance and reflexes already demonstrated in his RAF training. There's one story about the Mark 9 hastily completed for Sebring which demonstrates his ability. There was the usual Lotus panic to get the car ready in time to catch the boat. The exhausted crew dropped it down onto the Hornsey workshop floor but as they wheeled it out they found to their horror that the steering box had gone in upside-down; steer left and the wheels turned right, steer right and they turned left!

The minutes were ticking away. If they stripped out the box they'd miss the boat. Colin was brisk as ever. 'Leave it', he snapped, 'I'll see if it's drivable.' He set off gingerly round the block, reversing all his steering movements. 'I reckon I can manage that', he announced, and set off to the docks, weaving along the straights to keep himself attuned to the back-to-front steering. That takes a special kind of co-ordination, and nerve. ACBC had both . . .

For 1956, Colin and the Costin brothers developed their legendary Lotus 11 sports car which would sweep all before it. By this time Colin had decided his cars would carry Type, not Mark

numbers since Mark 11 looked very much like the Roman-numeral 'Mark II' despite the new 11 design being nothing like a mere revised version of the Lotus Mark I. Hence Lotus publicity projected the latest model as the 'Lotus Eleven', the succeeding *Type* 12 became Colin's first single-seater, and then he produced his radical new moulded glass-fibre monocoque Type 14 Elite GT. This fragile beauty, styled by Colin's friend Peter Kirwan-Taylor, both projected Lotus onto the serious production car stage, and almost destroyed the company . . .

Colin and Hazel's first child, a daughter — Jane — was born in 1956, sister Sarah following 20 months later and brother Clive in 1962, five years after her.

During these formative years the often rotund 'Chunky' Chapman — he fought a lifelong battle against overweight — really cemented his reputation for sharpness and roguery, and mercurial design genius.

He was Britain's top chassis man. As early as 1955 Derek Wootton was working for Tony Vandervell's Formula 1 team when Vandervell was at a loss to know how to improve his cars' handling, so Derek recommended Colin Chapman. Hard-nosed old Vandervell appreciated anybody who called a spade a spade and who got straight down to business without pussy-footing around. That was entirely

Chapman's way. He examined the existing Cooper-designed Vanwall frame at length and said finally: 'You'd do best by starting again from scratch'. He spelled out why. Vandervell commissioned him to design a new spaceframe chassis, Colin introduced Frank Costin to do the body design for it and so the ultimately World Championship-winning teardrop-shaped Vanwall was born.

Subsequently BRM called in Colin as suspension consultant to lead them out of the wilderness with their four-cylinder front-engined P25 cars. All stepping-stones on Lotus' own way into Formula 1.

Certainly the shrewd and quick-thinking Colin also upset many people, but very few could ever nail him down. He had an extraordinary facility for explaining his actions and manoeuvrings in such a detailed and persuasive manner that even the most aggrieved customer would usually end up sympathizing with Chunky's problems in running a specialized performance car company . . . they'd go away home and only later come to, shake-off the spell and realize they'd been turned over *again* . . .

That facility became a standing joke where Colin was concerned. Everyone in racing knew what he was like, and if you made allowances then you might emerge with a decent deal and certainly a potential race-winning car.

The Elite was designed in 1956-57 and was not ready for full-scale production until early 1959 when Lotus moved into their brand-new purpose-built factory at Delamare Road, Cheshunt, in Hertfordshire, just north of the capital.

The plant was running before its official opening on Wednesday, October 14, 1959. Now Lotus Engineering was split into three separate companies under Chapman control. Lotus Components produced the road and race kit cars, Lotus Cars produced the Elite, whose production successors were to be designed by Lotus Developments. Team Lotus, the racing team, remained a separate entity — Colin's own baby.

At Cheshunt in 1959-60, Colin appreciated he could not afford to manufacture the complex Elite moulded shells. So he sub-contracted GRP specialists Maximar — a company experienced in moulding boat hulls — to supply the first 250 from Lotus moulds. But quality was so bad that in September 1959 an alternative order was placed with Bristol Aeroplane Plastics Ltd for new Series II Elite shells, delivery beginning in July 1960.

The Elite project was financially a disaster. In 1959 Lotus lost £29,062 and in 1960 the predicted cash flow from US Elite sales didn't materialize. Like its founder, Lotus had always had a reputation for sailing close to the wind. Typically, when its lads went to Climax to collect FWE engines for the Elite they had to wait while Climax's accounts staff first cashed the cheque . . .

At one stage Bristol Aeroplane was set to foreclose on the Lotus bodyshell debt of £100,000. But Peter Kirwan-Taylor, by profession a Hill Samuel merchant banker, found an 'in' to Bristol's

'The Guv' goes testing. This is Colin at Silverstone late in 1960 with the Lotus 19 rear-engined sports-racing car.

finance director and saved the day by renegotiation.

Lotus Components' racing car and Lotus Seven kit sales kept Cheshunt alive. Team won its first outright F2 and F1 races that season, and the Chapman/Lotus Formula 1 legend had been launched.

Through 1961 the backbone-chassised Elan was developed, emerging at Earls Court in October '62. Where Lotus had lost — by Colin's own reckoning — 'around £100 on every Elite sold', Elan sales were well in profit. The Lotus-Ford twin-cam engine had been introduced, and was productionized by Ford.

Here Colin had pulled another of his famous strokes. He had commissioned ex-*Autocar* magazine technical editor-cum-Coventry Climax engine designer Harry Mundy to draw the new head. He gave Harry the choice of either a flat fee — reputedly £50! — or a royalty on each head sold. Somehow, I *can't* imagine how, Harry got the impression that only a handful would be made for racing, so he took the flat fee. Then Ford showed an interest, and tens of thousands were made to Lotus' profit. . .

By 1964, Group Lotus was a serious motor manufacturer, selling 1,195 Elans — more in one year than the entire Elite run. Group turned a profit of £113,000. A close relationship with Ford was benefiting both, Lotus commercially, Ford promotionally.

Through the 'sixties Group Lotus blossomed. It outgrew Cheshunt. An ideal new site was found on Hethel Aerodrome, near Wymondham in Norfolk. A new 151,000 square foot factory was commissioned, Group moving there in 1966.

During their last year at Cheshunt, they'd set new records for the third consecutive year, building 2,505 cars — including 986 Lotus-Cortinas — turning-over a record £2,156,000 and boosting profit by £97,000 to £251,000.

The Chapman family had lived in Beech Hill Avenue, Hadley Wood during the latter days at Cheshunt, now in Norfolk Colin had his dream house built for him at East Carleton, fussing and clucking about every detail, at one point having fresh-built walls demolished and begun again because he didn't like the brick. While it was being built the family lived in Kent House, just outside Norwich, which in his impatience he evidently hated.

By 1968 at Hethel, Group profitability had soared from 11.5 per cent to 16.5 per cent. The Lotus name was world-famous with its Formula 1 World Championship titles, Indianapolis 500-Miles track classic success and that growing range of magnificent-handling and quick, if often delicate, plastic-bodied sporting cars.

And the more experienced he became, and the more committed to so many projects involving both racing and road cars, the more vivid and mercurial Colin seemed. He always had a short fuse.

One classic story which demonstrates Colin's extraordinary impatience-cum-driving skill involved the Team Lotus trip to Reims for the 1960 French GP. At that time Team used a small Ford Zephyr-engined transporter which was invariably wildly overloaded, and even then still had to tow a double-deck two-car four-wheeled trailer.

One of its problems was that it could only surmount the loading ramp into one of the Channel Air Bridge Bristol Freighters if its intrepid driver gave it peak revs and then popped the clutch. Quite regularly the engine would judder wildly and poke its fan through the radiator. It did this trick during a typical last-minute dash to the French GP at Reims, mechanic Dick Scammell and his mate Mel finding themselves stranded at Le Touquet with the radiator ruined.

Eventually Colin arrived in his Raymond Mays-modified Ford Zephyr saloon. It ran multiple Amal carburettors and was a very quick car. They abandoned the transporter, hitched the two-car trailer, plus the kit from the truck, onto the Zephyr's tow-ball and rushed off.

At the first corner the entire rig speared straight on, with Dick cowering under the dash while Colin sorted it all out, muttering 'No brakes . . . no brakes', oblivious to the *c.* 2-ton trailer pushing from behind.

Colin was a fine and brave driver. The rig was soon up around 85mph and Dick recalls the journey along the undulating roads of northern France as a kind of obstacle race. The faster Colin drove the more the trailer weaved. Dick swears Frenchmen were pulling off the road ahead as they saw Team Lotus approaching, slewing from verge to verge, throttle nailed to the floor by the Guv'nor's large right foot.

Over one crest a fork loomed-up. Colin demanded directions and young Dick grabbed for the map. 'I was very young and overawed by it all, and couldn't pronounce the road signs. I ummed and aahed and Colin suddenly snatched the map, controlled a big weave with the other hand and yelled "I suppose I've got to read the bloody map as well!". I think more by luck than judgment we took the right fork'.

Somehow Colin found his way down a single-track lane, Dick was looking for something under the dash when he heard him mutter: 'She's just got to stop this time!', whereupon heavy braking jammed him down against the parcel shelf. When he finally struggled upright there was a farm tractor with very wide trailer blocking the lane ahead. Team's trailer was almost on its ear half up the bank behind the Zephyr as the phlegmatic Frenchman chugged impassively past . . .

Now Colin was purple with rage. Determined to make up time he hacked his way through traffic. Overtaking one big lorry the trailer took a desperate swing and Dick just knew all was lost: 'You could see the side of the trailer out through the side windows of the car and there was no way anybody could get it back into shape . . . but Colin did.'

This treatment was too much. A few kilometres further and a terrific bang and lurch announced that the trailer had thrown a wheel. The remaining wheel that side looked OK, so Dick pumped its tyre up to 50psi while Colin stamped about glancing at his watch, and a lorry driver stopped to return the missing brake drum.

Colin resumed his wild drive, unabashed, but the remaining wheel could only stand a few more kilometres at 85mph and an even louder bang, a lurch and a fearful grating noise announced its departure.

Now Colin 'did his crust'. 'You bloody FOOL!' he ranted at Dick, 'you over-tightened those wheel nuts, you must have done . . .'

Fortunately for Dick, there were the nuts still on their studs, the tortured steel wheel having pulled clean off over them. Now the trailer still had two wheels left, but both were on the same side. There were still miles to go.

Miraculously, the two 18s had survived all this undamaged, so then Colin had them unloaded and put Dick in one, Mel in the other to drive them on the open road. The trailer wheels were fitted one each side and Colin set off to tow it along behind. Some peasants from the fields were recruited to push-start the Lotuses and since they'd never seen such cars before, much less push-started them, the 18s' take-off left a cloud of rubber-smoke hanging over a heap of French farm-hands lying in the middle of the *Route Nationale*.

Eventually they all arrived safely in the Reims-Gueux paddock, with Colin beginning to stream and suffer the hay-fever which dogged him throughout his life. It had been a typical Team trip . . .

Colin once told me reflectively: 'It seems that the more successful you become, the more detractors you attract'. He never quite relished stories against himself, but he could always join in the laughter and sometimes when he and Andrew Ferguson would start reminiscing amongst a group of other Lotus old-hands the Guv' himself would laugh 'til the tears streamed down his face.

Until the end of his racing days he always enjoyed being the leader of the gang, as Leo Wybrott — Team's chief mechanic in 1969-70 — recalled: 'He would give us fearful rollickings if things went wrong, but he always liked to feel that it was his lads who'd had the wildest night out, or his lads who needed bailing out of jail! It seemed that if you worked for Team Lotus you acquired a special sort of licence and it seemed to hold you aloof from Lotus Cars and other racing people. I sensed that no matter what you did, or what trouble you found yourself in, Colin could somehow protect you, and I often thought he admired some of the wild acts his

Team boys would perform . . .'

Herbie Blash, mechanic 1968-71, recalling the 1969 Monaco GP: 'Colin had missed practice due to the Indianapolis race and arrived at 7 o'clock race morning. As he arrived at our garage near Nice we were busy loading the cars into the transporter to take them across to Monte Carlo . . . We very proudly showed him our latest construction, a rear wing we had constructed during practice. Colin immediately stopped us loading the cars and took us to the cafe next to the garage. He then proceeded to design a new rear wing on the tablecloth.

'I protested, saying we only had two hours before we had to be at the circuit. He then said that if he didn't have properly designed rear wings he'd rather not race, he was that dedicated to his cars winning and not just coming second.

'We rushed straight into the job with Colin working alongside us. By the time we reached Monte Carlo all the access roads had been closed. We unloaded the cars and finally got them onto the track just as the warm-up lap started. Our only pit equipment was a signalling board as once the race started we couldn't reach the transporter again, and Graham won his fifth Monaco GP and his team-mate Dickie Attwood finished third . . .'

Rex Hart, mechanic 1971-79: 'I saw Colin Chapman in many moods . . . He was a hard taskmaster, always wanted his money's worth out of his men, but he was hard on himself as well. I remember the look of shock on his face when Ronnie popped his car onto pole in Brazil, our second race of that year, as he realized how much competition there would be in the team, but deep down he loved it.

'There was the time testing at Silverstone with no motor-home, so he organized and laid out the lunch on the ramps at the back of the truck, not quite the sort of thing most MDs of large companies would do . . .'

David Lazenby: 'One of his greatest attributes was his ability to lift people and inspire them to greater efforts in the face of impossible odds . . . and he had an ability to take knife-edged impossible decisions and be right. At Indy in 1965 the night before the race he recalculated fuel jets for the Ford 4-cam engine in such a way as to run the whole race with only two stops for fuel — if he had been wrong the engine would have blown. As it was, he was exactly right and Jim Clark ran to that convincing victory.'

Mechanic Bob Sparshott recalls another episode at Indy that year which showed Colin at his best: 'We were working flat-out in the garage one evening when we had a visit from a party of Ford executives. Ford were supplying engines fully dyno-tested and ready to fit, but we had been having problems with them . . .

'As the visitors entered, an engine was being removed from its crate, Colin interrupted his conversation with the Ford head man, walked across to the engine and asked David Lazenby: "Do they all come in like this with no inlet trumpets or throttle equipment?". A very white-faced Laz confirmed that all the engine ancillaries had to be changed over each time.

'At this Colin made one of the most spectacular moves I have ever seen, he jumped up onto the box lid and delivered a speech that Sir Laurence Olivier would have been proud of.

'He said there was no way in which we could or would win Indy unless engines came in complete and that otherwise we might as well pack up and go home. We were all taken completely by surprise, as were the visitors from Ford — there were never again any incomplete engines . . .'

In his later years, having achieved one personal ambition by becoming a millionaire by the age of 40 — when Lotus Cars Ltd became a public company — Colin built a reputation as a very generous employer, both personally and financially.

One day in 1974, Peter Warr had been driving down to a test session at Snetterton with Ralph Bellamy beside him when a US Army truck pulled out of a side turning in their path. There was no avoiding a terrible accident, which smashed Peter's legs. He recalled floating in and out of consciousness in intensive care, 'suddenly aware of a nurse saying to somebody "No you can't come in here, no really sir, he's not well enough to receive visitors" and Colin's voice telling her he was coming in anyway because he had something for me. I certainly didn't feel like talking to him but there he was clutching this enormous cardboard box. I remember he asked how I was feeling and telling me not to worry about anything to do with the team, just to concentrate on recovery. And then as he turned to go he said "Here, you'll be needing this" and plonking down this enormous box and explaining to the nurse how it all worked.

'It was a portable colour television, which you just couldn't obtain for love nor money in those days, yet somehow he'd got hold of one and brought it in specially for me . . .'

After Colin's death, into the mid-eighties, Peter himself would occasionally be rubbished by some in Formula 1 as 'that flash so-and-so with the gold Rolex'. He did always wear a gold Rolex watch, but there was a very good reason why: 'After I'd been with Lotus for 10 years Colin presented me with a watch which he'd had suitably engraved. I treasured that watch until one day we were flying back from somewhere in one of Colin's light 'planes and we landed at Heathrow. Now Heathrow never liked light aircraft arriving there, but Colin had some good reason to want to land there instead of anywhere less busy or important, but as we landed there was a thump-thump and a lurch and we'd had a puncture. We stopped on the runway and jumped out to have a look at the damage, but the control tower people were jumping up and down and bawling at us to clear the runway. So we scrambled back on board and Colin taxied off onto the grass and we eventually got it all sorted out.

'We were just leaving the airport when I suddenly realized I'd lost my watch, the strap must have burst and it had fallen off without my noticing it, somewhere out on the runway. Colin asked what was the matter when I started cursing and I told him. There was no going back to hunt for it so I just put it down to bitter experience, the watch was lost . . .

'A few days later Colin walked past my desk and left a box on it, saying in passing "That's for you".

'It was the gold Rolex, inscribed from the Guv'nor. And *that's* why I now wear it all the time . . .'

Another side of Colin was his vanity. One time at Monaco Tony Southgate was confronted by a furious Colin who became so angry about something that he threw his cap on the ground and jumped up and down on it. Tony tried to control it, but couldn't help himself. He began to laugh.

'Colin realized he'd made a fool of himself but he wouldn't bend down to pick up his own cap in front of me. He called one of the mechanics over and ordered him to pick it up instead . . .'

Tony had blotted his own copybook with The Guv' soon after joining Team from Shadow. At a meeting they had been discussing modifications for the next race and how all the work necessary could be squeezed into the time available. Tony had piped-up unwisely to say: 'Well, we'll just have to do as much as we can and leave what's left over to the race after that . . .' There was a deathly hush. That wasn't the Team Lotus way at all . . .

Few people were on the receiving end of as many regular pastings from 'The White Tornado', as Tony Southgate christened Colin, as Group PR man Don McLauchlan. 'I normally got fired at least every month, and if six or eight weeks went by without my being fired I used to worry about it.' Sometimes he was certainly ordered to achieve the impossible.

Once, after flying over recently-acquired Ketteringham Hall, Colin had noticed that it still appeared to be carrying wartime camouflage. After landing he buttonholed Don. 'Get onto the US Embassy in Grosvenor Square', he ordered, 'Ask for the Air Attaché and tell him to get somebody up here straight away to scrape that camouflage paint off my building!'

Another time Hethel was expecting a Royal visitor and Colin wanted the main foyer approach to the factory tidied up. The lawns there were wet and spongey after incessant rain, so Don decided paving should be laid to carry a red carpet. Colin would only sanction that if the slabs were to be lifted immediately afterwards and the turves replaced.

'Then he wanted some flag-poles, must have flag-poles. Don! Get some flag-poles up! So I had some flag-poles put up and next day I was sitting at my desk in our huge open-plan office which everybody shares and where very little goes on without everybody noticing when suddenly there was Colin telling me very loudly that he had a bone to pick with me and that I should follow him, Right Now.

'So I was marched out through the front door to the far side of the service road. "Now look at those flag-poles", he said, "I want them moved immediately". I said you can't have them moved immediately, they're set in concrete. "Look at the poles against the front door!", he yelled. "Do you see anything strange about them?." And I said "Yes, the door is offset between them, they are not evenly spaced". And he said "Exactly!" and fired me.

'But then I called up maintenance and asked them to turn on the fountains which stand there, and as the fountains began to play — as they would during the visit — Colin could see how they and the flag-poles *were* evenly-spaced, and it was the fountains which caught the eye, not the door.

'There was a long pause, then he just grunted and said "Mmm — I suppose you think you've won that one then!." . . . and off he marched.'

Andrew Ferguson recalled how, one time at Indy in the mid-'sixties, the Old Man paused wearily in the middle of a typically hectic day riven with mechanical disaster and political strife . . . to share a philosophical moment.

'He turned to me and said: "You know Andrew, we're mad going racing like this. What do we do it for? We've got £150,000 capital investment here for a return of about 2 per cent . . . it's stupid.

'Point is, we couldn't have as much fun doing anything else . . .".'

The Australian, Peter Collins, who took Peter Warr's old place as team manager for three seasons, 1979-81, went through all the traumas with Chapman of Team's bad times through that period, and recalled his view of the Old Man's strengths and weaknesses like this:

'He had this absolutely incredible ability to motivate people, to get 110 per cent out of them when they only thought they could produce 105 per cent. He was a fantastic teacher, partly by example, but also by making it clear that if you wanted to do the job properly, then you'd better find out how to do it yourself. He never told you if you were doing things correctly, but if you were doing things wrong, you'd soon find out.

'The flipside of the coin was that his maximum interest only came when there was a project which was technically different; the 80 and the twin-chassis 88. If it was a conservative quantity, a progression from the previous year's car, he couldn't summon much enthusiasm for it. Like the 81, a ground-effect car with sliding skirts. Not interested. He liked to break new ground and be adventurous.'

The noisy controversy which submerged and eventually banned the 88 concept fundamentally affected Colin's attitude to Formula 1 for his final season-and-a-half.

Peter Collins again: 'He couldn't see any reason why that car wasn't legal, and from that point onwards there was no stopping him . . . He saw it as what Formula 1 was all about; pioneering, innovation, minimum restriction on the things you could do. When he lost the battle over it, I think it pretty well killed his interest and enthusiasm for

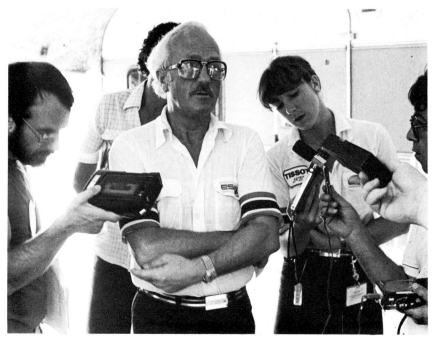

Disgust, dismay and disillusionment are written all over Colin Chapman's face as he holds a press conference following the banning of the 88 from the Brazilian GP – the second race in succession from which this ingenious design had been excluded. Two weeks later the same thing would happen in Argentina, whereupon Chapman would pack his bags and leave, his patience exhausted.

Grand Prix racing. It made life very difficult for him from that point on. He'd pioneered a lot of things during his career and he'd never been beaten like this. In fact he became so single-minded about it that he rather lost his sense of reality over the 88 problem . . . That reality was that he would not get it accepted simply because there were too many people banked up on the other side . . .'

Towards the end, none of the energy but some of the old magic Midas touch seemed to have waned. Colin would still fizz around his empire at a frantic pace, but problems abounded and they were not such as could be solved magically with flair and brilliance.

Even before Team's fortunes slumped in 1979, the rest of Group Lotus was having a thin time. In 1968-69 Lotus Cars had first developed its own engine, the LV-series, based on a GM-Vauxhall slant-four. But in '69 a rare strike interrupted Hethel production and the Government's financial 'squeeze' cut profit for the first time in years. Despite building a record 4,506 cars, with a record turnover of £5,285,000, profit fell to the 1967 level.

Group continued to invest heavily in 1970, their £300,000 body laminating plant becoming the most modern in Europe, but from over 900 employees at the start of the year it slimmed to about 650 by its end. Profitability plummeted to 6.5 per cent, and plans were laid for taking the product line up-market, away from the sports car enthusiast towards the high-paid young executive sector.

The new Elite was released with its completely new-style bodyshell and Lotus-made engine. Group had aimed high, virtually doubling the price range of its cars overnight. Almost immediately the 1974 Oil Crisis struck, the economy went into spasm, and Group was exposed way out on a fragile limb.

Hethel's staff was drastically reduced as stocks lay unsold. It was the worst time, staff down around 300, minimal production. Through the mid-'seventies Group struggled on. But Team's exploits ensured that the image survived and it attracted a growing volume of research and development work from outside customers.

Through the summer of 1978 Team Lotus dominated Formula 1 with the 79s on the crest of the wave, winning the World Championship titles yet again. Otherwise, 1978 was pretty bad for Lotus overall. Group financing had always been precarious, with Colin's loyal finance director Fred Bushell somehow balancing the books. Capital had been assembled for years from a mish-mash of small inputs. Now Fred came up with more stable long-term support from American Express, who used Group to spearhead their move into the UK merchant banking risk business.

Then De Lorean rode into town. At that time Lotus stock was so depressed that Group was valued at only some £3 million, *less* than Porsche had just *quoted* De Lorean to develop his car!

Colin wanted Group's high-tech capabilities to form a kind of British Porsche, providing rapid-reaction R&D for the inevitably less-flexible giants of the motor industry worldwide. Both Chapman and Bushell had serious reservations about the project which John De Lorean depicted, but the prospect of redesigning the American's dream car into a practicable proposition could bring just the financial injection Group desperately needed.

Short-term the De Lorean deal did just that. Long-term the project's ultimate collapse involved the Lotus name in grotesque scandal and rumour. Much of that was centred upon the elaborate financial structures erected ostensibly to protect Group from the effects of any possible US product-liability damages suit in which a legal settlement considered equitable by America's ludicrous standards could easily wipe-out Lotus overnight.

Serious damage was also caused simply by the immense effort required to design a production De Lorean virtually from scratch in just 22 months. Concentration upon that project crippled Lotus development of its own future model line.

What money did reach Group from De Lorean paid well for their massive 100 per cent effort on DMC's behalf. The work tailed off during 1981 by which time Lotus had designed a practicable car, in effect from a clean sheet of paper, in a matter of mere months.

Industry moguls — notably in Detroit — recognized this as an outstanding performance, and as an advertisement it succeeded in persuading them to enlist Lotus R&D's services. But meantime Lotus Cars' own markets had collapsed in the world recession. In 1980 they built a mere 365 cars, but struggled on, propped-up by R&D profits. Then came DMC's collapse, John De Lorean's arrest and the scandal which followed.

Through Colin's last months his creation was beset on all sides. American Express had taken fright at Group's dwindling assets sometime earlier and had pulled the plug. Group was now deep in the red, and some of the DMC mud was beginning to stick. Some of the Government funding behind DMC had been destined for Lotus and payments had been made into one end of the system which had failed to emerge at Group's end. Intensive investigation by the DMC receivers, the tax authorities and a Parliamentary committee nailed John De Lorean quite effectively but still 'the missing millions' were not fully accounted for. Rumours abounded.

Ultimately Group Lotus would be totally cleared and it is not within my remit to comment further. Suffice to say here that pressures on 'The Guv' had been intense. Perhaps most damaging of all to Lotus Cars, the vital US market was dead as a dodo. At a December '82 dinner in London, Colin saw an old acquaintance, David Wickins, rough-tongued, rugged head of British Car Auctions and a man known for his acquisition and revival of under-valued ailing companies. Wickins greeted him with a knowing 'How's it going?'. Colin mentioned in passing 'I might give you a call in a few weeks' time', but he did not live to make it.

He died at East Carleton Manor in the early hours of the morning on December 16, 1982, having spent the previous day in Paris on business before flying home. He was only 54, he'd always fought a battle with his weight, but seemed very fit. His massive heart attack struck therefore without any warning. It was over quickly.

Anthony Colin Bruce Chapman, CBE, RDI, BSc (Eng), FRSA, was buried at a private funeral in the small village churchyard of St Mary's, East Carleton, on December 22 and a packed public Memorial Service dedicated to him was held in Norwich Cathedral six weeks later, on Saturday, February 12.

Team's veteran chief mechanic, Bob Dance, struck just the right note in his piece in the tribute issue of *Lotus World* which followed. He had joined Lotus in 1960, and stayed with Team until the end of 1969, then returned in December '76 and is still with them as I write. At Rio in '84 he was talking quietly with Nigel Mansell when Ken Tyrrell walked by, saw them in conversation and interrupted, just to tell the driver 'I don't know what he is saying, but you listen to him, because you can bet it is worth listening to . . .'

In *Lotus World* Bob wrote: 'Just before the start at Monaco I said to the Guv, "Well, here we go again, I wonder what result we will get today?" During our brief chat we saw the Ferrari boys having a bit of a drama and he quipped that we had at least another 30 years to go to get up to Enzo Ferrari's record.

'Another part of a conversation that stuck in my mind was when he told me "No-one is indispensable" and that he expected things to carry on even if he was not around.

'So when we received the stunning news from Peter Warr at that Snetterton test, these two remarks immediately came back to mind, and I thought, well, we'd better get on with the job, and I am sure with the enthusiasm of the Chapman family, and the support of our sponsors, our strong team will still be a force to be reckoned with for many seasons to come . . .'

As usual, he was right.

David Wickins did take command of Group and ensure its survival, eventually in early 1986 being instrumental in selling control to General Motors. Fred Bushell and Hazel Chapman, with continued sponsorship support from Imperial, ensured Team's survival with Peter Warr in executive control. Gerard Ducarouge became chief engineer and within a year the black-and-gold was back on pole position.

Within three years Team was winning again and within four the opposition was jumping up and down and muttering about Lotus being 'up to something, they're bending the rules without breaking them, how can they continually qualify so quickly . . .?'.

Colin would have loved that, perhaps even more than merely winning, for to win alone without that buccaneering style had never quite been sweet enough.

DESIGNERS AND DESIGNING

'Everything you get done in this life really depends to some degree
upon team effort, but first you have to create the team . . .'

Colin Chapman

'He was inclined to trim designs down until they were too light and
fragile to be reliable, but his conceptual thinking and genius was
just unmatched . . .'

Len Terry

Colin Chapman was, of course, the dominant influence on Lotus major-formula racing car designs throughout his life. In general terms he framed the general concept of all Lotus cars, but in his last 10 years, and occasionally even earlier, this conceptual thinking would be framed more as a series of questions which he set before his design staff, then leaving them to do the donkeywork in finding the answers.

Thereafter his innate talent would blossom as his remarkable eye for a better way of doing things would hone a design, trimming and pruning and streamlining it down to the viable minimum, in which every single component would wherever possible combine with its neighbours to perform somehow more than the obvious number of vital functions.

He was himself a very fine draughtsman and he had the artistic talent to sketch designs and ideas three-dimensionally so that even someone with the most feeble grasp of how to read an engineering drawing could still see clearly what he was driving at.

Where Team Lotus cars were concerned, Colin was very much the irresistible driving force behind his staff's quick-fire development and detailing of any design. He drove them hard, but he was always prepared to drive himself just as hard, and in the latter days they knew that if they delivered the goods he was a generous employer.

Over the years, he worked with a number of other design engineers and draughtsmen. He wielded the ultimate power of life or death over any design, and every detail of it . . . but how much attention and time he devoted to them depended totally upon the other contemporary pressures upon him.

Like so many great designers he worked best when he had a like-minded partner alongside him to bounce ideas back and forth. Well, perhaps 'partner'

is too strong a word, for essentially there was seldom any question about who was The Boss. With another perhaps more cautious designer's mind in train to recognize fallacious thinking or weak points in any of his concepts, Colin Chapman could lead the world . . .

But before aspiring to such domination, it was initially a case of 'today the 750 Formula, tomorrow ze vorld!'

In the early days of Lotus, the Allen brothers provided Colin's necessary foil as well as four more hands, useful premises and a lot more muscle. At Lotus Engineering, 'Mac' Mackintosh and Peter Ross brought their aeronautical design engineering expertize to Colin's assistance. They all grew together. From 1954 to '62, Mike Costin always provided the hard-nosed practical development sense and tireless will to get cars prepared properly while still managing somehow to meet Colin's impossible deadlines.

He once told me: 'My time with Lotus I remember really as just a blurr, but the one thing I do clearly recall being very chuffed about is curing the frothing in the 6's carburettors by sawing through the inlet manifold branches, and then pushing the halves back together again joined by sawn-off lengths of rubber hose, which killed the vibration . . .'

Ian Jones detailed many of Colin's late-'fifties designs, like the Type 12 Formula 2 car, but one of Chapman's most significant collaborators was then Len Terry. Len was building his own Terrier 1,172cc sports-racing special, basing the first on one built originally by John Teychenne of Progress Chassis and Lotus fame. Len worked as Colin's design draughtsman at Hornsey for a princely £12 a week. He and Colin never got on really well together. Both had strong ideas of what was right. Len freely describes himself as 'being very Bolshie in those days, I'd argue with anybody if I thought I was right'. But both he and Chapman were good draughtsmen, and Len shared Colin's creative ability to sketch clearly in 3D which enabled all concerned to visualize clearly what they were arguing about.

Len recalled simply: 'Colin was brilliant. There's no other word for it. He'd occasionally come into me and maybe I'd got a problem translating one of his schemes and I'd start to explain why this bit couldn't fit in where he wanted it because that bit had to go there, and so on. And many times I'd be doing this and before I'd even finished the explanation he'd come up with the most elegant and practical solution. His mind was so quick he could rush on far ahead of my explanation, grasping exactly the problems I was trying to describe, and even before I had finished explaining it all he had then gone on right through the next process, which was to come up with a solution.

'That's brilliance, there's no doubt in my mind on that score.

'Generally speaking, although we often struck sparks off each other personally, we had a very good design relationship. When he was thinking out an original design he'd usually work at home and draft out a one-fifth scale general arrangement drawing, plan, sideview and cross-sections if necessary, to demonstrate what he wanted, and he'd bring that in for me to work-up and detail properly-scaled drawings, and at that stage we'd find the snags. And then we'd start to work out the solutions between us. I'd come up with a few and he'd come up with more . . .'

Len had two stints with Lotus, the first from March 1958 to August '59 and the second from September 1962 to May 1965. He left the first time to undertake private consultancy work, which sat uneasily with being employed full-time by Lotus, and he returned after hurting himself in a nasty accident at Oulton Park in 1961, while driving his Terrier Mark 2, on loan from its new owner. Mike Costin had put him in touch with Alpine of Dieppe, who wanted a Le Mans car designed, Len began doing freelance work for Lotus at that time and then, when Mike left to go full-time in Cosworth Engineering, Colin invited the crew-cut Len Terry to return in his place, as chief designer.

That rather put chief draughtsman Alan Styman's nose out of joint, and after having detailed the original, epochal Lotus 25, he had left, as would his colleague Ron Hickman — who eventually achieved fame and a Chapman-style fortune by inventing the Workmate DIY aid, and assiduously protecting the patents he held on it.

It had been during Len's first stint with Lotus that the Type 17 sports-racing car had been one source of friction between him and Colin: 'Eric Broadley's pretty little Lolas had blown off the Lotus 11s in 1,100cc sports car racing, so for 1959 Colin laid out the Type 17 as a tiny little car using Chapman-strut — or MacPherson-strut — suspension on all four wheels. He brought his scheme into me, saying "This one's going to make the Lola look like a London bus".

'He was right, it did, but it wouldn't work. The strut suspension was OK at the rear where there was plenty of height for a nice long strut, but to keep the car's noseline low you could only use very short struts there. After studying the scheme for a long time I finally concluded they wouldn't work, because there's a lot of sideload generated at the front into corners and as the sideload came on I suspected the suspension struts would bind. Like a bicycle pump, if you pump the handle straight in-and-out, it moves easily. But you put a sideload on the handle and you'll find the shaft binds on the cylinder and there's a lot of stiction between the two.

'I told Colin I thought this would happen, but he wouldn't have it. Then in practice we found that as soon as the 17 looked at a corner sideload came on, the front suspension locked up and you got terrific understeer as the front tyres unstuck and began to slide. The problem then was that once the tyres had lost adhesion there was no sideload to make the suspension stick, so it started working again, the front tyres — to which you'd just applied more lock to compensate for the understeer — would suddenly grip and instantaneously the tail would come round like a whiplash!

'By the middle of 1959 I was off to work for Syd Greene to modify his son Keith's 17 to double-wishbone front end, but before I could do it Colin recalled all the customer 17s and they were all converted to double wishbones at Lotus' expense. The trouble then was that the front of the chassis had been tailored to support the struts, so fitting wishbones to it was all a compromise and it wasn't until right at the end of the season that the modified cars finally came good.

'I'd tried to explain it to him but he wouldn't have it.'

Len recalls two other exceptions to the rule of Colin's hot-blooded kind of brilliance:

'On the Lotus-Cortina he'd located the live back axle by a triangulated A-bracket low in the middle and radius-arms either side. I'd used a similar system on my Terrier Mark 2, but on the Cortina Colin used tubular radius-arms and the A-bracket was also in tube. They were mounted in very stiff rubber bushings so when the car rolled it actually tried to twist each of those tubular links which were stiff torsionally, which meant they acted as a kind of giant rear anti-roll bar and gave the car enormous rear roll-stiffness.

'Colin and Jimmy were going off to Snetterton testing and I'd argued this out with Colin, predicting the car would oversteer like a pig, but again he wouldn't have it, it was just me being Bolshie.

'Day after the test I asked him what it was like and he said "Oh it oversteered like a pig, it was looking into corners before I'd reached them". I said: "Just like the man said", to which he replied: "Well, you sort it out then!".

'So I mounted the A-bracket on a very heavily-threaded trunnion so it could skew without adding roll-stiffness and we made the radius-arms out of channel-section which could also twist relatively easily to eliminate roll stiffness and it worked.'

That was one of his first jobs after returning to Cheshunt in 1962. Subsequently he argued incessantly with Colin again over the Lotus 30: 'I think Colin was perhaps a bit jealous of the Ford GT work going to Broadley when we'd had the Lotus-Ford Indy contract and so many other links with Ford. The 30 was in many ways fated to go the same way as the 17. It's ironic, but it seemed whenever Colin tried to put one over on Lola it all went wrong.

'If you believed everything that was written about the Elan backbone chassis its stiffness was around 4,000lb/ft per degree, but I think one was properly tested at not much more than a quarter of that. By that time the 30, which was to take a big Ford V8 engine, had been designed along the same principles. Where the Elan chassis formed a 'Y' shape the 30's was like a tuning fork with parallel extensions beyond the arms of the 'Y'. They were originally only channel-section, which allowed them to flex, and the bodywork was one giant glass-fibre moulding like a saddle with hatches in it which sat over the backbone and bolted to it.

'Like the 17 it was a lovely-looking thing, but when Colin gave me his scheme and said: "Study that and comment" I filled two foolscap sheets with close-spaced notes. But he stuck to his guns. The only thing he was prepared to change was to make the chassis arm extensions box-section instead of channel, while the backbone was still to be made of very thin-gauge sheet and so I told him I wanted no part of it, and refused to work on the thing . . .

'Sure enough, the early 30 chassis were so flimsy their panelling would just "oil-can" as soon as a load was applied to them, and some took on a permanent set as soon as they'd been run! The one-piece body was so inaccessible with its little hatches that setting-up and general work on the car was terribly difficult and time-consuming, the little 13-inch wheels had twee little 1½-litre F1-sized brakes inside them, tucked away from cooling air . . . and it was all a recipe for disaster.

'But believe me, those three designs were very much the exceptions to the rule. He was inclined to trim designs down until they were too light and fragile to be reliable, but his conceptual thinking and genius was just unmatched . . . it was an education just to have worked with him.'

Len's replacement was Maurice Phillipe, ex-De Havilland, which looks more and more like the Lotus apprentices' school, then Ford of Dagenham, for whom he had been briefly project manager on Anglia 1200 development.

He had built his own stressed-skin monocoque-chassised 1172 car, the MPS, in 1954-55, on which Lotus Engineering did most of the necessary welding, thus bringing Maurice for the first time into direct contact with Colin Chapman. After National Service in the RAF, Maurice returned to De Havilland and in his spare time built his own spaceframe-chassised front-engined FJ car, which he called the Delta. He entered it for the 1960 Easter Monday Brands Hatch meeting, and promptly crashed in Saturday practice. He rebuilt it completely that night and through the Sunday, then in the rainswept Monday race the leader spun his Lotus and most of the pack avoided him, until Maurice and a Caravelle rushed out of the murk to torpedo the spinning car fair and square. The Delta was written-off again, and the spinning leading car's driver? . . . Peter Warr.

Maurice subsequently raced the ex-Cosworth Lotus 7 with considerable success before Colin Chapman's secretary called out of the blue 'asking if I'd like to come up and have a chat with you-know-who . . . with a view to . . . so I joined Lotus in September 1965 as the design team — it consisted of one.'

A determined, quietly tough character, Maurice could evidently keep his end up in Colin's company without triggering the occasional blazing rows which Len Terry and Colin both probably enjoyed. He described the initial design process in his seven years with Team as 'a discussion between Colin and I on basic design features, with both of us suggesting innovations and bouncing ideas off each other. Once the basic design parameters had been finalized in discussion and by comparing sketches and ideas I got down to work with the draughtsmen to detail the design, and the team mechanics could then begin construction.

'With my background in the aeronautical industry and his lifelong interest in aeroplanes we had a lot in common and a lot of aeronautical principles inevitably appeared in the cars which we produced.'

Maurice eventually headed a small design and draughting team at Hethel which included Mike Pilbeam — ex-BRM and soon to return to them as chief chassis designer — John Baldwin from Handley-Page Aircraft, who would go on in Formula 1 and Indycar racing design, and John Stock, ex-Hawker Siddeley Aviation in Australia.

One characteristic which Chapman and Phillippe shared was a dislike for over-design, for complexity. Unnecessary weight was anathema to both of them. Maurice's post-Lotus career would be studded by a number of trimmed-to-the-bone and occasionally fragile designs in the Chapman tradition. After Team, Maurice moved on — with Dick Scammell and Andrew Ferguson — to the American Vel's Parnelli concern to complete their VPJ-series of Indy cars, ultimately producing a Formula 1 car which, had it been a Lotus, would have fulfilled Colin's 1974 requirement for a '100lb lighter 72' . . . had they only stayed together . . . it was a ravishing beauty and exquisitely well-built, but the team ran out of money.

Ralph Bellamy took Maurice's place, an Australian engineer, ex-Brabham in two stints which had sandwiched a period at McLaren. Early in 1973 he received a call from Peter Warr inviting him to work for Team. His response was unequivocal: 'I had always regarded the chief designer's jobs at Lotus and Ferrari as the top jobs in the business. I just could not turn down an offer like that.'

Quite unlike Len Terry, and perhaps also without the hard ambitious competitiveness which had made Maurice Phillippe such a good club-racing driver in his own right, Ralph was a naturally quiet, introspective and uncombative character. Partly as a consequence, he spent a fairly torrid time with Team, but recalled: 'It was immediately obvious that we had an almost unique advantage over our adversaries in that there were two of us' — himself and the Old Man — 'who could discuss problems or bounce new ideas off one another. For an engineer it's nice to work for a man who understands engineering problems, but this can be a two-edged sword at times.'

The creeping obsolescence of the 72s combined with the new 1973 deformable structure and fuel system regulations made a new F1 car the complete answer. It seemed logical to do a Formula 2 car first because Texaco had just come up with sponsorship for Emerson Fittipaldi and Ronnie Peterson to run an F2 programme with Novamotor-Lotus engines, and then use that design's cockpit area and entire front end, suspension and brakes for the F1 to follow.

'We built the Texaco Star F2s to this plan, and their career is forgettable to say the least! To my knowledge, though, these were the first modern cars to site their radiators fore-and-aft ahead of the rear wheels . . . and it was in areas like this that Colin was at his best, giving full encouragement for any unconventional ideas he thought stood a chance. We tested the system in Specialised Mouldings' wind-tunnel, and this was the first time I worked with Peter Wright, who ran the SM facility, and who later worked with us on the Lotus 78.'

The Stars' engines proved so unreliable that they never found out whether the chassis layout was any good or not.

Martin Waide designed the deformable-regulation mods for the 72 to involve as few changes as possible and Ralph then produced to Colin's brief the ill-begotten Type 76. For the Spanish GP

Ronnie qualified second quickest and Jacky Ickx fifth, and Ronnie led while Ickx ran fourth splitting the Ferraris. But everyone preferred the 72s and the 76s were set aside.

This marked the low ebb of the Bellamy period with Team, but in hindsight Ralph considered: 'One — the 76 failed to meet the requirement to be lighter than the 72, particularly with the electronic clutch fitted' — as Colin had insisted. 'Two — it would never have had any performance advantage over the 72 because one design requirement was that it should be just *like* the 72! Three — it was better-engineered than the 72. Four — it did suffer brake problems. Five — there were handling problems because I lightened part of the rear suspension too much, which allowed flexion and poor toe-in control. Six — by mid-year Goodyear were developing tyres unsuited to the low-unsprung-weight front suspension of the Types 72 and 76. We were not to recognize this fact and its significance until too late.'

Colin then seconded Ralph to Ketteringham Hall to realize one of his long-cherished ambitions, the Formula 1 Lotus gearbox. 'The job was to design an F1 gearbox 40lb lighter than the current Hewland. If you consider the FG weighed 100lb and was frail and unreliable in Formula 1 then the chances of reducing its weight by 40 per cent and increasing its strength were almost nil if the layout was unchanged. But Colin specified gear selector mechanism inside the gears . . . and this to some extent was the key to the big weight reduction. Colin, Tony Rudd and I came up with a number of different mechanisms to do this. I roughly laid out the gearbox I thought would do the job, but it was too large for Colin, particularly the crownwheel-and-pinion which I made even bigger than the Hewland in the interests of reliablity. He specified the far smaller one used in the ZF 'box from the Type 49s. I disagreed strongly but was overruled . . .'

The undersized CWP and the frail selector mechanism put forward by Getrag proved to be this ingenious Lotus gearbox's downfall, but Tony Rudd — Group Engineering Director and an old hand who had 'seen it all before' — characterized Ralph as 'a brilliant stressman' but significantly 'not very good in an argument, when he tends to clam up and not force through his point of view.' That had never been a problem for his predecessors — especially Len! — and forcefulness had never been a handicap within Team Lotus.

Ralph wrestled with another impossible task in 1975, to keep the obsolescent 72s competitive. He escaped from the terrible road accident which seriously injured Peter Warr with only severe shock. Thereafter, 'we tried umpteen changes. Don't think the poor results of 1975 were because we were disinterested and not trying. In fact we were trying very hard indeed, because we had to

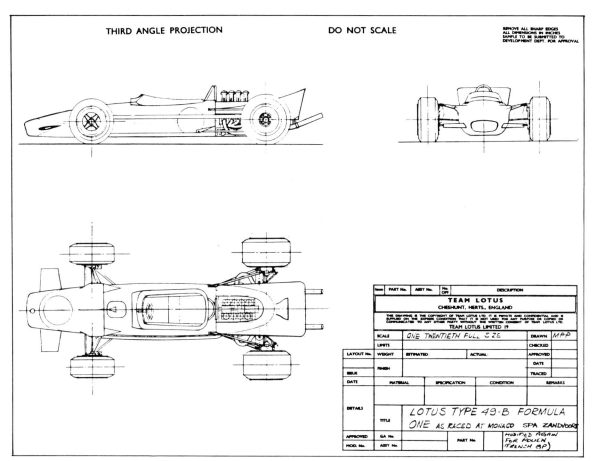

Lotus 49B (drawn 1968).

The illustrations on this and the opposite page have been compiled from a series of general arrangement drawings supplied by Club Team Lotus, the factory-based Club that caters for Lotus enthusiasts worldwide. Prints of these and other drawings of single-seater cars that have constituted major milestones in Lotus' racing history can be obtained by application to Club Team Lotus, Ketteringham Hall, Wymondham, Norfolk NR18 9RS (Tel: 0603 810849), who will quote prices for three sizes: A1 – 44in × 24in; A2 – 34in × 17in; A4 – 12in × 9in.

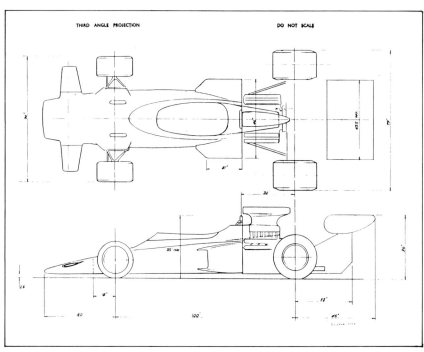

Lotus 72 (drawn 1972).

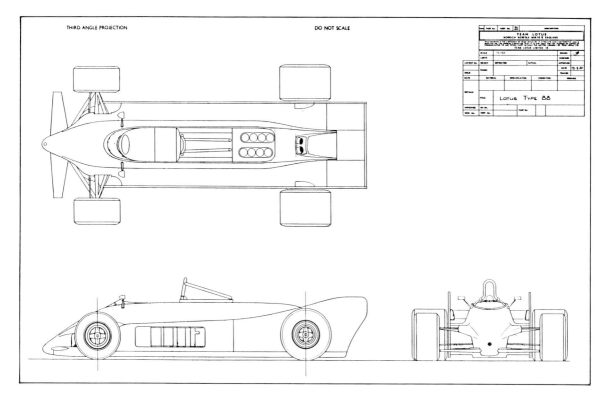

Lotus 88 (drawn 1981).

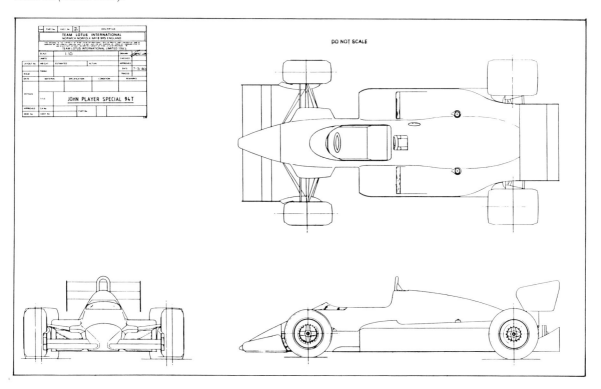

Lotus 94T (drawn 1983).

249

find out what was wrong with the 72 and correct it rather than just blindly build the same errors into the new 77 for 1976.

'Perhaps one bright spot that year was our successful introduction of the first pit-road driver-to-crew communications system in Formula 1, which has now become standard. Colin's idea, of course . . .'

In November 1975 Colin briefed Ralph to devote himself to Type 78 development at Ketteringham Hall, working to the spec worked-up by The Guv' and Tony Rudd. Colin detailed design draughtsmen Geoff Aldridge and Martin Ogilvie to produce his Type 77 racing research car meantime.

Of the 78 project Ralph told me: 'The success of its complex aerodynamics would have been impossible without Peter Wright, and Tony Rudd was of immense help. As the administrator in charge of Ketteringham Hall, he ensured all the necessary facilities and people were made available, *and* he provided the political umbrella under which we could all work.

'The value of his engineering wisdom goes without saying. It's remarkable how little Colin was involved beyond his original specification. Once he thought we were on the right track, he left us to it . . . Of course, there were times of crisis in the passenger car and boat companies, and he was deeply involved in designing two new powerboats which left very little time for our project.'

The 78 could have raced any time from Monza '76 on, but Colin held it back for the new year to deny his rivals a free winter's development in which to catch up relatively free of calendar pressures.

Then, in February '77, Ralph found himself abruptly shuffled sideways into Lotus Cars to fix some development problems on the production Esprit, while Martin Ogilvie and Geoff Aldridge would be detailed to design the 79. That October he left Lotus to join Emerson Fittipaldi's Copersucar operation, and his talents would eventually blossom with March in minor-formula and Indycar racing.

Martin Ogilvie, who would become Team's chief designer into the 'eighties, was an honours degree engineering graduate of Birmingham University. He had spent five years with Girling brakes, the last three of them as their sole designer on the racing side. He had been responsible for the AR5 and Lockheed twin-disc brake designs, but the budget was always minimal and it took ages to get things done. While on a consultative visit to Lotus one day in 1974 Martin had asked Ralph Bellamy if there was a job going. 'There was and I jumped at it. Mike Cooke, ex-Rolls-Royce joined at the same time. I just worked in the design office until Colin divided the operation and sent Ralph to Ketteringham Hall, eventually to design the 78, while Geoff Aldridge and I were briefed meantime to do the 77. Geoff and I then did the 79 and 80 between us before he left and I became chief designer from the Type 81 onwards.'

Team's design staff had always been compact and tight-knit, and by ordinary industrial standards grossly overworked. But they worked well. In the Ducarouge era into 1986 Martin ran the Ketteringham design office with a staff of only three. He handled chassis and body designs; Gene Varnier, ex-Tyrrell, was responsible for suspension, brakes and drive-lines; Mike Coughlan, ex-Tiga, covered gearboxes and some aerodynamic work, while into the final season of our period a young Imperial College graduate, Julian Robertson, had just joined the strength to handle the design office's computer work.

But perhaps nearest of all to Colin's conceptual and original-thinking ability of his close design collaborators was Peter Wright — 'the boffin'. He was another honours graduate in mechanical engineering, this time from Cambridge University, who had joined BRM at Bourne upon graduation, to become Tony Rudd's personal assistant. He had started there in 1967 just as the fearsome H16-cylinder engine was at last coming on song. 'It was a very interesting baptism. I worked essentially on chassis and suspensions, then became involved in aerodynamic study and eventually ran BRM's wind-tunnel programme at Imperial College. It was at that time that we began to cook up designs using the air passing beneath parts of the car bodies, the early days of ground-effects aerodynamic study.'

That programme crunched to a halt in mid-'69 as Tony Rudd left BRM, moving to Lotus, and not long after his departure Peter Wright left as well to join Peter Jackson's Specialised Mouldings company as aerodynamicist, setting-up and running their wind-tunnel facility at Huntingdon to specialize in aerodynamic study and design, essentially in racing car applications. He also learned an awful lot about moulded GRP and the possibilities of other related composite materials.

After four years or so with SM, he followed Rudd to Lotus, where he would run their composites technology development company, Technocraft. He directed development of composites manufacturing processes, but they did not handle carbon composites at that time, that would come later with Team, culminating in Peter's development of the revolutionary Type 88 carbon/Kevlar composite tub, and its immediate successors.

'I began working on the racing side effectively in my spare time, helping Ralph Bellamy on research for the 78, and then with Technocraft's work complete and the processes which we had developed in use, I began to concentrate on the Imperial College wind-tunnel programme.'

Peter only ever worked with Team as a self-employed freelance consultant, but in harness with them he became the true originator of ground-effects racing car design. Then, during the heyday of the 79 and more so during the troubles which followed with the 80, the legal wrangling over the

86/88 'twin-chassis' concept, and on into the initiation of active suspension in 1982 he worked very closely with Chapman, who recognized his innate conceptual brilliance and ultimately made him Director of Research & Development and a full director of Team Lotus International Ltd.

Peter says of his own abilities: 'I'm not a designer and I never have been. I am an R&D man, and developing ideas is really what I'm best at.' He attracted his critics, none challenging his Chapman-style ability, but some suggesting he was more comfortable in theory than practice. There's a measure of truth in that, but it doesn't entirely hold water, for successful R&D involves solving the practical problems to make theory work in practice, and Wright had spent most of his professional life very successfully doing just that.

'The most satisfying period I spent with Team was undoubtedly the development of ground-effects aerodynamics, followed by the active suspension experiments which were really brought by authority's attempts to stop ground-effects working, first by banning sliding skirts and then the 88 concept.

The Lotus active suspension system which was seen as the next logical response to FISA's sliding-skirt restrictions, which had tried to render ground-effects aerodynamics inoperable.

'Then overnight FISA removed ground-effects almost completely with their flat-bottom ruling and with it went the essential need for active suspension. We were trying it on the one remaining Cosworth car because there was nothing to lose, but with the second turbo on the way and flat-bottoms in anyway there was then no good reason to proceed with it in Formula 1.

'It had to be redesigned to fit on the new turbo car anyway, which simply wasn't worth doing at that time, yet coincidentally the exposure had attracted big-industry interest for production development, so I became wrapped-up in that R&D project instead, and got out of racing.

'And I must say that has been most stimulating and rewarding, because outside Formula 1 there are in effect *no* restrictions on what you can attempt to do. You are not working within the tight envelope of restrictive and largely irrational regulations . . . and you can try *anything*.'

He had relinquished his Team Lotus duties in 1983 when the active suspension system was withdrawn from Formula 1, and he began instead its intensive development for road car use under the Lotus Engineering R&D company banner. General Motors was just one client company which became fascinated by the immense potential of 'Active', and this interest would lead indirectly to their purchasing control of Group Lotus in 1986.

As perhaps the most naturally gifted of all those who had collaborated with Colin Chapman in racing car design, Peter had been described to me as being nearest-equal to the Old Man's innate skill.

But he rejected that idea: 'Once Colin or anybody like him had reached that status there was simply no way he could spend the time to detail and develop ideas. It is very easy to have ideas, very easy indeed, but the special skill is to have the insight to pick the right idea for further development. Colin had that.

'Out of 10 different ideas he could pick the good ones which would reward time and money spent on their development, and once he'd picked them he would push, and pull, and he had the faith to go on forcing them through and putting money into the programme even if it might still face real problems until they had been overcome and the idea had borne some fruit.

'He was very seldom wrong. Very few people have the ability to do that . . . and in that ability — he was very special. . .'

GERARD DUCAROUGE
— CHIEF ENGINEER

**'Gerard is, quite simply, our trump card — he is as important to the
team today as Colin was when he was alive . . .'**

Peter Warr

After the collapse of his team's best-laid plans for
their second-generation ground-effects car, the
Type 80, and subsequently for the twin-chassis
Type 88 concept — in that case so acrimoniously —
Colin Chapman really lost heart where Formula 1
was concerned. In many ways this was hardly
surprising. He had split his time between several
extraordinarily divergent businesses for many years.
Now into the early-'eighties almost every one of
those interests was struggling against competition
which was fiercer than ever before.

Through 1981 Colin was literally beset on all
sides. Group Lotus was suffering intense
difficulties, and effectively the least of his worries
was how to make Team Lotus competitive again in
Formula 1.

Partly because of this, he had already realized that
Team needed a 24-hours-a-day chief engineer, a
man as steeped in Formula 1 state-of-the-art
technology and lore as he had been in the early-
'sixties, but as much on top of the requirements of
contemporary Formula 1 as were Gordon Murray
of Brabham or Patrick Head of Williams.

The man he eventually considered best-qualified
for the post was the peripatetic French engineer
Gerard Ducarouge. He had an extraordinarily deep
grounding in motor racing which combined the
reliable, endurance-racing basics of what had made
Matra Sports' string of Le Mans 24-Hour race wins
possible in the early-'seventies, with Formula 1
achievement in his concept for the 1979 second-
generation ground-effects Ligier-Cosworth JS11s,
which had proved such a brilliant overnight success
while Team's Lotus 80 ideas had flopped.

Way back in Lotus 72 days Team had been testing
one day at Ricard when they needed a component
welded quickly. Peter Warr went off to the Matra
Sports workshops beside the circuit to ask for help.
Ducarouge was running the show there. Typically,
he could not have been more friendly nor more

helpful. While Team's welding was being done,
Peter was given a brief guided tour of the shop.

He recalled how: 'There was this immaculate little
factory making everything and doing everything to
aviation standards of workmanship, quality and
inspection. Gerard showed me round, showed me
their beautifully-constructed monocoque sports
cars, their special Porsche-made gearboxes and all
the Le Mans 24-Hours stuff. They had neat little
trolleys to carry all sub-assemblies around,
everything was clinically ordered and clinically
correct, the storeman had huge general arrangement
drawings with all components keyed and numbered
so they could be located easily — it all looked like
just the way a serious racing car factory should be
run . . . . I told Colin about what I had seen, and he
became very interested, it was all very, very
impressive to us.

'Years later, Gerard went from Matra to Ligier,
we saw him regularly around the circuits and we
used to sit across the table from him at FOCA
meetings and got to know him quite well. Then
suddenly he was out of Ligier and went to Alfa
Romeo. Colin contacted him about that time,
asking him to come and join us, but he already had
the Alfa contract. Colin still wanted him, he really
thought Gerard was the man for us, and after the
Austrian GP '82 — which Elio won in our car —
Gerard flew back with us in our helicopter and
private aeroplane to have a look round
Ketteringham Hall. By that time Colin was
determined he should join us, but Gerard still had
that Alfa contract, and for his own reasons he turned
us down.

'Then Colin died, but in the Spring of '83 at the
French GP which was run early that season Gerard
had his bust-up with Alfa Romeo and became
available. I pestered the life out of him to come and
join us now that he was free, and friends like Jabby
Crombac niggled at him and told him that working

in England wouldn't be so bad, and eventually we broke down his reservations and he came to join us immediately after the Belgian GP . . . and within five weeks the combination of his experience and grasp of what was needed and our human resource of a brilliant build team produced the cars which turned our fortunes round and assured our future . . . the 94Ts.'

Ducarouge had already done a laudable job of bringing Alfa Romeo some decent results. Now, in far more spectacular style, his arrival had turned Team Lotus round from also-ran to front-runner.

And he was neither a formally-qualified automotive engineer nor a master-artiste at the drawing board. In fact his background was in aeronautical engineering, specifically in aerodynamics. He had qualified at College with a *Baccalaureat Technique et Mathematique* and studied at the *École National Technique d'Aeronautique* at Ville de'Avray, west of Paris, achieving a *Degree Supérieur*.

'I intended to go into the aerospace industry', he explained, 'and I chose Nord Aviation to work on missiles, ground-to-air, air-to-ground, air-to-air, all kinds, you know? I worked in Nord Aviation's test centre close to Paris making static tests on missiles which initially was very interesting, but after a while I became restless. I am a man who likes to travel, I enjoy the change of surroundings, not always to be doing the same routine things day after day. I wanted to go to work in the field, live-firing missiles on the South American test range which the company used, and after one year with Nord Aviation I was waiting to be transferred there, but for months the transfer had not come.

'I was unhappy and then I saw a small advertisement from the Matra racing department for a technician and I applied and got the job. This was really very soon after the start of Matra Sports. It was December '65 and they had been running less than a year with Formula 3 cars, and I began work for them immediately with sports cars my main activity, although we were also just starting to build Formula 2 cars for 1966 and improved Formula 3 cars also.

'I then stayed with Matra Sports right until they stopped racing altogether at the end of 1974.'

His ability to speak reasonable English was unusual amongst the Matra Sports technical staff and that made him an ideal choice for the endurance division whose Le Mans cars were at that time powered by 2-litre BRM V8 engines. Gerard handled technical liaison with the British manufacturer and loved every minute of the sports-prototype racing in which he became involved.

'Endurance racing is fantastic because of the team work. From this point of view I still miss it today, you feel much more involved than in Formula 1, and really get the feeling of taking part in the race from start to finish.'

The man who helped to return JPS Team Lotus to the front of the starting grid. Gerard Ducarouge quickly gained the confidence of his new colleagues at Ketteringham Hall and did much to restore team morale during the difficult season following Colin Chapman's death.

Curiously, throughout his nine seasons' service with Matra Sports Gerard never had anything to do with their Formula 1 programme, although by 1968, when the V12-engined MS11 made its debut at Monaco, he was already head of prototype development.

He told his compatriot, former racing driver-turned-journalist José Rosinski: 'I learned my trade on the shop floor, watching and benefiting from the experience of others. To start with, as I was a good draughtsman, they put me in the drawing office . . . But I am really a down-to-earth man. Little by little I started suggesting small modifications, mainly of a practical nature, to make the mechanics' job easier or the cars more reliable.'

He also demonstrated an organizational flair which Matra Sports' management recognized, making him head of operations, in which capacity he subsequently masterminded Matra's hat-trick of Le Mans 24-Hour race wins in 1972-3-4 and their two World Championship titles of 1973-74. Thereafter Matra Sports' racing career ended with them securely at the top of the pile.

'At that time I found myself with two alternatives before me; to be relocated within the Group in their space division — which was the safe option — or to accept an offer from Guy Ligier, who was putting together a Formula 1 team.

'One of the marvellous things about Matra was that they always had funds available. Nothing was too expensive or too much of a luxury, as long as it was well justified and in those conditions a perfectionist like me is in seventh heaven. On the other hand I was only a small fish in a big pond — an important one perhaps, but nothing more. Ligier gave me the chance now to take control of everything.'

The move was utterly logical, for Ligier's new French Formula 1 team for 1976 was going to be sponsored by the SEITA tobacco company's Gitanes brand, which had already enjoyed a successful relationship with Matra Sports, whose V12 engine was being reworked for the new Ligier JS5, which became the first Formula 1 design with which Gerard Ducarouge was directly involved.

For the next six seasons Gerard was totally identified with the Ligier team, of which he was the leading technical light and an integral character alongside tough — occasionally rough — old Guy Ligier himself. They won in Formula 1 with the Matra V12 engine, and a little luck, before changing horses to the Cosworth DFV for 1979, when Gerard's rugged concept for the JS11 model proved man enough to handle the vast aerodynamic downloads which its second-generation ground-effects design generated. The result was utter dominance in the first two GPs of the new season, but the further the season progressed the more problems Ligier encountered and their effectiveness tailed off.

Gerard describes the JS11 as 'my most satisfying professional achievement, to date.'

What was the key to the cars' startling performance?

'What we had done was analyze what Colin Chapman's team had achieved in introducing us to ground-effects aerodynamics. They had introduced something new to the Formula 1 scene and won with this new concept. What I did in 1979 was to research more deeply into the idea than Team Lotus did at that time. They worked on the aerodynamics first and kept the chassis and suspension apart from that second. I tried to do the best possible and strongest chassis first, and then put a development of the new Chapman idea onto it. And it worked.

'At the beginning of the '79 season we were way ahead of the others. But they copied us after six months, they overtook us, simply because we had run out of money and could not continue with our development programme. We were very few people compared with most other Formula 1 teams and we were trying to run a whole year's racing on only six months' money . . . was impossible to keep ahead.'

Into 1981 a revised Matra V12 engine was back in the latest Ligier chassis and Talbot was backing the Vichy-based operation. But mid-season, like a bolt from the blue, Gerard was out of the team.

'I still to this day do not really understand what happened', he would recall, 'I was completely unsuspecting, we had just raced at Silverstone, Laffite was going well in the Championship, Talbot's money was quite good, we had more people to do the work and there was no sign of a problem at all. When we got back to home base after that race I went to see Guy Ligier for our usual

discussion about how things had gone and he suddenly said something like: "We should first discuss tomorrow and the day after and I think it's best that you should leave the team . . ."!

'I was stunned. It left all kind of big questions which I did not understand, but Jean-Pierre Jabouille had just joined the team as well with his own ideas on development; he is Jacques Laffite's brother-in-law and . . . I don't know . . . you understand?

'It was a terrible wrench. I went through a bad time, without doubt the worst time of my life.'

Ligier had wielded the axe on his long-time friend and confidant apparently without compunction, though certainly with remorse. The rift between the two would in fact heal quite rapidly, and Gerard's return to Vichy was subsequently rumoured more than once. Ligier himself was not short in praise: 'Above all else Gerard is a tremendous worker, and is passionately involved in his work.' With the Ligier team, the Boss would say, 'he was everywhere, doing everything'.

Ducarouge was quickly taken on by Autodelta, to help turn around the fortunes of their quasi-works Alfa Romeo Formula 1 team. 'That was a terrible wasted opportunity. Everything started well. I came into action at Zandvoort, at the end of August, and Giacomelli, who hadn't scored a single point until then through the previous 11 Grands Prix, came in third at Montreal and fourth at Las Vegas, only just saving the season for the team.

The Frenchman's carefully-coiffed hair-dos and penchant for brightly-coloured clothes initially roused Alfa driver Mario Andretti's grave suspicion. In the first few weeks he would refer to him as 'that damn peacock'. By the end of the season Mario's tune had changed: 'Gerard's OK', he would say, 'in fact he works more like Colin Chapman than any other race engineer I've ever worked with.'

Unfortunately, *Ducarosso* as the Italian *paparazzi* nicknamed him was regarded by some powerful factions within the Italian team more as an upstart incomer, a foreigner. His relationship with chief engineer Carlo Chiti, in particular, rapidly deteriorated despite Andrea de Cesaris being able to put one of Gerard's 1982 Alfas onto pole position at Long Beach and lead the race — before wiping it out against a wall.

'In Milan, when I got there the chassis side was unorganized, the engine side was quite good, but soon I began building new workshops to get them all organized, and persuading the whole team to go about their racing in a far more methodical manner than they had before. I really enjoyed living and working in Italy, but I had known before I went there that being part of an Italian team is never easy for an outsider and I knew this might be so for me with a very strong person at the top like Chiti.

'But my new buildings were never to be used. At the end of the season the President of Alfa Romeo

called me in to tell me that the Formula 1 effort had been handed to the Pavanello Euroracing team for 1983. I went to join them with the team and was devastated to discover that all I could do was to start all over again from virtually nothing.

'That was difficult. I am philosophical about these things, but here we had in control people coming from Formula 3 to Formula 1 who were used to managing an operation with five people and here they suddenly had an operation with 50. They were faced by new big problems while I organized building my second new Formula 1 workshop within a year.

'I asked Pavanello to invest money in testing, in development and wind-tunnel research and he instead explained how he wanted to make cutbacks and economies. We were not at all on the same wavelength . . . you cannot *win* in Formula 1 when you handicap yourself like that.'

The curious incident of first qualifying for the 1983 French GP, Andrea de Cesaris' Euroracing Alfa Romeo and its fire extinguisher bottles followed.

He was credited with fastest time in that session, but the scrutineers then discovered that his car had been running underweight because its onboard extinguisher system was empty. The driver was disqualified, fingers were pointed at Ducarouge — it's rumoured by those who had tipped off the scrutineers in the first place — and for the second time in two years he was summarily fired, in mid-season.

This time Alfa Romeo's ultimately fatal loss was Team Lotus' gain.

'I had already been taken to Ketteringham Hall by Colin Chapman and Peter Warr to see how Team Lotus worked and where it was based. That invitation in August 1982 was extremely flattering for me. I was still with Alfa Romeo at the time. I had had normal Formula 1 contact with Colin and Peter, but otherwise our first proper contact had been in the middle of that year in the Nikko Hotel in Paris, and then the more serious contact immediately after the Austrian GP when they brought me to Ketteringham to see their castle!

'I tell you that that was the biggest possible surprise for me. You see for me Colin Chapman was *absolutely* the top man in Formula 1 history. I cannot tell you how much respect I had for him. To me he was *Mr Formula 1*, and everything about Team Lotus was always in the forefront of advanced development — sure, even if sometimes it had gone wrong for them — and so Team Lotus to me was ultra-modern, and then to see all these modern facilities disguised in many little rooms inside this wonderful great castle was just *amazing!*

'I was used to the industrial factory atmosphere of Matra and Ligier and Alfa Romeo, and it was very difficult to make any direct comparisons in my mind, everything I had seen was just so extraordinary because of the background of the park and the woods and the countryside all around.'

Colin had shown him into one of the Hall's large oak-trimmed rooms with its fine furnishings and had said: 'Gerard, this is your office'.

But the French engineer had felt unable to accept, although 'to start with I was so proud to be approached by Colin I cannot tell you — but it was very difficult for me to analyze what would be best because Colin for me was so great a personality and so great an engineer that I was worried how I could work in his team.

'I just feared that living with a man who had such a forceful personality would be difficult. For the same reason, I cannot see myself at Ferrari.

'I was not at that stage ready to say "yes", but I must emphasize how proud I felt to be even asked!'

Tragically, it was partly Colin's death which cleared his preferred new chief engineer's path to Ketteringham Hall six months later.

Five weeks passed between Gerard's dismissal by Euroracing and his arrival in Norfolk, and in just five more weeks he firmly cemented his relationship with the old hands of Team Lotus in their extraordinary and successful Type 94T crash programme.

Those hastily-designed-and-built new cars brilliantly salvaged some success from Team's first season without Colin's influence, their first with Renault turbocharged engines and their first on Pirelli's under-developed and so far generally uncompetitive racing tyres.

'That was for me the biggest challenge I've ever had', Gerard confirmed.

His success in turning Team's fortunes round so effectively, and pushing them back into the regular Formula 1 limelight through 1984-86, secured his name and reputation amongst the media as something of a 'Miracle Man'.

Gerard himself is at pains to dismiss such hyperbole. 'I must tell you I certainly do not picture myself at all in this way. I am just an ordinary technician who is lucky enough to be able to be involved entirely in a very specialized area of technology and to work hard at it as many hours as I can. This is not magic, I am not a magician of any kind, nor a miracle worker; those things which have been written are flattering, but they are entirely too much . . . ha, you say over the top?'

He had known from the beginning he would find problems in working in rural England. For a start his wife Colette remained in Paris, sharing his life only at Grand Prix weekends: 'I have to say I was actually disappointed to leave Italy, which I liked very much, mainly because we French are closer to the Italian mentality than to the English one . . . Now I live on my own in Norwich, which is a nice town — sure — but a very quiet town and that leaves me with no social activity outside the team, and that I do find quite hard sometimes.'

At the end of 1983 Renault's number 1 driver Alain Prost had in fact proposed a scheme to Régie President Bernard Hanon which might have attracted the Gallic Ducarouge back to Gaul. After Renault's late-season catastrophes had just blown his and their world title hopes, his idea was for the chassis department to be moved down to Ricard with Gerard in charge.

The engineer told José Rosinski: 'Renault had everything necessary to succeed in Formula 1, on the condition that they distanced themselves from the tight hold of the hierarchy and worked in a much more autonomous way', but as José put it 'the project never took off, Prost left France, and Ducarouge never went back'.

Despite this flamboyant and gregarious man's isolation in Norwich, he remained a character who attracts friends. One of his most obvious attributes is his open charm. He is simply an extremely likeable man who in Lotus' case charmed everyone into quickly giving him as much support as they had formerly given the Old Man.

When he first took up residence in the Hall he spent his first few days meeting everybody and absorbing their knowledge, beliefs and methodology. He would admit 'I am not a specialist in composite materials', but would add 'I think I am a specialist in suspension, suspension geometry and aerodynamics too'.

He would demonstrate his different way of working in the moving-ground quarter-scale wind-tunnel at Kensington's Imperial College, and back it up with further full-scale testing in the high-speed airstream *Soufflérie* at St Cyr, Paris. His influence and experience rubbed off on every member of the team while he in turn listened to absorb everything.

There was thus a rapid mutual trade-off between the engineer and his new team. He patiently — and tactfully — expounded his own views and explained what he called his 'Golden Rules — basic practices and theories which I never want to go away from, although they develop in detail all the time'.

From what I have heard from Team's old hands it seems most of them listened spellbound during that initial honeymoon period, realization slowly dawning of how far off the pace their thinking had fallen.

Through 1984-86, the years of reviving hard Team Lotus success, Gerard — in his mid-40s — emerged as a consummate gatherer of information, spending hours on the telephone to a network of old-established contacts, maintaining a broad-based feel for everything that was new in Formula 1. He hardly ever drew a line on a sheet of draughting paper, but he would worry out a design concept and watch tirelessly over the drawing office staff's shoulders while they massaged his ideas towards three-dimensional form.

In overall charge, Gerard Ducarouge's greatest strength was his immense experience of ploys tried, avenues explored, what will work and what will not. This fund of knowledge had been founded in his nine formative seasons with Matra Sports. During that time they had enjoyed the funding and the will to experiment, research and test almost any idea which surfaced just in case something about it might prove of value. Ducarouge inherited that priceless basic asset — a near unerring feel for what not to do. Such deep experience was pure gold, the foundation in fact of Gerard's Golden Rules, and with Team Lotus in the mid-'eighties they — and their author — now found true fulfilment.

PETER WARR
— TEAM DIRECTOR

'Peter is very efficient, he gets the job done — he's just the best team
manager in Formula 1 . . .'

Walter Wolf

After Colin Chapman's premature death on December 16, 1982, Team Lotus International Ltd became *de facto* the property of his widow Hazel Chapman and of Colin's long-serving — and long-suffering — friend and Group Lotus Finance Director Fred Bushell. Team as such had no formal connection with Group. Whereas Group Lotus was a publicly-quoted company with shares bought and sold on the Stock Exchange, Team Lotus was entirely privately-owned by Mrs Chapman and Bushell. And upon Colin's death, Peter Warr, the team director, was given the possibly thankless task of ensuring Lotus' continuing participation and future progress in Formula 1.

At that time Peter could already look back over a twice-interrupted Lotus career to which he had already devoted half his life. Born on June 18, 1938, he had joined the Lotus Engineering Co Ltd in August 1958 when it was still based behind Stan Chapman's pub at Hornsey and he was only a fresh-faced 20-year-old. Team itself was at that time living from hand-to-mouth through its maiden season of Formula 1 racing with the Type 12s while Engineering was in production with its Type 11 sports-racing cars and 7 kits and the Elite programme was — intermittently — running up.

Peter had appeared at Hornsey fresh from National Service in the Army. He had actually served in the Royal Horse Artillery, which regiment had won certain notoriety by being inadvertently described in a BBC radio live commentary as 'The Royal Arse Hortillery'.

Peter's time with the Hortillery had been cut short by a knee injury which eventually put him into the RAF rehabilitation centre at Leatherhead 'where Rob Walker invited us to visit his workshop at Dorking to see his racing cars'. Finally the injury was judged bad enough for him to be invalided out of the Army.

'They gave me six weeks invalid and demob leave', he recalled, 'during which time I wrote to all the car manufacturers I could think of simply because cars were my great interest. I was still waiting for the replies when I went up to Hornsey just to have a look round Lotus Engineering. I was fairly enthralled by all the activity there when someone said "don't just stand there, give us a hand", and I found I had started working for them! Just like that.

'I was taken on formally next day, starting work at £500 per annum as assistant to Colin Bennett, the sales manager.'

Lotus Engineering still concentrated at that time upon competition and kit cars, the 7s and 11s, soon the 15s and 17s too, and through selling to enthusiasts Peter became closely acquainted with the racing world.

There were about 30 people on the staff at Hornsey when he joined. A tiny development unit down the road in Edmonton was working on the forthcoming Elite, 'so all together there was a lot of activity on numerous fronts and everybody was caught up in all aspects of it'.

Colin had commissioned construction of his company's new purpose-built factory in Delamare Road, Cheshunt, and the Lotus companies moved there in mid-1959 to cope with the predicted increase in production brought about by the Elite programme. The way the concern was organized in its new home at Cheshunt, there was a natural and logical split between Lotus Cars Ltd, which had been set-up to build road cars like the Elite, and Lotus Components, which built the racers and kit-cars. Peter worked for Components under general manager Norman 'Nobby' Clarke and with Roy Badcock in charge of production.

Tragically, quite soon after moving, Nobby suffered a fatal heart-attack, and still in his very early-20s Peter found himself running Components' sales and commercial side alongside

Roy Badcock, still running production.

'I was very interested and hugely involved. I had set my sights on racing my own Lotus and bought the 7 which had been built specially for Graham Hill to run at Boxing Day Brands '59. It had a good Climax engine and at Brands Graham had actually blown-off all the streamlined proper sports-racing cars in pouring rain and won. It had then become our factory road-test car, then I bought it, raced it for a couple of seasons and had a lot of fun before graduating to Formula Junior.

'Two things happened. I always had to buy the last car of the previous year's production because Colin would never let anyone who worked for the company have the pick of the delivery. That meant I could never buy the first of the new year's batch of cars; I always had to take on the last of the preceding year's. Those were the days when our doors got beaten down from February to late-May with customers wanting us to build 100 cars in six weeks for the start of the season.

'Colin's restriction on what I could buy for my own use was actually an advantage in a way because the last car of the previous season's batch always had the fullest specification, with all the development extras built into it.'

Talking to Peter about this period he unconsciously illustrated just how far Colin Chapman could manipulate his people without their realizing it. What to anybody else would have been a normal-period weekend off was recalled like this: 'And I did a deal with Colin under which he *allowed*' (my italics, DCN) 'me to leave the factory early on Friday evening, rush to the Continent for a race meeting, come back home on the midnight boat Sunday and be back in the office Monday morning.

'I carried a selection of Lotus spares in my van to provide a Lotus presence at the circuit, and this allowed me the means to go racing and I got to know a lot of racing folk very well. It was great fun, and a very exciting time . . .'

Peter soon discovered he was not going to be World Champion as a driver. But he travelled a lot and raced widely with some success, including two trips to Suzuka in Japan, once with a Junior, once victoriously with a Lotus 23B sports. After not quite five seasons' active competition he finally retired from driving in 1964.

By that time more companies were sharing the production racing car cake, so profit margins all round were tacked back. 'In 1960 we had built around 125 Lotus 18s, but by 1963 with the Lotus 27 we made only about 25 . . . Lotus Components' production had been largely responsible for keeping the Lotus companies alive during the dramas of the Elite, but towards the end life was becoming very difficult. The 7 was still trundling on, but the car scheduled to replace the 7 eventually became the Lotus Europa because it showed so much promise in development that it was seen as a potential threat

Peter Warr in his driving days at the wheel of the ex-Graham Hill and factory demonstration 1,100cc Lotus 7-Climax at Silverstone in June 1960.

to Elan sales. Therefore the specification was upped and the price raised to get away from the Elan market and suddenly it was a Lotus Cars production not a Components car at all.

'At virtually the same time we found we had outgrown Delamare road, the local council wouldn't allow us to build any more there so Colin went hunting for a new home and found it in Norfolk, for excellent reasons.

'I was then involved in the early planning of the new Hethel plant there, planning the logistics of moving our people and plant while ensuring minimum disruption to production, and I also had the job of selling the idea of moving to the workforce at Cheshunt. Unfortunately, in selling the idea to them I totally convinced myself that I didn't want to go!'

He was still only 27, he enjoyed the electricity of living in London, felt he would miss his friends and social life there and had some natural reluctance to see the Lotus which he knew and had grown up with grow any bigger. 'I just didn't fancy working for the big megalith if that's what it was going to become.'

Ever since that day when he had first joined the staff at Hornsey the plum job he had really dreamed of landing was that of managing Team Lotus. Initially that had been Stan Chapman's job, and when he stood down it had gone to Andrew Ferguson, fresh from the Camoradi Team and before that ex-Cooper.

'Andrew and I had become good friends. He was still there so that job wasn't available and I decided I wanted to go into business on my own, largely just to see if I could make it outside Lotus.'

He went into partnership with an old racing chum

The youthful Peter Warr earned international success as a racing driver. Here he is garlanded after winning the 25th International Eifelrennen at the Nürburgring in his Lotus 20.

named Ken Lyon and for three years ran a model and hobbies import business. It was fun, but he found that 'the real world' outside the sizzling always-electric atmosphere of Lotus was agonizingly, frustratingly slow.

Then one day in 1969 Andrew Ferguson telephoned him and said he was leaving Team, the job Peter had always wanted would be available. Peter instantly called Colin, who was out, left a message with his secretary and Colin quickly called back.

'Whether Colin was psychic — which he very often seemed to be, because he always had an *incredible* feel for what was about to happen — or whether by that time Andrew had told him I was interested, I don't know, but without any preamble he just invited me straight up to Hethel and I signed-up there and then, while trying hard not to appear *too* keen.'

Peter had been with Lotus through the greater part of the Jimmy Clark era. 'Now we had another fantastic period. I started with Team the day after Graham broke his legs at Watkins Glen and Jochen Rindt won his first GP there, and then we went through the 1970 Championship season with all its success and euphoria and then its tragic end, and all through the Lotus 72 era to the end of '75 with Emerson and Ronnie Peterson and another Driver's World title and two more Constructors' Championships. We all enjoyed a sense of real achievement, being part of a team which for the greater part of that period was always right up there amongst the very best.'

Through 1975, however, it had been a classic case of a bridge too far for the 72s, and into 1976 Peter had been with Team for seven seasons and some of

the excitement was beginning to pall: 'It's vain to say so, but by 1976 I couldn't help but feel that I tended to be in trouble when it all blew-up, while Colin got the glory if it all went like clockwork and the cars won. That was a bad season for us, which meant I felt increasingly belaboured. Don't misunderstand that, Colin was just incredible as an employer. He was incredibly generous both financially and in other ways, but I had just been around long enough to start wondering if it needed him and his magic to be successful.

'Against the background of this psychology, I had been approached in the paddock at Brands Hatch during the British GP by this very loud guy with a funny accent who said "I wanna word with you" and virtually dragged me bodily behind a mobile home and said "I want you to come and work with me, come and have dinner tonight, bring your wife . . .". That was Walter Wolf, whose new Wolf-Williams team was at that time in all kinds of trouble.

'He took us to dinner at the London Hilton and laid before us a picture of a racing team and an ambition and the wherewithal to do something which was very simple and straightforward, and fairly staggering in its concept.

'You see that was the end of the private owner era. You just couldn't make it in Formula 1 on your own any more, as Hesketh had discovered. But here was Walter Wolf describing a team concentrating its efforts upon one driver, and building, developing and racing its own cars, which he would fund totally.

'He already had Harvey Postlethwaite to design a new car for him and now his approach to me gave me the opportunity to see if I could run a racing team without Colin behind me. So I told Colin at Monza that I would be leaving at the end of the season.

'He was very upset. We did have a close relationship within the team, not outside it, but certainly within it, and he knew how I'd tackle a problem; we'd been through some difficult times together and we had won a lot of races. He felt it would upset the smooth running of the team, but was typically generous because he realized I really did want to go. I told him I wanted to go for at least three years, and he finally said: "Let's not treat it as a resignation, let's treat it as a leave of absence . . ." And we ended the season with Mario's win at Fuji, and the prototype 78 had been looking very good on test, so that wasn't a bad point at which to leave . . . Team's fortunes had sunk very low, and now they had surged back up again, so by no means was I abandoning a sinking ship — in fact quite the reverse. I left on a high note for everybody.'

Peter joined Walter Wolf Racing in the former Williams factory at Bennett Road, Reading, immediately after that Japanese GP trip. By that time Harvey had already completed design of the

Peter Warr the Grand Prix winner. This is the 1963 Japanese GP in which he was first past the post in his Lotus 23.

new 1977 Wolf cars which Jody Scheckter would drive for the team. Peter obviously knew of Team's Lotus 78 'wing-car' thinking and naturally discussed his knowledge with Harvey, but the tough-minded engineer was convinced that a good conventional car driven by Scheckter could win the championship and he was right — the new Wolf car winning on its debut in Argentina, adding two more wins at Monaco and Mosport Park and numerous good placings. 'With one car and one driver we finished second in the Championship and but for two fuel pump problems we would probably have won it.'

By the end of 1977 there was still a general feeling that the Lotus 78 was too slow in a straight line, but in the first 1978 race at Buenos Aires, Mario's 78 won on that quite high-speed circuit and the Wolf team returned home with Harvey telling Peter: 'If we don't have a wing car ready for the European season we aren't going to be in the hunt.'

So they hastily built a ground-effects car which incorporated several innovations, but being late on the ground-effects scene left Wolf, and every other team apart from Lotus, trailing behind and having to catch up that year.

'Initially we had regarded 1977 — in which we had still won those three GPs — as only a shake-down season, and we really intended to go for it in '78, but that was the year of Lotus ground-effects and against that magic ingredient we weren't in such good shape.

'By the end of it, Wolf was beginning to run out of steam, Jody wanted to go to Ferrari, having received a fantastic offer from them. That was really our own fault.

'At that time we didn't have any sensible onboard recording apparatus for test and development, so we rang up Ferrari and asked if we could test on their Fiorano track, to have access to their corner-timing equipment. They of course took all the measurements of Jody driving our car and realized just how quick he was against their flat-12s, even in a Ford-engined car, and that really made them sit up and take notice. So Jody went to Ferrari for 1979 and won the World Championship, and I have to say that we were all delighted for him.

'But meanwhile, during 1979 Walter had found

he could no longer handle the bill for running his team privately. He had always liked the star personality association. He wasn't a man to take on an unknown young driver and bring him on. That wasn't his way. Consequently we ran James Hunt, which brought us Olympus Cameras sponsorship, and being commercially sponsored like that was actually a bit against the grain because we had become the last of the intrepid independents; we could run our programme as we wanted, build as many cars as we liked, we had no sponsors' ties — so 1979 went a little against the ethic of Walter Wolf Racing as originally conceived.

'Then we soon found that James' heart was no longer in it and although Harvey did an advanced new monocoque for us, introducing the folded aluminium honeycomb sheet form of construction, it wasn't really a competitive car. James suddenly decided to retire in mid-season. The Ligiers had been very quick and then Depailler had his hang-gliding accident and Ligier were suddenly looking for a driver, so James was interested in taking the drive, retired or otherwise.

'Now he'd omitted to read his contract, which stated that if he should retire and then decide to return within five years he would have to fulfill the rest of his contract with us. We wouldn't give him the release he needed to join Ligier, and Gerard Ducarouge of Ligier was a strong member of FOCA at that time and he agreed he would not take James without our approval.

'That still left us without a driver, so I jetted to America on Concorde, went to a funny little CanAm race at Elkhart Lake, sat in Paul Newman's motorhome and signed-up a Finn named Keke Rosberg. He did jolly well considering the car was not that good, but then Walter decided to stop. Unlike many people who have come into motor racing and then dropped out, he paid-up all his bills before he left, utterly correct and proper.

'I had 34 people at Bennett Road relying on me for jobs, and the only deal I could strike to ensure their future was to merge with Fittipaldi from Slough. I did the deal with Emerson — whom I knew very well of course from our time together in Team Lotus — and his brother Wilson and we combined in the Reading shop, assimilating a few of their people, Emerson bringing sponsorship for himself and for Rosberg as second driver. We were up and running. Emerson and I had a long-lasting and very good relationship, but it only took the 1980 season to destroy it *completely*.

'At the end of 1973 it had been evident to us at Lotus that Emerson was no longer the demon racer he had once been, much of the original panache and sharpness seemed to be fading. Now through 1980 we found he wanted to be driver, designer, team manager, everything. Wilson was a very competent businessman, well able to cope competently with major matters, but he was in Brazil looking after the family farm and the Mercedes dealership and so on and just couldn't get to Europe often enough to make his younger brother concentrate upon what he should have been doing, which was driving.

'I had signed a two-year contract with Emerson, but Harvey quickly realized there was no future for him there and he told me at Monaco '81 that he'd accepted a Ferrari job. And that was the beginning of the end.

'We ran out the end of the season amid fantasies of wealthy Brazilian friends fronting-up with fantastic sponsorship, but nothing concrete happening and I was most unhappy with the whole situation and I finally told Emerson I would be leaving when my contract expired at the end of the year.

'Colin got wind of what was going on and rang me up and said simply: "Leave of absence is over, come back here".

At 43, Peter was married — wife Yvonne — with two children, and after his five-season absence from Team Lotus, he found it a very different organization to that which he had left.

'Back in 1976 we had already set up the then-new R&D department at Ketteringham Hall, and even then it was obvious that having R&D remote from the racing team itself was not very efficient, so I had recommended that Team should also move as soon as possible from Potash Lane to Ketteringham. That had happened in my absence.'

Upon his return Peter found morale understandably indifferent. Team had been run 'an odd way', with the Australian Peter Collins as competitions manager and freelance consultant Peter Wright largely in sole technical charge since Nigel Bennett had left. Team had been drifting, Colin searching — when he could find the time — for the next spectacular leap forward, which he was fated not to find.

The 1982 Austrian GP win — albeit so fortunate — was the highlight of Peter's first season back at Lotus, but that December a small-hours telephone call brought him the chilling news of Colin's death.

'It's still difficult to explain my feelings adequately', he would reflect in later years, 'like most of the people here the first reaction was simple disbelief. It was an utterly stunning blow, but we had to pick up the team and go on because that's what Colin would have expected of us, and logically of course there was no alternative. We had contractual commitments and we couldn't just sit there and let everything collapse while we felt sorry for ourselves.'

During that 1982 season Colin's advance plans for the mid-'eighties had been progressed by Peter Warr. He had gone hunting for a turbocharged engine, talking first to BMW, who said they'd love to assist but at that stage simply could not because they were fully-extended by their Brabham commitments. The only other major-company turbocharged engine available was Renault's. Consequently Peter negotiated the deal through Gerard Larrousse to project Team into turbocharged Formula 1 racing, and when the race engineers had returned from testing or GPs saying in effect, 'we've got to have radial-ply tyres for ride-height purposes, we're suffering from tyres which grow at speed and lose us ground-effect', it was Peter's job again to secure a supply.

'I talked to Michelin, who said "No way, we cannot service any more teams than we have already", and then Pirelli found us and we found them simultaneously; they were interested in taking on a major team, the terms were terrific — I'm sure it was financially the biggest tyre contract ever written — and with great enthusiasm we signed, but through 1983 we found it was an absolute no-hoper . . . until Pirelli came up with quite good qualifying tyres for the two races which were crucial to our future, at Silverstone and Brands Hatch.

'So after Colin's death we staggered into 1983 with a no-no car, tyres not working properly and trying to learn all about turbo engines and how to use them.'

It wasn't a baptism, but it was certainly fiery.

Just like the Old Man, Peter Warr could be a hard man. He had never suffered fools gladly. He could become excitable under pressure. He certainly developed vivid likes and dislikes. He was by no means everybody's favourite in Formula 1. He would habitually correct any minor verbal inexactitude uttered in his hearing. He would admit 'somebody says something out of place and I'm on to it like that', making a snapping gesture with his fingers. One gets the impression that his very first meeting with Nigel Mansell, whom Colin had encouraged to view himself as an established star driver, struck sparks off both parties, which was an unfortunate start.

The Birmingham driver would develop very much into a Graham Hill of the 'eighties, but his time with Team Lotus — though punctuated with a number of good drives — was generally as fraught as had been Graham's first stint with Team during its early Formula 1 days in 1958-59. Elio de Angelis was another natural good number 2 driver serving with number 1 status. He developed a consistent

Peter with Johnny Dumfries, whom he signed as Ayrton Senna's number 2 for the 1986 season. It was to provide the Scottish earl with invaluable experience in his baptism year of Formula 1 racing.

ability to bring his cars home in the points, but was never a natural winner.

Colin had committed himself to them both as joint number 1 drivers, which meant in effect Team having to prepare four cars for every race to provide them each with a spare. His faith in Nigel Mansell — which the driver ultimately fulfilled with Williams in 1985-86 — had accepted some contractual obligations which Peter Warr came to rue: 'Nigel was always saying "It's written in my contract" . . .'

Peter recalled: 'Colin used to say that in any one year there are three, possibly four drivers in the running for the World Championship who always had to be regarded as natural Grand Prix winners. Our drivers when I returned to Lotus in 1982 didn't figure in that elite group. In effect we did have two number 2s and it stayed that way until 1985 when we took on Ayrton Senna. His class was so obvious that when he joined us that season I had offered him number 1 status, with Elio to decide if he wanted to stay, but he turned it down, preferring to be joint number 1 in what was still only his second season of Formula 1 racing, so that he could still learn his

trade . . . but he soon made it clear he was *the* number 1 out on the track . . .'

Peter had in fact negotiated with Toleman driver Derek Warwick to replace Mansell for 1984, but the Hampshireman had changed his mind at the last moment and moved to Renault instead when Prost abruptly left them to join McLaren. That same month — October '83 — Peter had invited Formula 3 star Ayrton Senna to Ketteringham Hall for a look-round, but Gerard Ducarouge's 1984 Lotus 95Ts would retrieve Team's real stature that season still driven by de Angelis and Mansell.

Finally, for '85 Nigel moved to Williams where he found the relaxed and supportive atmosphere he needed to emerge as a consistent winner. In his place Peter signed-on Senna, who won Team's first GP since Austria '82 and really projected the Lotus-Renault 97Ts to the top. Elio de Angelis just ran out of breath trying to keep up and was outclassed; and would leave for Brabham and what would prove to be his tragically short last season.

Peter then wanted Warwick — out of a job following Renault's works team closure — to join Senna for '86, but the single-minded young Brazilian vetoed the idea, and Peter just knew he was so good — 'In my experience the most complete racing driver since Jimmy Clark' — that he was prepared to let him have his way

That's not to say he did not try — almost interminably — to argue Senna round, but Ayrton was 'a man who is frighteningly and single-mindedly devoted to success' and for complex yet essentially very practical reasons he simply wouldn't have it. The promising young Scots Earl, Johnny Dumfries, was taken on as novice number 2 instead, and Peter Warr found himself the butt of a considerable public controversy for rejecting Derek Warwick's services, and bowing to the Brazilian's wishes.

Short-term that was a no-win situation, until the involved full story emerged — both Senna and Dumfries did well in Team's F1 cars and Warwick shone in his new endurance-racing drive with Jaguar, then returned to Formula 1 by joining Brabham in the aftermath of Elio de Angelis' fatal accident in post-Monaco testing at Ricard.

Into 1986, Team's Lotus-Renault 98Ts were on a par with Williams-Honda and McLaren-TAG Turbo, very much at the top of the Formula 1 pile, with Peter Warr's organizational and administration skills providing an effective framework in which Gerard Ducarouge's technical direction and Ayrton Senna's exceptional driving talents could both flourish.

Team Lotus could well have died along with its founder in 1982-83, but the Old Man had picked and propagated his lieutenants well . . . and in some ways, quite genuinely, even into 1987, they were still doing it all 'for him'.

APPENDIX I

Racing Record; Lotus 12-Lotus 98T

1957

I have included this purely Formula 2 season of Lotus single-seater racing since it involves the early career of the Lotus 12s and provides a prelude to their Formula 1 debut in 1958. For many years records of these early cars were unavailable, and outsiders were usually told they had been mislaid in the move from Cheshunt to Hethel in 1966, or maybe even earlier in the move from Hornsey to Cheshunt in 1959.

Then, late in April 1978, Lotus' long-serving Roy Badcock made available to Richard Bourne two filing cabinets containing some of the original sales record cards for the type 12s, a few of the type 16s, most type 18s and 24s plus many other types. From these it appears that the '300-series' numbers of the front-engined cars (at least) were applied post-completion. Cards survive for ten of the dozen type 12s built. Three of them show that different numbers were applied originally — thus Brooke's '354' began life as 'F2/7', Dennis Taylor's '355' was 'F2/6' and Vogele's (written 'Voegler' on the card) '356' was 'F2/9'. The Brooke and Keith Greene cars' careers took in club races, while the following list shows only Internationals or particularly significant National events. Team cars' careers are as suggested by circumstantial evidence.

22-4-57—Lavant Cup, Goodwood—12-laps

Rtd	Cliff Allison	12-Climax	352

9-6-57—Whit-Sunday Brands Hatch—10-laps

2nd	Herbert Mackay-Fraser	12-Climax	351
Rtd	Cliff Allison	12-Climax	352

10-6-57—Whit-Monday Crystal Palace—Two 10-lap Heats

Rtd	Cliff Allison	12-Climax	352
Rtd	Herbert Mackay-Fraser	12-Climax	351

14-7-57—Coupe de Vitesse, Reims-Gueux, France—40-laps

Rtd	Cliff Allison	12-Climax	352 or '3
Rtd	Dennis Taylor	12-Climax	355*

Records show this car completed 9-7-57, engine FPF No 1009.

5-8-57—Rochester Trophy, Brands Hatch—Two 10-lap Heats

Rtd	Dennis Taylor	12-Climax	355
DNS	Cliff Allison	12-Climax	352 or '3

14-9-57—BRDC International Trophy, Silverstone—Two 15-lap Heats, 35-lap Final

Heat One

Rtd	Cliff Allison	12-Climax	357*

Works car, completed 12-9-57

Heat Two

7th	Henry Taylor/Allison	12-Climax	353
9th	Dennis Taylor	12-Climax	355
Rtd	Keith Hall	12-Climax	352

Final

Rtd	Allison	12-Climax	353
Rtd	Dennis Taylor	12-Climax	355

28-9-57—Woodcote Cup, Goodwood—10-laps

3rd	Cliff Allison	12-Climax	357
5th	Graham Hill	12-Climax	353
Rtd	Keith Hall	12-Climax	352

5-10-57—Gold Cup, Oulton Park—50-laps

2nd	Cliff Allison	12-Climax	357

11th	Graham Hill	12-Climax	353
12th	Keith Hall	12-Climax	352
Rtd	Dennis Taylor	12-Climax	355

1958

7-4-58—Lavant Cup, Goodwood—15-laps

2nd FL	Graham Hill	12-Climax	353
3rd	Cliff Allison	12-Climax	357
Rtd	Dennis Taylor	12-Climax	355

7-4-58—Glover Trophy F1, Goodwood—42-laps*

4th	Cliff Allison	12-Climax F2	357
Rtd	Graham Hill	12-Climax F2	353

Race admitting 1.5-litre F2 cars as make-weights.

19-4-58—Aintree '200' F2 class—67-laps

4th	Graham Hill	12-Climax	353
5th	Cliff Allison	12-Climax	357
10th	Dennis Taylor	12-Climax	355

3-5-58—BRDC International Trophy, Silverstone—50-laps

6th (1st F2)	Cliff Allison	12-Climax F2	357
8th	Graham Hill	12-Climax F1*	353
15th	Dennis Taylor	12-Climax F2	355
Rtd	Ivor Bueb	12-Climax F2	359

Fitted with 1.96-litre Coventry-Climax FPF engine

18-5-58—MONACO GP, Monte Carlo—100-laps

6th	Cliff Allison	12-Climax 1.9	357
Rtd	Graham Hill	12-Climax 1.9	353

26-5-58—DUTCH GP, Zandvoort—75-laps

6th	Cliff Allison	12-Climax 2.2*	357
Rtd	Graham Hill	12-Climax 1.9	353

First use of the intermediate 2207cc engine, spare at Monaco

27-5-58—Crystal Palace Trophy F2—Two 15-lap Heats, 25-lap Final

Heat One

1st FL	Ivor Bueb	12-Climax	359*
Rtd	Les Leston	12-Climax	360**

Bueb's high-tailed car, completed 29-4-58, engine FPF No 1024, also won Helsinki F2.
**John Fisher's car. Mechanic Wally Varley recalls completing it at Hornsey for this race, Leston breaking down on the warming-up lap. Lotus records, however, show completion 30-5-58 and 'shipping' 31-5-58 — after this meeting. Fisher also owned ex-works 353, but 'later' . . .*

Heat Two

3rd	Dennis Taylor	12-Climax	355
Rtd	Anthony Brooke	12-Climax	354*

Records show no completion date (1957) for this car, but FPF engine No 1019.

Final

4th	Ivor Bueb	12-Climax	359
9th	Dennis Taylor	12-Climax	355

8-6-58—Brands Hatch F2—Two 10-lap Heats

5th	Dennis Taylor	12-Climax	355
7th	Les Leston	12-Climax	360

2nd = FL	Dennis Taylor	12-Climax	355
10th	Les Leston	12-Climax	360

Taylor 2nd and Leston 8th on aggregate.

15-6-58—BELGIAN GP, Spa-Francorchamps—24-laps

4th	Cliff Allison	12-Climax 2.2	357
Rtd	Graham Hill	12-Climax 1.9	353

15-6-58—Prix de Paris F2, Montlhéry, France

Rtd	Ivor Bueb	12-Climax	359

5-7-58—Crystal Palace F2—Two 10-lap Heats

2nd PP	Ivor Bueb	12-Climax	359
2nd	Ivor Bueb	12-Climax	359

2nd on Aggregate.

7-7-58—FRENCH GP, Reims-Gueux—50-laps

Rtd	Cliff Allison	12-Climax 2.2	357
Rtd	Graham Hill	16-Climax 1.9	363

7-7-58—Coupe de Vitesse F2, Reims-Gueux—25-laps

'13th'	Graham Hill	12-Climax	352
15th	Les Leston	12-Climax	360
Rtd	Dennis Taylor	12-Climax	355
Rtd	Cliff Allison	16-Climax	362*

This car subsequently written-off after its Portuguese GP accident, and the number re-allocated to John Fisher's new 1958 London Motor Show car—which was completed slowly that year having been given the number '364' when laid down.

20-7-58—BRITISH GP, Silverstone—75-laps

Rtd	Cliff Allison	12-Climax 2.2	357
Rtd	Graham Hill	16-Climax 1.9	362
Rtd	Alan Stacey	16-Climax 1.9	363

21-7-58—Caen GP, Le Prairie, France—86-laps

Rtd	Les Leston	12-Climax F2	360

27-7-58—Vanwall Trophy, Snetterton—20-laps

Rtd	Anthony Brooke	12-Climax	354

27-7-58—Coupe d'Auvergne F2, Clermont-Ferrand, France 20-laps

2nd FL	Ivor Bueb	12-Climax	359
15th	Dennis Taylor	12-Climax	355
Rtd	'Michy'	12-Climax	353*

This was the second-string Fisher car, bought ex-works and driven by a local ace in place of Leston and 360, both slightly bent after inversion (following engine seizure) at Caen.

3-8-58—GERMAN GP, Nurburgring—15-laps

'5th' F1	Cliff Allison	16-Climax 1.9	362
Rtd	Graham Hill	16-Climax F2	363
Rtd	Ivor Bueb	12-Climax F2	359

4-8-58—Kent Trophy, Brands Hatch F2—Two 21-lap Heats

7th	Dennis Taylor	12-Climax	355
9th	Ivor Bueb	12-Climax	359
12th	Keith Greene	12-Climax	361
Rtd	Cliff Allison	12-Climax	357
Rtd	Graham Hill	12-Climax	352

Heat Two

6th	Taylor	
8th	Greene	
Rtd	Bueb	
DNS	Allison and Hill in the works cars	

On aggregate: Taylor 6th; Greene 9th.

24-8-58—PORTUGUESE GP, Oporto—50-laps

Rtd	Graham Hill	16-Climax 2.2	363
DNS	Cliff Allison	16-Climax 1.9	362*

Car wrecked in practice accident, repaired frame believed to be that supplied to Anthony Brooke for his Lotus 16 'special', 1959.

30-8-58—Kentish '100' F2, Brands Hatch—Two 42-lap Heats

5th*	Cliff Allison	12-Climax	357
9th	Ivor Bueb	12-Climax	359
12th	Dennis Taylor	12-Climax	355
Rtd	Graham Hill	16-Climax	363
DNS	Les Leston	12-Climax	360

Aggregate results.

7-9-58—ITALIAN GP, Monza—70-laps

6th*	Graham Hill	16-Climax 2.2	363
7th*	Cliff Allison	12-Climax 1.5	357

Subsequently elevated to 5th and 6th as Gregory/Shelby Maserati was disqualified.

21-9-58—AVUSrennen F2, Berlin, Germany

Rtd	Cliff Allison	12-Climax	357

—	Ivor Bueb	12-Climax	359
—	Dennis Taylor	12-Climax	355

5-10-58—Coupe du Salon F2, Montlhéry, France—20-laps

Rtd	Ivor Bueb	12-Climax	359

19-10-58—MOROCCAN GP, Ain-Diab, Casablanca—53-laps

10th	Cliff Allison	12-Climax 1.9	357
16th	Graham Hill	16-Climax 1.9	363

1959

Research for this season has been more time-consuming than any other since Lotus 16s are now historic racing cars and claims and counter-claims have fogged the real story.

Three Lotus 16s were completed in 1958. The first two were numbered '362' and '363', the former was written-off and the third (laid down as '364') took the earlier number for sale. The surviving works car '363' was sold to David Piper, so Team Lotus had to build new cars for the 1959 season.

Legend has it that they built four, yet in 1960 two ex-Hill cars and two ex-Ireland cars were sold, and Lotus had one left over. There were five. Since Lotus' retrospective 300-series numbering pays no heed to chronology I have renumbered these cars as follows for clarity's sake.

16/1 — Prototype 1959 F1/2 car for Graham Hill, debut Easter Goodwood actually numbered 'F1/X' — sold to David Piper 1960, supposedly as '368'.

16/2 — Debut Silverstone International Trophy 1959, driven by Hill, and became Ireland's regular F1 car. Modified to double-wishbone front suspension for Sebring — almost certainly the Utley/Hicks 1960 car.

16/3 — Debut Silverstone International Trophy F2 class 1959, driven by Ireland. His own F2 car — almost certainly to Finney 1960.

16/4 — Debut Crystal Palace F2 1959, driven by Alan Stacey. His own F2 car — retained at Cheshunt 1960-64.

16/5 — Debut French GP 1959, driven by Ireland and became Hill's regular F1 car until Portuguese GP collision. Rebuilt with double-wishbone front suspension for Sebring — Hill returning to 16/1 meanwhile — to Mike Taylor 1960.

Subsequent ownerships indicate that 16/5 became the Wilks/Roberts/Halford historic racing '365' and 16/4 is definitely the Boorer/Dawson-Damer historic racing '366'. Keith Finney's 1960 invoice for his type 16 bears the chassis number '336' — which is a Lotus 11 sports-car serial! Innes Ireland Ltd operated a team of sports-racers. Photographic evidence and Team personnel memories make me 'virtually certain' of the individual car careers as listed below.

30-3-59—Lavant Cup F2, Goodwood—15-laps

4th	Graham Hill	12-Climax	357
9th	Bruce Halford	16-Climax	362(2)
13th	Dennis Taylor	12-Climax	355

30-3-59—Glover Trophy F1, Goodwood—42-laps

9th	David Piper	16-Climax 1.9	363
Rtd	Graham Hill	16-Climax 2.5	16/1

11-4-59—British Empire Trophy F2, Oulton Park—40-laps

16th	Bob Hicks	12-Climax	357
17th	Dennis Taylor	12-Climax	355
18th	Anthony Brooke	12-Climax	354
Rtd	Graham Hill	16-Climax	16/1
Rtd	Bruce Halford	16-Climax	362(2)
Rtd	Bill Allen	12-Climax	360

18-4-59—Aintree '200' F1/F2—67-laps

11th (5th F1)	Graham Hill	16-Climax 2.5	16/1
12th (last)	Dennis Taylor	12-Climax F2	355
Rtd	Bruce Halford	16-Climax F2	362(2)
Rtd	David Piper	16-Climax F2	363

25-4-59—Syracuse GP F2, Sicily—55-laps

8th	David Piper	16-Climax	363
Rtd	Graham Hill	16-Climax	16/1
Rtd	Bruce Halford	16-Climax	362(2)
Rtd	Maria Teresa de Filippis	12-Climax	353
Rtd	Willie Zimmermann	12-Climax	356

2-5-59—BRDC International Trophy, Silverstone F1/F2—50-laps

4th F2	Innes Ireland	16-Climax F2	16/3
14th (8th F1)	Pete Lovely	16-Climax 2.2	16/1
Rtd	Graham Hill	16-Climax 2.5	16/2

10-5-59—MONACO GP, Monte Carlo—100-laps

Rtd	Graham Hill	16-Climax 2.5	16/1
Rtd	Bruce Halford	16-Climax F2	362(2)
DNQ	Pete Lovely	16-Climax 2.5	16/2

18-5-59—Pau GP F2, France—80-laps

12th	Bob Hicks	12-Climax	357

18-5-59—London Trophy F2, Crystal Palace—36-laps

5th	Dennis Taylor	12-Climax	355
11th	Alan Stacey	16-Climax	16/4
Rtd	David Piper	16-Climax	363
Rtd	Innes Ireland	16-Climax	16/3
Rtd	Bruce Halford	12-Climax	353
DNS	J. D. Lewis	12-Climax	359

31-5-59—DUTCH GP, Zandvoort—75-laps

4th	Innes Ireland	16-Climax 2.5	16/2
7th	Graham Hill	16-Climax 2.5	16/1

28-6-59—Mallory Park F2, England—30-laps

9th	Anthony Brooke	12-Climax	354
Rtd	Graham Hill	16-Climax	16/1
11th	Bob Hicks	12-Climax	357
DNS	Albert Gay	12-Climax	361

5-7-59—FRENCH GP, Reims-Gueux—50-laps

Rtd	Graham Hill	16-Climax 2.5	16/2
Rtd	Innes Ireland	16-Climax 2.5	16/5

5-7-59—Coupe de Vitesse F2, Reims-Gueux—25-laps

7th			
7th	Innes Ireland	16-Climax	16/3
Rtd	Graham Hill	16-Climax	16/1
Rtd	Bruce Halford	16-Climax	362(2)

12-7-59—Rouen GP F2, Les Essarts, France—35-laps

7th	Graham Hill	16-Climax	16/1
'12th'	Bruce Halford	16-Climax	362(2)
'13th'	Alan Stacey	16-Climax	16/4
Rtd	Innes Ireland	16-Climax	16/3

18-7-59—BRITISH GP, Aintree—75-laps

8th	Alan Stacey	16-Climax	16/2
9th	Graham Hill	16-Climax	16/5
Rtd	David Piper	16-Climax F2	363

26-7-59—Coupe d'Auvergne F2, Clermont-Ferrand, France—26-laps

6th	Graham Hill	16-Climax	16/1
9th	Bob Hicks	12-Climax	357
Rtd	Bruce Halford	16-Climax	362(2)

2-8-59—GERMAN GP, AVUS, Berlin—Two 30-lap Heats

Rtd (H1)	Graham Hill	16-Climax	16/5
Rtd (H1)	Innes Ireland	16-Climax	16/2

3-8-59—John Davy Trophy F2, Brands Hatch—Two 25-lap Heats

Rtd	Graham Hill	16-Climax	16/1
Rtd	David Piper	16-Climax	363
Rtd	Dennis Taylor	12-Climax	355

23-8-59—Preis von Zeltweg F2, Knittelfeld, Austria—59-laps

2nd	David Piper	16-Climax	363

23-8-59—PORTUGUESE GP, Monsanto Park, Lisbon—62-laps

Rtd	Graham Hill	16-Climax	16/5*
Rtd	Innes Ireland	16-Climax	16/2

*Wrecked in collision.

29-8-59—Kentish '100' F2, Brands Hatch—Two 42-lap Heats

Heat One

2nd	Graham Hill	16-Climax	16/1
9th	Alan Stacey	16-Climax	16/4
11th	Innes Ireland	16-Climax	16/3
Rtd	David Piper	16-Climax	363

Heat Two

2nd FL	Hill
Rtd	Stacey
DNS	Ireland

Aggregate

2nd = FL	Hill		
DNQ	Bruce Halford	16-Climax	362(2)
DNQ	Dennis Taylor	12-Climax	355
DNP	Peter Monteverdi	12-Climax	356*
DNP	Albert Gay	12-Climax	361**

*Swiss-entered by 'Ecurie Hoba', presumably ex-Vogele '356'. Monteverdi later built the MBM Formula cars, then his extremely exotic luxury saloons.
**Ex-Keith Greene car entered by 'Ecurie Gay-Yimkin'.

13-9-59—ITALIAN GP, Monza—72-laps

Rtd	Graham Hill	16-Climax	16/1
Rtd	Innes Ireland	16-Climax	16/2

26-9-59—Gold Cup, Oulton Park, England—55-laps

5th	Graham Hill	16-Climax	16/1
7th	David Piper	16-Climax	363

27-9-59—Coupe du Salon, Montlhéry, France—26-laps

Rtd	Bob Hicks	12-Climax	357

11-10-59—Silver City Trophy F1/F2, Snetterton—25-laps

4th	David Piper	16-Climax 1.9	363
Rtd	Graham Hill	16-Climax 2.5	16/1
Rtd	Innes Ireland	16-Climax 2.5	16/2

12-12-59—UNITED STATES GP, Sebring, Florida—42-laps

5th	Innes Ireland	16-Climax	16/5
Rtd	Alan Stacey	16-Climax	16/2

N.B. By this time 16/1 (perhaps '368') had been sold to David Piper and was headed for New Zealand.

1960

7-2-60—ARGENTINE GP, Buenos Aires—80-laps

6th	Innes Ireland	18-Climax	369
9th	Rodriguez Larreta	16-Climax	16/5
Rtd	Alan Stacey	16-Climax	16/2

14-2-60—Buenos Aires City GP, Cordoba, Argentina—75-laps

Rtd	Alan Stacey/Ireland	16-Climax	16/2
Rtd	Ireland	16-Climax	16/5
DNS	Innes Ireland	18-Climax	369

18-4-60—Glover Trophy F1, Goodwood—42-laps

1st FL	Innes Ireland	18-Climax	371
Rtd	Alan Stacey	18-Climax	369
Rtd	Mike Taylor	16-Climax	16/5

14-5-60—BRDC International Trophy, Silverstone—50-laps

1st FL	Innes Ireland	18-Climax	371
4th	Alan Stacey	18-Climax	370
17th	Mike Taylor	18-Climax	369
Rtd	John Surtees	18-Climax	373
Rtd	David Piper	18-Climax	368

29-5-60—MONACO GP, Monte Carlo—100-laps

1st PP	Stirling Moss	18-Climax	376
Rtd	Innes Ireland	18-Climax	371
Rtd	Alan Stacey	18-Climax	370
Rtd	John Surtees	18-Climax	373

6-6-60—DUTCH GP, Zandvoort—75-laps

2nd	Innes Ireland	18-Climax	371
4th PP FL	Stirling Moss	18-Climax	376
Rtd	Alan Stacey	18-Climax	370
Rtd	Jim Clark	18-Climax	373

19-6-60—BELGIAN GP, Spa-Francorchamps—36-laps

5th	Jim Clark	18-Climax	373
Rtd = FL	Innes Ireland	18-Climax	371

Crashed	Alan Stacey	18-Climax	370
DNS	Stirling Moss	18-Climax	376
DNS	Mike Taylor	18-Climax	369

3-7-60—FRENCH GP, Reims-Gueux—50-laps

5th	Jim Clark	18-Climax	373
6th	Ron Flockhart	18-Climax	374
7th	Innes Ireland	18-Climax	371
DNS	David Piper	16-Climax	368

16-7-60—BRITISH GP, Silverstone—77-laps

2nd	John Surtees	18-Climax	373
3rd	Innes Ireland	18-Climax	371
12th	David Piper	16-Climax	368
16th	Jim Clark	18-Climax	374

1-8-60—Silver City Trophy F1, Brands Hatch—50-laps

6th	John Surtees	18-Climax	373
Rtd PP = FL	Jim Clark	18-Climax	374
Rtd	Innes Ireland	18-Climax	371
Rtd	David Piper	18-Climax	368

14-8-60—PORTUGUESE GP, Oporto—35-laps

3rd	Jim Clark	18-Climax	374
6th	Innes Ireland	18-Climax	371
Rtd PP FL	John Surtees	18-Climax	373
DIS	Stirling Moss	18-Climax	376*

*Presumed to be the new car taking the number of its predecessor written-off after Spa, rebuilt around a new frame, or possibly '906'. or '912'—had white screen moulding.

4-9-60—ITALIAN GP, Monza—No British works team entries

17-9-60—Lombank Trophy, Snetterton—37-laps

1st	Innes Ireland	18-Climax	372
2nd FL	Jim Clark	18-Climax	374
11th	Keith Finney	16-Climax F2	16/3 ('367')
12th	Marcus Niven	12-Climax F2	367
14th	Bob Hicks	16-Climax F2	16/2 ('364')
Rtd	John Surtees	18-Climax	373
DNS	Tony Brooks	18-Vanwall	901

24-9-60—Gold Cup, Oulton Park—60-laps

1st PP	Stirling Moss	18-Climax	376*
Rtd	Innes Ireland	18-Climax	372
Rtd FL	Jim Clark	18-Climax	374
Rtd	John Surtees	18-Climax	373
Rtd	Ian Burgess	18-Maserati	902

*Black screen surround

9-10-60—Watkins Glen Formule Libre GP, USA—100-laps

1st PP	Stirling Moss	18-Climax	'376'*
10th	Harry Entwhistle	15-Climax sports	
Rtd	Syd Kaback	15-Climax sports	

*White screen surround

20-11-60—UNITED STATES GP, Riverside, California—75-laps

1st PP	Stirling Moss	18-Climax	'376'*
2nd	Innes Ireland	18-Climax	372
7th	Jim Hall	18-Climax	907
16th	Jim Clark	18-Climax	371
Rtd	John Surtees	18-Climax	373

*Black screen surround

N.B.—Team Lotus 18s with 1.5-litre Climax engines also won the following Formula 2 races this season:
2-4-60 Oulton Park—Innes Ireland 369
18-4-60 Lavant Cup, Goodwood—Innes Ireland 370
6-6-60 Crystal Palace—Trevor Taylor 372
27-8-60 Kentish '100', Brands Hatch—Jim Clark 372
Also: 11-9-60 Roskilde, Denmark—Ireland 3rd 372; 9-10-60 Coupe du Salon, Montlhéry—Richard Utley 3rd (16-Climax 364); 23-4-60, Norfolk Trophy, Snetterton—David Piper 3rd (16-Climax 368).

1961

This season was the first of 1½-litre Formula 1 racing, and this table also includes the four British InterContinental Formula events run for 2½-litre cars surviving from 1960.

25-3-61—Lombank Trophy InterContinental, Snetterton—37-laps

2nd	Cliff Allison	18-Climax 2.5	915
Rtd FL	Innes Ireland	18-Climax 2.5	374

26-3-61—Lombank Trophy, Snetterton—37-laps

2nd	Cliff Allison	18-Climax	915
4th	Henry Taylor	18-Climax	916
6th	Jim Clark	18-Climax	371
7th	Tim Parnell	18-Climax	904
Rtd PP = FL	Innes Ireland	18-Climax	374

3-4-61—Lavant Cup InterContinental, Goodwood—21-laps

Rtd	Dan Gurney	18-Climax 2.5	903

3-4-61—Glover Trophy, Goodwood—42-laps

4th PP	Stirling Moss	18-Climax	'912'
5th	Innes Ireland	18-Climax	372
6th	Henry Taylor	18-Climax	916
7th	Tony Marsh	18-Climax	909
8th	Cliff Allison	18-Climax	915

3-4-61—Pau GP, France—100-laps

1st FL	Jim Clark	18-Climax	371
2nd	Jo Bonnier	18-Climax	914
9th	Trevor Taylor	18-Climax	374
10th	Wolfgang Seidel	18-Climax	373
Rtd	Ian Burgess	18-Climax	908

9-3-61—Brussels GP, Heysel, Belgium—Three 22-lap Heats
Heat One

5th	Tony Marsh	18-Climax	909
6th	Innes Ireland	18-Climax	371
7th	Cliff Allison	18-Climax	915
11th	Ian Burgess	18-Climax	908
14th	Stirling Moss	18-Climax	906*

*The black screen surround car, definitely '906' possibly Ex-Tasman, US GP and Gold Cup car while white surround car was possibly '912'—otherwise 4-cyl cars were virtually identical.

Heat Two		**Heat Three**	
3rd	Marsh	2nd FL	Moss
4th	Ireland	4th	Marsh
6th	Allison	6th	Allison
7th	Burgess	7th	Burgess
8th	Moss	10th	Ireland

Aggregate

3rd	Marsh		
5th	Allison		
6th	Ireland		
7th	Moss		
8th	Burgess		
Rtd	Clark	18-Climax	374
Rtd	Wolfgang Seidel	18-Climax	373
Rtd	Andre Pilette	18-Climax	904
Rtd	Henry Taylor	18-Climax	916

16-3-61—Vienna Preis, Aspern aerodrome, Austria—55-laps

1st PP FL	Stirling Moss	18-Climax	906
2nd	Wolfgang Seidel	18-Climax	373
3rd	Ernesto Prinoth	18-Climax	913
6th	Tim Parnell	18-Climax	904
Rtd	Gerry Ashmore	18-Climax	919

22-4-61—Aintree '200', England—50-laps

7th	Tony Marsh	18-Climax	909
9th	Jim Clark	18-Climax	372
10th	Innes Ireland	18-Climax	371
11th	Gerry Ashmore	18-Climax	919
14th	Dan Gurney	18-Climax	903
15th	Cliff Allison	18-Climax	915
19th	Trevor Taylor	18-Climax	374
Rtd	Michel May	18-Climax	914
Rtd	Tim Parnell	18-Climax	904
Rtd	Peter Procter	16-Climax	'B1'
Rtd	Henry Taylor	18-Climax	916
Rtd	Ian Burgess	18-Climax	908

25-4-61—Syracuse GP, Sicily—56-laps

6th	Jim Clark	18-Climax	374
8th	Stirling Moss	18-Climax	906
10th	Wolfgang Seidel	18-Climax	373
Rtd	Innes Ireland	18-Climax	371
DNS	Ernesto Prinoth	18-Climax	913

14-5-61—MONACO GP, Monte Carlo—100-laps

1st PP = FL	Stirling Moss	18-Climax	912
8th	Cliff Allison	18-Climax	916

10th	Jim Clark	21-Climax	930
Rtd	Michel May	18-Climax	914
DNS	Innes Ireland	21-Climax	931
DNQ	Henry Taylor	18-Climax	915

6-5-61—BRDC International Trophy InterContinental, Silverstone—80-laps
4th	Henry Taylor	18-Climax 2.5	916
12th	Innes Ireland	18-Climax 2.5	371
Rtd	Jim Clark	18-Climax 2.5	374
Rtd	Cliff Allison	18-Climax 2.5	915
Rtd	Tim Parnell	18-Climax 2.5	918/2

14-5-61—Naples GP, Possilippo, Italy—60-laps
2nd PP	Gerry Ashmore	18-Climax	919
4th	Ian Burgess	18-Climax	908
8th	Tim Parnell	18-Climax	904
9th	Ernesto Prinoth	18-Climax	913

22-5-61—DUTCH GP, Zandvoort—75-laps
3rd FL	Jim Clark	21-Climax	930
4th	Stirling Moss	18-Climax	912
13th	Trevor Taylor	18-Climax	371
DNS	Ian Burgess	18-Climax	905

22-5-61—London Trophy, Crystal Palace—37-laps
2nd = FL	Henry Taylor	18-Climax	916
3rd	Tony Marsh	18-Climax	909
5th	Wolfgang Seidel	18-Climax	373
8th	Cliff Allison	18-Climax	915

3-6-61—Silver City Trophy, Brands Hatch—76-laps
1st PP FL	Stirling Moss	18/21-Climax	918
2nd	Jim Clark	21-Climax	930
5th	Dan Gurney	18-Climax	903
6th	Tony Marsh	18-Climax	909
7th	Tim Parnell	18-Climax	904
8th	Henry Taylor	18-Climax	916
9th	Trevor Taylor	18-Climax	371
11th	Jo Bonnier	18/21-Climax	917
Rtd	Wolfgang Seidel	18-Climax	373
Rtd	Michel May	18-Climax	914

18-6-61—BELGIAN GP, Spa-Francorchamps—30-laps
8th	Stirling Moss	18/21-Climax	912
12th	Jim Clark	21-Climax	932
Rtd	Innes Ireland	21-Climax	933
Rtd	Lucien Bianchi	18-Climax	373
Rtd	Willy Mairesse	18-Climax	909
DNQ	Tony Marsh	18-Climax	909
DNQ	Wolfgang Seidel	18-Climax	373
DNQ	Ian Burgess	18-Climax	918

8-7-61—British Empire Trophy InterContinental, Silverstone—52-laps
5th	Jim Clark	18-Climax 2.5	372
9th	Innes Ireland	18-Climax 2.5	371
10th	Lucien Bianchi/Henry Taylor	18-Climax 2.5	915
Rtd	Henry Taylor	18-Climax 2.5	916
Rtd	Tim Parnell	18-Climax 2.5	904

2-7-61—FRENCH GP, Reims-Gueux—52-laps
3rd	Jim Clark	21-Climax	932
4th	Innes Ireland	21-Climax	933
10th	Henry Taylor	18/21-Climax	916
11th	Michel May	18-Climax	914
14th	Ian Burgess	18-Climax	905
Rtd	Stirling Moss	18/21-Climax	912
Rtd	Willy Mairesse	21-Climax	930
T-car	Juan-Manuel Bordeu	18/21-Climax	915
DNS	Wolfgang Seidel	18-Climax	373
Rtd	Lucien Bianchi	18/21-Climax	917

15-7-61—BRITISH GP, Aintree—75-laps
10th	Innes Ireland	21-Climax	933
13th	Tony Maggs	18-Climax	903
14th	Ian Burgess	18-Climax	905
17th	Wolfgang Seidel	18-Climax	373
Rtd	Jim Clark	21-Climax	932
Rtd	Lucien Bianchi	18/21-Climax	917
Rtd	Stirling Moss	18/21-Climax	912
Rtd	Tony Marsh	18-Climax	909
Rtd	Tim Parnell	18-Climax	904
Rtd	Gerry Ashmore	18-Climax	919
Rtd	Henry Taylor	18/21-Climax	916

23-7-61—Solitude GP, Stuttgart, West Germany—25-laps
1st	Innes Ireland	21-Climax	933
7th	Jim Clark	21-Climax	932
9th	Trevor Taylor	21-Climax	930
Rtd	Michel May	18-Climax	914
Rtd	Wolfgang Seidel	18-Climax	373
Rtd	Stirling Moss	18/21-Climax	917

6-8-61—GERMAN GP, Nurburgring—15-laps
1st	Stirling Moss	18/21-Climax	912
4th	Jim Clark	21-Climax	930
11th	Tony Maggs	18-Climax	903
15th	Tony Marsh	18-Climax	909
16th	Gerry Ashmore	18-Climax	919
Rtd	Wolfgang Seidel	18-Climax	373
Rtd	Innes Ireland	21-Climax	933
DNS	Michel May	18-Climax	914

7-8-61—Guards Trophy InterContinental, Brands Hatch—76-laps
2nd	Jim Clark	18-Climax	372
Rtd	Innes Ireland	18-Climax 2.5	371
Rtd	Masten Gregory	18-Climax 2.5	916
Rtd	Dan Gurney	18-Climax 2.5	915
Rtd	Bruce Halford	18-Climax 2.5	374

20-8-61—Karlskoga Kannonloppet, Sweden—30-laps
1st = FL	Stirling Moss	18/21-Climax	918
5th	Tim Parnell	18-Climax	904
Rtd	Carl Hammarlund	18/21-Climax	917
Rtd	Innes Ireland	18-Climax	371
Rtd PP	Jim Clark	21-Climax	930

26/27-8-61 — Danish GP, Roskilde—One 20-lap, two 30-lap Heats
Heat One
1st PP FL	Stirling Moss	18/21-Climax	916
3rd	Innes Ireland	21-Climax	930
6th	Jim Clark	18-Climax	371
7th	Henry Taylor	17/21-Climax	917
8th	Masten Gregory	18/2-Climax	918
10th	Tim Parnell	18-Climax	904

Heat Two		Heat Three	
1st PP FL	Moss	1st PP FL	Moss
2nd	Ireland	2nd	Ireland
5th	Parnell	4th	Clark
6th	Taylor	5th	Taylor
Rtd	Clark	6th	Parnell
		DNS	Gregory

Aggregate
1st	Moss
2nd	Ireland
4th	Taylor
5th	Parnell
7th	Clark
Rtd	Gregory

3-9-61—Modena GP, Italy—100-laps
1st PP FL	Stirling Moss	18/21-Climax	912
4th	Jim Clark	21-Climax	933
Rtd	Giorgio Scarlatti	18-Maserati	902
Rtd	Henry Taylor	18/21-Climax	918
DNQ*	Innes Ireland	21-Climax	934
DNQ	Wolfgang Seidel	18-Climax	373
DNQ	Tim Parnell	18-Climax	904

Set faster time than Bussinello's De Tomaso and Scarlatti but excluded to allow these Italian drivers a start amongst the 14-car field.

10-9-61—ITALIAN GP—Monza—43-laps
11th	Tim Parnell	18-Climax	904
12th	Henry Taylor	18/21-Climax	918
Rtd	Stirling Moss	21-Climax	933
Rtd	Prince Gaetano Starrabba	Maserati	902
Rtd	Masten Gregory	18/21-Climax	917
Rtd	Innes Ireland	18/21-Climax	912
Rtd	Wolfgang Seidel	18-Climax	373
Rtd	Jim Clark	21-Climax	934
Rtd	Gerry Ashmore	18-Climax	919

17-9-61—Zeltweg Flugplatzrennen, Austria—80-laps
1st PP FL	Innes Ireland	21-Climax	933
4th	Jim Clark	21-Climax	930
7th	Tim Parnell	18-Climax	904

| Rtd | Ernesto Prinoth | 18-Climax | 913 |
| Rtd | Wolfgang Seidel | 18-Climax | 373 |

23-9-61—Gold Cup, Oulton Park—60-laps
5th	Masten Gregory	18/21-Climax	917
8th	Henry Taylor	18/21-Climax	918
10th	Wolfgang Seidel	18-Climax	373
Rtd	Tim Parnell	18-Climax	904
Rtd	Innes Ireland	21-Climax	933
Rtd	Jim Clark	21-Climax	930
Rtd	Trevor Taylor	18-Climax	371

1-10-61—Lewis-Evans Trophy, Brands Hatch—30-laps
| 3rd | Tim Parnell | 18-Climax | 904 |
| Rtd | Peter Procter | 16-Climax | 'B1' |

8-10-61—UNITED STATES GP, Watkins Glen—100-laps
1st	Innes Ireland	21-Climax	933
7th	Jim Clark	21-Climax	930
9th	Peter Ryan	18/21-Climax	372
11th	Olivier Gendebien/Masten Gregory	18/21-Climax	918
Rtd	Jim Hall	18/21-Climax	371
Rtd	Lloyd Ruby	18-Climax	907
Rtd	Stirling Moss	18/21-Climax	912
Rtd	Masten Gregory	18/21-Climax	917

10-10-61—Coppa Italia, Vallelunga, Italy—Two 30-lap Heats
Heat One
| 2nd | Ernesto Prinoth | 18-Climax | 913 |
| 8th | Gaetano Starrabba | 18-Maserati | 902 |

Heat Two
| 2nd | Prinoth |
| '8th' | Starrabba |

Aggregate
| 2nd | Prinoth |
| 8th | Starrabba |

9-12-61—Rand GP, Kyalami, South Africa—75-laps
1st PP	Jim Clark	21-Climax	937
2nd	Trevor Taylor	21-Climax	933
7th	Syd van der Vyver	18-Alfa Romeo	FJ
9th	Bob van Niekerk	18-Ford	FJ
Rtd	Jack Holme	18-Climax	FJ-720
Rtd	Gene Bosman	15-Alfa Romeo	sports
Rtd	Helmut Menzler	18-Borgward	911
Rtd	Bernie Podmore	18-Ford	FJ
Rtd	Masten Gregory	18/21-Climax	917

17-12-61—Natal GP, Westmead, South Africa—89-laps
1st PP	Jim Clark	21-Climax	937
2nd FL	Stirling Moss	18/21-Climax	918
5th	Syd van der Vyver	18-Alfa Romeo	FJ
Rtd	Masten Gregory	18/21-Climax	917
Rtd	Trevor Taylor	21-Climax	933
Rtd	Bob van Niekerk	18-Ford	FJ
Rtd	Neville Lederle	18-Ford	FJ
Rtd	Helmut Menzler	18-Borgward	911

26-12-61—South African GP, East London—80-laps
1st PP FL	Jim Clark	21-Climax	937
2nd	Stirling Moss	18/21-Climax	918
6th	Syd van der Vyver	18-Alfa Romeo	FJ
9th	Bob van Niekerk	18-Ford	FJ
10th	Helmut Menzler	18-Borgward	911
Rtd	Bernie Podmore	18-Ford	FJ
Rtd	Masten Gregory	18/21-Climax	916
Rtd	Trevor Taylor	21-Climax	933
Rtd	Gene Bosman	15-Alfa Romeo	sports

1962
2-1-62—Cape GP, Killarney, South Africa—60-laps
1st	Trevor Taylor	21-Climax	933
2nd PP FL	Jim Clark	21-Climax	937
4th	Masten Gregory	18/21-Climax	917
7th	Syd van der Vyver	18-Alfa Romeo	FJ
10th	Helmut Menzler	18-Borgward	911
11th	Bob van Niekerk	18-Ford	FJ
13th	Bernie Podmore	18-Ford	FJ
14th	Neville Lederle	18-Ford	FJ

1-4-62—Brussels GP, Heysel, Belgium—Three 22-lap Heats
Heat One
2nd FL	Stirling Moss	18/21-Climax V8	906
7th	Innes Ireland	18/21-Climax	916
13th	Jo Siffert	22-Ford	22-J-7
15th	Trevor Taylor	21-Climax	938
Rtd PP	Jim Clark	24-Climax V8	948
Rtd	Masten Gregory	18/21-Climax	917

Heat Two
3rd	Ireland
7th	Siffert
'Rtd'	T. Taylor
Rtd	Moss

Heat Three
3rd	Ireland
4th	T. Taylor
6th	Siffert

Aggregate
3rd	Ireland
6th	Siffert
10th	T. Taylor
FL	Moss

14-4-62—Lombank Trophy, Snetterton—50-laps
1st	Jim Clark	24-Climax V8	948
5th	Tony Shelly	18/21-Climax	'P1'
7th PP FL	Stirling Moss	18/21-Climax V8	906
Rtd	Masten Gregory	18/21-Climax	917
Rtd	Innes Ireland	18/21-Climax	916
Rtd	Trevor Taylor	21-Climax	938
Rtd	Tim Parnell	18/21-Climax	'P2'

23-4-62—Lavant Cup, Goodwood (4-cyl F1 cars)—21-laps
3rd	Tony Shelly	18/21-Climax	'P1'
5th	Jay Chamberlain	18-Climax	908
Rtd	Gunther Seifert	18-Climax	373
Rtd	Gerry Ashmore	18/21-Climax	919

23-4-62—Glover Trophy, Goodwood—42-laps
3rd	Innes Ireland	18/21-Climax	916
5th	Masten Gregory	18/21-Climax	917
6th	Tony Shelly	18/21-Climax	'P1'
9th	Gerry Ashmore	18/21-Climax	919
Rtd	Jay Chamberlain	18-Climax	905
Rtd PP = FL*	Stirling Moss	18/21-Climax V8	906

Moss' final near-fatal accident occurred in this event

23-4-62—Pau GP, France—100-laps
1st	Maurice Trintignant	18/21-Climax	918
6th	Nino Vaccarella	18/21-Climax	912
7th	Jo Siffert	21-Climax	938
11th	Trevor Taylor	24-Climax V8	950
Rtd	Jack Brabham	21-Climax	936
Rtd PP FL	Jim Clark	24-Climax V8	948

28-4-62—Aintree '200'—Liverpool—50-laps
1st PP FL	Jim Clark	24-Climax V8	948
5th	Trevor Taylor	24-Climax V8	950
7th	Tony Shelly	18/21-Climax	'P1'
9th	Tim Parnell	18/21-Climax	'P2'
11th	David Piper	18/21-Climax	919
12th	Gunther Seifert	18-Climax	373
DIS	Jay Chamberlain	18-Climax	908
Rtd	Jack Brabham	21-Climax	936
Rtd	Innes Ireland	18/21-Climax	916
Rtd	Masten Gregory	18/21-Climax	917

12-5-62—BRDC International Trophy, Silverstone—52-laps
2nd FL	Jim Clark	24-Climax V8	948
6th	Jack Brabham	24-Climax V8	947
8th	Masten Gregory	24-Climax V8	942
10th	Trevor Taylor	24-Climax V8	950
16th	Jay Chamberlain	18-Climax	908
17th	David Piper	18/21-Climax	919
Rtd	Tony Shelly	18/21—Climax	'P1'
Rtd	Tim Parnell	18/21-Climax	'P2'
Rtd	Nino Vaccarella	18/21-Climax	912
Rtd	Maurice Trintignant	18/21-Climax	918
T-car	Brabham	21-Climax	936

20-5-62—DUTCH GP, Zandvoort—80-laps
2nd	Trevor Taylor	24-Climax V8	948
9th	Jim Clark	25-Climax V8	R1
Rtd	Innes Ireland	24-Climax V8	942
Rtd	Masten Gregory	18/21-Climax	917
Rtd	Jack Brabham	24-Climax V8	947

20-5-62—Naples GP, Possillippo, Italy—60-laps
6th	Tony Shelly	18/21-Climax	'P1'
7th	Tim Parnell	18/21-Climax	'P2'
8th	David Piper	18/21-Climax	919
Rtd	Gaetano Starrabba	18-Climax	905

DNS	Jay Chamberlain	18-Climax	908
DNS	Gunther Seifert	18-Climax	373
WDN	Jo Siffert	21-Climax	—

3-6-62—MONACO GP, Monte Carlo—100-laps

Rtd	Jack Brabham	24-Climax V8	947
Rtd	Innes Ireland	24-Climax V8	943
Rtd PP FL	Jim Clark	25-Climax V8	R1
Rtd	Trevor Taylor	24-Climax V8	948
Rtd	Maurice Trintignant	24-Climax V8	940
DNQ	Jo Siffert	21-Climax	938
DNQ	Masten Gregory	24-BRM V8	944
DNQ	Nino Vaccarella	18/21-Climax	912

11-6-62—International 2,000 Guineas, Mallory Park—75-laps

2nd	Jack Brabham	24-Climax V8	947
3rd	Graham Hill	18/21-Climax	918
5th	Masten Gregory	18/21-Climax	917
7th	Colin Davis	18/21-Climax	912
8th	Tony Shelly	18/21-Climax	'P1'
Rtd	John Dalton	18/21-Climax	'P2'
Rtd PP	Jim Clark	25-Climax V8	R1
WDN	Peter Arundell	Team Lotus	—
WDN		Team Lotus	—

11-6-62—Crystal Palace Trophy, London—36-laps

1st FL	Innes Ireland	24-BRM V8	944
5th	Brian Hart	20-Ford	—
6thj	David Piper	18/21-Climax	919
Rtd	Graham Eden	18-Climax	909
Rtd	Jay Chamberlain	18-Climax	908
Rtd	Gunther Seifert	18-Climax	373
Rtd	Trevor Taylor	24-BRM V8	950
DNS	Philip Robinson	18-Climax	—

17-6-62—BELGIAN GP, Spa-Francorchamps—32-laps

1st FL	Jim Clark	25-Climax V8	R1
6th	Jack Brabham	24-Climax V8	947
8th	Maurice Trintignant	24-Climax V8	940
9th	Lucien Bianchi	18/21-Climax	918
10th	Jo Siffert	21-Climax	938
11th	John Campbell-Jones	18-Climax	373
Rtd	Trevor Taylor	24-Climax V8	948
Rtd	Masten Gregory	24-BRM V8	944
Rtd	Innes Ireland	24-Climax V8	943
DNS	Dan Gurney	24-BRM V8	950

1-7-62—Reims GP, Reims-Gueux, France—50-laps

3rd	Innes Ireland	24-Climax V8	943
4th	Jack Brabham	24-Climax V8	947
5th	Maurice Trintignant	24-Climax V8	940
9th	Jo Siffert	21-Climax	938
Rtd	Masten Gregory	24-BRM V8	944
Rtd	Tony Shelly	18/21-Climax	'P1'
Rtd	Trevor Taylor	24-Climax V8	949
Rtd PP	Jim Clark	25-Climax V8	R1
Rtd	Carlo Mario Abate	18/21-Climax	912
Rtd	Peter Arundell/Clark	24-BRM V8	950

8-7-62—FRENCH GP, Rouen-Les-Essarts—54-laps

7th	Maurice Trintignant	24-Climax V8	940
8th	Trevor Taylor	25-Climax V8	R1
Rtd PP	Jim Clark	25-Climax V8	R2
Rtd	Masten Gregory	24-BRM V8	944
Rtd	Jack Brabham	24-Climax V8	947
Rtd	Jo Siffert	24-Climax V8	950
Rtd	Innes Ireland	24-Climax V8	942

15-7-62—Solitude GP, Stuttgart, West Germany—25-laps

3rd	Trevor Taylor	24-Climax V8	949
6th	Gerhard Mitter	21-Climax	938
NC	Gunther Seifert	18-Climax	373
Rtd	Jo Siffert	24-BRM V8	950
Rtd	Kurt Kuhnke	18-Climax	914
Rtd PP	Jim Clark	25-Climax V8	R2
T-car	Mitter	18-Climax	373
DNS	Peter Arundell	24-Climax V8	—
DNS	Innes Ireland	24-Climax V8	—
DNS	Masten Gregory	24-BRM V8	—
DNS	Wolfgang Seidel	24-BRM V8	—

21-7-62—BRITISH GP, Aintree—75-laps

1st PP FL	Jim Clark	25-Climax V8	R2
5th	Jack Brabham	24-Climax V8	947
7th	Masten Gregory	24-Climax V8	942

8th	Trevor Taylor	24-Climax V8	949
15th	Jay Chamberlain	18-Climax	905
16th	Innes Ireland	24-Climax V8	943
Rtd	Wolfgang Seidel	24-BRM V8	946
Rtd	Tony Shelly	18/21-Climax	'P1'

5-8-62—GERMAN GP, Nurburgring—15-laps

4th	Jim Clark	25-Climax V8	R2
12th	Jo Siffert	21-Climax	938
Rtd	Maurice Trintignant	24-Climax V8	940
Rtd	Heinz Schiller	24-BRM V8	950
Rtd	Trevor Taylor	24-Climax V8	949
DNQ	Wolfgang Seidel	24-BRM V8	946
DNQ	Tony Shelly	18/21-Climax	'P1'
DNQ	Jay Chamberlain	18-Climax	905
DNQ	Gunther Seifert	18-Climax	373

12-8-62—Kannonloppet, Karlskoga, Sweden—30-laps

1st	Masten Gregory	24-BRM V8	944
4th FL	Innes Ireland	24-Climax V8	942
Rtd	Olle Nygren	18-Climax	908
Rtd	Graham Hill	24-Climax V8	940

19-8-62—Mediterranean GP, Enna, Sicily—50-laps

4th	Jo Siffert	21-Climax	938
8th	Wolfgang Seidel	24-BRM V8	946
9th	Gunther Seifert	18-Climax	373
Rtd	Nino Vaccarella	18/21-Climax	912
DNS	Heini Walter	24-BRM V8	950
DNS	Jay Chamberlain	18-Climax	908
DNS	Kurt Kuhnke	18-Borgward	—
DNS	Peter Arundell	24-BRM V8	—

25/26-8-62—Danish GP, Roskildering, Copenhagen—20-laps, two 30-laps

Heat One

1st PP FL	Jack Brabham	24-Climax V8	947
2nd	Masten Gregory	24-BRM V8	944
3rd	Innes Ireland	24-Climax V8	942
8th	Gary Hocking	18/21-Climax	'P2'
9th	Wolfgang Seidel	24-BRM V8	946
10th	Trevor Taylor	25-Climax V8	R2
Rtd	Jay Chamberlain	18-Climax	908

Heat Two

1st	Brabham
2nd	Ireland
4th	Gregory
5th	Taylor
6th	Seidel
8th	Hocking

Heat Three

1st	Brabham
2nd	Gregory
3rd	Ireland
4th	Hocking
5th	Taylor
7th	Seidel
9th	Chamberlain

Aggregate

1st	Brabham
2nd	Gregory
3rd	Ireland
4th	Hocking
6th	Taylor
8th	Seidel
9th	Chamberlain

1-9-62—Gold Cup, Oulton Park—73-laps

1st FL	Jim Clark	25-Climax V8	R2
5th	Tony Shelly	18/21-Climax	'P1'
6th	Masten Gregory	24-BRM V8	945
8th	Gerry Ashmore	18/21-Climax	919
10th	Gunther Seifert	18-Climax	373
Rtd	Philip Robinson	18/21-Climax	904
Rtd	Jo Bonnier	24-Climax V8	940
Rtd	Trevor Taylor	24-Climax V8	R3
Rtd	Innes Ireland	24-Climax V8	942
Rtd	Graham Eden	18-Climax	909
Rtd	Gary Hocking	18/21-Climax	'P2'
DNS	Chris Ashmore	18-Climax	—
DNS	Wolfgang Seidel	24-BRM V8	946
T-car	Trevor Taylor	24-Climax V8	949

16-9-62—ITALIAN GP, Monza—86-laps

9th	Nino Vaccarella	24-Climax V8	941
12th	Masten Gregory	24-BRM V8	944
Rtd	Innes Ireland	24-Climax V8	942
Rtd	Trevor Taylor	25-Climax V8	R2
Rtd	Maurice Trintignant	24-Climax V8	940
Rtd PP	Jim Clark	25-Climax V8	R3
DNQ	Gerry Ashmore	18-Climax	919

DNQ	Jo Siffert	24-BRM V8	950
DNQ	Ernesto Prinoth	18-Climax	913
DNQ	Jay Chamberlain	18-Climax	905
DNQ	Tony Shelly	24-BRM V8	946

7-10-62—UNITED STATES GP, Watkins Glen—100-laps

1st	Jim Clark	25-Climax V8	R3
6th	Masten Gregory	24-BRM V8	944
8th	Innes Ireland	24-Climax V8	942
9th	Roger Penske	24-Climax V8	943
10th	Rob Schroeder	24-Climax V8	940
12th	Trevor Taylor	25-Climax V8	R2
Rtd	Maurice Trintignant	24-Climax V8	941
DNS	Jim Hall	21-Climax	936

4-11-62—Mexican GP, Magdalena Mixhuca, Mexico City—60-laps

1st FL	Jim Clark/Trevor Taylor	25-Climax V8	R2
3rd	Innes Ireland	24-Climax V8	942
4th	Jim Hall	21-Climax	936
5th	Masten Gregory	24-BRM V8	944
6th	Bob Schroeder	24-Climax V8	940
8th	Homer Rader	18/21-Climax	371
9th	Jay Chamberlain	18-Climax	908
Rtd	Wolfgang Seidel	24-BRM V8	946
DIS PP	Jim Clark	25-Climax V8	R3
Rtd	Roger Penske	24-Climax V8	943
Rtd	Walt Hansgen	18-Climax	372
Rtd	John Surtees	24-Climax V8	947
DNS*	Ricardo Rodriguez	24-Climax	941

Fatally injured in practice accident with this car

15-12-62—Rand GP, Kyalami, South Africa—50-laps

1st PP FL	Jim Clark	25-Climax V8	R3
2nd	Trevor Taylor	25-Climax V8	R2
4th	Gary Hocking	24-Climax V8	940
5th	Neville Lederle	21-Climax	939
10th	Brausch Niemann	7!-Ford	—
11th	Ernie Pieterse	21-Climax	937
12th	Bernard Podmore	20-Climax	20-J-952
14th	Bob van Niekerk	22-Climax	22-J-37
Rtd	Innes Ireland	24-Climax V8	942
Rtd	Syd van der Vyver	24-Climax V8	947
DNS	Vern McWilliams	18-Borgward	911
DNS	Peter van Niekerk	18-Ford	—
DNS	Lionel Wilmot	20-Ford	20-J-876
DNS	Dave Charlton	20-Ford	20-J-867
DNS	Jack Holme	18-Climax	FJ-720
DNS	Gary Hocking	18/21-Climax	'P2'

22-12-62—Natal GP, Westmead—Two 22-lap Heats, 33-lap Final

Heat One

3rd	Syd van der Vyver	24-Climax	947
8th	Jack Holme	18-Climax	FJ-720
9th	Peter van Niekerk	18-Ford	—
12th PP	Jim Clark	25-Climax V8	R4
13th	Bernard Podmore	20-Climax	20-J-952
14th	Vern McWilliams	18-Borgward	911
Rtd	Brausch Niemann	7-Ford	—

Heat Two

1st	Trevor Taylor	25-Climax V8	R2
3rd	Neville Lederle	21-Climax	939
5th	Ernie Pieterse	21-Climax	937
6th	Bob van Niekerk	22-Climax	22-J-37
Rtd	Dave Charlton	20-Ford	20-J-867
Rtd	Bill Scheepers	18-Alfa Romeo	—

Final

1st FL	Taylor		
2nd	Clark		
4th	Lederle		
5th	Pieterse		
11th	Bob van Niekerk		
14th	Holme		
Rtd	Van der Vyver		
Rtd	Peter van Niekerk		
DNS*	Gary Hocking	24-Climax V8	940
DNS	Lionel Wilmot	20-Ford	—

Fatally injured in practice accident with this car

29-12-62—SOUTH AFRICAN GP, East London—82-laps

5th	Innes Ireland	24-Climax V8	942
6th	Neville Lederle	21-Climax	939
10th	Ernie Pieterse	21-Climax	937
Rtd PP FL	Jim Clark	25-Climax V8	R5
Rtd	Trevor Taylor	25-Climax V8	R2

1963

30-3-63—Lombank Trophy, Snetterton—50-laps

2nd PP	Jim Clark	25-Climax V8	R3
3rd	Innes Ireland	24-Climax V8	944
6th	Jim Hall	24-BRM V8	945
7th	Adam Wyllie	18/21-Climax	918
Rtd	Tim Parnell	24-BRM V8	'P1'
Rtd	Philip Robinson	18/21-Climax	904
DNS	Trevor Taylor	25-Climax V8	—
DNS	Jo Siffert	24-BRM V8	950
WDN	Jack Pearce	22-Climax	—
WDN	Ron Carter	18-Climax	—

15-4-63—Glover Trophy, Goodwood—42-laps

1st	Innes Ireland	24-BRM V8	944
3rd	Tony Maggs	24-Climax V8	943
4th	Jim Hall	24-BRM V8	945
8th	Philip Robinson	18/21-Climax	904
DNS	Gunter Seifert	24-BRM V8	—
DNS	Ian Raby	24-BRM V8	—

15-4-63—Pau GP, France—100-laps

1st PP FL	Jim Clark	25-Climax V8	R5
2nd	Trevor Taylor	25-Climax V8	R3
5th	Herbert Muller	21-Climax	938
6th	Andre Pilette	18/21-Climax	916
Rtd	Bernard Collomb	24-Climax V8	949
Rtd	Maurice Trintignant	24-Climax V8	941
Rtd	Jo Siffert	24-BRM V8	950
Rtd	Tim Parnell	18/21-Climax	917

21-4-63—Imola GP, Castellacis, Italy—50-laps

1st PP	Jim Clark	25-Climax V8	R5
2nd	Jo Siffert	24-BRM V8	950
8th	Ernesto Prinoth	18-Climax	913
9th FL	Trevor Taylor	25-Climax V8	R3
Rtd	Gaetano Starrabba	18-Maserati	905
Rtd	Bernard Collomb	24-Climax V8	949
DNS	Giancarlo Baghetti	21-Climax	938
DNS	Gunther Seifert	24-BRM V8	946
DNS	Andre Pilette	18/21-Climax	—

25-4-63—Syracuse GP, Sicily—56-laps

1st PP FL	Jo Siffert	24-BRM V8	950
5th	Jo Bonnier	24-Climax V8	941
6th	Gaetano Starrabba	18-Maserati	905
Rtd	Bernard Collomb	24-Climax V8	949
Rtd	Gunther Seifert	24-BRM V8	946
WDN	Phil Hill	24-BRM V8	—
WDN	Jim Clark	25-Climax V8	—
WDN	Trevor Taylor	25-Climax V8	—

27-4-63—Aintree '200', Liverpool—50-laps

2nd	Innes Ireland	24-BRM V8	944
3rd FL	Trevor Taylor/Jim Clark	25-Climax V8	R3
7th PP	Jim Clark/Trevor Taylor	25-Climax V8	R5
8th	Jimmy Blumer	24-Climax V8	943
Rtd	Jim Hall	24-BRM V8	945
Rtd	Philip Robinson	18/21-Climax	904
Rtd	Jock Russell	18/21-Climax	918
Rtd	Tim Parnell	18/21-Climax	917
Rtd	John Campbell-Jones	24-BRM V8	'P1'
DNS	Andre Pilette	18/21-Climax	916

11-5-63—BRDC International Trophy, Silverstone—52-laps

1st	Jim Clark	25-Climax V8	R5
3rd	Trevor Taylor	25-Climax V8	R3
4th PP FL	Innes Ireland	24-BRM V8	944
Rtd	John Campbell-Jones	24-BRM V8	'P1'
Rtd	Philip Robinson	18/21-Climax	904
Rtd	Tim Parnell	18/21-Climax	915
Rtd	Jim Hall	24-BRM V8	945
WDN	Peter Arundell	25-Climax V8	—
WDN	Andre Pilette	18/21-Climax	916

19-5-63—Rome GP, Vallelunga, Italy—Two 40-lap Heats

Heat One

5th	Gaetano Starrabba	18-Maserati	905
7th	Clement Barrau	21-Climax	938
8th	Gunther Seifert	24-BRM V8	946
12th	John Campbell-Jones	24-BRM V8	'P1'
13th	Bernard Collomb	24-Climax V8	949
Rtd	Tim Parnell	18/21-Climax	915

Heat Two

4th	Parnell	
6th	Starrabba	
7th	Barrau	
9th	Campbell-Jones	
11th	Seifert	

Aggregate

5th	Starrabba		
6th	Barrau		
9th	Parnell		
10th	Seifert		
11th	Campbell-Jones		
DNS	Kurt Kuhnke	18-Borgward	914
DNS	Ernst Maring	18-Borgward	373
WDN	Andre Pilette	18/21-Climax	—
WDN	Philip Robinson	18/21-Climax	—
WDN	Jo Siffert	24-BRM V8	950

26-5-63—MONACO GP, Monte Carlo—100-laps

6th	Trevor Taylor	25-Climax V8	R5
8th(Rtd) PP	Jim Clark	25-Climax V8	R4
9th UNC	Jack Brabham	25-Climax V8	R3
Rtd	Innes Ireland	24-BRM V8	944
Rtd	Jim Hall	24-BRM V8	945
Rtd	Jo Siffert	24-BRM V8	950
DNQ	Bernard Collomb	24-Climax V8	949

9-6-63—BELGIAN GP, Spa-Francorchamps—32-laps

1st FL	Jim Clark	25-Climax V8	R4
Rtd	Jim Hall	24-BRM V8	945
Rtd	Jo Siffert	24-BRM V8	950
Rtd	Trevor Taylor	25-Climax V8	R3
T-car	Innes Ireland	24-BRM V8	944

23-6-63—DUTCH GP, Zandvoort—80-laps

1st PP FL	Jim Clark	25-Climax V8	R4
7th	Jo Siffert	24-BRM V8	950
8th	Jim Hall	24-BRM V8	944
10th	Trevor Taylor	25-Climax V8	R2
T-car	Chris Amon	24-Climax V8	943
T-car	Innes Ireland	24-BRM V8	944

30-6-63—FRENCH GP, Reims-Gueux—53-laps

1st PP FL	Jim Clark	25-Climax V8	R4
6th	Jo Siffert	24-BRM V8	950
8th	Maurice Trintignant	24-Climax V8	942
11th	Jim Hall	24-BRM V8	945
13th(Rtd)	Trevor Taylor	25-Climax V8	R2
Rtd	Phil Hill	24-BRM V8	951
Rtd	Masten Gregory	24-BRM V8	952
DNS	Peter Arundell	25-Climax V8	R3

20-7-63—BRITISH GP, Silverstone—82-laps

1st PP	Jim Clark	25-Climax V8	R4
6th	Jim Hall	24-BRM V8	945
8th	Mike Hailwood	24-Climax V8	942
11th	Masten Gregory	24-BRM V8	'P1'
Rtd	Jo Siffert	24-BRM V8	950
Rtd	Trevor Taylor	25-Climax V8	R2
T-car	Innes Ireland	24-BRM V8	944

28-7-63—Solitude GP, Stuttgart, West Germay—25-laps

2nd	Peter Arundell	25-Climax V8	R2
6th	Jim Hall	24-BRM V8	945
11th	Bernard Collomb	24-Climax V8	949
12th	Andre Pilette	18/21-Climax	917
NC	Philip Robinson	18/21-Climax	904
NC	Gunther Seifert	24-BRM V8	946
NC PP FL	Jim Clark	25-Climax V8	R4
Rtd	Kurt Kuhnke	18-Borgward	914
Rtd	Ron Carter	18/21-Climax	915
Rtd	Tim Parnell	24-BRM V8	'P1'
Rtd	Trevor Taylor	25-Climax V8	R3
Rtd	Phil Hill	24-BRM V8	951
Rtd	Ernst Maring	18-Borgward	373
Rtd	Jo Siffert	24-BRM V8	950

4-8-63—GERMAN GP, Nurburing—15-laps

2nd PP	Jim Clark	25-Climax V8	R4
5th	Jim Hall	24-BRM V8	945
8th	Trevor Taylor	25-Climax V8	R2
9th(Rtd)	Jo Siffert	24-BRM V8	950
10th	Bernard Collomb	24-Climax V8	949
Rtd	Innes Ireland	24-BRM V8	944
DNQ	Tim Parnell	18-Climax	915
DNQ	Andre Pilette	18/21-Climax	917
DNQ	Kurt Kuhnke	'BKL-Borgward'	914

11-8-63—Kannonloppet, Karlskoga, Sweden—Two 20-lap Heats

Heats One

1st FL	Jim Clark	25-Climax V8	R3
2nd	Trevor Taylor	25-Climax V8	R2
7th	Masten Gregory	24-BRM V8	'P1'
10th	Ernst Maring	18-Borgward	373
11th	Andre Pilette	18/21-Climax	917
13th	Clement Barrau	21-Climax	938
14th	Kurt Kuhnke	18-Borgward	914

Heat Two

2nd	Taylor
3rd	Clark
6th	Gregory
10th	Pilette
12th	Barrau
Rtd	Kuhnke
Rtd	Maring

Aggregate

1st	Clark
2nd	Taylor
6th	Gregory
10th	Pilette
12th	Barrau

18-8-63—Mediterranean GP, Enna, Sicily—60-laps

2nd	Peter Arundell	25-Climax V8	R3
5th	Jo Siffert	24-BRM V8	950
9th	Andre Wicky	24-BRM V8	951
10th	Bernard Collomb	24-Climax V8	949
Rtd	Giacomo 'Geki' Russo	27-Ford	—
Rtd	Carmelo Genovese	22-Ford	22-J-28
Rtd	Trevor Taylor	25-Climax V8	R2
DNS	Gaetano Starrabba	18-Maserati	905

1-9-63—Austrian GP, Zeltweg—80-laps

'5th'	Bernard Collomb	24-Climax V8	949
6th	Tim Parnell	24-BRM V8	'P1'
7th	Gunther Seifert	24-BRM V8	946
'8th'	Innes Ireland	24-BRM V8	944
9th	Andre Pilette	18/21-Climax	917
Rtd	Jim Hall	24-BRM V8	945
Rtd PP	Jim Clark	25-Climax V8	R6
Rtd	Ernesto Prinoth	18-Climax	913
Rtd	Jo Siffert	24-BRM V8	950
WDN	Peter Arundell	25-Climax V8	R3

8-9-63—ITALIAN GP, Monza—86-laps

1st FL	Jim Clark	25-Climax V8	R4
8th	Jim Hall	24-BRM V8	945
13th(Rtd)	Mike Spence	25-Climax V8	R3
Rtd	Jo Siffert	24-BRM V8	950
Rtd	Masten Gregory	24-BRM V8	'P1'
DNQ	Andre Pilette	18/21-Climax	917

21-9-63—Gold Cup, Oulton Park—73-laps

1st PP FL	Jim Clark	25-Climax V8	R4
9th	Peter Revson	24-BRM V8	941
'11th'	Jo Siffert	24-BRM V8	950
12th	Andre Pilette	18/21-Climax	917
'13th'	Innes Ireland	24-BRM V8	944
'14th'	Bernard Collomb	24-Climax V8	949
Rtd	Trevor Taylor	25-Climax V8	R6
Rtd	Masten Gregory	24-BRM V8	'P1'
Rtd	Mike Beckwith	24-BRM V8	945
WDN	Peter Arundell	25-Climax V8	—

6-10-63—UNITED STATES GP, Watkins Glen—110-laps

3rd FL	Jim Clark	25-Climax V8	R4
10th(Rtd)	Jim Hall	24-BRM V8	944
Rtd	Jo Siffert	24-BRM V8	950
Rtd	Rodger Ward	24-BRM V8	'P1'
Rtd	Pedro Rodriguez	25-Climax V8	R3
Rtd	Trevor Taylor	25-Climax V8	R6
Rtd	Hap Sharp	24-BRM V8	940

20-10-63—MEXICAN GP, Mexico City—56-Laps

1st PP FL	Jim Clark	25-Climax V8	R4
7th	Hap Sharp	24-BRM V8	940

8th	Jim Hall	24-BRM V8	944
9th	Jo Siffert	24-BRM V8	950
Rtd	Pedro Rodriguez	25-Climax V8	R3
Rtd	Trevor Taylor	25-Climax V8	R6
Rtd	Chris Amon	24-BRM V8	'P1'

14-12-63—Rand GP, Kyalami, South Africa—Two 25-Lap Heats
Heat One

7th	Ernie Pieterse	21-Climax	937
'10th'	Brausch Niemann	22-Ford	22-J-17
11th	Paddy Driver	24-BRM V8	946
13th	Dave Charlton	20-Ford	20-J-867
'16th'	Jack Holme	18-Climax	F-J-720
17th	Trevor Taylor	25-Climax V8	R7
19th	Jim Clark	25-Climax V8	R4
Rtd	Clive Puzey	18/21-Climax	'P2'

Heat Two		**Aggregate**	
5th	Clark	5th	Pieterse
6th	Taylor	7th	Driver
8th	Pieterse	10th	Taylor
9th	Driver Rtd Niemann	11th	Charlton
14th	Holme	13th	Holme
17th	Charlton	16th	Clark

28-12-63—SOUTH AFRICAN GP, East London—85-laps

1st PP	Jim Clark	25-Climax V8	R4
8th	Trevor Taylor	25-Climax V8	R7
14th	Brausch Niemann	22-Ford	22-J-17
Rtd	Ernie Pieterse	21-Climax	937
DNS	Paddy Driver	24-BRM V8	946

1964

14-3-64—Daily Mirror Trophy, Snetterton—35-laps

5th	Chris Amon	25-BRM V8	R3
Rtd	Bernard Collomb	24-Climax V8	949
Rtd	Jock Russell	18/21-Climax	918
Rtd	Trevor Taylor	24-BRM V8	944
Rtd	Mike Hailwood	25-BRM V8	R7
Rtd PP	Jim Clark	25-Climax V8	R6
Rtd FL	Peter Arundell	25-Climax V8	R4
Rtd	Peter Revson	24-BRM V8	'P1'

30-3-64—News of the World Trophy, Goodwood—42-laps

1st	Jim Clark	25-Climax V8	R6
2nd	Peter Arundell	25-Climax V8	R4
3rd	Trevor Taylor	24-BRM V8	944
5th	Mike Hailwood	24-BRM V8	R7
8th	Peter Revson	24-BRM V8	'P1'
Rtd	Bernard Collomb	24-Climax V8	949
WDN	Chris Amon	25-BRM V8	R3
WDN	Andre Wicky	24-BRM V8	—

12-4-64—Syracuse GP, Sicily—40-laps

3rd	Mike Spence/Peter Arundell	25-Climax V8	R4
5th	Chris Amon	25-BRM V8	R3
7th	Mike Hailwood	25-BRM V8	R7
Rtd	Peter Revson	24-BRM V8	'P1'
Rtd	Peter Arundell/Spence	25-Climax V8	R6
DNS	Jo Siffert	24-BRM V8	950
DNS	Andre Wicky	24-BRM V8	951

18-4-64—Aintree '200', Liverpool—67-laps

3rd	Peter Arundell	25-Climax V8	R6
6th	Mike Spence	32-Cosworth F2	32-F2-1
'12th'	Brian Hart	22-Cosworth F2	22-J-36
14th	John Fenning	27-Ford F2	27-JM-32
Rtd	Chris Amon	25-BRM V8	R3
Rtd	Mike Hailwood	25-BRM V8	R7
Rtd FL	Jim Clark	33-Climax V8	R8
WDN	Peter Revson	24-BRM V8	'P1'
WDN	Jo Siffert	24-BRM V8	950

2-5-64—BRDC International Trophy, Silverstone—52-laps

3rd	Peter Arundell	25-Climax V8	R4
5th	Chris Amon	25-BRM V8	R3
6th	Mike Hailwood	25-BRM V8	R7

9th	Peter Revson	24-BRM V8	'P1'
11th	Jo Siffert	24-BRM V8	950
Rtd	Jim Clark	25-Climax V8	R6

10-5-64—MONACO GP, Monte Carlo—100-laps

3rd	Peter Arundell	25-Climax V8	R4
'4th' PP	Jim Clark	25-Climax V8	R6
6th	Mike Hailwood	25-BRM V8	R7
8th	Jo Siffert	24-BRM V8	950
DNQ	Chris Amon	25-BRM V8	R3
DNQ	Peter Revson	24-BRM V8	'P1'
DNQ	Bernard Collomb	24-Climax V8	949
DNS	Innes Ireland	BRM V8	944

24-5-64—DUTCH GP, Zandvoort—80-laps

1st FL	Jim Clark	25-Climax V8	R6
3rd	Peter Arundell	25-Climax V8	R4
5th	Chris Amon	25-BRM V8	R3
'12th'	Mike Hailwood	25-BRM V8	R7

14-6-64—BELGIAN GP, Spa-Francorchamps—32-laps

1st	Jim Clark	25-Climax V8	R6
9th	Peter Arundell	25-Climax V8	R4
DIS	Peter Revson	24-BRM V8	'P1'
Rtd	Chris Amon	25-BRM V8	R3

28-6-64—FRENCH GP, Rouen-Les-Essarts—57-laps

4th	Peter Arundell	25-Climax V8	R4
8th	Mike Hailwood	25-BRM V8	R7
10th	Chris Amon	25-BRM V8	R3
Rtd PP	Jim Clark	25-Climax V8	R6

11-7-64—BRITISH GP, Brands Hatch—80-laps

1st PP FL	Jim Clark	25-Climax V8	R6
9th	Mike Spence	25-Climax V8	R4
Rtd	Peter Arundell	24-BRM V8	'P1'
Rtd	Mike Hailwood	25-BRM V8	R7
Rtd	Chris Amon	25-BRM V8	R3
Rtd	Trevor Taylor		945

19-7-64—Solitude GP, Stuttgart, West Germany—20-laps

1st PP FL	Jim Clark	33-Climax V8	R8
4th	Peter Arundell	24-BRM V8	'P1'
6th	Trevor Taylor	24-BRM V8	945
9th	Mike Hailwood	25-BRM V8	R7
10th	Ernst Maring	18-'BKL-Borgward'	919
Rtd*	Chris Amon	25-BRM V8	R3
Rtd*	Gerhard Mitter	25-Climax V8	R4
Rtd*	Joachim Diel	18-Borgward	914
Rtd*	Mike Spence	25-Climax V8	R6

*All crashed in rain on opening lap, with four other cars

2-8-64—GERMAN GP, Nurburgring—15-laps

8th	Mike Spence	33-Climax V8	R8
9th	Gerhard Mitter	25-Climax V8	R6
'11th'	Chris Amon	25-BRM V8	R3
'14th'	Peter Revson	24-BRM V8	'P1'
Rtd	Jim Clark	33-Climax V8	R9
Rtd	Mike Hailwood	25-BRM V8	R7

16-8-64—Mediterranean GP, Enna, Sicily—60-laps

2nd	Jim Clark	25-Climax V8	R6
4th	Chris Amon	25-BRM V8	R3
5th FL	Mike spence	25-Climax V8	R4
6th	Peter Revson	24-BRM V8	'P1'
Rtd	Mike Hailwood	25-BRM V8	R7
Rtd	Luigi Malanca	27-Ford	27-JM-10
DNS	Brian Gubby	24-Climax V8	943
WDN	Giacomo 'Geki' Russo	24-—	—

23-8-64—AUSTRIAN GP, Zeltweg—105-laps

8th	Mike Hailwood	25-BRM V8	R3
Rtd	Mike Spence	33-Climax V8	R8
Rtd	Jim Clark	33-Climax V8	R9
Rtd	Chris Amon	25-Climax V8	R4

6-9-64—ITALIAN GP, Monza—78-laps

6th	Mike Spence	33-Climax V8	R8
13th	Peter Revson	24-BRM V8	'P1'
13th	Jim Clark	25-Climax V8	R6
Rtd	Mike Hailwood	25-Lotus-BRM V8	R4

4-10-64—UNITED STATES GP, Watkins Glen—110-laps

| 5th | Walt Hansgen | 33-Climax V8 | R8 |
| '7th' FL | Mike Spence/Jim Clark | 33-Climax V8 | R9 |

272

'8th'	Mike Hailwood	25-BRM V8	R7
Rtd PP	Jim Clark/Mike Spence	25-Climax V8	R6
Rtd	Chris Amon	25-BRM V8	R4

20-10-64—MEXICAN GP, Mexico City—65-laps

4th	Mike Spence	25-Climax V8	R6
'5th' PP FL	Jim Clark	33-Climax V8	R9
10th	Moises Solana	33-Climax V8	R8
Rtd	Chris Amon	25-BRM V8	R4
Rtd	Mike Hailwood	25-BRM V8	R7

12-12-64—Rand GP, Kyalami, South Africa—Two 25-lap Heats

Heat One

2nd FL	Mike Spence	33-Climax V8	R9
9th	Brausch Niemann	22-Ford	22-J-17
10th	Clive Puzey	18/21-Climax	'P2'
13th	Bob Hay	20-Ford	20-J-876
15th	Neville Lederle	21-Climax	952
Rtd PP	Jackie Stewart	33-Climax V8	R10
Rtd	Ernie Pieterse	21-Climax	937
DNS	Tony Maggs	25-BRM V8	R4
DNS	Dave Charlton	20-Ford	20-J-867

Heat Two

		Aggregate	
1st FL	Stewart	5th	Niemann
6th	Niemann	7th	Puzey
8th	Lederle	9th	Hay
9th	Puzey	10th	Lederle
11th	Hay	16th	Spence
Rtd	Spence	17th	Stewart

1965

1-1-65—SOUTH AFRICAN GP, East London—85-laps

1st PP FL	Jim Clark	33-Climax V8	R10
4th	Mike Spence	33-Climax V8	R9
11th	Tony Maggs	25-BRM V8	R4
DNQ	Neville Lederle	21-Climax	952
DNQ	Brausch Niemann	22-Ford	22-J-17
DNQ	Ernie Pieterse	21-Climax	937
DNQ	Clive Puzey	18/21-Climax	'P2'

13-3-65—Race of Champions, Brands Hatch—Two 40-lap Heats

Heat One

1st PP FL	Jim Clark	33-Climax V8	R10
3rd	Mike Spence	33-Climax V8	R9
10th	Dick Attwood	25-BRM V8	R3
Rtd	Mike Hailwood	25-BRM V8	R7
DNS*	Paul Hawkins	33-Climax V8	R8
T-car	Clark	33-Climax V8	R11

Reserve entry

Heat Two

		Aggregate	
1st	Spence	1st	Spence
Rtd	Hailwood	10th	Hawkins
Rtd FL PP	Clark		
Rtd	Attwood		
10th	Hawkins		

4-4-65—Syracuse GP, Sicily—56-laps

1st PP FL	Jim Clark	33-Climax V8	R11
7th	Bernard Collomb	24-Climax V8	949
9th	Andre Wicky	24-BRM V8	951
Rtd	Innes Ireland	25-BRM V8	R3
Rtd	Mike Hailwood	25-BRM V8	R7
Rtd	Mike Spence	33-Climax V8	R9
WDN	Paul Hawkins	25-Climax V8	R8

19-4-65—Sunday Mirror Trophy, Goodwood—42-laps

1st = FL	Jim Clark	25-Climax V8	R6
6th	Dick Attwood	25-BRM V8	R3
Rtd	Paul Hawkins	33-Climax V8	R8
DNS*	Mike Spence	33-Climax V8	R9
WDN	Mike Hailwood	25-BRM V8	—

Actually wheeled from grid with fuel-injection trouble

15-5-65—BRDC International Trophy, Silverstone—52-laps

3rd	Mike Spence	33-Climax V8	R9
4th	Pedro Rodriguez	25-BRM V8	R6
8th	Dick Attwood	25-BRM V8	R3

9th	Mike Hailwood	25-BRM V8	R7
10th	Paul Hawkins	33-Climax V8	R8

30-5-65—MONACO GP, Monte Carlo—100-laps

10th(Rtd)	Paul Hawkins	33-Climax V8	R8
Rtd	Richard Attwood	25-BRM V8	R3
Rtd	Mike Hailwood	25-BRM V8	R7

13-6-65—BELGIAN GP, Spa-Francorchamps—32-laps

1st FL	Jim Clark	33-Climax V8	R11
7th	Mike Spence	33-Climax V8	R9
13th	Innes Ireland	25-BRM V8	R7
14th(Rtd)	Dick Attwood	25-BRM V8	R4

27-6-65—FRENCH GP, Clermont-Ferrand—40-laps

1st PP FL	Jim Clark	25-Climax V8	R6
7th	Mike Spence	33-Climax V8	R9
Rtd	Chris Amon	25-BRM V8	R3
Rtd	Innes Ireland	25-BRM V8	R7

10-7-65—BRITISH GP, Silverstone—80-laps

1st PP	Jim Clark	33-Climax V8	R11
4th*	Mike Spence	33-Climax V8	R9
13th	Richard Attwood	25-BRM V8	R3
Rtd	Innes Ireland	25-BRM V8	R7
DNS	Brian Gubby	24-Climax V8	943

18-7-65—DUTCH GP, Zandvoort—80-laps

1st FL	Jim Clark	33-Climax V8	R9
8th	Mike Spence	25-Climax V8	R6
10th	Innes Ireland	25-BRM V8	R7
12th	Richard Attwood	25-BRM V8	R3

1-8-65—GERMAN GP, Nurburgring—15-laps

1st PP FL	Jim Clark	33-Climax V8	R11
Rtd	Gerhard Mitter	25-Climax V8	R6
Rtd	Mike Spence	33-Climax V8	R9
Rtd	Richard Attwood	25-BRM V8	R3
Rtd	Chris Amon	25-BRM V8	R7
Rtd	Paul Hawkins	33-Climax V8	R8

15-8-65—Mediterranean GP, Enna, Sicily—60-laps

2nd FL PP	Jim Clark	25-Climax V8	R6
5th	Innes Ireland	25-BRM V8	R7
Rtd	Mike Spence	33-Climax V8	R9
Rtd	Chris Amon	25-BRM V8	R3
DNS	Colin Davis	18-Climax	913
WDN	Paul Hawkins	33-Climax V8	R8
WDN	Brian Gubby	24-Climax V8	943

12-9-65—ITALIAN GP, Monza—76-laps

6th	Richard Attwood	25-BRM V8	R3
9th	Innes Ireland	25-BRM V8	R13
'10th'PP FL	Jim Clark	33-Climax V8	R11
11th(Rtd)	Mike Spence	33-Climax V8	R9
Rtd	Giacomo 'Geki' Russo	25-Climax V8	R6

3-10-65—UNITED STATES GP, Watkins Glen—110-laps

10th	Richard Attwood	25-BRM V8	R3
12th	Moises Solana	25-Climax V8	R6
Rtd	Jim Clark	33-Climax V8	R11
Rtd	Innes Ireland	25-BRM V8	R13
Rtd	Mike Spence	33-Climax V8	R9

24-10-65—MEXICAN GP, Mexico City—65-laps

3rd	Mike Spence	33-Climax V8	R9
6th	Richard Attwood	25-BRM V8	R3
Rtd	Moises Solana	25-Climax V8	R6
Rtd	Bob Bondurant	25-BRM V8	R13
Rtd PP	Jim Clark	33-Climax V8	R11

5-12-65—Rand GP, Kyalami, South Africa—50-laps

3rd	Paul Hawkins	25-Climax 2.7	R3
6th	Innes Ireland	25-BRM V8 2.0	R4
9th	Clive Puzey	18/21-Climax 2.5	'P2'
Rtd	Jo Bonnier	25-Climax V8	R6
Rtd	Jackie Pretorius	21-Climax 2.0	959
Rtd	Brausch Niemann	22-Ford 1.6	—
DNS	Dave Charlton	22-Ford 1.6	—

1966

2-1-66—South African GP, East London—60-laps

1st	Mike Spence	33-Climax V8 2.0	R11
3rd	Peter Arundell	33-Climax V8	R9
7th	Clive Puzey	18/21-Climax 2.7	'P2'

9th	Jackie Pretorius	21-Climax 2.0	959
Rtd	David Prophet	24-Maserati 2.8	—
Rtd	Jo Bonnier	25-Climax V8	R6
Rtd	Innes Ireland	25-BRM V8 2.0	R4
Rtd	Paul Hawkins	25-Climax 2.7	R3

1-5-66—Syracuse GP, Sicily—56-laps

3rd	David Hobbs	25-BRM V8	R4
Rtd	Giancarlo Baghetti	25-Climax V8	R6
Rtd	Paul Hawkins	25-Climax 2.7	R3

14-5-66—BRDC International Trophy, Silverstone—35-laps

8th	Paul Hawkins	25-Climax 2.7	R3
Rtd	Mike Spence	25-BRM V8	R4

22-5-66—MONACO GP, Monte Carlo—100-laps

Rtd PP	Jim Clark	33-Climax V8	R11
Rtd	Mike Spence	25-BRM V8	R13
T-car	Phil Hill	25-Climax V8	R6
T-car	Jo Bonnier	25-Climax 2.7	R3

12-6-66—BELGIAN GP, Spa-Francorchamps—28-laps

Rtd	Mike Spence	25-BRM V8	R13
Rtd	Jim Clark	33-Climax V8	R11
DNS	Peter Arundell	43-BRM H16	43/1

3-7-66—FRENCH GP, Reims-Gueux—48-laps

Rtd	Pedro Rodriguez	33-Climax V8	R11
Rtd	Mike Spence	25-BRM V8	R13
Rtd	Peter Arundell	43-BRM H16	43/1
DNS	Jim Clark	33-Climax V8	R11

16-7-66—BRITISH GP, Brands Hatch—80-laps

4th	Jim Clark	33-Climax V8	R14
Rtd	Peter Arundell	33-BRM V8	R11
Rtd	Mike Spence	25-BRM V8	R13

24-7-66—DUTCH GP, Zandvoort—90-laps

3rd	Jim Clark	33-Climax V8	R14
5th	Mike Spence	25-BRM V8	R13
Rtd	Peter Arundell	33-BRM V8	R11

7-8-66—GERMAN GP, Nurburgring—15-laps

12th	Peter Arundell	33-BRM V8	R11
Rtd	Mike Spence	25-BRM V8	R13
Rtd PP	Jim Clark	33-Climax V8	R14
Rtd	Pedro Rodriguez	'4'-Cosworth	44-F-3*
Rtd	Piers Courage	'4'-Cosworth	44-F-2*
DNS	Gerhard Mitter	'4'-Cosworth	44-F-1*

Formula 2 cars in race run concurrently with Formula 1 Grand Prix

4-9-66—ITALIAN GP, Monza—68-laps

5th	Mike Spence	25-BRM V8	R13
8th	Peter Arundell	33-BRM V8	R11
9th	Giacomo 'Geki' Russo	33-Climax V8	R14
Rtd	Jim Clark	43-BRM H16	43/1
T-car	Giancarlo Baghetti	25-BRM V8	R3

17-9-66—Gold Cup, Oulton Park—40-laps

3rd	Jim Clark	33-Climax 2.0	R14
Rtd	Mike Spence	33-BRM V8	R13
DNS	Peter Arundell	33-Climax 2.0	R14
DNS	Jim Clark	43-BRM H16	43/1

2-10-66—UNITED STATES GP, Watkins Glen—108-laps

1st	Jim Clark	43-BRM H16	43/1
6th	Peter Arundell	33-Climax V8	R14
Rtd	Mike Spence	25-BRM V8	R3
Rtd	Pedro Rodriguez	33-BRM V8	R11

23-10-66—MEXICAN GP, Mexico City—65-laps

7th	Peter Arundell	33-BRM V8	R11
Rtd	Pedro Rodriguez	33-Climax V8	R14
Rtd	Jim Clark	43-BRM H16	43/1
DNS	Mike Spence	25-BRM V8	R3

2-1-67—SOUTH AFRICAN GP, Kyalami—80-laps

Rtd	Piers Courage	25-BRM V8 2.1	R3
Rtd	Jim Clark	43-BRM H16	43/2
Rtd	Graham Hill	43-BRM H16	43/1

12-3-67—Race of Champions, Brands Hatch—Two 10-lap Heats, 40-laps
Heat One

13th	Chris Irwin	25-BRM V8 2.0	R13

Heat Two

11th	Irwin

Final

6th	Irwin

15-4-67—Spring Cup, Oulton Park—Two 10-lap Heats, 30-lap Final
Heat One

4th	Graham Hill	48-Cosworth F2	48/1
6th	Jack Oliver	41-Cosworth F2	—
7th	Piers Courage	25-BRM V8 2.0	R13

Heat Two

7th	Oliver
Rtd	Hill
Rtd	Courage

Final

4th	Oliver	
8th	Hill	F2 FL
Rtd	Courage	

29-4-67—BRDC International Trophy, Silverstone—52-laps

4th	Graham Hill	33-BRM V8 2.1	R11
7th	Chris Irwin	25-BRM V8 2.1	R13

7-5-67—MONACO GP, Monte Carlo—100-laps

2nd	Graham Hill	33-BRM V8	R11
Rtd FL	Jim Clark	33-Climax V8	R14

21-5-67—Syracuse GP, Sicily—56-laps

4th	Chris Irwin	25-BRM V8 2.1	R13

4-6-67—DUTCH GP, Zandvoort—90-laps

1st FL	Jim Clark	49-Ford V8	49/R2
7th	Chris Irwin	25-BRM V8	R13
Rtd PP	Graham Hill	49-Ford V8	49/R1

18-6-67—BELGIAN GP, Spa-Francorchamps—28-laps

6th PP	Jim Clark	40-Ford V8	49/R2
Rtd	Graham Hill	49-Ford V8	49-R1

2-7-67—FRENCH GP, Bugatti Circuit Le Mans—80-laps

Rtd	Jim Clark	49-Ford V8	49/R2
Rtd PP FL	Graham Hill	49-Ford V8	49/R1

15-7-67—BRITISH GP, Silverstone—80-laps

1st PP	Jim Clark	49-Ford V8	49/R2
Rtd	Graham Hill	49-Ford V8	49/R3
T-car	Graham Hill	49-Ford V8	49/R1

6-8-67—GERMAN GP, Nurburgring—15-laps

5th	Jackie Oliver	48-Cosworth '4'	48/3
Rtd	Graham Hill	49-Ford V8	49/R1
Rtd PP	Jim Clark	49-Ford V8	49/R2
T-car	Graham Hill	49-Ford V8	49/R3

27-8-67—CANADIAN GP, Mosport Park—90-laps

4th	Graham Hill	49-Ford V8	49/R3
11th	Mike Fisher	33-BRM V8	R11
Rtd	Eppie Weitzes	49-Ford V8	49/R1
Rtd PP FL	Jim Clark	49-Ford V8	49/R2

10-9-67—ITALIAN GP, Monza—68-laps

3rd PP FL	Jim Clark	49-Ford V8	49/R2
Rtd	Graham Hill	49-Ford V8	49/R3
Rtd	Giancarlo Baghetti	49-Ford V8	49/R1

16-9-67—Gold Cup, Oulton Park F1/F2—45-laps

2nd	Graham Hill	48-Cosworth F2	48/1
Rtd	Jack Oliver	41B-Cosworth F2	—

1-10-67—UNITED STATES GP, Watkins Glen—108-laps

1st	Jim Clark	49-Ford V8	49/R2
2nd PP FL	Graham Hill	49-Ford V8	49/R3
Rtd	Moises Solana	49-Ford V8	49/R1

22-10-67—MEXICAN GP, Mexico City—65-laps

1st PP FL	Jim Clark	49-Ford V8	49/R1
Rtd	Moises Solana	49-Ford V8	49/R2
Rtd	Graham Hill	49-Ford V8	49/R3
DNS	Mike Fisher	33-BRM V8	R11

12-11-67—Madrid GP, Jarama, Spain—60-laps

1st PP FL	Jim Clark	49-Ford V8	49/1
2nd	Graham Hill	49-Ford V8	49/2
DNS	Alex Soler-Roig	48-Cosworth F2	48/1

1968
1-1-68—SOUTH AFRICAN GP, Kyalami—80-laps

1st PP FL	Jim Clark	49-Ford V8	49/R4
2nd	Graham Hill	49-Ford V8	49/R3

17-3-68—Race of Champions, Brands Hatch—50-laps
Rtd   Graham Hill   49-Ford V8   49/5

27-4-68—BRDC International Trophy, Silverstone—52-laps
Rtd   Graham Hill   49-Ford V8   49/1
Rtd   Jo Siffert   49-Ford V8   49/2

12-5-68—SPANISH GP, Jarama—90-laps
1st   Graham Hill   49-Ford V8   49/R1
Rtd   Jo Siffert   49-Ford V8   49/R2

26-5-68—MONACO GP, Monte Carlo—80-laps
1st PP   Graham Hill   49B-Ford V8   49B/R5
Rtd   Jo Siffert   49-Ford V8   49/R2
Rtd   Jackie Oliver   49-Ford V8   49/R1

9-6-68—BELGIAN GP, Spa-Francorchamps—28-laps
5th   Jackie Oliver   49B-Ford V8   49B/R6
'7th'   Jo Siffert   49-Ford V8   49/R2
Rtd   Graham Hill   49B-Ford V8   49B/R5

23-6-68—DUTCH GP, Zandvoort—90-laps
9th (Rtd)   Graham Hill   49B-Ford V8   49B/R5
UNC   Jackie Oliver   49B-Ford V8   49B/R6
Rtd   Jo Siffert   49-Ford V8   49/R2

7-7-68—FRENCH GP, Rouen-Les Essarts—60-laps
11th   Jo Siffert   49-Ford V8   49/R2
Rtd   Graham Hill   49B-Ford V8   49B/R5
DNS   Jackie Oliver   49B-Ford V8   49B/R6

20-7-68—BRITISH GP, Brands Hatch—80-laps
1st FL   Jo Siffert   49B-Ford V8   49B/R7
Rtd   Jackie Oliver   49B-Ford V8   49B/R2
Rtd PP   Graham Hill   49B-Ford V8   49B/R5

4-8-68—GERMAN GP, Nurburgring—14-laps
2nd   Graham Hill   49B-Ford V8   49B/R5
11th   Jackie Oliver   49B-Ford V8   49B/R2
Rtd   Jo Siffert   49B-Ford V8   49B/R7

17-8-68—Gold Cup, Oulton Park—40-laps
3rd   Jack Oliver   49B-Ford   49B/2
Rtd PP   Graham Hill   49B-Ford V8   49B/5

8-9-68—ITALIAN GP, Monza—68-laps
Rtd   Jo Siffert   49B-Ford V8   49B/R7
Rtd FL   Jackie Oliver   49B-Ford V8   49B/R5
Rtd   Graham Hill   49B-Ford V8   49B/R6*
DNS   Mario Andretti   49B-Ford V8   48B/R5
*Car rebuilt with new monocoque chassis

22-9-68—CANADIAN GP, St Jovite—90-laps
4th   Graham Hill   49B Ford-V8   49B/R6
Rtd   Jackie Oliver   49B-Ford V8   49B/R2
Rtd FL   Jo Siffert   49B-Ford V8   49B/R7
Rtd   Bill Brack   49B-Ford V8   49B/R5

6-10-68—UNITED STATES GP, Watkins Glen—108-laps
2nd   Graham Hill   49B-Ford V8   49B/R6
5th   Jo Siffert   49B-Ford V8   49B/R7
Rtd PP   Mario Andretti   49B-Ford V8   49B/R5
DNS   Jackie Oliver   49B-Ford V8   49B/R2

3-11-68—MEXICAN GP, Mexico City—65-laps
1st   Graham Hill   49B-Ford V8   49B/R6
3rd   Jackie Oliver   49B-Ford V8   49B/R5
6th PP FL   Jo Siffert   49B-Ford V8   49B/R7
Rtd   Moises Solana   49B-Ford V8   49B/R2

1969
1-3-69—SOUTH AFRICAN GP, Kyalami—80-laps
2nd   Graham Hill   49B-Ford V8   49B/R6
4th   Jo Siffert   49B-Ford V8   49B/R7
Rtd   Jochen Rindt   49B-Ford V8   49B/R9
Rtd   John Love   49-Ford V8   49/R3
Rtd   Mario Andretti   49B-Ford V8   49B/R11

16-3-69—Race of Champions, Brands Hatch—50-laps
2nd PP   Graham Hill   49B-Ford V8   49B/6
Rtd FL   Jochen Rindt   49B-Ford V8   49B/9
6th   Pete Lovely   49B-Ford V8   49B/11
4th   Jo Siffert   49B-Ford V8   49B/7

30-3-69—International Trophy, Silverstone—52-laps
2nd   Jochen Rindt   49B-Ford V8   49B/9
7th   Graham Hill   49B-Ford V8   49B/6
11th   Jo Siffert   49B-Ford V8   49B/7
Rtd   Pete Lovely   49B-Ford V8   49B/11

13-4-69—Madrid GP F1/5000, Jarama, Spain—40-laps
3rd   Jock Russell   43-Ford V8 5.0   43/1
Rtd   Rob Lamplough   43-Ford V8 5.0   43/2
Rtd   Max Mosley   59-Cosworth F2   59---

4-5-69—SPANISH GP, Barcelona—90-laps
Rtd   Jo Siffert   49B-Ford V8   49B/R7
Rtd PP FL   Jochen Rindt   49B-Ford V8   49B/R9
Rtd   Graham Hill   49B-Ford V8   49B/R6

8-6-69—MONACO GP, Monte Carlo—80-laps
1st   Graham Hill   49B-Ford V8   49B/R10
3rd   Jo Siffert   49B-Ford V8   49B/R7
4th   Richard Attwood   49-Ford V8   49/R8

21-6-69—DUTCH GP, Zandvoort—90-laps
2nd   Jo Siffert   49B-Ford V8   49B/R7
7th   Graham Hill   49B-Ford V8   49B/R10
Rtd PP   Jochen Rindt   49B-Ford V8   49B/R6*
*Car rebuilt with new monocoque chassis

6-7-69—FRENCH GP, Clermont-Ferrand—38-laps
6th   Graham Hill   49B-Ford V8   49B/R10
9th   Jo Siffert   49B-Ford V8   49B/R7
Rtd   Jochen Rindt   49B-Ford V8   49B/R6
Rtd   John Miles   63-Ford V8   63/2

19-7-69—BRITISH GP, Silverstone—84-laps
4th PP   Jochen Rindt   49B-Ford V8   49B/R6
7th   Graham Hill   49B-Ford V8   49B/R8
8th   Jo Siffert   49B-Ford V8   49B/R7
10th   John Miles   63-Ford V8   63/2
Rtd   Jo Bonnier   63-Ford V8   63/1

3-8-69—GERMAN GP, Nurburgring—14-laps
4th   Graham Hill   49B-Ford V8   49B/R10
8th   Rolf Stommelen   '4'-Cosworth   59-F2-19*
11th (Rtd)   Jo Siffert   49B-Ford V8   49B/R7
Rtd   Jochen Rindt   49B-Ford V8   49B/R6
Rtd   Jo Bonnier   49B-Ford V8   49B/R8
Rtd   Mario Andretti   63-Ford V8   63/2
DNS   Hans Herrmann   '4'-Cosworth   59-F2-20*
*Formula 2 cars in race run concurrently with Formula 1 Grand Prix.

16-8-69—Gold Cup, Oulton Park—40-laps
2nd   Jochen Rindt   63-Ford V8   63/1
Rtd   Graham Hill   59-Cosworth F2   ----

8-9-69—ITALIAN GP, Monza—68-laps
2nd PP   Jochen Rindt   49B-Ford V8   49B/R6
8th (Rtd)   Jo Siffert   49B-Ford V8   49B/R7
9th (Rtd)   Graham Hill   49B-Ford V8   49B/R10
Rtd   John Miles   63-Ford V8   63/1

20-9-69—CANADIAN GP, Mosport Park—90-laps
3rd   Jochen Rindt   49B-Ford V8   49B/R6
7th   Pete Lovely   49B-Ford V8   49B/R11
Rtd   Graham Hill   49B-Ford V8   49B/R10
Rtd   Jo Siffert   49B-Ford V8   49B/R7
Rtd   John Miles   63-Ford V8   63/2

5-10-69—UNITED STATES GP, Watkins Glen—108-laps
1st PP FL   Jochen Rindt   49B-Ford V8   49B/R6
Rtd   Graham Hill   49B-Ford V8   49B/R10
Rtd   Pete Lovely   49B-Ford V8   49B/R11
Rtd   Mario Andretti   63-Ford V8   63/2
Rtd   Jo Siffert   49B-Ford V8   49B/R7

19-10-69—MEXICAN GP, Mexico City—65-laps

9th	Pete Lovely	49B-Ford V8	49B/R11
Rtd	Jochen Rindt	49B-Ford V8	49B/R6
Rtd	Jo Siffert	49B-Ford V8	49B/R7
Rtd	John Miles	63-Ford V8	63/2

1970

7-3-70—SOUTH AFRICAN GP, Kyalami—80-laps

5th	John Miles	49C-Ford V8	49B/R10
6th	Graham Hill	49C-Ford V8	49B/R7
8th	John Love	49-Ford V8	49/R3
12th (Rtd)	Dave Charlton	49C-Ford V8	49B/R8
13th (Rtd)	Jochen Rindt	49C-Ford V8	49B/R6
T-car	Brian Redman	49C-Ford V8	49B/R7

22-3-70—Race of Champions, Brands Hatch—50-laps

2nd	Jochen Rindt	49C-Ford V8	49C/6
5th	Graham Hill	49C-Ford V8	49C/7
Rtd	Pete Lovely	49B-Ford V8	49B/11

19-4-70—SPANISH GP, Jarama—90-laps

4th	Graham Hill	49C-Ford V8	49B/R7
Rtd	Jochen Rindt	72-Ford V8	72-2
DNQ	John Miles	72-Ford V8	72-1
DNQ	Alex Soler-Roig	49C-Ford V8	49B/R10

26-4-70—BRDC International Trophy, F1/5000, Silverstone—Two 26-laps Heats

9th	Graham Hill	49C-Ford V8	49C/7
13th	Pete Lovely	49B-Ford V8	49B/11
Rtd	Jochen Rindt	72-Ford V8	72/2
Rtd	John Miles	72-Ford V8	72/1

10-5-70—MONACO GP, Monte Carlo—80-laps

1st FL	Jochen Rindt	49C-Ford V8	49B/R6
5th	Graham Hill	49C-Ford V8	49B/R10
DNQ	John Miles	49B-Ford V8	49B/R10
DNS	Graham Hill	49C-Ford V8	49B-R7

7-6-70—BELGIAN GP, Spa-Francorchamps—28-laps

Rtd	Graham Hill	49C-Ford V8	49B/R7
Rtd	John Miles	72-Ford V8	72/1
Rtd	Jochen Rindt	49C-Ford V8	49B/R6
DNQ	Alex Soler-Roig	72-Ford V8	72/2

21-6-70—DUTCH GP, Zandvoort—80-laps

1st PP	Jochen Rindt	72-Ford V8	72/2
7th	John Miles	72-Ford V8	72/1
Unc	Graham Hill	49C-Ford V8	49B/R7
DNQ	Pete Lovely	49B-Ford V8	49B/R11

5-7-70—FRENCH GP, Clermont-Ferrand—38-laps

1st	Jochen Rindt	72-Ford V8	72/2
8th	John Miles	72-Ford V8	72/1
10th	Graham Hill	49C-Ford V8	49B/R7
DNQ	Alex Soler-Roig	49C-Ford V8	49B/R6
DNQ	Pete Lovely	49B-Ford V8	49B/R11

18-7-70—BRITISH GP, Brands Hatch—80-laps

1st PP	Jochen Rindt	72-Ford V8	72/2
6th	Graham Hill	49C-Ford V8	49B/R7
8th	Emerson Fittipaldi	49C-Ford V8	49B/R10
'10th'	Pete Lovely	49B-Ford V8	49B/R11
Rtd	John Miles	72-Ford V8	72/1

2-8-70—GERMAN GP, Hockenheimring—50-laps

1st	Jochen Rindt	72-Ford V8	72/2
4th	Emerson Fittipaldi	49C-Ford V8	49B/R10
Rtd	Graham Hill	49C-Ford V8	49B/R7
Rtd	John Miles	72-Ford V8	72/3

16-8-70—AUSTRIAN GP, Osterreichring—60-laps

15th	Emerson Fittipaldi	49C-Ford V8	49B/R10
Rtd PP	Jochen Rindt	72-Ford V8	72/2
Rtd	John Miles	72-Ford V8	72/3

22-8-70—Gold Cup, Oulton Park—Two 20-lap Heats

Heat One

3rd	Jochen Rindt	72-Ford V8	72/2
Rtd	Graham Hill	72-Ford V8	72/4

Heat Two		Aggregate	
1st FL	Rindt	2nd	Rindt
DNS	Hill	18th	Hill

16-8-70—ITALIAN GP, Monza—68-laps

†	Jochen Rindt	72-Ford V8	72/2
DNS	Graham Hill	72-Ford V8	72/4
DNS	John Miles	72-Ford V8	72/3
DNS	Emerson Fittipaldi	72-Ford V8	72/5

20-9-70—CANADIAN GP, St Jovite—90-laps

Unc	Graham Hill	72-Ford V8	72/4

4-10-70—UNITED STATES GP, Watkins Glen—108-laps

1st	Emerson Fittipaldi	72-Ford V8	72/5
3rd	Reine Wisell	72-Ford V8	72/3
Rtd	Graham Hill	72-Ford V8	72/4
DNQ	Pete Lovely	49B-Ford V8	49B/R11

18-10-70—MEXICAN GP, Mexico City—65-laps

Unc	Reine Wisell	72-Ford V8	72/3
Rtd	Graham Hill	72-Ford V8	72/4
Rtd	Emerson Fittipaldi	72-Ford V8	72/5

1971

24-1-71—Argentine GP, Buenos Aires—Two 50-lap Heats

Heat One

5th FL	Reine Wisell	72-Ford V8	72/3
8th	Wilson Fittipaldi	49C-Ford V8	49C/6
10th	Emerson Fittipaldi	72-Ford V8	72/5

Heat Two		Aggregate	
Rtd	Wisell	7th	Wisell
Rtd	W.Fittipaldi	9th	W. Fittipaldi
Unc	E. Fittipaldi	NC	E. Fittipaldi

6-3-71—SOUTH AFRICAN GP, Kyalami—79-laps

4th	Reine Wisell	72-Ford V8	72/3
Rtd	Emerson Fittipaldi	72-Ford V8	72/5

21-3-71—Race of Champions, Brands Hatch—50-laps

Rtd	Reine Wisell	72-Ford V8	72/3
Rtd	Emerson Fittipaldi	56B-P&W Turbine	56B/1
Rtd	Tony Trimmer	72-Ford V8	72/5
DNS	Tony Trimmer	49C-Ford V8	49C/6

28-3-71—Questor GP, Ontario Motor Speedway, Calif, USA—Two 32-lap Heats

Heat One

Rtd	Emerson Fittipaldi	72-Ford V8	72/5
Rtd	Reine Wisell	72-Ford V8	72/3
Rtd	George Follmer	70-Ford V8 5.0	—
DNS	Pete Lovely	49C-Ford V8	49C/11

Aggregate		Heat Two	
21st	Fittipaldi	No Lotus starters	
27th	Wisell		
30th	Follmer		

9-4-71—Rothmans Trophy, Oulton Park—40-laps

6th	Tony Trimmer	49C-Ford V8	49C/6
7th	Emerson Fittipaldi	72-Ford V8	72/5
Rtd	Reine Wisell	56B-P&W Turbine	56B/1

18-4-71—SPANISH GP, Barcelona—75-laps

12th	Reine Wisell	72-Ford V8	72/3
13th	Emerson Fittipaldi	72-Ford V8	72/5

8-5-71—BRDC International Trophy, Silverstone—Two 26-laps Heats

Heat One

7th	Reine Wisell	72-Ford V8	72/3
22nd	Jock Russell	70-Ford V8 5.0	—
Rtd	Emerson Fittipaldi	56B-P&W Turbine	56B/1

Heat Two				Aggregate	
3rd	Fittipaldi		13th	Wisell	
'18th'	Wisell		Unc	Fittipaldi	
DNS	Russell		Unc	Russell	

23-5-71—MONACO GP, Monte Carlo—80-laps

5th	Emerson Fittipaldi	72-Ford V8	72/5
Rtd	Reine Wisell	72-Ford V8	72/3

13-6-71—Rindt Memorial Race, Hockenheim, West Germany—35-laps

9th	Dave Walker	72-Ford V8	72/5
10th	Reine Wisell	72-Ford V8	72/3
DNS	Dave Walker	56B-P&W Turbine	56B/1
DNS	Tony Trimmer	72-Ford V8	72/5

20-6-71—DUTCH GP, Zandvoort—70-laps

Dis	Reine Wisell	72-Ford V8	72/3
Rtd	Dave Walker	56B-P&W turbine	56B/1

4-7-71—FRENCH GP, Paul Ricard Circuit, Le Castellet—55-laps

3rd	Emerson Fittipaldi	72-Ford V8	72/5
6th	Reine Wisell	72-Ford V8	72/3

17-7-71—BRITISH GP, Silverstone—68-laps

3rd	Emerson Fittipaldi	72-Ford V8	72/5
Unc	Reine Wisell	56B-P&W turbine	56B/1
Rtd	Dave Charlton	72-Ford V8	72/3

1-8-71—GERMAN GP, Nurburgring—12-laps

8th	Reine Wisell	72-Ford V8	72/6
Rtd	Emerson Fittipaldi	72-Ford V8	72/5

15-8-71—AUSTRIAN GP, Osterreichring—54-laps

2nd	Emerson Fittipaldi	72-Ford V8	72/5
4th	Reine Wisell	72-Ford V8	72/6

21-8-71—Gold Cup, Oulton Park—Two 20-lap Heats
Heat One

Rtd	Jock Russell	70-Ford V8 5.0	—

5-9-71—ITALIAN GP, Monza—55-laps

8th	Emerson Fittipaldi	56B-P&W turbine	56B/1

19-9-71—CANADIAN GP, Mosport Park—64-laps

5th	Reine Wisell	72-Ford V8	72/6
7th	Emerson Fittipaldi	72-Ford V8	72/5
Unc	Pete Lovely	69-Ford V8	69-F2-5*

*Special built by Lovely using front end of ex-Rindt Lotus 69 Formula 2 car and rear-end of Lovely's 49B/R11

3-10-71—UNITED STATES GP, Watkins Glen—59-laps

19th	Emerson Fittipaldi	72-Ford V8	72/5
20th	Pete Lovely	69-Ford V8	69-F2-5
Rtd	Reine Wisell	72-Ford V8	72/6

24-10-71—Rothmans Victory race, Brands Hatch—14-laps*

2nd FL	Emerson Fittipaldi	72-Ford V8	72/5

*Race stopped after Jo Siffert's fatal BRM accident.

1972

23-1-72—ARGENTINE GP, Buenos Aires—95-laps

Dis	Dave Walker	72D-Ford V8	72D/6
Rtd	Emerson Fittipaldi	72D-Ford V8	72D/5

4-3-72—SOUTH AFRICAN GP, Kyalami—79-laps

2nd	Emerson Fittipaldi	72D-Ford V8	72D/5
10th	Dave Walker	72D-Ford V8	72D/6
Rtd	Dave Charlton	72D-Ford V8	72D/3

19-3-72—Race of Champions, Brands Hatch-40-laps

1st PP FL	Emerson Fittipaldi	72-Ford V8	72D/5
10th	Dave Walker	72-Ford V8	72D/6
DNQ	Jock Russell	70-Ford V8*	70/R3

*F5000 car in combined F1/5000 race.

30-3-72—Brazilian GP, Interlagos, Sao Paulo-37-laps

5th	Dave Walker	72-Ford V8	72D/6
Rtd PP FL	Emerson Fittipaldi	72-Ford V8	72D/7

23-4-72—BRDC International Trophy, Silverstone—40-laps

1st PP	Emerson Fittipaldi	72D-Ford V8	72D/7
DNS	Dave Walker	72D-Ford V8	72D/6
Rtd	Jock Russell	70-Ford V8 5.0	—

1-5-72—SPANISH GP, Jarama, Madrid—90-laps

1st	Emerson Fittipaldi	72D-Ford V8	72D/7
'9th'	Dave Walker	72D-Ford V8	72D/5

14-5-72—MONACO GP, Monte Carlo—80-laps

3rd	Emerson Fittipaldi	72D-Ford V8	72D/7
14th	Dave Walker	72D-Ford V8	72D/5

29-5-72—Gold Cup, Oulton Park—40-laps

2nd	Emerson Fittipaldi	72D-Ford V8	72D/5
Rtd	Dave Walker	72D-Ford V8	72D/6

4-6-72—BELGIAN GP, Nivelles-Baulers—85-laps

1st PP	Emerson Fittipaldi	72D-Ford V8	72D/7
14th	Dave Walker	72D-Ford V8	72D/6
T-car	Fittipaldi	72D-Ford V8	72D/5

18-6-72—Gran Premio Repubblica Italiana, Vallelunga, Rome—80-laps

1st PP FL	Emerson Fittipaldi	72D-Ford V8	72D/5

2-7-72—FRENCH GP, Clermont-Ferrand—38-laps

2nd	Emerson Fittipaldi	72D-Ford V8	72D/7
'18th'	Dave Walker	72D-Ford V8	72D/6
T-car	Fittipaldi	72D-Ford V8	72D/5
DNQ	Dave Charlton	72D-Ford V8	72D/3

15-7-72—BRITISH GP, Brands Hatch—76-laps

1st	Emerson Fittipaldi	72D-Ford V8	72D/7
Rtd	Dave Walker	72D-Ford V8	72D/6
Rtd	Dave Charlton	72D-Ford V8	72D/3
T-car	Fittipaldi	72D-Ford V8	72D/5
Wdn	Tony Trimmer	Lotus	—

30-7-72—GERMAN GP, Nurburgring—14-laps

Rtd	Dave Charlton	72D-Ford V8	72D/3
Rtd	Dave Walker	72D-Ford V8	72D/6
Rtd	Emerson Fittipaldi	72D-Ford V8	72D/7
T-car	Fittipaldi	72D-Ford V8	72D/5

13-8-72—AUSTRIAN GP, Osterreichring—54-laps

1st PP	Emerson Fittipaldi	72D-Ford V8	72D/5
Rtd	Dave Walker	72D-Ford V8	72D/6
T-car	Fittipaldi	72D-Ford V8	72D/7

28-8-72—Rothmans 50,000 Libre, Brands Hatch—118-laps

1st PP FL	Emerson Fittipaldi	72D-Ford V8	72D/5

10-9-72—ITALIAN GP, Monza—55-laps

1st	Emerson Fittipaldi	72D-Ford V8	72D/5*

*Single World Wide Racing entry, 72D/7 damaged in transporter crash on way to Monza to give Fittipaldi choice of cars.

24-9-72—CANADIAN GP, Mosport Park—80-laps

11th	Emerson Fittipaldi	72D-Ford V8	72D/7
Rtd	Reine Wisell	72D-Ford V8	72D/6
T-car	Fittipaldi	72D-Ford V8	72D/5

8-10-72—UNITED STATES GP, Watkins Glen—59-laps

10th	Reine Wisell	72D-Ford V8	72D/6
Rtd	Emerson Fittipaldi	72D-Ford V8	72D/5
Rtd	Dave Walker	72D-Ford V8	72D/7
T-car	Fittipaldi	72D-Ford V8	72D/7

22-10-72—John Player Challenge Trophy, Brands Hatch—40-laps

Rtd PP FL	Emerson Fittipaldi	72D-Ford V8	72D/7

1973

28-1-73—ARGENTINE GP, Buenos Aires—96-laps

1st FL	Emerson Fittipaldi	72D-Ford V8	72D/7
Rtd	Ronnie Peterson	72D-Ford V8	72D/8

11-2-73—BRAZILIAN GP, Interlagos, Sao Paulo—40-laps

1st FL	Emerson Fittipaldi	72D-Ford V8	72D/7
Rtd PP	Ronnie Peterson	72D-Ford V8	72D/8

3-3-73—SOUTH AFRICAN GP, Kyalami—79-laps

3rd FL	Emerson Fittipaldi	72D-Ford V8	72D/7
11th	Ronnie Peterson	72D-Ford V8	72D/8
Rtd	Dave Charlton	72D-Ford V8	72D/3

18-3-73—Race of Champions, Brands Hatch—40-laps

Rtd	Emerson Fittipaldi	72E-Ford V8	72E/5
Rtd = FL	Ronnie Peterson	72E-Ford V8	72E/6

8-4-73—BRDC International Trophy, Silverstone—40-laps

2nd FL	Ronnie Peterson	72E-Ford V8	72E/8
Rtd FP	Emerson Fittipaldi	72E-Ford V8	72E/5
DNS	Peterson	72E-Ford V8	72E/6*

*Crashed heavily in practice by Peterson.

29-4-73—SPANISH GP, Montjuich Park, Barcelona—75-laps

1st	Emerson Fittipaldi	72E-Ford V8	72E/5
Rtd PP FL	Ronnie Peterson	72E-Ford V8	72E/8
T-car	Fittipaldi	72E-Ford V8	72E/7

20-5-73—BELGIAN GP, Zolder, Limburg—70-laps

3rd	Emerson Fittipaldi	72E-Ford V8	72E/7
Rtd PP	Ronnie Peterson	72E-Ford V8	72E/6
DNS	Peterson	72E-Ford V8	72E/8
T-car	Fittipaldi	72E-Ford V8	72E/5

3-6-73—MONACO GP, Monte Carlo—80-laps

2nd FL	Emerson Fittipaldi	72E-Ford V8	72E/7
3rd	Ronnie Peterson	72E-Ford V8	72E/6
T-car	Fittipaldi	72E-Ford V8	72E/5

17-6-73—SWEDISH GP, Anderstorp—80-laps

2nd PP	Ronnie Peterson	72E-Ford V8	72E/6
'12th'	Emerson Fittipaldi	72E-Ford V8	72E/7
T-car	Fittipaldi	72E-Ford V8	72E/5
T-car	Peterson	72E-Ford V8	72E/8

1-7-73—FRENCH GP, Ricard-Castellet—54-laps

1st	Ronnie Peterson	72E-Ford V8	72E/6
Rtd	Emerson Fittipaldi	72E-Ford V8	72E/5
T-car	Fittipaldi	72E-Ford V8	72E/7
T-car	Peterson	72E-Ford V8	72E/8

14-7-73—BRITISH GP, Silverstone—67-laps

2nd PP	Ronnie Peterson	72E-Ford V8	72E/6
Rtd	Emerson Fittipaldi	72E-Ford V8	72E/5
T-car	Fittipaldi	72E-Ford V8	72E/7
T-car	Peterson	72E-Ford V8	72E/8

29-7-73—DUTCH GP, Zandvoort—72-laps

11th PP FL	Ronnie Peterson	72E-Ford V8	72E/6
Rtd	Emerson Fittipaldi	72E-Ford V8	72E/7
T-car	Fittipaldi	72E-Ford V8	72E/5*
T-car	Peterson	72E-Ford V8	72E/8

*Car severely damaged in Fittipaldi's practice accident.

5-8-73—GERMAN GP, Nurburgring—14-laps

6th	Emerson Fittipaldi	72E-Ford V8	72E/7
Rtd	Ronnie Peterson	72E-Ford V8	72E/6
T-car	Peterson	72E-Ford V8	72E/8

19-8-73—AUSTRIAN GP, Osterreichring—54-laps

1st	Ronnie Peterson	72E-Ford V8	72E/6
Rtd PP	Emerson Fittipaldi	72E-Ford V8	72E/7
T-car	Peterson	72E-Ford V8	72E/8

9-9-73—ITALIAN GP, Monza—65-laps

1st PP	Ronnie Peterson	72E-Ford V8	72E/6
2nd	Emerson Fittipaldi	72E-Ford V8	72E/7
T-car	Peterson	72E-Ford V8	72E/8

23-9-73—CANADIAN GP, Mosport Park—80-laps

2nd FL	Emerson Fittipaldi	72E-Ford V8	72E/7
Rtd PP	Ronnie Peterson	72E-Ford V8	72E/6
T-car	Peterson	72E-Ford V8	72E/8

7-10-73—UNITED STATES GP, Watkins Glen—59-laps

1st PP	Ronnie Peterson	72E-Ford V8	72E/6
6th	Emerson Fittipaldi	72E-Ford V8	72E/7
T-car	Peterson	72E-Ford V8	72E/8

1974

13-1-74—ARGENTINE GP, Buenos Aires—53-laps

13th PP	Ronnie Peterson	72E-Ford V8	72E/8
Rtd	Jacky Ickx	72E-Ford V8	'72E/5'

27-1-74—BRAZILIAN GP, Interlagos, Sao Paulo—32-laps

3rd	Jacky Ickx	73E-Ford V8	'72E/5'
6th	Ronnie Peterson	72E-Ford V8	72E/8

3-2-74—Presidente Medici GP, 40-laps

No Lotus entries

17-3-74—Race of Champions, Brands Hatch—40-laps

1st FL	Jacky Ickx	72E-Ford V8	'72E/5'

30-3-74—SOUTH AFRICAN GP, Kyalami—78-laps

13th	Ian Scheckter	72E-Ford V8	72E/6
Rtd	Ronnie Peterson	76-Ford V8	JPS9
Rtd	Jacky Ickx	76-Ford V8	JPS10
Wdn	John McNicol	72D-Ford V8	72D/3
Rtd	Paddy Driver	72E-Ford V8	72E/7
T-car	Peterson & Ickx	72E-Ford V8	72E/8

7-4-74—BRDC International Trophy, Silverstone—40-laps

Rtd	Ronnie Peterson	76-Ford V8	JPS9

28-4-74—SPANISH GP, Jarama, Madrid—Two Hours—84-laps

Rtd	Jacky Ickx	76-Ford V8	JPS10
Rtd	Ronnie Peterson	76-Ford V8	JPS9
T-car	Peterson	72E-Ford V8	72E/8

12-5-74—BELGIAN GP, Nivelles-Baulers—85-laps

Rtd	Ronnie Peterson	76-Ford V8	JPS9
Rtd	Jacky Ickx	76-Ford V8	JPS10
T-car	Peterson	72E-Ford V8	72E/8

26-5-74—MONACO GP, Monte Carlo—80-laps

1st FL	Ronnie Peterson	72E-Ford V8	72E/8
Rtd	Jacky Ickx	72E-Ford V8	'72E/5'
T-car	Ickx	76-Ford V8	JPS10

9-6-74—SWEDISH GP, Anderstorp—80-laps

Rtd	Ronnie Peterson	72E-Ford V8	72E/8
Rtd	Jacky Ickx	72E-Ford V8	'72E/5'
T-car	Peterson	76-Ford V8	JPS9

23-6-74—DUTCH GP, Zandvoort—75-laps

8th FL	Ronnie Peterson	72E-Ford V8	72E/8
11th	Jacky Ickx	72E-Ford V8	'72E/5'
T-car	Ickx	76-Ford V8	JPS10

7-7-74—FRENCH GP, Dijon-Prenois—80-laps

1st	Ronnie Peterson	72E-Ford V8	72E/8
5th	Jacky Ickx	72E-Ford V8	'72E/5'
T-car	Peterson	76-Ford V8	JPS10

20-7-74—BRITISH GP, Brands Hatch—75-laps

3rd	Jacky Ickx	72E-Ford V8	'72E/5'
10th*	Ronnie Peterson	72E-Ford V8	72E/8

* = Lauda's Ferrari pole-position time.

4-8-74—GERMAN GP, Nurburgring—14-laps

4th	Ronnie Peterson	76-Ford V8	JPS10
5th	Jacky Ickx	72E-Ford V8	'72E/5'
T-car	Peterson	72E-Ford V8	72E/8

18-8-74—AUSTRIAN GP, Osterreichring—54-laps

Rtd	Jacky Ickx	76-Ford V8	JPS10
Rtd	Ronnie Peterson	72E-Ford V8	72E/8
T-car	Ickx	72E-Ford V8	'72E/5'
T-car	Peterson	76-Ford V8	JPS9

8-9-74—ITALIAN GP, Monza—52-laps

1st	Ronnie Peterson	72E-Ford V8	72E/8
Rtd	Jacky Ickx	76-Ford V8	JPS10
T-car	Peterson	76-Ford V8	JPS9

22-9-74—CANADIAN GP, Mosport Park—80-laps

3rd	Ronnie Peterson	72E-Ford V8	72E/8
13th	Jacky Ickx	72E-Ford V8	'72E/5'
T-car	Ickx	76-Ford V8	JPS9

6-10-74—UNITED STATES GP, Watkins Glen—59-laps

Dis	Tim Schenken	76-Ford V8	JPS9
Rtd	Jacky Ickx	72E-Ford V8	'72E/5'
Rtd	Ronnie Peterson	72E-Ford V8	72E/8

1975

12-1-75—ARGENTINE GP, Buenos Aires—53-laps

8th	Jacky Ickx	72E-Ford V8	'72E/5'
Rtd	Ronnie Peterson	72E-Ford V8	72E/8

278

26-1-75—BRAZILIAN GP, Interlagos, Sao Paulo—40-laps
| 9th | Jacky Ickx | 72E-Ford V8 | '72E/5' |
| 15th | Ronnie Peterson | 72E-Ford V8 | 72E/8 |

1-3-75—SOUTH AFRICAN GP, Kyalami—78-laps
10th	Ronnie Peterson	72E-Ford V8	72E/9
11th	Guy Tunmer	72E-Ford V8	72E/7
12th	Jacky Ickx	72E-Ford V8	'72E/5'
13th	Eddie Keizan	72E-Ford V8	72E/6

16-3-75—Race of Champions, Brands Hatch—40-laps
| 3rd | Ronnie Peterson | 72E-Ford V8 | 72E/9 |
| 4th | Jacky Ickx | 72E-Ford V8 | '72E/5' |

13-4-75—BRDC International Trophy, Silverstone—40-laps
| DNS* | Ronnie Peterson | 72E-Ford V8 | 72E/9 |
| DNS** | Jim Crawford | 72E-Ford V8 | '72E/5' |

*Engine failure in warm-up — **Practice crash, after testing crash and hasty rebuild, severely damaged 'R5'.*

27-4-75—SPANISH GP, Montjuich Park, Barcelona—29-laps*
2nd	Jacky Ickx	72E-Ford V8	'72E/5'
Rtd	Ronnie Peterson	72E-Ford V8	72E/9
T-car	Peterson	72E-Ford V8	72E/8

Race stopped following Stommelen's Hill accident crowd casualties

11-5-75—MONACO GP, Monte Carlo—Two hours—75-laps
4th	Ronnie Peterson	72E-Ford V8	72E/9
8th	Jacky Ickx	72E-Ford V8	'72E/5'
T-car	Peterson	72E-Ford V8	72E/8

25-5-75—BELGIAN GP, Zolder—70-laps
Rtd	Jacky Ickx	72E-Ford V8	'72E/5'
Rtd	Ronnie Peterson	72E-Ford V8	72E/9
T-car	Peterson	72E-Ford V8	72E/8

8-6-75—SWEDISH GP, Anderstorp—80-laps
9th	Ronnie Peterson	72E-Ford V8	72E/9
15th	Jacky Ickx	72E-Ford V8	'72E/5'
T-car	Peterson	72E-Ford V8	72E/8

22-6-75—DUTCH GP, Zandvoort—75-laps
| Rtd | Ronnie Peterson | 72E-Ford V8 | 72E/9 |
| Rtd | Jacky Ickx | 72E-Ford V8 | '72E/5' |

6-7-75—FRENCH GP, Ricard-Castellet—54-laps
10th	Ronnie Peterson	72E-Ford V8	72E/9
Rtd	Jacky Ickx	72E-Ford V8	'72E/5'
T-car	Peterson	72E-Ford V8	72E/5

19-7-75—BRITISH GP, Silverstone—56-laps*
'16th'*	Brian Henton	72E-Ford V8	72F/5
Rtd	Ronnie Peterson	72E-Ford V8	72E/9
Rtd*	Jim Crawford	72E-Ford V8	72F/8

Race stopped after rain showers caused cars including R5 and R8 to crash.

3-8-75—GERMAN GP, Nurburgring, 14-laps
| Rtd | Ronnie Peterson | 72E-Ford V8 | 72E/9 |
| Rtd | John Watson | 72F-Ford V8 | 72F/8 |

17-8-75—AUSTRIAN GP, Osterreichring—29-laps*
5th	Ronnie Peterson	72E-Ford V8	72E/9
DNS	Brian Henton	72F-Ford V8	72F/5
T-car	Peterson & Henton	72F-Ford V8	72F/8

Race stopped after downpour "flooded circuit"

24-8-75—"Swiss GP", Dijon-Prenois—60-laps
| 4th | Ronnie Peterson | 72E-Ford V8 | 72E/9 |

7-9-75—ITALIAN GP, Monza—52-laps
| 13th | Jim Crawford | 72F-Ford V8 | 72F/8 |
| Rtd | Ronnie Peterson | 72E-Ford V8 | 72E/9 |

5-10-75—UNITED STATES GP, Watkins Glen—59-laps
| 5th | Ronnie Peterson | 72E-Ford V8 | 72E/9 |
| 12th | Brian Henton | 72F-Ford V8 | 72F/5 |

1976

25-1-76—BRAZILIAN GP, Interlagos, Sao Paulo—40-laps
| Rtd | Ronnie Peterson | 77-Ford V8 | JPS12 |
| Rtd | Mario Andretti | 77-Ford V8 | JPS11 |

6-3-76—SOUTH AFRICAN GP, Kyalami—78-laps
| 10th | Bob Evans | 77-Ford V8 | JPS12 |

| Rtd | Gunnar Nilsson | 77-Ford V8 | JPS11 |

14-3-76—Race of Champions, Brands Hatch—40-laps
| 8th | Gunnar Nilsson | 77-Ford V8 | JPS11 |
| Rtd | Bob Evans | 77-Ford V8 | JPS12 |

27-3-76—UNITED STATES GP WEST, Long Beach, Cal.—80-laps
| Rtd | Gunnar Nilsson | 77-Ford V8 | JPS11 |
| DNQ | Bob Evans | 77-Ford V8 | JPS12 |

11-4-76—BRDC International Trophy, Silverstone—40-laps
| 6th | Gunnar Nilsson | 77-Ford V8 | JPS12 |

2-5-76—SPANISH GP, Jarama, Madrid—75-laps
| 3rd | Gunnar Nilsson | 77-Ford V8 | JPS12 |
| Rtd | Mario Andretti | 77-Ford V8 | JPS11 |

16-5-76—BELGIAN GP, Zolder, Limbourg—70-laps
| Rtd | Gunnar Nilsson | 77-Ford V8 | JPS12 |
| Rtd | Mario Andretti | 77-Ford V8 | JPS11 |

30-5-76—MONACO GP, Monte Carlo—78-laps
| Rtd | Gunnar Nilsson | 77-Ford V8 | JPS12 |

13-6-76—SWEDISH GP, Anderstorp—72-laps
| Rtd | Gunnar Nilsson | 77-Ford V8 | JPS12 |
| Rtd* | Mario Andretti | 77-Ford V8 | JPS11 |

2nd fastest qualifier in practice, on front row of grid

4-7-76—FRENCH GP, Ricard-Castellet—54-laps
5th	Mario Andretti	77-Ford V8	JPS11
Rtd	Gunnar Nilsson	77-Ford V8	JPS12
T-car	Andretti	77-Ford V8	JPS14

18-7-76—BRITISH GP, Brands Hatch—76-laps
Rtd	Mario Andretti	77-Ford V8	JPS11
Rtd	Gunnar Nilsson	77-Ford V8	JPS12
T-car	Andretti & Nilsson	77-Ford V8	JPS14

1-8-76—GERMAN GP, Nurburgring—14-laps
5th	Gunnar Nilsson	77-Ford V8	JPS12
12th	Mario Andretti	77-Ford V8	JPS14
T-car	Andretti	77-Ford V8	JPS11

15-8-76—AUSTRIAN GP, Osterreichring—54-laps
3rd	Gunnar Nilsson	77-Ford V8	JPS12
5th	Mario Andretti	77-Ford V8	JPS14
T-car	Andretti & Nilsson	77-Ford V8	JPS11

29-8-76—DUTCH GP, Zandvoort—75-laps
3rd	Mario Andretti	77-Ford V8	JPS11
Rtd	Gunnar Nilsson	77-Ford V8	JPS12
T-car	Andretti	77-Ford V8	JPS14

12-9-76—ITALIAN GP, Monza—52-laps
13th	Gunnar Nilsson	77-Ford V8	JPS12
Rtd	Mario Andretti	77-Ford V8	JPS14
T-car	Andretti	77-Ford V8	JPS11

3-10-76—CANADIAN GP, Mosport Park—80-laps
3rd	Mario Andretti	77-Ford V8	JPS11
12th	Gunnar Nilsson	77-Ford V8	JPS12
T-car	Andretti	77-Ford V8	JPS14

10-10-76—UNITED STATES GP, Watkins Glen—59-laps
Rtd	Gunnar Nilsson	77-Ford V8	JPS12
Rtd	Mario Andretti	77-Ford V8	JPS11
T-car	Andretti	77-Ford V8	JPS14

24-10-76—JAPANESE GP, Mount Fuji Speedway—73-laps
| 1st PP | Mario Andretti | 77-Ford V8 | JPS11 |
| 6th | Gunnar Nilsson | 77-Ford V8 | JPS12 |

1977

9-1-77—ARGENTINE GP, Buenos Aires—53-laps
5th	Mario Andretti	78-Ford V8	JPS15
DNS	Gunnar Nilsson	78-Ford V8	JPS15
T-car	Andretti	78-Ford V8	JPS16*

Monocoque damaged by onboard extinguisher explosion in practice.

23-1-77—BRAZILIAN GP, Interlagos, Sao Paulo—40-laps
| 5th | Gunnar Nilsson | 78-Ford V8 | JPS15 |
| Rtd | Mario Andretti | 78-Ford V8 | JPS16* |

Car rebuilt for race after damaged by fire in practice.

5-3-77—SOUTH AFRICAN GP, Kyalami—78-laps

12th	Gunnar Nilsson	78-Ford V8	JPS15
Rtd	Mario Andretti	78-Ford V8	JPS16

20-3-77—Race of Champions, Brands Hatch—40-laps

Rtd*	Mario Andretti	78-Ford V8	JPS16

2nd fastest qualifier in practice, started from front grid row

3-4-77—UNITED STATES GP WEST, Long Beach, California

1st*	Mario Andretti	78-Ford V8	JPS17
8th	Gunnar Nilsson	78-Ford V8	JPS16

2nd fastest qualifier in practice.

T-car	Andretti	78-Ford V8	JPS15

8-5-77—SPANISH GP, Jarama, Madrid—75-laps

1st PP	Mario Andretti	78-Ford V8	JPS17
5th	Gunnar Nilsson	78-Ford V8	JPS16

22-5-77—MONACO GP, Monte Carlo—76-laps

5th	Mario Andretti	78-Ford V8	JPS17
Rtd	Gunnar Nilsson	78-Ford V8	JPS16
T-car	Andretti	78-Ford V8	JPS15

5-6-77—BELGIAN GP, Zolder, Limbourg—70-laps

1st FL	Gunnar Nilsson	78-Ford V8	JPS16
Rtd PP	Mario Andretti	78-Ford V8	JPS17
T-car	Nilsson	78-Ford V8	JPS15

19-6-77—SWEDISH GP, Anderstorp—72-laps

6th PP FL	Mario Andretti	78-Ford V8	JPS17
Rtd	Gunnar Nilsson	78-Ford V8	JPS16
T-car	Andretti	78-Ford V8	JPS15

3-7-77—FRENCH GP, Dijon-Prenois—80-laps

1st PP FL	Mario Andretti	78-Ford V8	JPS17
4th	Gunnar Nilsson	78-Ford V8	JPS16
T-car	Andretti	78-Ford V8	JPS15

16-7-77—BRITISH GP, Silverstone—68-laps

3rd	Gunnar Nilsson	78-Ford V8	JPS16
Rtd	Mario Andretti	78-Ford V8	JPS17

31-7-77—GERMAN GP, Hockenheimring—47-laps

Rtd	Gunnar Nilsson	78-Ford V8	JPS18
Rtd	Mario Andretti	78-Ford V8	JPS17
T-car	Andretti	78-Ford V8	JPS16

14-8-77—AUSTRIAN GP, Osterreichring—54-laps

Rtd	Mario Andretti	78-Ford V8	JPS17
Rtd	Gunnar Nilsson	78-Ford V8	JPS16
T-car	Nilsson	78-Ford V8	JPS18

28-8-77—DUTCH GP, Zandvoort—75-laps

Rtd	Gunnar Nilsson	78-Ford V8	JPS18
Rtd PP	Mario Andretti	78-Ford V8	JPS17
T-car	Nilsson	78-Ford V8	JPS16

11-9-77—ITALIAN GP, Monza—52-laps

1st FL	Mario Andretti	78-Ford V8	JPS17
Rtd	Gunnar Nilsson	78-Ford V8	JPS16

2-10-77—UNITED STATES GP EAST, Watkins Glen—59-laps

2nd	Mario Andretti	78-Ford V8	JPS17
Rtd	Gunnar Nilsson	78-Ford V8	JPS18

9-10-77—CANADIAN GP, Mosport Park, Toronto—80-laps

'9th' PP FL	Mario Andretti	78-Ford V8	JPS17
Rtd	Gunnar Nilsson	78-Ford V8	JPS18

23-10-77—JAPANESE GP, Mount Fuji Speedway—73-laps

Rtd	Gunnar Nilsson	78-Ford V8	JPS18
Rtd PP	Mario Andretti	78-Ford V8	JPS17

1978

15-1-78—ARGENTINE GP, Buenos Aires—53-laps

1st PP	Mario Andretti	78-Ford V8	78/3
5th	Ronnie Peterson	78-Ford V8	78/2
DNQ	Hector Rebaque	78-Ford V8	78/1

29-1-78—BRAZILIAN GP, Jacarepagua, Rio de Janeiro—63-laps

4th	Mario Andretti	78-Ford V8	78/3
Rtd PP	Ronnie Peterson	78-Ford V8	78/2
Rtd	Hector Rebaque	78-Ford V8	78/1

4-3-78—SOUTH AFRICAN GP, Kyalami—78-laps

1st	Ronnie Peterson	78-Ford V8	78/2
7th FL	Mario Andretti	78-Ford V8	78/3
10th	Hector Rebaque	78-Ford V8	78/1

18-3-78—BRDC International Trophy, Silverstone—40-laps

Rtd PP	Ronnie Peterson	78-Ford V8	78/2
Rtd	Mario Andretti	79-Ford V8	79/2

2-4-78—UNIITED STATES GP (WEST), Long Beach, California-80.5-laps

2nd	Mario Andretti	78-Ford V8	78/3
4th	Ronnie Peterson	78-Ford V8	78/2
DNQ	Hector Rebaque	78-Ford V8	78/1
T-car	Mario Andretti	78-Ford V8	78/4

7-5-78—MONACO GP, Monte Carlo—75-laps

11th	Mario Andretti	78-Ford V8	78/3
Rtd	Ronnie Peterson	78-Ford V8	78/2
DNQ	Hector Rebaque	78-Ford V8	78/4
T-car	Andretti	79-Ford V8	79/2

21-5-78—BELGIAN GP, Zolder—70-laps

1st PP	Mario Andretti	79-Ford V8	79/2
2nd FL	Ronnie Peterson	78-Ford V8	78/2
Spare	Andretti	78-Ford V8	78/3

4-6-78—SPANISH GP, Jarama—75-laps

1st PP FL	Mario Andretti	79-Ford V8	79/3
2nd	Ronnie Peterson	79-Ford V8	79/2
Rtd	Hector Rebaque	78-Ford V8	78/1
T-car	Rebaque	78-Ford V8	78/4

17-6-78—SWEDISH GP, Anderstorp—70-laps

Rtd PP	Mario Andretti	79-Ford V8	79/3
3rd*	Ronnie Peterson	79-Ford V8	79/2
12th	Hector Rebaque	78-Ford V8	78/4

Winner was Lauda's controversial 'Fan' Brabham—later rendered illegal.

2-7-78—FRENCH GP, Ricard-Castellet—54-laps

1st	Mario Andretti	79-Ford V8	79/3
2nd	Ronnie Peterson	79-Ford V8	79/2
DNQ	Hector Rebaque	78-Ford V8	78/4

16-7-78—BRITISH GP, Brands Hatch-76-laps

Rtd PP	Ronnie Peterson	79-Ford V8	79/2
Rtd	Hector Rebaque	78-Ford V8	78/4
Rtd	Mario Andretti	79-Ford V8	79/3

30-7-78—GERMAN GP, Hockenheim-45-laps

1st PP	Mario Andretti	79-Ford V8	79/3
Rtd FL	Ronnie Peterson	79-Ford V8	79/2
6th	Hector Rebaque	78-Ford V8	78/4

13-8-78—AUSTRIAN GP, Osterreichring-54-laps*

1st PP FL	Ronnie Peterson	79-Ford V8	79/2
Rtd*	Mario Andretti	79-Ford V8	79/3
Rtd*	Hector Rebaque	78-Ford V8	78/4

Race stopped due to heavy rain after first 7 laps during which both Andretti and Rebaque crashed. Race was restarted over remaining 47 laps, result decided on aggregate overall.

27-8-78—DUTCH GP, Zandvoort-75-laps

1st PP	Mario Andretti	79-Ford V8	79/4
2nd	Ronnie Peterson	79-Ford V8	79/2
11th	Hector Rebaque	78-Ford V8	78/4

10-9-78—ITALIAN GP, Monza-40-laps*

6th** PP FL	Mario Andretti	79-Ford V8	79/4
Rtd	Ronnie Peterson	79-Ford V8	78/3
DNQ	Hector Rebaque	78-Ford V8	78/4

Race stopped by first-lap multiple accident which fatally injured Peterson, restarted over 40-laps instead of scheduled 52 in order to finish before dusk.
**Andretti won on the road from Villeneuve's Ferrari but both were penalized one minute for jumping the start.*

1-10-78—UNITED STATES GP, Watkins Glen-59-laps

Rtd PP*	Mario Andretti	79-Ford V8	79/3
15th FL	Jean-Pierre Jarier	79-Ford V8	79/1
Rtd	Hector Rebaque	78-Ford V8	78/2

Andretti qualified 79/4 on pole before crashing, raced spare car.

8-10-78—CANADIAN GP, Ile Notre Dame, Montreal-70-laps

10th	Mario Andretti	79-Ford V8	79/4
Rtd PP	Jean-Pierre Jarier	79-Ford V8	79/3
DNQ	Hector Rebaque	78-Ford V8	78/2

1979

21-1-79—ARGENTINE GP, Buenos Aires-53-laps

2nd	Carlos Reutemann	79-Ford V8	79/2
5th	Mario Andretti	79-Ford V8	79/3*
Rtd	Hector Rebaque	79-Ford V8	79/1
	Mario Andretti	79-Ford V8	79/4
T-car	Rebaque	78-Ford V8	78/4

*Actually the T-car, used by Andretti at the re-start following damage to 79/4 in first-lap multiple accident.

4-2-79—BRAZILIAN GP, Interlagos-40-laps

3rd	Carlos Reutemann	79-Ford V8	79/2
Rtd	Mario Andretti	79-Ford V8	79/4
DNQ	Hector Rebaque	79-Ford V8	79/1
T-car	Reutemann	79-Ford V8	79/3
T-car	Rebaque	78-Ford V8	78/4

3-3-79—SOUTH AFRICAN GP, Kyalami-78-laps

4th	Mario Andretti	79-Ford V8	79/5
5th	Carlos Reutemann	79-Ford V8	79/2
Rtd	Hector Rebaque	79-Ford V8	79/1

8-4-79—UNITED STATES GP WEST, Long beach, California-80-laps

4th	Mario Andretti	79-Ford V8	79/5
Rtd*	Carlos Reutemann	79-Ford V8	79/2
Rtd	Hector Rebaque	79-Ford V8	79/1
T-car	Andretti	79-Ford V8	79/4

*Second fastest qualifier in practice but started from pit lane.

15-4-79—Race of Champions, Brands Hatch-40-laps

3rd*	Mario Andretti	79-Ford V8	79/3
Rtd	Emileo de Villota	78-Ford V8	78/1
T-car	Andretti	80-Ford V8	80/1

*Fastest qualifier in practice.

29-4-79—SPANISH GP, Jarama-75-laps

2nd	Carlos Reutemann	79-Ford V8	79/2
3rd	Mario Andretti	80-Ford V8	80/1
Rtd	Hector Rebaque	79-Ford V8	79/1
T-car		79-Ford V8	79/4
T-car		79-Ford V8	79/5

13-5-79—BELGIAN GP, Zolder-70-laps

4th	Carlos Reutemann	79-Ford V8	79/2
Rtd	Mario Andretti	79-Ford V8	79/5*
Rtd	Hector Rebaque	79-Ford V8	79/1
	Andretti	80-Ford V8	80/1
T-car	Rebaque	78-Ford V8	78/4

*Andretti raced T-car 79/5 after crashing 80/1 during practice.

27-5-79—MONACO GP, Monte Carlo-76-laps

3rd	Carlos Reutemann	79-Ford V8	79/4*
Rtd	Mario Andretti	80-Ford V8	80/1
	Carlos Reutemann	79-Ford V8	79/2
T-car	Andretti	79-Ford V8	79/5

*Reutemann raced T-car 79/4 after damaging 79/2 during practice.

1-7-79—FRENCH GP, Dijon-Prenois-80-laps

12th	Hector Rebaque	79-Ford V8	79/1
13th†	Carlos Reutemann	79-Ford V8	79/4
Rtd	Mario Andretti	80-Ford V8	80/1
	Andretti	80-Ford V8	80/2*
T-car	Reutemann	79-Ford V8	79/5
T-car	Rebaque	78-Ford V8	78/4

*Intended as race car but Andretti used T-car 80/1 instead.
†Finished race in pits with accident damage.

14-7-79—BRITISH GP, Silverstone-68-laps

8th	Carlos Reutemann	79-Ford V8	79/5
9th	Hector Rebaque	79-Ford V8	79/1
Rtd	Mario Andretti	79-Ford V8	79/4
T-car	Andretti	80-Ford V8	80/1
T-car	Reutemann	79-Ford V8	79/3
T-car	Rebaque	78-Ford V8	78/4

29-7-79—GERMAN GP, Hockenheim-45-laps

Rtd	Mario Andretti	79-Ford V8	79/5
Rtd	Carlos Reutemann	79-Ford V8	79/3*
Rtd	Hector Rebaque	79-Ford V8	79/1
	Reutemann	79-Ford V8	79/4

T-car	Rebaque	78-Ford V8	78/4

*Reutemann raced T-car 79/3 after damaging 79/4 during practice.

12-8-79—AUSTRIAN GP, Osterreichring-54-laps

Rtd	Mario Andretti	79-Ford V8	79/5
Rtd	Carlos Reutemann	79-Ford V8	79/4
DNQ	Hector Rebaque	79-Ford V8	79/1
	Andretti	79-Ford V8	79/2*
T-car	Rebaque	78-Ford V8	78/4

*Intended as race car but Andretti used T-car 79/5 instead.

26-8-79—DUTCH GP, Zandvoort-75-laps

7th	Hector Rebaque	79-Ford V8	79/1
Rtd	Mario Andretti	79-Ford V8	79/2
Rtd	Carlos Reutemann	79-Ford V8	79/4
T-car	Andretti	79-Ford V8	79/5

9-9-79—ITALIAN GP, Monza-50-laps

5th	Mario Andretti	79-Ford V8	79/5
7th	Carlos Reutemann	79-Ford V8	79/4
T-car	Andretti	79-Ford V8	79/2
T-car	Hector Rebaque	79-Ford V8	79/1*

*Rebaque failed in his first attempt to qualify the Rebaque HR100 manufactured by his own team. Lotus 79/1 became the T-car.

16-9-79—Dino Ferrari GP, Imola, Italy-40-laps

2nd	Carlos Reutemann	79-Ford V8	79/2

30-9-79—CANADIAN GP Ile Notre-Dame, Montreal-72-laps

10th†	Mario Andretti	79-Ford V8	79/5
Rtd	Carlos Reutemann	79-Ford V8	79/3
	Reutemann	79-Ford V8	79/4*

*Intended as race car but Reutemann raced T-car 79/3 instead.
†Out of fuel after 66 laps.

7-10-79—UNITED STATES GP EAST, Watkins Glen-59-laps

Rtd	Mario Andretti	79-Ford V8	79/5
Rtd	Carlos Reutemann	79-Ford V8	79/3
	Reutemann	79-Ford V8	79/4*

*Intended as race car but Reutemann raced T-car 79/3 instead.

1980

13-1-80—ARGENTINE GP, Buenos Aires-53-laps

Rtd	Mario Andretti	81-Ford V8	81/2
Rtd	Elio de Angelis	81-Ford V8	81/1

27-1-80—BRAZILIAN GP, Interlagos-40-laps

2nd	Elio de Angelis	81-Ford V8	81/1
Rtd	Mario Andretti	81-Ford V8	81/2

1-3-80—SOUTH AFRICAN GP, Kyalami-78-laps

12th	Mario Andretti	81-Ford V8	81/2
Rtd	Elio de Angelis	81-Ford V8	81/1
T-car	Andretti	81-Ford V8	81/3

30-3-80—UNITED STATES GP WEST, Long Beach, Cal.-80-laps

Rtd	Mario Andretti	81-Ford V8	81/2
Rtd	Elio de Angelis	81-Ford V8	81/3
T-car	Andretti	81-Ford V8	81/1

4-5-80—BELGIAN GP, Zolder-72-laps

10th*	Elio de Angelis	81-Ford V8	81/3
Rtd	Mario Andretti	81-Ford V8	81/1
T-car	Andretti	81-Ford V8	81/2

*Accident on 70th lap.

18-5-80—MONACO GP, Monte Carlo-76-laps

7th	Mario Andretti	81-Ford V8	81/2
9th*	Elio de Angelis	81-Ford V8	81/3
T-car	Andretti	81-Ford V8	81/4
T-car	De Angelis	81-Ford V8	81/1

*Accident on 69th lap.

1-6-80—SPANISH GP, Jarama-80-laps

3rd	Elio de Angelis	81-Ford V8	81/3
Rtd	Mario Andretti	81-Ford V8	81/2
T-car		81-Ford V8	81/1

29-6-80—FRENCH GP, Paul Ricard-54-laps

Rtd	Mario Andretti	81-Ford V8	81/1
Rtd	Elio de Angelis	81-Ford V8	81/3
T-car		81-Ford V8	81/2

13-7-80—BRITISH GP, Brands Hatch-76-laps

Rtd	Mario Andretti	81-Ford V8	81/1

Rtd	Elio de Angelis	81-Ford V8	81/2
	De Angelis	81-Ford V8	81/3*

Intended as race car but de Angelis raced T-car 81/2 instead.

10-8-80—GERMAN GP, Hockenheim-45-laps

7th	Mario Andretti	81-Ford V8	81/1
16th†	Elio de Angelis	81-Ford V8	81/3
T-car		81-Ford V8	81/2
		81B-Ford V8	81/B*

*Using the rebuilt monocoque of 81/4 (crashed by Andretti at Monaco), a heavily revised 81, designated 81/B, was completed in the paddock, but not used during race weekend.
†Stopped on 43rd lap with seized wheel bearing.

17-8-80—AUSTRIAN GP Osterreichring-54-laps

6th	Elio de Angelis	81-Ford V8	81/3
Rtd	Mario Andretti	81-Ford V8	81/1
Rtd	*Nigel Mansell	81B-Ford V8	81/B
T-car	Andretti	81-Ford V8	81/2

*Mansell used 81/3 to qualify for a place on the grid after failing to do so with 81/B.

31-8-80—DUTCH GP, Zandvoort-72-laps

8th*	Mario Andretti	81-Ford V8	81/1
Rtd	Elio de Angelis	81-Ford V8	81/3
Rtd	Nigel Mansell	81B-Ford V8	81/B
T-car	Mansell and Andretti	81-Ford V8	81/2

*Out of fuel after 70 laps.

14-9-80—ITALIAN GP, Imola—60-laps

4th	Elio de Angelis	81-Ford V8	81/3
Rtd	Mario Andretti	81-Ford V8	81/1
DNQ	Nigel Mansell	81B-Ford V8	81/B
T-car	Mansell	81-Ford V8	81/2

29-9-80—CANADIAN GP, Ile Notre-Dame, Montreal—70-laps

10th	Elio de Angelis	81-Ford V8	81/2
Rtd	Mario Andretti	81-Ford V8	81/3*
	Andretti	81-Ford V8	81/1

*Actually the T-car, raced by Andretti at the re-start following damage to 81/1 in first-lap multiple accident.

5-10-80—UNITED STATES GP EAST, Watkins Glen-59-laps

4th	Elio de Angelis	81-Ford V8	81/2
6th	Mario Andretti	81-Ford V8	81/3

1981

7-2-81—SOUTH AFRICAN GP, Kyalami-77-laps

3rd	Elio de Angelis	81-Ford V8	81/3
10th	Nigel Mansell	81-Ford V8	81/2
T-car		81-Ford V8	81/1

15-3-81—UNITED STATES GP WEST, Long Beach, Cal.—80-laps

Rtd	Elio de Angelis	81-Ford V8	81/3
Rtd	Nigel Mansell	81-Ford V8	81/2
	de Angelis	88-Ford V8	88/1*

*Used by de Angelis during practice in between arguments and protests over the car's legality. It was intended to race the car, assuming it qualified, but de Angelis used 81/3 once 88/1 had been excluded from the meeting.

29-3-81—BRAZILIAN GP, Jacarepagua, Rio de Janeiro-62-laps

5th	Elio de Angelis	81-Ford V8	81/3
11th	Nigel Mansell	81-Ford V8	81/2
	de Angelis	88-Ford V8	88/1*

*Used by de Angelis during practice until excluded by organizers.

12-4-81—ARGENTINE GP, Buenos Aires-53-laps

6th	Elio de Angelis	81-Ford V8	81/3
Rtd	Nigel Mansell	81-Ford V8	81/2
	de Angelis	88-Ford V8	88/1*

*Failed to pass scrutineering.

3-5-81—SAN MARINO GP, Imola, Italy-60-laps

Team Essex Lotus withdrew cars for Elio de Angelis and Nigel Mansell following FIA International Court of Appeal decision on April 23 to ban the Lotus 88.

17-5-81—BELGIAN GP, Zolder-54-laps

3rd	Nigel Mansell	81-Ford V8	81/1
5th	Elio de Angelis	81-Ford V8	81/3
T-car		81-Ford V8	81/2

31-5-81—MONACO GP, Monte Carlo-76-laps

Rtd	Elio de Angelis	87-Ford V8	87/2
Rtd	Nigel Mansell	87-Ford V8	87/1
T-car		81-Ford V8	81/2

21-6-81—SPANISH GP, Jarama-80-laps

5th	Elio de Angelis	87-Ford V8	87/2
6th	Nigel Mansell	87-Ford V8	87/1
T-car		81-Ford V8	81/2

5-7-81—FRENCH GP, Dijon-80-laps

6th	Elio de Angelis	87-Ford V8	87/2
7th	Nigel Mansell	87-Ford V8	87/1
T-car		81-Ford V8	81/2

Race stopped after 58 laps due to downpour and restarted.

18-7-81—BRITISH GP, Silverstone-68-laps

Rtd	Elio de Angelis	87-Ford V8	87/3
DNQ	Nigel Mansell	87-Ford V8	87/2*
	de Angelis	88B-Ford V8	88B/4
	Mansell	88B-Ford V8	88B/2
T-car		88B-Ford V8	88B/1

*Began practice as 88B/2 but converted back to 87/2 once Type 88 and its derivatives had been declared illegal. De Angelis began practice with 88B/4 (a new chassis) and 87/3 was brought from Hethel following the ban on the Type 88.

2-8-81—GERMAN GP, HOCKENHEIM-45-laps

7th	Elio de Angelis	87-Ford V8	87/3
Rtd	Nigel Mansell	87-Ford V8	87/4*
T-car		87-Ford V8	87/2

*Converted from 88B/4.

16-8-81—AUSTRIAN GP, Osterreichring-53-laps

7th	Elio de Angelis	87-Ford V8	87/3
Rtd	Nigel Mansell	87-Ford V8	87/4
T-car	Mansell	87-Ford V8	87/2

30-8-81—DUTCH GP, Zandvoort-72-laps

5th	Elio de Angelis	87-Ford V8	87/3
Rtd	Nigel Mansell	87-Ford V8	87/4
T-car	Mansell	87-Ford V8	87/2

13-9-81—ITALIAN GP, Monza-52-laps

4th	Elio de Angelis	87-Ford V8	87/3
Rtd	Nigel Mansell	87-Ford V8	87/4
T-car	Mansell	87-Ford V8	87/5

27-9-81—CANADIAN GP, Ile Notre Dame, Montreal-63-laps

6th	Elio de Angelis	87-Ford V8	87/3
Rtd	Nigel Mansell	87-Ford V8	87/5
T-car		87-Ford V8	87/2

17-10-81—CAESARS PALACE GP, Las Vegas, Nevada-75-laps

4th	Nigel Mansell	87-Ford V8	87/5
Rtd	Elio de Angelis	87-Ford V8	87/3
T-car	Mansell	87-Ford V8	87/5

1982

23-1-82—SOUTH AFRICAN GP, Kyalami-77-laps

8th	Elio de Angelis	87B-Ford V8	87B/3
Rtd	Nigel Mansell	87B-Ford V8	87B/5
T-car	de Angelis	87-Ford V8	87/4
T-car	Mansell	87-Ford V8	87/2

21-3-82—BRAZILIAN GP, Jacarepagua, Rio de Janeiro-63-laps

3rd*	Nigel Mansell	91-Ford V8	91/7
Rtd	Elio de Angelis	91-Ford V8	91/6
T-car		87B-Ford V8	87B/3

*5th on the road but Piquet (1st) and Rosberg (2nd) disqualified.

4-4-82—UNITED STATES GP, LONG BEACH, California-75-laps

5th	Elio de Angelis	91-Ford V8	91/6
7th	Nigel Mansell	91-Ford V8	91/7
T-car		87B-Ford V8	87B/3

25-4-82—SAN MARINO GP, Imola, Italy-60-laps

De Angelis and Mansell withdrawn in line with boycott by FOCA.

9-5-82-BELGIAN GP, Zolder-70-laps

4th*	Elio de Angelis	91-Ford V8	91/6
Rtd	Nigel Mansell	91-Ford V8	91/7
T-car		91-Ford V8	91/8

*5th on the road but Lauda (3rd) disqualified.

23-5-82—MONACO GP, Monte Carlo-76-laps

4th	Nigel Mansell	91-Ford V8	91/7
5th	Elio de Angelis	91-Ford V8	91/6
T-car	de Angelis	91-Ford V8	91/8
T-car	Mansell	91-Ford V8	91/9

6-6-82—UNITED STATES GP, DETROIT, Michigan-62-laps

Rtd	Elio de Angelis	91-Ford V8	91/9
Rtd	Nigel Mansell	91-Ford V8	91/7
		91-Ford V8	91/6*

Intended as race car but de Angelis used T-car 91/9 instead.

13-6-82—CANADIAN GP, Ile Notre Dame, Montreal-70-laps

4th	Elio de Angelis	91-Ford V8	91/6
Rtd	Nigel Mansell	91-Ford V8	91/7
T-car		91-Ford V8	91/9

3-7-82—DUTCH GP, Zandvoort-72-laps

Rtd	Elio de Angelis	91-Ford V8	91/6
DNQ	Roberto Moreno	91-Ford V8	91/7
T-car	de Angelis	91-Ford V8	91/8
T-car	Moreno	91-Ford V8	91/9

18-7-82—BRITISH GP, Brands Hatch-76-laps

4th	Elio de Angelis	91-Ford V8	91/8
Rtd	Nigel Mansell	91-Ford V8	91/7
T-car	Mansell	91-Ford V8	91/6
T-car	de Angelis	91-Ford V8	91/5*

Converted from 87/5.

25-7-82—FRENCH GP, Paul Ricard-54-laps

12th	Geoff Lees	91-Ford V8	91/6
Rtd	Elio de Angelis	91-Ford V8	91/8
	Lees	91-Ford V8	91/7*
T-car	de Angelis	91-Ford V8	91/5

Intended as race car but Lees raced T-car 91/6 instead.

8-8-82—GERMAN GP, Hockenheim-45-laps

9th	Nigel Mansell	91-Ford V8	91/7
Rtd	Elio de Angelis	91-Ford V8	91/8
T-car	de Angelis	91-Ford V8	91/6
T-car	Mansell	91-Ford V8	91/5

15-8-82—AUSTRIAN GP, Osterreichring-53-laps

1st	Elio de Angelis	91-Ford V8	91/8
Rtd	Nigel Mansell	91-Ford V8	91/7
T-car	de Angelis	91-Ford V8	91/6
T-car	Mansell	91-Ford V8	91/5

29-8-82—SWISS GP, Dijon, France-80-laps

6th	Elio de Angelis	91-Ford V8	91/8
8th	Nigel Mansell	91-Ford V8	91/7
T-car	de Angelis	91-Ford V8	91/6
T-car	Mansell	91-ford V8	91/9

12-9-82—ITALIAN GP, Monza-52-laps

7th	Nigel Mansell	91-Ford V8	91/7
Rtd	Elio de Angelis	91-Ford V8	91/8
T-car	de Angelis	91-Ford V8	91/6
T-car	Mansell	91-Ford V8	91/9

25-9-82—CAESARS PALACE GP, Las Vegas, Nevada-75-laps

Rtd	Elio de Angelis	91-Ford V8	91/6
Rtd	Nigel Mansell	91-Ford V8	91/8
	Mansell	91-Ford V8	91/10*

Intended as race car but Mansell raced T-car 91/8 instead.

1983

13-3-83—BRAZILIAN GP, Rio de Janeiro-63-laps

12th	Nigel Mansell	92-Ford V8	92/10
Disq	Elio de Angelis	93T-Renault V6 t/c	93T/1

27-3-83—UNITED STATES GP (WEST), Long Beach, Cal.-75-laps

12th	Nigel Mansell	92-Ford V8	92/10
Rtd	Elio de Angelis	93T-Renault V6 t/c	93T/1

17-4-83—FRENCH GP, Ricard-Castellet-54-laps

Rtd	Nigel Mansell	92-Ford V8	92/10
Rtd	Elio de Angelis	93T-Renault V6 t/c	93T/1

1-5-83—SAN MARINO GP, Imola, Italy-60-laps

12th†	Nigel Mansell	92-Ford V8	92/10
Rtd	Elio de Angelis	93T-Renault V6 t/c	93T/1

†Accident on 57th lap.

15-5-83—MONACO GP, Monte Carlo-76-laps

Rtd	Nigel Mansell	92-Ford V8	92/10
Rtd	Elio de Angelis	93T-Renault V6 t/c	93T/1

22-5-83—BELGIAN GP, Spa-Francorchamps-40-laps

9th	Elio de Angelis	93T-Renault V6 t/c	93T/1
Rtd	Nigel Mansell	92-Ford V8	92/10

5-6-83—DETROIT GP, Michigan, USA-60-laps

6th	Nigel Mansell	92-Ford V8	92/10
Rtd	Elio de Angelis	93T-Renault V6 t/c	93T/1

12-6-83—CANADIAN GP, Ile Notre Dame, Montreal-70-laps

Rtd	Nigel Mansell	92-Ford V8	92/10
Rtd	Elio de Angelis	93T-Renault V6 t/c	93T/1

16-7-83—BRITISH GP, Silverstone-67-laps

4th	Nigel Mansell	94T-Renault V6 t/c	94T/2
Rtd	Elio de Angelis	94T-Renault V6 t/c	94T/1

17-8-83—GERMAN GP, Hockenheimring-45-laps

Rtd	Nigel Mansell	94T-Renault V6	94T/2
Rtd	Elio de Angelis	94T-Renault V6	94T/1

14-8-83—AUSTRIAN GP, Osterreichring-53-laps

5th	Nigel Mansell	94T-Renault V6	94T/2
Rtd	Elio de Angelis	94T-Renault V6	94T/1

28-8-83—DUTCH GP, Zandvoort-72-laps

Rtd	Nigel Mansell	94T-Renault V6	94T/2
Rtd	Elio de Angelis	94T-Renault V6	94T/3

11-9-83—ITALIAN GP, Monza-52-laps

5th	Elio de Angelis	94T-Renault V6	94T/1
8th	Nigel Mansell	94T-Renault V6	94T/2

25-9-83—EUROPEAN GP, Brands Hatch, GB-76-laps

3rd FL	Nigel Mansell	94T-Renault V6	94T/2
Rtd PP	Elio de Angelis	94T-Renault V6	94T/1

15-10-83—SOUTH AFRICAN GP, Kyalami-77-laps

UNC	Nigel Mansell	94T-Renault V6	94T/2
Rtd	Elio de Angelis	94T-Renault V6	94T/3

1984

25-3-84—BRAZILIAN GP, Rio de Janeiro-61-laps

3rd PP	Elio de Angelis	95T-Renault V6	95T/3
Rtd	Nigel Mansell	95T-Renault	95T/2

7-4-84—SOUTH AFRICAN GP, Kyalami-75-laps

7th	Elio de Angelis	95T-Renault V6	95T/3
Rtd	Nigel Mansel	95T-Renault V6	95T/2

29-4-84—BELGIAN GP, Zolder-70-laps

5th	Elio de Angelis	95T-Renault V6	95T/3
Rtd	Nigel Mansell	95T-Renault V6	95T/2

6-5-84—SAN MARINO GP, Imola, Italy-60-laps

3rd	Elio de Angelis	95T-Renault	95T/3
Rtd	Nigel Mansell	95T-Renault	95T/1

20-5-84—FRENCH GP, Dijon-Prenois-79-laps

3rd	Nigel Mansell	95T-Renault V6	95T/2
5th	Elio de Angelis	95T-Renault V6	95T/3

3-6-84—MONACO GP, Monte Carlo-31-laps*

6th	Elio de Angelis	95T-Renault V6	95T/3
Rtd	Nigel Mansell	95T-Renault V6	95T/2

Rain shortened race from scheduled 78 laps.

17-6-84—CANADIAN GP, Ile Notre Dame, Montreal-70-laps

4th	Elio de Angelis	95T-Renault V6	95T/4
6th	Nigel Mansell	95T-Renault V6	95T/2

24-6-84—DETROIT GP, Michigan, USA-63-laps

3rd	Elio de Angelis	95T-Renault V6	95T/4
Rtd	Nigel Mansell	95T-Renault V6	95T/2

8-7-84—DALLAS GP, Texas, USA-67-laps

3rd	Elio de Angelis	95T-Renault V6	95T/3
6th† PP	Nigel Mansell	95T-Renault V6	95T/2

†Broken gearbox on 65th lap, Mansell collapsed when attempting to push car across line.

22-7-84—BRITISH GP, Brands Hatch-71-laps

4th	Elio de Angelis	95T-Renault V6	95T/3
Rtd	Nigel Mansell	95T-Renault V6	95T/2

5-8-84—GERMAN GP, Hockenheimring-44-laps

4th	Nigel Mansell	95T-Renault V6	95T/2
Rtd	Elio de Angelis	95T-Renault V6	95T/3

19-8-84—AUSTRIAN GP, Osterreichring-51-laps

Rtd	Elio de Angelis	95T-Renault V6	95T/3
Rtd	Nigel Mansell	95T-Renault V6	95T/2

26-8-84—DUTCH GP, Zandvoort-71-laps

3rd	Nigel Mansell	95T-Renault V6	95T/2
4th	Elio de Angelis	95T-Renault V6	95T/3

9-9-84—ITALIAN GP, Monza-51-laps

Rtd	Elio de Angelis	95T-Renault V6	95T/3
Rtd	Nigel Mansell	95T-Renault V6	95T/2

7-10-84—EUROPEAN GP, New Nurburgring-67-laps

Rtd	Elio de Angelis	95T-Renault V6	95T/3
Rtd	Nigel Mansell	95T-Renault V6	95T/2

21-10-84—PORTUGUESE GP, Estoril-70-laps

5th	Elio de Angelis	95T-Renault V6	95T/4
Rtd	Nigel Mansel	95T-Renault V6	95T/2

Car 94/1 used as spare at Rio, 95T/1 became Team spare from Rio to Monaco, joined by 95T/4 spare from Dijon.

1985
7-4-85—BRAZILIAN GP, Rio de Janeiro-61-laps

3rd	Elio de Angelis	97T-Renault V6	97T/3
Rtd	Ayrton Senna	97T-Renault V6	97T/2

21-4-85—PORTUGUESE GP, Estoril-67-laps

1st PP FL	Ayrton Senna	97T-Renault V6	97T/2
4th	Elio de Angelis	97T-Renault V6	97T/3

5-5-85—SAN MARINO GP, Imola, Italy-60-laps

1st	Elio de Angelis*	97T-Renault V6	97T/1
7th† PP	Ayrton Senna	97T-Renault V6	97T/2

*After disqualification of McLaren which won on road.
†Out of fuel on 58th lap.

19-5-85—MONACO GP, Monte Carlo-78-laps

3rd	Elio de Angelis	97T-Renault V6	97T/1
Rtd PP	Ayrton Senna	97T-Renault V6	97T/2

16-6-85—CANADIAN GP, Ile Notre Dame, Montreal-70-laps

5th PP	Elio de Angelis	97T-Renault V6	97T/3
16th FL	Ayrton Senna	97T-Renault V6	97T/2

23-6-85—DETROIT GP, Michigan, USA-63-laps

5th	Elio de Angelis	97T-Renault V6	97T/3
Rtd PP FL	Ayrton Senna	97T-Renault V6	97T/2

7-7-85—FRENCH GP, Ricard-Castellet-53-laps

5th	Elio de Angelis	97T-Renault V6	97T/3
Rtd	Ayrton Senna	97T-Renault V6	97T/4

21-7-85—BRITISH GP, Silverstone-65-laps

10th*	Ayrton Senna	97T-Renault V6	97T/4
Rtd	Elio de Angelis	97T-Renault V6	97T/3

*Stopped on circuit on 61st lap.

4-8-85—GERMAN GP, New Nurburgring-67-laps

Rtd	Ayrton Senna	97T-Renault V6	97T/4
Rtd	Elio de Angelis	97T-Renault V6	97T/3

18-8-85—AUSTRIAN GP, Osterreichring-52-laps

2nd	Ayrton Senna	97T-Renault V6	97T/4
5th	Elio de Angelis	97T-Renault V6	97T/2

25-8-85—DUTCH GP, Zandvoort-70-laps

3rd	Ayrton Senna	97T-Renault V6	97T/4
5th	Elio de Angelis	97T-Renault V6	97T/3

8-9-85—ITALIAN GP, Monza-51-laps

3rd PP	Ayrton Senna	97T-Renault V6	97T/4
6th	Elio de Angelis	97T-Renault V6	97T/3

15-9-85—BELGIAN GP, Spa-Francorchamps-43-laps

1st	Ayrton Senna	97T-Renault V6	97T/4
Rtd	Elio de Angelis	97T-Renault V6	97T/3

6-10-85—EUROPEAN GP, Brands Hatch-75-laps

2nd PP	Ayrton Senna	97T-Renault V6	97T/4
5th	Elio de Angelis	97T-Renault V6	97T/3

19-10-85—SOUTH AFRICAN GP, Kyalami-75-laps

Rtd	Ayrton Senna	97T-Renault V6	97T/4
Rtd	Elio de Angelis	97T-Renault V6	97T/3

3-11-85—AUSTRALIAN GP, Adelaide-82-laps

Rtd PP	Ayrton Senna	97T-Renault V6	97T/4
Disq	Elio de Angelis	97T-Renault V6	97T/3

Chassis 97T/1 spare car Rio to Monaco, 97T/4 spare mid-season, 97T/2 late-season.

1986
23-3-86—BRAZILIAN GP, Jacarepagua, Rio de Janeiro-61-laps

2nd PP	Ayrton Senna	98T-Renault V6 turbo	98T/3
9th	Johnny Dumfries	98T-Renault V6 turbo	98T/2

13-4-86—SPANISH GP, Jerez-72-laps

1st PP	Ayrton Senna	98T-Renault V6 turbo	98T/3
Rtd	Johnny Dumfries	98T-Renault V6 turbo	98T/2

27-4-86—SAN MARINO GP, Imola, Italy-60-laps

Rtd PP	Ayrton Senna	98T-Renault V6 turbo	98T/3
Rtd	Johnny Dumfries	98T-Renault V6 turbo	98T/2

11-5-86—MONACO GP, Monte Carlo-78-laps

3rd	Ayrton Senna	98T-Renault V6 turbo	98T/3
DNQ	Johnny Dumfries	98T-Renault V6 turbo	98T/2

25-5-86—BELGIAN GP, Spa-Francorchamps-43-laps

2nd PP	Ayrton Senna	98T-Renault V6 turbo	98T/3
Rtd	Johnny Dumfries	98T-Renault V6 turbo	98T/2

15-6-86—CANADIAN GP, Ile Notre Dame, Montreal-69-laps

5th	Ayrton Senna	98T-Renault V6 turbo	98T/3
Rtd	Johnny Dumfries	98T-Renault V6 turbo	98T/1

22-6-86—DETROIT GP, Detroit, Michigan, USA-63-laps

1st PP	Ayrton Senna	98T-Renault V6 turbo	98T/3
7th	Johnny Dumfries	98T-Renault V6 turbo	98T/2

6-7-86—FRENCH GP, Ricard-Castellet-80-laps

Rtd* PP	Ayrton Senna	98T-Renault V6 turbo	98T/3
Rtd	Johnny Dumfries	98T-Renault V6 turbo	98T/2

* Car damaged in accident.

13-7-86—BRITISH GP, Brands Hatch-75-laps

Rtd	Ayrton Senna	98T-Renault V6 turbo	98T/1*
7th	Johnny Dumfries	98T-Renault V6 turbo	98T/2

* Regular qualifying car preferred for race instead of new 98T/4.

KEY:
PP-Pole position; FL-Fastest lap; Rtd-Retired; Unc-Finished but too far behind to be classified; '10th'-placed but not running at finish; DNS-Did not start; DNQ-Did not qualify; DNP-Did not practice; T-car-Training or practice car; Wdn—Entry withdrawn.

Indianapolis Record; 1963-1969

Lotus cars appeared in seven Indianapolis 500-Mile races from 1963 to 1969. The drivers and cars, their qualifying speeds, grid positions, finishing positions and average speeds or retirement reasons were as follows:

1963

No '92' Jim Clark	29-Ford	Qualifying speed 149.750mph (5th) Finished 2nd at 142.752mph
No '93' Dan Gurney	29-Ford	Qualifying speed 149.019mph (12th) Finished 7th at 140.071mph
No '91' Dan Gurney	29-Ford	Wrecked in qualifying crash

1964

No '12' Dan Gurney	34-Ford	Qualifying speed 154.487mph (6th) Placed 17th—withdrawn at 110-laps
No '6' Jim Clark	34-Ford	Qualifying speed 158-828mph (POLE) Placed 24th—tyre/suspension failure at 47-laps, led
No '51' Bobby Marshman	29-Ford	Qualifying speed 157-857mph (2nd) Placed 25th—oil lead at 39-laps, led

284

1965

No '82'	Jim Clark	38-Ford	Qualifying speed 160.729mph (2nd) WON at 150.686mph
No '98'	Parnelli Jones	Lotus/ Kuzma 34-Ford	Qualified 158.625mph (5th) Finished 2nd at 149.200mph
No '74'	Al Miller	29-Ford	Qualifying speed 157.805mph (7th) Finished 4th at 146.581mph
No '83'	Bobby Jones	38-Ford	Qualifying speed 155.481mph (22nd) Flagged-off 7th, 197-laps completed
No '1'	A. J. Foyt	34-Ford	Qualifying speed 161.233mph (POLE) Placed 15th—drop gears at 115-laps
No '17'	Dan Gurney	38-Ford	Qualifying speed 158.898mph (3rd) Placed 26th—timing gears at 42-laps

1966

No '19'	Jim Clark	38-Ford	Qualifying speed 164-114mph (2nd) Finished 2nd at 143.843mph
No '18'	Al Unser	38-Ford	Qualifying speed 162.372mph (23rd) Placed 12th—crashed at 161-laps
No '2'	A. J. Foyt	38-Ford	Qualifying speed 161.355mph (18th) Placed 26th—collision at start
No '75'	Al Miller	29-Ford	Qualifying speed 158.681mph (30th) Placed 30th—collision at start

1967

No '22'	Larry Dickson	38-Ford	Qualifying speed 162.543mph (21st) Placed 15th—spun out at 180-laps
No '31'	Jim Clark	38-Ford	Qualifying speed 163.213mph (16th) Placed 31st—burned piston at 35-laps
No '81'	Graham Hill	42F-Ford	Qualifying speed 163.317mph (31st) Placed 32nd—burned piston at 23-laps

1968

No '60'	Joe Leonard	56-P&W	Qualifying speed 171.599mph (POLE) Placed 12th—fuel-pump shaft at 191-laps
No '20'	Art Pollard	56-P&W	Qualifying speed 166.297mph (11th) Placed 13th—fuel-pump shaft at 188-laps
No '70'	Graham Hill	56-P&W	Qualifying speed 171.208mph (2nd) Placed 19th—crashed at 110-laps

1969

No '40'	Art Pollard	'56-Offy'	Qualifying speed 167.123mph (12th) Placed 31st—transmission at 7-laps
No '64'	Mario Andretti	64-Ford	Wrecked in practice crash due to hub failure
No '70'	Graham Hill	64-Ford	Withdrawn after delays caused by above
No '80'	Jochen Rindt	64-Ford	Withdrawn as above

Tasman Record; 1960-1969

1960
9-1-60—New Zealand GP, Ardmore, Auckland

7th	Jim Palmer	11-Climax sports 1.96
Rtd	David Piper	16-Climax 2.5
—	Arnold Stafford	16-Climax 1.96

Preliminary race

| 3rd | Piper | |

23-1-60—Lady Wigram Trophy, Christchurch, NZ

| 2nd | David Piper | 16-Climax 2.5 |
| 6th | Jim Palmer | 11-Climax sports 1.96 |

30-1-60—Dunedin races, New Zealand

4th	Jim Palmer	11-Climax sports 1.96
7th	Johnnie Windleburn	11-Climax sports 1100
Rtd	David Piper	16-Climax 2.5-ran 2nd

5-2-60—Teretonga Trophy, Invercargill, NZ

| 2nd PP FL | David Piper | 16-Climax 2.5 |

Preliminary race

| 1st | David Piper | 16-Climax 2.5 |

1961
7-1-61—New Zealand GP, Ardmore, Auckland

7th	Jim Clark	18-Climax 2.5
Rtd PP	Stirling Moss	18-Climax 2.5-led
Rtd	Innes Ireland	18-Climax 2.5
Rtd	John Surtees	18-Climax 2.5
Rtd	Roy Salvadori	18-Climax 2.5

Heat 1

| 1st FL | Moss | |

Heat 2

| 2nd | Ireland | |

14-1-61—Vic Hudson Trophy, Levin, NZ

| 2nd | Roy Salvadori | 18-Climax 2.5 |

21-1-61—Lady Wigram Trophy, Christchurch, NZ

2nd	Stirling Moss	18-Climax 2.5
Rtd PP	Jim Clark	18-Climax 2.5
Rtd	John Surtees	18-Climax 2.5
Rtd	Roy Salvadori	18-Climax 2.5

29-1-61—Warwick Farm '100', Sydney, Australia

| 1st PP | Stirling Moss | 18-Climax 2.5 |
| 2nd | Innes Ireland | 18-Climax 2.5 |

4-2-61—Teretonga Trophy, Invercargill, NZ

| 2nd FL | Roy Salvadori | 18-Climax 2.5 |
| 6th | Jim Palmer | 18-Climax FJ |

'Flying Farewell' race

| 1st | Roy Salvadori | 18-Climax 2.5 |

1962
6-1-62—New Zealand GP, Ardmore, Auckland

| 1st FL | Stirling Moss | 21-Climax 2.5 |
| Rtd | Ron Flockhart | 18-Climax 2.5 |

20-1-62—Lady Wigram Trophy, Christchurch, NZ

1st FL	Stirling Moss	21-Climax 2.5
Rtd	Ron Flockhart	18-Climax 2.5
Rtd	Jim Palmer	20-Ford Classic 1.5
Rtd	Ross Greenville	18-Ford Classic 1.5

27-1-62—Teretonga Trophy, Invercargill, NZ

| 4th | Jim Palmer | 20-Ford Classic 1.5 |

4-2-62—Warwick Farm '100', Sydney, Australia

| 5th | Ron Flockhart | 18-Climax 2.5 |
| Rtd | Leo Geoghegan | 20-Ford FJ |

1963
5-1-63—New Zealand GP, Pukekohe, Auckland

| Rtd | Tony Shelly | 18/21-Climax 2.7* |

*4th in prelim, penalized 1-min for jumped GP start, ran 3rd before retirement.

12-1-63—Vic Hudson Trophy, Levin, NZ

| Rtd | Tony Shelly | 18/21-Climax 2.7 |

19-1-63—Lady Wigram Trophy, Christchurch, NZ

| Rtd | Tony Shelly | 18/21-Climax 2.7 |

26-1-63—Teretonga Trophy, Invercargill, NZ

| 6th | Tony Shelly | 18/21-Climax 2.7 |

1-3-63—'Examiner' Trophy, Longford, Tasmania
5th   Tony Shelly   18/21-Climax 2.7

10-3-63—Sandown Park International, Melbourne, Australia
6th   Tony Shelly   18/21-Climax 2.7

1964
11-1-64—New Zealand GP, Pukekohe, Auckland
6th   Tony Shelly   18/21-Climax 2.5

Preliminary race
4th   Tony Shelly   18/21-Climax 2.5

18-1-64—Lady Wigram Trophy, Christchurch, NZ
6th   Tony Shelly   18/21-Climax 2.5

Preliminary race
3rd   Tony Shelly   18/21-Climax 2.5

25-1-64—Teretonga Trophy, Invercargill, NZ
4th   Tony Shelly   18/21-Climax 2.5

Preliminary race
4th   Tony Shelly   18/21-Climax 2.5

1965
9-1-65—New Zealand GP, Pukekohe, Auckland
Rtd   Jim Clark   32B-Climax 2.5*

Preliminary race
1st   Jim Clark   32B-Climax 2.5
Rammed by McLaren's Cooper.

16-1-65—Gold Leaf International, Levin, NZ
1st PP FL   Jim Clark   32B-Climax 2.5

Preliminary race
1st FL   Jim Clark   32B-Climax 2.5

23-1-65—Lady Wigram Trophy, Christchurch, NZ
1st PP   Jim Clark   32B-Climax 2.5

Preliminary race
1st FL   Jim Clark   32B-Climax 2.5

30-1-65—Teretonga Trophy, Invercargill, NZ
1st PP FL   Jim Clark   32B-Climax 2.5

Preliminary race
1st PP FL   Jim Clark   32B-Climax 2.5

14-2-65—Warwick Farm '100', Sydney, Australia
1st FL   Jim Clark   32B-Climax 2.5

21-2-65—Sandown Park International, Melbourne, Australia
2nd   Jim Clark   32B-Climax 2.5

1-3-65—Australian GP, Longford, Tasmania
5th   Jim Clark   32B-Climax 2.5

'Examiner' Trophy
8th   Jim Clark   32B-Climax 2.5

7-3-65—Lakeside '99', Brisbane, Australia
1st PP FL   Jim Clark   32B-Climax 2.5

1966
8-1-66—New Zealand GP, Pukekohe, Auckland
3rd   Jim Palmer   32B-Climax 2.5
Rtd   Jim Clark   39-Climax 2.5*
Stripped first gear at start.

15-1-66—Gold Leaf International, Levin, NZ
2nd   Jim Clark   39-Climax 2.5
5th   Jim Palmer   32B-Climax 2.5

22-1-66—Lady Wigram Trophy, Christchurch, NZ
3rd   Jim Palmer   32B-Climax 2.5
Rtd   Jim Clark   39-Climax 2.5*
Collision with Gardner's Brabham.

Preliminary races
2nd   Jim Clark   39-Climax 2.5
3rd   Jim Palmer   32B-Climax 2.5

29-1-66—Teretonga Trophy, Invercargill, NZ
3rd   Jim Palmer   32B-Climax 2.5
Rtd   Jim Clark   39-Climax 2.5*
Off on oil when leading.

Preliminary race
1st=   Jim Clark   39-Climax 2.5*
6th   Jim Palmer   32B-Climax 2.5
9th   John Riley   18/21-Climax 2.5**
Dead-heat with Stewart's BRM.
**Ex-Shelly car.*

14-2-65—Warwick Farm '100', Sydney, Australia
1st PP FL   Jim Clark   39-Climax 2.5*
6th   Jim Palmer   32B-Climax 2.5
On Firestone tyres.

20-2-66—Australian GP, Lakeside, Brisbane
3rd   Jim Clark   39-Climax 2.5
4th   Jim Palmer   32B-Climax 2.5

Preliminary race
2nd   Jim Clark   39-Climax 2.5
4th   Jim Palmer   32B-Climax 2.5

27-2-66—Sandown Park International, Melbourne, Australia
2nd   Jim Clark   39-Climax 2.5
4th   Jim Palmer   32B-Climax 2.5

Preliminary race
2nd   Jim Clark   39-Climax 2.5
5th   Jim Palmer   32B-Climax 2.5

6-3-66—South Pacific Trophy, Longford, Tasmania
4th   Jim Palmer   32B-Climax 2.5
7th   Jim Clark   39-Climax 2.5*
After plug-change.

'Examiner' 45 preliminary race
3rd   Jim Clark   39-Climax 2.5
4th   Jim Palmer   32B-Climax 2.5

1967
7-1-67—New Zealand GP, Pukekohe, Auckland
2nd FL   Jim Clark   33-Climax V8 2.0*
Lost body panelling.

14-1-67—Vic Hudson Trophy, Levin, NZ
1st PP FL   Jim Clark   33-Climax V8 2.0

21-1-67—Lady Wigram Trophy, Christchurch, NZ
1st   Jim Clark   33-Climax V8 2.0

28-1-67—Teretonga Trophy, Invercargill, NZ
1st PP FL   Jim Clark   33-Climax V8 2.0

12-2-67—Lakeside, Brisbane, Australia
1st PP FL   Jim Clark   33-Climax V8 2.0
Rtd   Greg Cusack   32B-Climax 2.5
Rtd   Leo Geoghegan   39-Climax 2.5

19-2-67—Australian GP, Warwick Farm, Sydney
2nd   Jim Clark   33-Climax V8 2.0
5th   Leo Geoghegan   39-Climax 2.5
Rtd   Graham Hill   48-Cosworth FVA 1.6*
Crownwheel & pinion failure in F2 prototype car.

26-2-67—Sandown Park International, Melbourne, Australia
1st   Jim Clark   33-Climax V8 2.0
2nd   Leo Geoghegan   39-Climax 2.5

6-3-67—South Pacific Trophy, Longford, Tasmania
2nd   Jim Clark   33-Climax V8 2.0

Preliminary races
2nd Heat 1   Jim Clark   33-Climax V8 2.0
3rd Heat 2   Jim Clark   33-Climax V8 2.0
Rtd Heat 1   Leo Geoghegan   39-Climax 2.5

1968

8-1-68—New Zealand GP, Pukekohe, Auckland
Rtd PP   Jim Clark   49T-Ford V8 2.5*
Dropped valve in new DFW Cosworth-Ford engine.

13-1-68—Rothmans International, Levin, NZ
Rtd   Jim Clark   49T-Ford V8 2.5*
Damaged car, left course.

20-1-68—Lady Wigram Trophy, Christchurch, NZ
1st PP = FL Jim Clark   49T-Ford V8 2.5

27-1-68—Teretonga Trophy, Invercargill, NZ
2nd FL   Jim Clark   49T-Ford V8 2.5*
Lost time, knocked-off nose cone.

11-2-68—Rothmans '100', Surfers Paradise, Australia
1st   Jim Clark   49T-Ford V8 2.5
2nd   Graham Hill   49T-Ford V8 2.5
4th   Leo Geoghegan   39-Climax 2.5

18-2-68—Warwick Farm '100', Sydney, Australia
1st PP   Jim Clark   49T-Ford V8 2.5
2nd   Graham Hill   49T-Ford V8 2.5

25-2-68—Australian GP, Sandown Park, Melbourne
1st   Jim Clark   49T-Ford V8 2.5*
3rd   Graham Hill   49T-Ford V8 2.5
7th   Leo Geoghegan   39-Climax 2.5
Beat Chris Amon's Ferrari by 0.1-second—Jimmy's last Grand Prix victory . . . in style.

4-3-68—South Pacific Trophy, Longford, Tasmania
5th   Jim Clark   49T-Ford V8 2.5
6th   Graham Hill   49T-Ford V8 2.5
—   Mel McEwin   32B-Climax 2.5

1969

4-1-69—New Zealand GP, Pukekohe, Auckland
2nd FL   Jochen Rindt   49B-Ford V8 2.5
5th   Leo Geoghegan   39-Repco V8 2.5
Rtd   Graham Hill   49B-Ford V8 2.5

11-1-69—Rothmans International, Levin, NZ
4th   Leo Geoghegan   39-Repco V8 2.5
Rtd   Graham Hill   49B-Ford V8 2.5*
Rtd   Jochen Rindt   49B-Ford V8 2.5**
*Drive-shaft joint— **Spun twice, second time rolled car.*

Preliminary race
3rd   Graham Hill   49B-Ford V8 2.5*
4th   Jochen Rindt   49B-Ford V8 2.5*
Furious after pushing and shoving each other during race.
6th   Leo Geoghegan   39-Repco V8 2.5

18-1-69—Lady Wigram Trophy, Christchurch, NZ
1st PP = FL Jochen Rindt 49B-Ford V8 2.5
2nd   Graham Hill   49B-Ford V8 2.5

Preliminary race
1st FL   Graham Hill   49B-Ford V8 2.5
2nd PP   Jochen Rindt   49B-Ford V8 2.5

25-1-69—Rothmans International, Teretonga, Invercargill, NZ
2nd   Graham Hill   49B-Ford V8 2.5
Rtd PP   Jochen Rindt   49B-Ford V8 2.5*
Startline collision.

Preliminary race
1st PP FL Jochen Rindt   49B-Ford V8 2.5
6th   Graham Hill   49B-Ford V8 2.5

2-2-69—Australian GP, Lakeside, Brisbane
3rd   Leo Geoghegan   39-Repco V8 2.5*
4th   Graham Hill   49B-Ford V8 2.5**
Rtd   Jochen Rindt   49B-Ford V8 2.5
*Behind Amon/Bell Ferraris— **Stop to remove collapsed wing . . .*

9-2-69—Warwick Farm '100', Sydney, Australia
1st PP   Jochen Rindt   49B-Ford V8 2.5
5th   Leo Geoghegan   39B-Repco V8 2.5*
11th FL   Graham Hill   49B-Ford V8 2.5**
*With rear wing— **Rain water in the works.*

16-2-69—Sandown Park International, Melbourne, Australia
2nd PP   Jochen Rindt   49B-Ford V8 2.5*
6th   Graham Hill   49B-Ford V8 2.5**
—   Leo Geoghegan   39-Repco V8 2.5
*Beaten by Amon's Ferrari— **Stop, throttle linkage.*

NB *Hill's car throughout was truly a 49T, Rindt's Levin replacement a 49B.*

In 1970 the Tasman Championship was opened to Formula 5000 cars and F1-derived works participation ceased. Leo Geoghegan was 7th at Surfers' and Warwick Farm in his 39-Repco 2.5 in 1970 and John Roxburgh was 7th at Sandown in the veteran 32B-Climax. In 1971 Lotus Tasman cars were all private 59s, 69s and F5000 type 70s.

APPENDIX II
Lotus specifications 1956-1986

LOTUS 12   Engines 1475cc Climax F2 or 1960cc and 2207cc Climax F1. Wheelbase 7ft 4in; track 4ft 0in; overall length 10ft 11in; weight *c.* 660lbs.

LOTUS 16   Engines 1498cc Climax F2 or 1960cc, 2207cc and 2495cc F1. Wheelbase 7ft 4in; track 3ft 11in; overall length 11ft 8in; weight *c.* 1080lbs.

LOTUS 18   Engines (F1 variant) 2495cc Climax. Wheelbase 7ft 6in; track 4ft 4in (front) 4ft 5¼in (rear); overall length 11ft 8in; weight *c.* 980lbs.

LOTUS 21   Engine 1495cc Climax F1. Wheelbase 7ft 6in; track 4ft 5¼in; overall length 11ft 9in; weight *c.* 995lbs.

LOTUS 24   Engine 1497cc Climax F1 V8. Wheelbase 7ft 6in; track 4ft 5¼in; overall length 11ft 10in; weight 1000lbs.

LOTUS 25   Engine 1497cc Climax F1 V8. Dimensions as 24 except weight *c.* 995lbs.

LOTUS 29   Engine 4200cc Ford Indianapolis V8. Wheelbase 8ft 0in; max. track 4ft 5¼in; overall length 13ft 0in; weight *c.* 1250lbs.

LOTUS 32B   Engine 2495cc Climax Tasman 4-cyl. Wheelbase 7ft 6in; max. track 4ft 3½in; overall length 11ft 7in; weight *c.* 1000lbs.

LOTUS 33   Engine 1497cc Climax F1 V8. Wheelbase 7ft 8in; max. track 4ft 8in; overall length 11ft 10in; weight *c.* 995lbs.

LOTUS 34   Engine 4200cc Ford quad-cam Indianapolis V8. Wheelbase 8ft 0in; max. track 4ft 5¼in; overall length 13ft 0in; weight *c.* 1250 lbs.

LOTUS 38   Engine 4200cc Ford quad-cam Indianapolis V8. Wheelbase 8ft 0in; max. track 5ft 0in; overall length 13ft 0in; weight *c.* 1350lbs.

LOTUS 39   Engine 2495cc Climax Tasman 4-cyl. Wheelbase 7ft 7½in; max. track 4ft 8¼in; overall length 11ft 8in; weight *c.* 995lbs.

LOTUS 42F Engine 4200cc Ford quad-cam Indianapolis V8. Wheelbase 8ft 10in; max. track 4ft 8½in; overall length *c.* 13ft.

LOTUS 43 Engine 2996cc BRM H16. Wheelbase 8ft 0in; max. track 5ft 0in; overall length 13ft 6in; weight *c.* 1250lbs.

LOTUS 49 Engine 2993cc Cosworth-Ford DFV V8. Wheelbase 7ft 11in; max. track 5ft 1in; overall length 13ft 2in; weight *c.* 1102lbs.

LOTUS 49B As above except wheelbase 8ft 1in; front track widened to 5ft 2.6in; weight *c.* 1180lbs (1968) then 1190lbs (1969-70).

LOTUS 49T As above except engine 2499cc Cosworth-Ford DFW V8 Tasman.

LOTUS 56 Engine Pratt & Whitney 14.999 sq in intake annulus area ST6 gas turbine. Wheelbase 8ft 6in; max. track 5ft 2½in; overall length 14ft 2in; weight *c.* 1350lbs.

LOTUS 56B As above except engine 3-litre-equivalency 'F1' P&W turbine.

LOTUS 63 Engine 2993cc Cosworth-Ford DFV V8. Wheelbase 8ft 2in; max. track 4ft 11in; overall length 12ft 8in; weight *c.* 1170lbs.

LOTUS 64 Engine 2605cc turbocharged Ford Indianapolis V8. Wheelbase 8ft 4in;: max. track 4ft 2in; overall length 13ft 4in.

LOTUS 72 Engine 2993cc Cosworth-Ford DFV V8. Wheelbase 8ft 4in; max. track 4ft 9in; overall length 13ft 9in; weight *c.* 1170lbs, approaching 1280lbs by 1975 when 72 'F' variant wheelbase was 8ft 9in, max. track 5ft 2in.

LOTUS 76 Engine 2993cc Cosworth-Ford DFV V8. Wheelbase 8ft 5in; max. track 5ft 2in; weight *c.* 1268lbs.

LOTUS 77 Engine 2993cc Cosworth-Ford DFV V8. Wheelbase 9ft 4¼in/2850mm (and 8ft 11in/reduced to 8ft 10¼in/2700mm late-season; max. track 4ft 8in/1422mm (front) 5ft 1in/1550mm (rear); weight *c.* 1300lbs.

LOTUS 78 Engine 2993cc Cosworth-Ford DFV V8. Wheelbase 9ft 4¼in/2850mm (not 8ft 11in/2720mm as has been published); max. track *c.* 5ft 7in/1700mm (front) *c.* 5ft 3in/1600mm (rear); weight *c.* 1310lbs.

LOTUS 79 Engine 2993cc Cosworth-Ford DFV V8. Wheelbase 9ft 4¼in/2850mm; max. track *c.* 5ft 8in/1727mm (front); weight *c.* 1300lbs.

LOTUS 80 Engine 2993cc Cosworth-Ford DFV V8. Wheelbase 9ft 0in/2743mm; max. track *c.* 5ft 10in/1778mm; weight *c.* 1278lbs.

LOTUS 81 Engine 2993cc Cosworth-Ford DFV V8. Wheelbase 9ft 3in/2819mm; max. track *c.* 5ft 6in/1676mm (front); weight *c.* 1290lbs.

LOTUS 86 As above.

LOTUS 87 Engine 2993cc Cosworth-Ford DFV V8. Wheelbase 8ft 11in/2718mm; max. track *c.* 5ft 10in/1778mm (front); weight *c.* 1290lbs.

LOTUS 87B Engine 2993cc Cosworth-Ford DFV V8. Wheelbase 9ft 2in/2794mm; max. track *c.* 5ft 9in/1750mm (front); weight *c.* 1279lbs.

LOTUS 88/88B Engine 2993cc Cosworth-Ford DFV V8. Wheelbase 8ft 11in/2718mm; max. track *c.* 5ft 10in/1778mm (front); weight *c.* 1290lbs.

LOTUS 91 Engine 2993cc Cosworth-Ford DFV V8. Wheelbase 9ft 2in/2794mm; max. track *c.* 5ft 9in/1750mm (front); weight *c.* 1279lbs.

LOTUS 92 Engine 2994cc DFV/DFY V8. Wheelbase 9ft 2in/2794mm; max. track 5ft 9in/1750mm (front); weight *c.* 1191lbs.

LOTUS 93T Engine 1492cc Renault V6 turbo. Wheelbase 8ft 10in/2692mm; max. track *c.* 5ft 11in/1800mm; weight *c.* 1250lbs.

LOTUS 94T Engine 1492cc Renault V6 turbo. Wheelbase 8ft 10in/2692mm; max. track *c.* 5ft 11in/1800mm; weight *c.* 1250lbs.

LOTUS 95T Engine 1492cc Renault V6 turbo. Wheelbase 8ft 11in/2720mm; max. track *c.* 5ft 11in/1800mm (front); weight *c.* 1191lbs.

LOTUS 96 Engine 2643cc Cosworth DFX V8 turbo. Wheelbase 9ft 2in/2800mm; max track 5ft 7in/1700mm (front); weight *c.* 1503.51lbs

LOTUS 97T Engine 1494cc Renault V6 turbo. Wheelbase 8ft 11in/2720mm; max. track *c.* 5ft 11in/1800mm (front); weight *c.* 1191lbs.

LOTUS 98T Engine 1499cc Renault V6 turbo. Wheelbase 8ft 11in/2720mm; max. track *c.* 5ft 11in/1800mm (front); weight *c.* 1191lbs.